Politics as Performance

A Social History of the Telugu Cinema

The Indian Century

General Editors Ramachandra Guha and Sunil Khilnani

David Hardiman
Gandhi in His Time and Ours

Christophe Jaffrelot
Dr Ambedkar and Untouchability

Harish Damodaran
India's New Capitalists

Vasanthi Srinivasan
Gandhi's Conscience Keeper

Rajendra Vora
The World's First Anti-Dam Movement

Srinath Raghavan
War and Peace in Modern India

Irfan Ahmad
Islamism and Democracy in India

Mukul Sharma
Green and Saffron

Nico Slate
Colored Cosmopolitanism

Niraja Gopal Jayal
Citizenship and Its Discontents

Sarvepalli Gopal
Imperialists, Nationalists, Democrats

S.V. Srinivas
Politics as Performance: A Social History of the Telugu Cinema

Jahnavi Phalkey
Atomic State

POLITICS AS PERFORMANCE

A Social History of the Telugu Cinema

S.V. SRINIVAS

permanent black

in association with

THE NEW INDIA FOUNDATION

Published by

PERMANENT BLACK
'Himalayana', Mall Road, Ranikhet Cantt,
Ranikhet 263645
perblack@gmail.com

In association with
THE NEW INDIA FOUNDATION

Distributed by

ORIENT BLACKSWAN PRIVATE LTD
Bangalore Bhopal Bhubaneshwar Chandigarh
Chennai Ernakulam Guwahati Hyderabad Jaipur
Kolkata Lucknow Mumbai New Delhi Patna
www.orientblackswan.com

ISBN 81-7824-372-5

Typeset in Adobe Garamond
by Guru Typograph Technology, Crossings Republik, Gbd, 201009
Printed and bound by Sapra Brothers, New Delhi 110092

For

CSCS

the idea, the people, the institution

Contents

MAPS

Series Editors' Preface

The cinema is our great popular passion, cutting across class, caste, geographical, and generational boundaries. The making, watching, and conveying of films is a fundamental part of modern India's social, cultural, and even economic history. And yet, for all its significance in our individual and collective lives, the subject has been poorly served by writers and scholars. The literature is dominated by two very different genres—rumour-filled biographies of stars on the one hand, and post-modern deconstructions of the ideological limitations of their films on the other.

Low gossip and high (albeit indecipherable) theory—those are the extremes offered to the reader interested in Indian films and what they have meant to Indian history. Exceptions to these opposed but equally depressing trends are few. They include an excellent biography of Satyajit Ray by Andrew Robinson and Krishna Dutta, an impressive encyclopaedia of Indian cinema edited by Ashish Rajadhyaksha and Paul Willemen, and an insightful series of books on the aesthetic choices of directors and lyricists by Nasreen Munni Kabir. There are also some fine sociological studies of the impact of films in the Tamil country, where politics and cinema have intimately influenced one another.

Into a still somewhat arid landscape comes this groundbreaking book by S.V. Srinivas. He is a native of Vijayawada, a fluent speaker of Telugu who is yet conversant with scholarly and political trends elsewhere in India and the world. His background and training exquisitely match his subject, which is the social history of films in the Andhra country.

In the early decades of the twentieth century, a popular movement arose for the creation of a state of Telugu speakers out of the erstwhile

Madras Presidency (which was dominated by Tamil speakers). Steadily gathering force, the struggle finally bore fruit in 1953 through the creation of the Andhra State, later known as Andhra Pradesh. This had a snowballing effect, leading to the wholesale redrawing of the map of India on linguistic lines.

A passionate identification with the Telugu language thus powerfully impacted both the history and geography of modern India. And, in an oral culture, love of the language has been most eloquently and powerfully conveyed by films. The cinema became the vehicle by which the Telugu-speaking people defined themselves, both in a positive sense, and negatively, against the hegemonizing influence of films made in other languages.

S.V. Srinivas's book is attentive to the emotional, affectual dimensions of Telugu films. It traces the impact on films and film-making of folk and mythological traditions in the Andhra country. But this is much more than a cultural history. Two important chapters locate the making and distribution of films in the changing political economy of Andhra. The capital generated by commercial farming was transferred to more profitable uses in the city, via real estate and film production. From culture and economics the book moves on to politics, through a brilliant analysis of the election campaign of 1982–3, when the great film star N.T. Rama Rao created a political party single-handedly, and carried it to victory against the all-powerful Congress.

The book's rich diversity of themes is matched by its depth of sources. Archival materials, field studies, newspaper records, pamphlets, posters, and newspaper records are all scoured thoroughly, with these materials then assembled in a most readable and yet robustly analytical narrative. Through these means and methods S.V. Srinivas has written the first substantial social history of Indian cinema. In a field obsessed with the colonial period, he has also opened up the post-Independence history of Andhra Pradesh in new and extremely productive ways.

Politics as Performance should be read by anyone interested in India's great popular passion, or in the fascinating modern history of one of our largest and most populous states. It will, we think, also influence similar studies of other filmic traditions. Aspiring scholars of Malayalam cinema, Kannada cinema, Bhojpuri cinema,

Bengali cinema, and Punjabi cinema will read Srinivas's book with great interest. So might scholars of Hindi cinema, who have thus far not adequately answered some vital questions relating to their field. These include: How did the Partition of India affect the making of Hindi films in terms of their staffing patterns, sources of funding, and themes foregrounded or suppressed? What are the sources of capital for Hindi films and how have these changed over time? What are the connections between film-making in Mumbai and the politics and economics of that city? What role have Hindi films played in carrying the once-reviled Hindi language across Southern and Eastern India? Why—unlike their Tamil or Telugu counterparts—have even the biggest Hindi film stars been unable to leverage their charisma and fame for successful political careers?

To answer these and other questions, *Politics as Performance* may provide a guide and a model. For this is that rare book which both educates the general reader as well as inspires the serious scholar. We are proud to publish it in "The Indian Century."

RAMACHANDRA GUHA SUNIL KHILNANI

Acknowledgements

It is unlikely that I would have written this book without the New India Foundation fellowship. I am grateful to the Foundation for the fellowship and Ramachandra Guha for his support over the five years I took to complete the manuscript.

This book draws on research projects I carried out at the Centre for the Study of Culture and Society (CSCS), Bangalore. My present and former colleagues Ashish Rajadhyaksha, Tejaswini Niranjana, Sitharamam Kakarala (Ram), M. Madhava Prasad, Vivek Dhareshwar, and Janaki Nair offered valuable feedback at different stages of the research and writing process. Other colleagues who were in and out of CSCS, Anup Dhar, Aparna Balachandran, Lakshmi Arya, Mathew John, Milind Wakankar, Mrinalini Sebastian, Prasanta Chakravarty, Radhika P., Rochelle Pinto, Sanghamitra Misra, Sruti Chaganti, and Swagato Sarkar, and PhD students Ratheesh Radhakrishnan, Subhajit Chatterjee, Sujith Parayil, T. Vishnu Vardhan, and Ashwin Kumar were all participants in lively discussions that shaped this book. Working with my PhD students Vishnu, Nishant Shah, Zainab Bawa, and Kanthi Krishnamurthy helped me sort out my own writing problems.

Chapter 1 draws on conversations with Ashish and Ram. Sections of chapters 4 and 5 are traceable to extended arguments and debates with Vishnu and Ratheesh. Colleagues and students at CSCS patiently heard me present every single chapter of the manuscript between 2005 and 2012. Apart from managing a variety of crises that cropped up every once in a while, the CSCS Administrative Officer M.P. Nagaraj helped me catch up with "Auto Raja" (chapter 4). I thank S. Padmavathy of the Media Archive for help with digital resources of the archive; Maheshwari S., Pushpalatha Reddy, Vijayalakshmi J.S.,

Pavithrabai M.S. and other staff of the CSCS Library for helping me locate and access books and online material. Special thanks to Tejaswini, Ashish, and Madhav for their sustained interest in and engagement with my work.

Ravi Vasudevan and Moinak Biswas have been long-term interlocutors whose feedback I value. Ravi Vasudevan, Ravi Sundaram, Moinak, Subhajit, and Madhuja Mukherjee provided me opportunities to present my work to interested audiences in Delhi and Kolkata.

In Hyderabad, English and Foreign Languages University (EFLU), University of Hyderabad, and Anveshi were important locations for discussions that shaped this book. I could not have written this book in Hyderabad but friends from the city K. Satyanarayana, K. Murali, Uma Bhrugubanda, Rekha Pappu, G.L.N. Reddy, I. Mohan Krishna, R. Srivatsan, Satish Poduval, Madhumita Sinha, Susie Tharu, M.T. Ansari, V.B. Tharakeshwar, Hariprasad Athanickal, Nikhila H., Sowmya Dechamma, and E. Satya Prakash, and innumerable MA and PhD students in EFLU have contributed directly or indirectly to this book. Without the help of G.L.N. Reddy and K. Balaji, working on the Telugu film industry in Hyderabad would have been difficult, if not altogether impossible.

Many thanks to Deepak Singh for making me feel at home in Chandigarh. And, also, for giving me the opportunity to present my work in Panjab University, Chandigarh, on several occasions.

I would like to thank Bernard Bate, Uma Bhrugubanda, Swarnavel Pillai, and Krishna Sankar Kusuma for giving me copies of their unpublished PhD dissertations; Stephen Hughes for sharing his work on Tamil cinema in the 1930s; S. Theodore Baskaran, Madhav Prasad, and Ashish Rajadhyaksha for their published and unpublished work alike. A.R. Venkatachalapathy, Ananth, Ratheesh, Uma, Madhav, M. Sridhar, Lawrence Liang, Neela Badami, Ram, G.L.N. Reddy, and L.V. Lakshmi helped me locate films, books, essays, and other library resources related to this book.

Accessing film-related material was far from easy. Not least because the government archive in Hyderabad is neither particularly hospitable to researchers nor a good place for film historians. I am grateful to the staff of Chittaranjan and Bhramarambha Malleswari libraries of Vijayawada for allowing me to access their newspaper and film magazine collections. M.V. Rayudu (Manasu Collection) and B. Vijay-vardhan, who as luck would have it were conveniently located in Bangalore, have been generous with their enormous collections of material on the Telugu cinema. Several images reproduced here are from their collections.

Vijayawada-based distributor Muthyala Ramesh and exhibitor-distributor G. Vishwanath were welcoming and helpful. In Hyderabad D. Ramanaidu and D. Suresh Babu took time off their busy schedules to speak to me. I am grateful to all of them for the information and insights they provided.

Drafts of this book's chapters were presented or published earlier. I have benefited immensely from the feedback received from listeners, readers, and editors.

The opening arguments of the book were presented at the International Conference on Film Cultures: Historical Perspectives, organized by the Department of Cultural Studies, EFLU (2011). The first complete draft of what is now chapter 1 was published in *BioScope*. I thank Ravi Vasudevan, Moinak Biswas, and Rosie Thomas for their comments and suggestions.

Sections of chapter 2 were presented at the seminar on South Indian Cinemas: Culture, Resistance, Ideology, organized by the Centre for Comparative Literature and Department of Communications, University of Hyderabad (2008); and the seminar on Regional Film Industries: The Formative Years, organized by the Department of Cultural Studies, EFLU (2008). Early versions of this chapter were published in the journal *Lensight* and the edited volume *Cinemas of South India: Culture, Resistance, and Ideology*.

Chapter 3 began as a brief presentation on the "folk" in N. Pushpamala's Somberikatte Forum (Bangalore 1998). The section on the folklore film was presented in the Anveshi-CSCS Telugu Cinema Workshop in Hyderabad (1999) and appeared in *Deep Focus*. An early draft was written while I was a Senior Visiting Fellow at the Asia Research Institute (National University of Singapore), and published in *Postscript*.

The argument on mythological speech was initially made at the seminar on New Asian Cinema: Trans-Asian Frames at the Department of Film Studies, Jadavpur University, Kolkata (2007). The first cut of chapter 4 was presented at the South Asia Seminar Series on Media and Postcolonial Culture in India, organized by the South Asia Institute and Department of Radio, Television and Film, University of Texas, Austin (2010). The complete chapter was presented at the CSCS Work in Progress series (2011).

Sections of chapter 5 were presented as a lecture at EFLU, Hyderabad (2012). The complete chapter was presented at the CSCS Work in Progress series (2012). Sections of chapter 5 were published in *Economic and Political Weekly*. My thanks to Anant Maringanti and the reviewer(s) of the essay for their comments and constructive criticism.

The argument on pathetic performance was made at a lecture at the Centre for the Study of Developing Societies (CSDS), Delhi. The closing arguments were presented at the First Monday Lunch Series seminar organized by the Department of English, Georgetown University, Washington DC.

I thank Shanti Kumar of the University of Texas, Austin, and Prathama Banerjee of CSDS for the opportunities to present and discuss the most challenging sections of the book. The questions and feedback from participants in both venues in general, and Aditya Nigam and Ravi Vasudevan in particular, were useful to make the case for performative politics.

My thanks to Chua Beng Huat of the Asia Research Institute for the quality writing time in 2004–5 and Kuan-Hsing Chen for the wonderful months in Singapore. For all the conversations on politics and/or the popular I wish to thank my good friends, Meaghan Morris, Kim Soyoung, Stephen Chan, Yoshitaka Mori, and Takako Inoue.

I thank the Indian Council for Cultural Relations (ICCR) and Georgetown University, Washington, DC, for the visiting appointment as ICCR Professor of Indian Society and Culture 2012–13. My stay in Georgetown gave me the opportunity to review the final draft of the manuscript in a new context and setting. Henry Schwarz, Bernard Cook, Alejandro Yarza, and Samuel Robfogel deserve special thanks as supportive colleagues.

For the maps of Andhra Pradesh I thank Uma Bhattacharya.

I am overwhelmed by the care with which Ramachandra Guha read the manuscript and grateful to him for his suggestions. If it wasn't for Rukun Advani's editing skills, this would have been a less readable book.

Thanks to my parents and Ananth for their care and support during difficult times. In addition to everything else, Ananth also helped me with library work and research in Vijayawada.

Finally, a very warm thanks to Anita and Gauri for tolerating my movies, odd working hours, and absences.

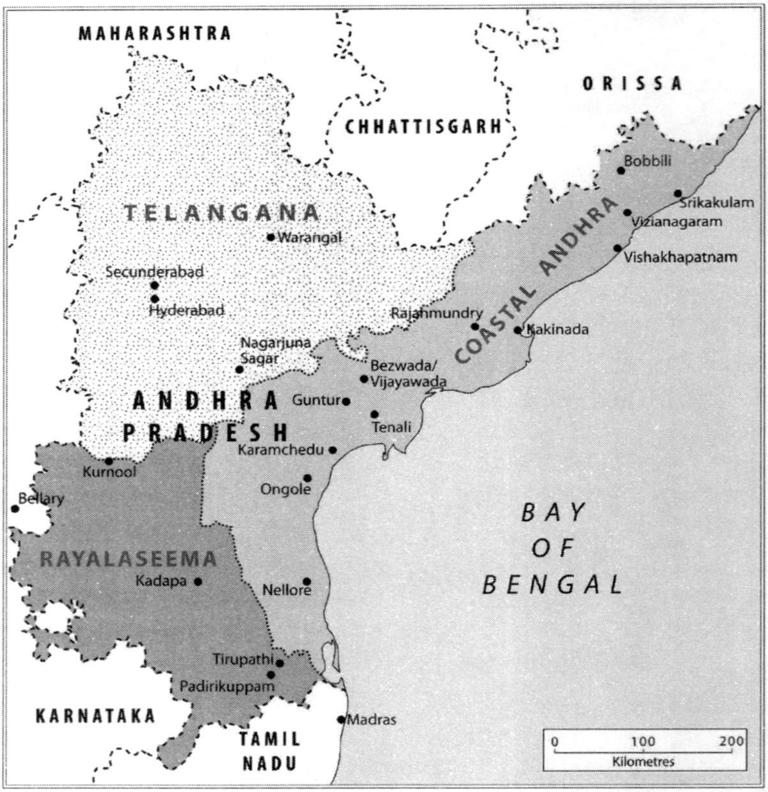

Map 1: Andhra Pradesh Regions

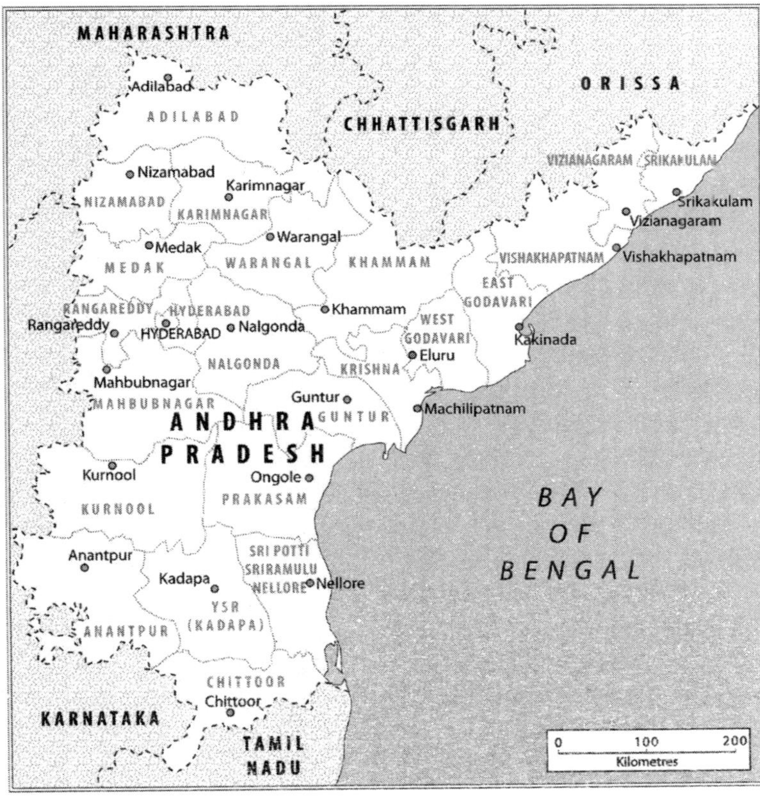

Map 2: Andhra Pradesh Districts

Introduction

What does the cinema tell us about a society and its politics? I believe the cinema is useful, indeed crucial, for understanding two key developments that shaped various aspects of life in post-Independence India in general, and the country's southern states in particular. These are, first, the rise to prominence of an elite which continues to dominate parts of the country to this day; and, second, the emergence of a new idiom of mass politics. This elite and the idiom—which together constitute what I have called "performative politics"—are both pan-Indian phenomena traceable to the colonial era but have resulted more largely from post-Independence economic policies, as also the dynamics of electoral politics. In fact, my view is that in relation to the regions that became Andhra Pradesh in 1956, where Telugu films were watched by ever-increasing numbers of people from the 1930s, the history of these developments cannot be told without reference to the cinema.

Telugu cinema, I argue, is directly implicated in the rise of the post-Independence ruling class–caste constellation, and more recently electoral mobilization. The degree of intimacy between cinema and politics is best appreciated when we examine the career of the man who represented the new elite politically. This was the film star Nandamuri Taraka Rama Rao (N.T. Rama Rao, "NTR," 1923–96), who crossed over to politics with nothing to show by way of qualifications except his roughly 300 films. I examine Telugu cinema in the fifty-year period from the 1930s to the early 1980s, beginning with the early career of the elite in the film industry and ending with the event that flags cinema's arrival as the foremost player in the economy and politics of the state: the election of NTR as chief minister in 1983.

The star, NTR, was born in a wealthy agricultural family in

Nimmakuru, Krishna district. It is remarkable how perfect an example he was of the new ruling elite of the state. His family lost most of its wealth during the Depression. In his teens NTR moved to Vijayawada, to his maternal aunt's family, there attending high school and college. As a college student he was drawn to the amateur theatre, and this led him eventually to the film industry.

In the 1930s and 1940s Madras Presidency zamindars (landlords with revenue collection privileges) belonging to the agricultural castes—more specifically the Kamma, Reddy, Kapu, Velama, and Raju castes—played an important role in establishing studios and cinema production infrastructure in the province's capital. By the early 1950s, roughly coinciding with the passing of the Abolition of Estates Act in 1948, non-zamindar entrepreneurs from these agricultural castes replaced the colonial elite as the prime movers of the film industry.

Two pioneers of the pre-Independence period who facilitated the shift away from zamindari investments were Gudavalli Ramabrahmam and B.N. Reddi. They were influential film-makers but also entrepreneurs who demonstrated that the cinema was a suitable investment destination for the capital that was beginning to migrate out of the Presidency countryside after the Depression made land-related investments risky. Ramabrahmam and Reddi presided over the setting up of production infrastructure in Madras, a city that attracted men and money. Ramabrahmam was instrumental in the establishment of Sarathy Films, in which the main investor was a Presidency zamindar. His reformist films laid the ground for cinema's engagement with politics, even as they foregrounded an issue that would frequently resurface in discussions of Telugu cinema: how can films—and by implication actors—be linguistically marked? The choice of stories, locations, sets, props, costumes, and of course the accents of actors—in short everything—had to be done to ensure that Telugu-language films were saturated with Telugu*ness*.

NTR's film career began in 1949. In 1950–1 he was launched as a star by Vijaya Pictures, around the time that this production company took over B.N. Reddi's Vauhini Studio. Soon, partly on the strength of NTR's success, Vijaya-Vauhini went on to become the most important studio and producer of Telugu cinema of the post-Independence period. NTR and his contemporary Akkineni Nageswara Rao (ANR) belonged to the Kamma caste. *Hero-dwayam* (star-twosome), as they came to be known, were now not only the biggest stars but also went on to set up their own production companies and, in the 1970s, film studios. Their growth as stars and entrepreneurs is symptomatic of the domination of the industry by the new elite of the erstwhile Presidency. It was an elite that had strong links to agriculture and related activities, and was non-Brahmin, non-Vaishya, and non-zamindar by origin. And what makes the cinema so crucial in Andhra Pradesh is that this elite did not limit itself to the cinema, nor to the old Presidency region, but extended its domination over the economy and politics of the state as a whole.

Paradoxically, the establishment of facilities for the production of sound films in Madras from the mid to late 1930s coincided with Ramabrahmam's realization—in as early as 1940—that the city was proving inimical to the on-screen representation of Teluguness. Actors, settings, and props required for showing the Telugu country were simply not to be found in Madras. And thus began the yearning for relocating the Telugu film industry out of Madras as well as the search for solutions to the problem of a cultural form that was not living up to its aesthetic-political potential.

Given the history of this cinema's Teluguness, NTR's claim in 1982, when he established the Telugu Desam Party (TDP), to represent the Telugu nation, is puzzling. He had little to show by way of qualifications to represent "Telugu" interests; as we shall see below, it was not NTR but his competitor ANR who was associated with the Telugu cause as defined by the industry. By the 1960s ANR and NTR had in fact come to be identified with what we can now recognize as alternative resolutions to the problem faced by Ramabrahmam. This was in part because over the next decade various factors changed the template on which Teluguness could be constructed. These included the attempts made by the Andhra Pradesh government to persuade investors from the old Presidency hinterland to invest in Hyderabad. The growing film industry was an obvious focus of the state government's efforts. A regime of loans and subsidies was instituted in 1964 to offset real and notional losses to producers who worked from Hyderabad. There were still good reasons for producers to remain in Madras where the studio set up by B.N. Reddi had, among other facilities, been expanded by its new owners to become India's largest; Hyderabad on the other hand had only one functioning studio, built by the owners of Sarathy Films in the late 1950s, and even this was more or less defunct by the early 1960s. It was ANR not NTR, who took the lead in speaking up for "Telugu" interests within the industry by coming out in support of relocation. NTR was seen as preferring to stay on in Madras and, for that reason, earned some bad press even at the time that he overtook ANR as the highest paid actor in the industry. And yet twenty years later it was NTR who, apparently with little prior warning or reflection, declared in public that his party would be called the Telugu Desam, and who went on to interpret every sign of poverty and underdevelopment as an insult heaped upon the Telugu "nation" by a "stepmotherly" Congress government at the centre. What enabled NTR to make a credible claim to being the representative of a linguistic community? What did his film career have to do with the claim?

In spite of the long history of the star politician as an object of social scientific analysis, there is precious little by way of a theoretically sound and empirically verifiable explanation of the NTR phenomenon. His political success has been variously attributed to his populist schemes (subsidized rice for the poor, for example) and ambient Telugu nationalist sentiments in the state. These claims do not withstand close scrutiny. Nor does the attribution of his political success to the numerous divine roles that he played in films. NTR announced his decision to form a political party in March 1982 without any clear idea of what its agenda would be. Indeed, naming it the Telugu Desam Party took observers by surprise, for neither his remarkable film career nor occasional but spectacular philanthropic actions had been read as having anything to do with Telugu nationalism. As for his roles as screen gods, while there is no doubt that he was the master of the mythological film, the genre itself was more or less out of currency by 1982. Moreover, the most successful NTR mythological was a film based loosely on the *Mahabharata* in which the star played Karna, Krishna, and Duryodhana. He directed and produced this film, ensuring that Duryodhana, the arch-villain, had the best lines.

Quite apart from the dubiousness of the assertion that the cinema can fool its audience into acting against their best interests, commentaries on NTR ignore the fact that in his early 1980s films the star, almost 60 years of age, had earned some notoriety for his sexually charged dance numbers with his heroines and cabaret specialists. The formation of the TDP and the launch of its election campaign did not result in any "cleaning up" of NTR's films. In short, his political success defies the available explanations of the star-politician's emergence in Andhra Pradesh, as also in the rest of South India. It has been assumed, for this region as a whole, that pre-existing frameworks for linguistic identity politics—such as for example Dravidian formations or Kannada organizations—were merely inherited by the cinema and that, at best, these pre-existing forms of politics had their agendas scaled up by the new entertainment.

NTR was by far the most popular South Indian film star in the early 1980s but, unlike his Tamil counterpart M.G. Ramachandran (MGR), he was not actively involved in politics before 1982. MGR was associated with Dravidian politics before his election to the state assembly in 1967; he became the chief minister of Tamil Nadu in 1977, twenty-odd years after he joined the Dravida Munnetra Kazhagam (DMK). It is therefore possible to suggest that the cinema played a far more critical role in the political success of NTR than MGR. What can NTR's career tell us about the star-politician that the commentaries on MGR have missed? The propagandist content of films is not what these stars banked on: this has been pointed out in studies on MGR but is all the more clear in relation to the Telugu cinema. NTR was a director and producer of some repute but he made no attempt to insert explicitly political or religious messages, not even in his "campaign films" released during the long campaign in 1982–3.

There are, therefore, good reasons to start the story of Telugu cinema's public career from the very beginning, reconstructing its history from the limited sources currently available in order to understand how it matters and what it means for contemporary Andhra Pradesh. For this reason I return to the late 1930s, when the film form known in India as "the social" was being established as *the* nationalist form by sound-era pioneers like Gudavalli Ramabrahmam, whose two classics, *Malapilla* (Untouchable Girl, 1938) and *Raitu Bidda* (Son of Farmer, 1939), laid down the protocols of engagement with Indian nationalism as well as linguistic identity. It is not an exaggeration to suggest that, to this day, neither caste nor the peasantry is represented in Telugu cinema in violation of the Ramabrahmam protocol: whereas there are innumerable direct references to Gandhian nationalist agendas (Gandhi Mahatmudu/Mahatma is invoked within minutes of *Malapilla*'s opening), linguistic identity is almost never mentioned. This is not to suggest that the language question was a non-issue for Telugu cinema. It is to suggest that it was an issue articulated by means other than those made familiar by Tamil cinema's DMK legacy, which generously laced the sound track with the word "Tamil" as adjective and noun. Looking for explicit references to linguistic identity, on the other hand, is definitely not the best way to approach the Telugu cinema.

A question thrown up by my material is whether the cinema's political work is different from that of other cultural forms and public institutions. I propose that it certainly is. The films and political crossovers of NTR allow this book to make the contrarian argument that the cinema did not borrow extant models of community formation from the political and literary domains. Nor did the film star have to draw on extant and easily identifiable strands of identity politics. Instead, this cinema threw open novel possibilities for the formation of collectives and naming them (in that order). Of particular relevance to the understanding of our present are developments in the post-Emergency period when this cinema, working in tandem with newspapers, played a constitutive role in the emergence of a new variety of populist politics.

NTR's election campaign in 1982–3 flags the moment of arrival of politics as a *performance* that succeeds or fails on the strength of its *emotional appeal*. What our star carried over from his screen career, especially from the period immediately preceding the formation of his TDP, is the capacity to invoke affect. His notion of Telugu identity was remarkably fuzzy, and, recalling one description of early silent cinema, his conception of political community was *indiscriminately inclusive* (Hansen 1991). Moreover, despite frequent references to heroic Telugu figures of the past, NTR did not have much in common with earlier representatives of linguistic identity politics.

A clarification is in order about what I mean by politics. I do not intend to restate the notion that a power grid surrounds us. When I refer to politics I have in mind mass mobilization and electoral politics. It is this link to a somewhat older and now unfashionable conception of politics which is a distinguishing feature of the Indian cinemas. Furthermore, if the perspective is that everything is political—as it is in certain strands of academic writing that pass for Cultural Studies—why bother with the specificities of cinema?

I would like instead to stake the claim that the cinema is political in ways that other domains of cultural representation are not. My conception of the performative is important for this book's central argument on cinema's political linkages. Role-playing is, of course, at the heart of our understanding of the performative, as is the acute awareness of a spectatorial presence. The performative act is addressed to *somebody*, and the form of its address is shaped by this awareness. In the case of both cinema and electoral politics the performer's addressee is the population—literally everyone who can be counted. Excess and exaggeration are easily noticeable features of the performance in the instance of NTR. But then, as Ravi Vasudevan's (2010) notion of "melodramatic" acting suggests, what is at issue is a *style* that had complex connections with notions of publicness; an idiom, not a cultural trait.

NTR's election campaign was characterized by a performativity straightforwardly traceable to his film career. His speeches in a pseudo-classical Telugu recalled both theatre and the popular cinema. His exaggerated gestures and gesticulations, and the strong emotional appeal of his campaign too, were "theatrical" and typical of his acting style in general. Together, these traits—lampooned by political opponents and earning him the nickname Drama Rao—facilitated a clean break with the earlier, non-media-savvy, political leadership. A decade and a half after his death, in spite of everything that has changed in Andhra Pradesh, politics continues to be centred on excessive, even extreme, utterances and symbolic gestures, and this mode of performativity has also become evident in other parts of of India. The cinema has had something to do with this turn in politics.

The 1983 election in Andhra Pradesh allows us to see how perfectly in sync the performative idiom, with its singular focus on the generation and transmission of affect, was with a new crop of newspapers established and run by the post-Independence elite. These newspapers catered to expanded markets and adopted aggressive reporting and editorial strategies that, among other things, gave pride of place to photojournalism. Tracking the political work of cinema thus leads us to an engagement with a major transformation of the other major public institution of modern India, whose very form and mode of address was now overdetermined by the economic and political ambitions of its owners.

~

In the past decade there have been several book-length studies on Indian cinema. There are clear signs of a growing academic interest in South Indian film too, indicated by the submission of Ph.D. dissertations (Bhrugubanda 2011, Kusuma 2010, Pillai 2010), the publication of full-length books (for example, Raghavendra 2011) and edited collections (Velayutham 2008, Dechamma and Satya Prakash 2010).

Nevertheless, for the most part, the literature on Indian cinema has shied away both from addressing social science disciplines and from engaging them in a productive debate on the contemporary. Take, for instance, our projects on film history. Over the past few years there has been a "historical turn" in research on the Indian cinemas, including Bengali, Hindi, Tamil, Malayalam, and Telugu. Researchers have unearthed a substantial body of fascinating archival material that allows comparisons to be made across the diverse film industries and cultures of India. We now know a great deal more about the early sound era, Indian film magazines, studios, stars, and technicians than ever before. The exceptions apart, such research—regardless of the richness of the material—tends to reconfirm what we already know about the time and place studied, as well as about categories such as nation, region, gender, and caste. There is in fact a real danger of film history emerging as a specialization within Film Studies, a second order historiography. This is a turn Film Studies cannot afford to take: difficult enough to justify in any setting, it is much more so in India, where the discipline has a limited institutional presence—just two full-fledged university departments. The task before us is therefore to expand our historiography by showing how history-writing is enriched by examining cinema. Hence the central problem with which this book is concerned—and one that most film students have chosen to ignore—is perhaps the most striking aspect of the country's film culture: the intimacy between cinema and politics. Notwithstanding the fact that in South India and the rest of the country star-politicians are growing by the election, there is little new writing on the subject other than the work of M. Madhava Prasad (1999, 2006, 2009), following upon earlier studies by Chidananda Das Gupta (1991), M.S.S. Pandian (1992), and Sara Dickey (1993).

Another area that this book addresses is the paucity of academic scholarship in English on Andhra Pradesh. From the perspective of all the human sciences, not just Film or Cultural Studies, the state has been understudied in comparison with both Kerala and Tamil Nadu. Other than Lisa Mitchell (2009), there has not been much quality academic writing on the state's politics, or on contemporary Telugu-language sources/materials, whether literary or pertaining to films and the media. As far as the cinema is concerned, apart from the works mentioned above, a few descriptive-ethnographic accounts in English are to be found in novels (Juluri 2010 and Devulapalli 2011).

The most respected analyst of the state's politics and society, K. Balagopal, a human rights activist, is no more. In many ways, this book is influenced by his essays and takes up some of the issues he raised in his perceptive commentaries on life in Andhra Pradesh. I do not discuss his writings on individual films but his thesis on Telugu cinema's political economy is demonstrated in the pages that follow.

State, Region, and Cinema

Andhra Pradesh was created in 1956 from three distinct regions: Coastal Andhra, Rayalaseema, and Telangana. These regions were earlier a part of the Madras Presidency and Hyderabad (or the Nizam's Dominions). While the Presidency was directly under the British colonial administration, Telangana was a princely state under "indirect" rule. Rayalaseema was a part of the Nizam's Dominions in the nineteenth century but was ceded to the British. Evidently, the Presidency and Telangana regions of the state were never fully integrated into a single political geographical entity. As we shall see in Chapter 2, there were back-to-back agitations (1969–73) demanding the formation of separate Telangana and Andhra states. The agitation in the Telangana region demanding statehood is far from new. So I cannot but ask what role the cinema has played in a state where the language question is complicated by tensions and conflicts between the constituent regions of a linguistic state. Region and caste have often recently figured in discussions of the Telugu film industry. That the industry has been controlled by Coastal Andhra entrepreneurs, the majority of whom belonged to the Kamma caste, is not news. Taking cognizance of this detail does not however make for an explanation of the work of the cinema. How then do we account for the *integrationist* economics and politics of Telugu cinema?

Its analysis of numerous Telugu films from the 1930s to the 1980s apart, this book examines a range of materials, including government reports, mainstream newspapers, film song booklets, film magazines, publications by film industry bodies, and "yellow" journals. A lot of this material has never before been the object of critical attention, whether academic or journalistic. Much of it is in fact unavailable in public libraries and the government-run archives in Hyderabad, for a handful of private collectors and institutions are the guardians of these invaluable resources on Telugu cinema. I have benefited immensely from the generosity of many such collectors who gave me access to their material. My location at the Centre for the Study of Culture and Society (CSCS), Bangalore, which assembled the very first public repository of Telugu film-related materials, also gave me privileged access to precious resources. In the decade since the CSCS Media Archive went online (http://www.cscsarchive.org), a far more comprehensive collection was assembled by M.V. Rayudu of the Manasu Foundation, Bangalore. Unfortunately, although I was able to tap Rayudu's collection, the archive was still under construction and much of it was inaccessible to users when the manuscript of this book was being finalized.

Of the five main chapters here, the first two outline the socio-economic and political context in which the Telugu film industry was established and developed. The rest examine film and related materials to reconstruct the social universe in and of the cinema. Briefly, the first chapter, focusing on the 1930s–50s, shows the making of an industry from what might be called peasant origins. NTR, as also all major stars from the 1950s to the present, belonged to the agrarian castes and rose from fairly modest origins to positions of enormous wealth and prestige. This chapter also outlines the early history of the sound film in South India, focusing on the economic significance of the cinema for entrepreneurs of peasant origin. The film industry, having been established by the colonial elites of the Madras Presidency—including traders from Vaishya backgrounds and zamindars belonging to the Sudra castes—now came under the control of a new category of investors who channelled agricultural surpluses into film production. At a time when a crisis in the rural economy forced villagers and capital to migrate towards the city, the cinema was among the few investment options available to a whole generation of inexperienced entrepreneurs from the countryside. The careers of the pioneers of sound film, including Gudavalli Ramabrahmam and B.N. Reddi, are illustrative here.

We see in the second chapter that even as Madras emerged as the production centre of Telugu cinema in the late 1930s, key industry representatives realized that this city was not suitable for a realistic rendering of Telugu people and their customs. The location of the production centre was seen to be a major obstacle for Telugu cinema's economic and aesthetic development, as also for efforts by film-makers to represent Teluguness on the screen. From this predicament emerged the foundational problem of Telugu cinema, the solution to which was to create an equilibrium between economic, aesthetic, and political criteria. The formation of Andhra Pradesh in 1956 shifted the equilibrium away for an aesthetics-centred formulation of Teluguness. While policy-makers sought to achieve economic integration between the regions by opening up Telangana, and Hyderabad in particular, as desirable destinations for surpluses generated by commercial agriculture in the Coastal Andhra region, cultural integration was largely achieved by the cinema, now fully under the control of peasant entrepreneurs. I show here how the film industry's rapid expansion was made possible by the opening up of the market in Telangana, largely untapped before the state's formation. With the integration of Telangana into the film market—as late as the 1970s—cinema became the first cultural form in modern times to be made at least notionally available to Telugu speakers across social and regional divides. The cinema was thus uniquely capable of addressing the Telugus as a whole. The establishment of an integrated film market laid the grounds for the emergence of a populist aesthetics whose primary concern was to maximize the viewership of films. An unintended consequence of this was that the cinema could claim to speak for the Telugu nation. Within a few years of this aesthetic-economic model's emergence, NTR made his decision to enter politics.

Like other Indian cinemas, Telugu cinema was invested in mobilizing the masses for nationalist politics. The third chapter tracks this cinema's interest in the masses along the axes of the altered political context in the post-Independence period, and the changes in film form and aesthetics that accompanied the creation of the first generation of male film stars in the 1950s. For a variety of reasons, NTR evolved into the star whose films extended the cinema's populist appeal. By the 1970s he was repeatedly cast as a representative of the masses marked by his distinguished ancestry. In the early 1980s it was this form, not mythologicals or propagandist films, that he used to aid his campaign.

The interesting question posed by NTR's career in the late 1970s and early 1980s, when he was evidently preparing for a crossover to politics, is how his films made political sense. What was the connection between films that made no explicit reference to linguistic identity politics and NTR's self-anointed role as the representative of the Telugu people? Chapter 4 examines NTR starrers from the late 1970s to understand how he came to be associated with a pseudo-classical Telugu because of his mastery of mythological roles. Even as the mythological waned in the 1970s, NTR, as director and producer of his own films, transformed the genre into a commentary on socio-political affairs, thus creating a link between the elevated or "classical" Telugu speech of the mythologicals and contemporary politics. Simultaneously, his social films cast him in dual roles wherein he played a vulgar, "eve-teasing" youth, and a tragic patriarch. The latter roles allowed the star to emerge as the centre of a film-viewing collective unified by the affect generated on the screen. Only much later did NTR make the claim that his constituency, which was in fact the audience of popular cinema, was the Telugu nation itself.

NTR's political success was a consequence of multiple convergences between popular cinema and print in Andhra Pradesh. His Telugu nationalist claims were facilitated and authenticated by the leading Telugu newspaper *Eenadu,* which insisted that the crowds rallying behind NTR during his nine-month-long election campaign were members of an injured Telugu race (*jati*). Like NTR, *Eenadu*'s proprietor was Kamma by caste and of peasant origin. More important, Telugu newspapers were in the process of extending their reach across the state, thus evolving from being the city-centred mouthpieces of an ageing nationalist elite to mass-circulated commodities that addressed new constituencies across region and class. With NTR's election, the print media began to acquire significant stakes in politics, not merely by endorsing a particular political party (which they did anyway in 1982–3) but also by transforming the election itself into an entertaining media event. The election received saturation coverage in every newspaper, even as *Eenadu*'s strategy of supporting NTR paid immediate dividends in the form of a sharp increase in circulation. This final chapter examines NTR's election campaign in some detail, drawing attention to the role played by *Eenadu* and other newspapers in the creation of a novel performative political idiom around the film star. NTR appeared on the political platform with such exaggerated gestures and an archaic mode of speech that—a bit like the protagonist in Woody Allen's *The Purple Rose of Cairo* (1985)—he gave the impression of having walked straight off the screen and into the world.

1

The Making of a Peasant Industry: 1930s–1950s

My history of the Telugu film industry begins with the sound era of the early 1930s, followed by the emergence of Madras as the production centre of Telugu films and the formation of the state of Andhra Pradesh in 1956. The fledgling film industry, which would soon become the focus of language-related discussions, was implicated in and made a notable contribution to a watershed event, namely, the rise to social, economic, and later political prominence of a caste–class constellation. This constellation has been variously categorized as provincial propertied (Balagopal 1987a), farmer-capitalist (Upadhya 1988a & b), and new capitalist (Damodaran 2008). In Andhra Pradesh the distinctiveness of the new elite lay in its peasant origin, not only as caste but also by occupation. The story of the rise of this elite cannot be told without reference to the cinema.

The entrepreneurs who took to the cinema in what is now Andhra Pradesh were part of an all-India phenomenon. Gail Omvedt, among the earliest to draw attention to what was in fact the rise of the country's post-Independence economic and political elite, observes: "After the coming of independence, rich peasants, landlords and the emerging capitalist farmers began to invest on a wider scale, rather than simply consuming surpluses. The establishment of tiny transport companies, tea shops, small flour mills, oil mills, brick kilns, etc., were all part of this process. Some moved into trade in direct competition with previous merchant classes/castes" (1981: 147).

The economic intimacy of this class with the cinema in Andhra Pradesh has been established by several commentators. Marking the elite's moment of arrival on the political scene was the formation of the TDP in 1982 by NTR, with his party winning a landmark election and forming the first non-Congress government in the state in the year following. With NTR's political success the genealogy of the new elite and the extent to which cinema contributed to its rise became a matter of public record. In a typical small town, remarks K. Balagopal, "the pride of place is taken by the twin symbols of Coastal Andhra: cinema halls that look like rice-mills and rice-mills that look like cinema halls, give or take a chimney stack" (1984: 1901). He goes on to assert that "all the surplus that is generated by the [Krishna–Godavari] delta agriculture goes in exactly two directions: agro-based industry and trade, and film production, distribution and exhibition" (1984: 1901).

The 1980s discussion of this class was broadly framed by what came to be known as the "mode of production" debate, in which the primary concern was the nature of transition (or the lack of it) between pre-capitalist and capitalist modes of production. My interest is not in whether a properly capitalist class emerged among peasants or whether it battled feudal interests. There seem better fish to fry by asking a different set of questions. For instance, it is a notable fact that film industries in this part of the world have produced hundreds of movies that do not, year after year, recover their production costs at the box office. How then may we understand the apparent lack of fit between this loss-making variety of cinema and a new investing elite? What allowed the cinema to play a role in the bildungsroman of this class of people? I suggest that the best method of explaining this is by tracking mobility—the mobility of men and money from agriculture and associated activities into new geographical areas and spheres of investment.

Locating the Peasant Question

"Peasant" is a term I use in spite of its vagueness as well as its Maoist associations. Balagopal points out that the term "is frequently used as un-discriminatingly as the Mughal and British revenue administrators used the terms *raiyat* or *ryot* [farmer]" (1986a: 1402). He adds that peasant castes, also referred to as "middle" or "intermediate" castes in the literature of the 1980s, "have been not only cultivators but also kings, feudatories, barons, overlords and revenue intermediaries . . ." (ibid.: 1403). Furthermore, there is evidence of cultivators among these castes engaging in violent struggles against feudal landlords of the same caste (ibid.). So I prefer to use "peasant," rather than the categories proposed by earlier commentators—such as "rural propertied classes," "farmer-capitalist," and "new capitalist"—because it allows me to flag the connection of the film industry's investors with land and agriculture in the period under consideration.

I would like to specify matters further. On account of the Telangana armed struggle against feudal oppression, as well as against the Indian state (1948–52), Andhra Pradesh has been the focus of a very different kind of "peasant question." My invocation of the peasant, however, is very specific and should not be confused with the rather more familiar "peasant question" in Communist debates. The peasants I refer to were neither poor nor insurgent. Moreover, my focus is on regions other than Telangana—for two reasons. First, I have not had access to material on the history of the film industry in the Telangana region before the formation of Andhra Pradesh. Second, developments internal to Telangana did not have a significant impact on the Madras-based film industry in the period under consideration. As we shall see, it was only after 1956 that Telangana became important for Telugu cinema, both as a market for films as well as a destination for investment.

My hypothesis is that, historically, the cinema in Andhra Pradesh has served as the point of entry into the realm of modern-day capitalism for a whole generation of entrepreneurs who traced their origins quite directly to the peasantry—small and medium landowners working on their land, and wealthy landlords with strong ties to land. The cinema was among the earliest, if not the first, industries that this group invested in.

Studies on Andhra Pradesh have tended to limit discussion of the economic significance of the cinema to its function as a destination of investment, and as a source of surplus for some among the Kamma caste from Coastal Andhra. Damodaran's (2008) account of the rise of "new capitalists," belonging to what he calls "non-traditional" backgrounds in post-Independence India, is perhaps the first study to extend the importance of the cinema beyond the Kammas to a wider cross-section of peasant castes in the state. Damodaran makes a useful distinction between castes with a history of involvement in trade and business—the Banias and other trading castes and communities, the traditional businessmen—and those castes that took to these in more recent times. It is the Komati caste that best fits Damodaran's definition of traditional businessmen. As he points out, businessmen and industrialists from non-traditional backgrounds were drawn from castes with agrarian origins, namely, the Kamma, Reddy, Raju, and to a lesser extent the Velama and Kapu. What is of direct relevance to my argument is his pointing out that the business pioneers among Kammas, Reddys, and Velamas invested in the film industry and played a key role in setting up this industry's infrastructure (Damodaran 2008: 99, 114, 119).

Damodaran, however, does no more than refer passingly to this development. Like earlier commentators on the political economy of the state, he simply lists cinema as one among many areas for investment, these ranging from sugar and tobacco to transport, government contracts, newspapers, and pickles. The routes of progress to prosperity and political prominence seem to have been varied. Even as Damodaran gathers interesting evidence in support of a larger argument about peasant castes and the cinema, he too ends up seeing the cinema as having to do primarily with the rise of one caste—the Kamma. There is some truth to this view; yet, in spite of the apparent obviousness of Kamma domination within the film industry, I would like to ask a more general question: was the cinema something more than just an incidental site for investments by those who did not belong to the traditional trading castes? The answer, as we shall see, is that it was much more than an incidental site.

There is no denying, as already noted, that non-Brahmin, non-Komati castes in general, and Kammas in particular, have dominated the Telugu film industry. However, the narrow focus on the caste origins of the industry obscures a key shift that occurred by the end of the 1930s–1950s period. The Telugu cinema's peasant connection cannot, I believe, be explained away by gesturing vaguely towards the peasant origins of the *castes* to which the industry's stakeholders belonged. As a matter of fact, there was a definite slipping of control over the film industry away from old money, which for historical reasons was held by zamindars. Ownership of the industry now passed to new money, generated by people who had no feudal antecedents whatsoever.

Situating my argument on the peasant industry against the background of recent research on the Madras studios, it becomes possible to see how significant socio-economic developments in Presidency Andhra were for the Madras film industry as a whole during the studio era. Not much is served by labouring the point that the Madras studios made films in several South Indian languages and, as such, do not fit neatly into the history of any single language cinema. Chakravarthy and Chakravarthy (2008) draw attention to the importance of caste factors in the rise to prominence of A.V. Meiyappan, the Nattukottai Chettiar who established the studio AVM Film Company in 1947. Nattukottai Chettiars, with their long-standing and well-established business credentials and presence across the Tamil-speaking areas of the Presidency (as well as in Ceylon and Malaya), are "traditional businessmen." A.V. Meiyappan is something of a textbook example of a businessman-turned-producer and studio owner. Rajadhyaksha and Willemen (1999: 47–8), and more recently Pillai (2010), note that A.V. Meiyappan inherited his father's store and expanded the business by selling cars and gramophone records. He then established a gramophone record label and began producing films in 1935 (Pillai 2010: 101–8).

Traditional businessmen from the Telugu-speaking districts of the Presidency had a far more limited role in setting up production companies and studios during the 1930s–1950s. Instead the ownership of the not-yet and not-quite-Telugu industry passed from zamindars to non-zamindar entrepreneurs whose caste backgrounds were similar to those of the zamindars. Post-zamindar entrepreneurs of the industry had increasing degrees of intimacy with agriculture and related activities, so much so that by 1956 the film industry was all set to become an industry of peasants, its investments directly from agriculture and allied activities. These activities were related to agriculture in the sense that those who accumulated agricultural surpluses typically carried them out, while continuing to grow crops and rear cattle. As historical accounts of the region have pointed out, such activities included rural moneylending as well as commodity trade and speculation.[1]

Pioneers of the Silent Era

There was no such thing as a "Telugu" film industry in the 1930s. While sound films in Telugu were a novelty in the early 1930s, and were marketed as such, neither the production process nor the distribution and exhibition networks of films allowed for any neat demarcation along linguistic lines. Nevertheless, sound triggered off demands made on behalf of a linguistically defined culture and community. By the late 1930s language became a factor in determining what kind of films should be made, where, how, and for whom. I therefore use "Telugu film industry" as a convenient label to refer to the production-related institutions and distribution-exhibition networks established by Presidency Telugus. For the most part, the films they produced were in Telugu.

Even from the limited sources available on the early history of film production and exhibition it is possible to suggest that, during the silent era, there was, first, a marginal Kamma presence in the film business; and, second, that the pioneers do not appear to have any direct link with agricultural and related surpluses. Raghupathi Venkaiah, widely recognized by Telugu film commentators as the "father" of the industry, was a Madras-based photographer from the agrarian Kapu caste.[2] He came into the film business as a travelling exhibitor of silent films. He then built the first Indian-owned permanent cinema hall in Madras, Gaiety, in 1914, and later the

[1] N.G. Ranga (1926) points out that by the 1920s there were already a number of Kamma agriculturists who were engaged in speculation and trade in agricultural commodities as well as moneylending (35–7).

[2] I am grateful to M.L. Kantha Rao, who researched the history of the Kapu caste (Kantha Rao 1999), for the information on Venkaiah's caste background. The backgrounds of Srinivasa Rao and Mangaraju, whose contributions to the industry are discussed below, were confirmed from members of their families in personal interviews with the author.

Crown and Globe theatres. Some years later his son, R. Prakash, set up a studio, Star of the East Film Company, in Madras, and became a producer-director of silent films in 1921 (Baskaran 1996: 3–5).

Pothina Srinivasa Rao is credited with the establishment of Maruthi, in Vijayawada (then known as Bezwada) in 1921, said to be the first permanent cinema hall in the Telugu-speaking regions of the Madras Presidency. He went on to direct what is believed to be the very first talkie made with "Telugu" investment in 1933. The film was produced in Bombay (Murari n.d.: 8). Rao was a businessman and theatre enthusiast belonging to the locally prominent Nagara caste (now categorized under OBC, Other Backward Classes).[3]

According to the available accounts, the very first locally owned distribution company was established by G.K. Mangaraju, a Komati rice trader turned pilgrim-tour operator, in the 1930s (Image 1). Komati, also known as Arya Vysya, is a trading caste engaged in a

Image 1: Photograph of the permanent exhibition on the history of Poorna in the Inox premises (Vijayawada). The poster on the left states that the company was established in 1932. Source: G. Vishwanath.

[3] See Parthasarathy 1997 for an account of the significance of the Nagara caste for Vijayawada.

variety of businesses over the Madras Presidency and beyond. Murari claims that Mangaraju got into the film industry in the late silent era (*circa* 1927) as an exhibitor. At some point between 1933 and 1937 Mangaraju established the distribution company Quality Pictures. In 1937 Quality Pictures went into film production. In 1940 the distribution company Poorna Pictures was established (Murari n.d.: 16–17). In spite of the continuing significance of Poorna Pictures for the industry, and the fact that Vijayawada city's first (Inox) multiplex is housed in a triple-theatre complex built by Mangaraju's descendants, neither exhibition nor distribution can be said to have been controlled by Komati entrepreneurs.

Madras and the Zamindar Era

The story of the new capitalists in the Telugu film industry and the internal upheaval within this category are closely linked to the growing prominence of Madras as the centre of Telugu film production. The film critic K.N.T. Sastry points out that the first sound film in Telugu, *Bhakta Prahlada* (H.M. Reddy, 1932) was made in Bombay (1993: 15). It was only some years later that sound film production facilities became available in Madras. The first of the studios in Madras equipped to handle sound film production was Srinivas Cinetone, established in 1934. This was followed by Vel Pictures, National Movietone, and Meenakshi Cinetone in 1935. The opening of these studios resulted in a spurt in talkie production in Tamil as well as Telugu and created the conditions for the establishment of Madras as the centre for the production of South Indian films in the years to come (Hughes 2010: 221).

Around 1933 ("*1933 prantallo*") Vel Pictures was established by a group of Madras-based exhibitors and funded by a Kamma zamindar from Krishna district, Yarlagadda Sivaramaprasad, the "Raja" of Challapalli (Murari n.d.: 9). In 1923 this Raja had helped set up Andhra Bank by providing financial resources for the venture. Among his other investments were a sugar factory and a company manufacturing precision tools (Damodaran 2008: 99). With the establishment of Vel Pictures the zamindar era in the Telugu film industry can be said to have begun. In Coastal Andhra, "Most of the early local industrialists of the 1930s to 1950s were from this class [zamindars], but because zamindars belong to the 'peasant' castes, they became role models for their enterprising caste brethren of more humble backgrounds" (Upadhya 1988a: 1378). Upadhya notes the transition from zamindar and rich landlord in the early part of the twentieth century, to the wealthy cultivator (who controlled landholdings that were smaller by comparison) in the years to come. The majority of her informants among industrialists in Visakhapatnam were from families with landholdings between 20 and 49 acres (1988b: 1434).

In the 1930s and 1940s Coastal Andhra zamindars of a variety of Sudra castes bankrolled the setting up of production infrastructure in Madras. In 1938 Venkataramaiah Apparao Bahadur, the Raja of Mirzapuram (a Krishna district zamindar from the Velama caste), built the second "Telugu" studio in Madras, Jaya Films. It was renamed Sobhanachala Studio in 1940 and became Venus Studio in 1955 (Mikkilineni 1975: 62). The Raja of Mirzapuram was the most prominent of the film-industry zamindars. He is said to have established a "small studio" (*chinna studio*) in Vijayawada in the late 1930s and produced three films there between 1938 and 1940 (Jaganmohan 2011: 59). The Raja, his actress wife Krishnaveni, and their daughter Anuradha between them produced dozens of successful films in Telugu, Tamil, and Kannada in the decades to come. The Raja also directed *Keelugurram* (1949), a bilingual production in Telugu and Tamil (Images 2 & 3).

A less-known zamindari enterprise in the Telugu film industry was the Andhra Cinetone studio in Visakhapatnam. It was set up in 1938 by R.S.R.K. Ranga Rao, who was the Raja of Bobbili (and of the Velama caste), and R.J.K. Ranga Rao, a zamindar of Chikkavaram. The studio made a bilingual production in Telugu and Bengali, *Bhakta Jayadeva* (Hiren Bose, 1938), and became defunct soon after (Murari n.d.: 26).[4]

During the 1930s three important players from the Kamma and

[4] Rajadhyaksha and Willemen (1999: 274) categorize *Jayadeva* as a Telugu film and make no mention of its Bengali version. They state that the film was made on a big budget but was commercially unsuccessful.

Image 2: Advertisement for the Mirzapuram Raja's Sobhanachala Production, *Gollabhama* (C. Pullaiah, 1947) in the Telugu film magazine *Roopavani* (February 1946: 2).

Reddy castes but not from zamindari backgrounds came into the film industry, laying the foundations for the second phase of development. They are Akkineni Lakshmi Vara Prasad (L.V. Prasad), Gudavalli Ramabrahmam, and Bommireddi Narasimha Reddi (B.N. Reddi). L.V. Prasad left his village for Bombay in 1930 when the Depression

Image 3: Songbook of *Keelugurram* featuring Akkineni Nageswara Rao (Raja of Mirzapuram, 1949). Source: B. Vijayvardhan.

led his well-to-do Kamma agricultural family to file for bankruptcy (Sastry 1993: 6). He became H.M. Reddy's assistant in the Imperial Film Company, which produced the first talkies in Hindi/Hindustani, Tamil, and Telugu. Prasad had bit parts in all three. In the 1930s he was an actor and director of some repute, but on the whole a rather minor player in the industry. Over the next three decades, however, he became a producer and also set up film laboratories in Bombay, Madras, and Hyderabad (Sastry 1993; Damodaran 2008, Images 4 & 5).

Prasad established a trend that a number of other Kamma men,

4

5

Images 4 & 5: Advertisements of Sarathy's critically acclaimed social *Grihapravesam* (L.V. Prasad, 1946) in *Roopavani*. The film was L.V. Prasad's debut as director and also featured him. May 1946, back cover (top) and September 1946 inside back cover (bottom).

who become key players in the industry, followed in the years to come. The category of entrepreneur of which he was representative is the first-generation migrant who traces his origin directly to families of rich or poor cultivators (but cultivators nevertheless). Prasad came to play an increasingly important role in the industry from the 1940s and became a hyper-visible presence. Casual observers get the impression that entrepreneurs like him arrived directly from fields and cattle-sheds to acquire major stakes in the industry. This is partly because both the superstars of the 1950s, ANR and NTR, were born into agricultural families and went on to set up production companies and studios in addition to becoming stars. Likewise, the younger star, Krishna, who joined the industry in the 1960s, began producing films in the 1970s and established a studio in the 1980s.

In NTR's case, very much as in L.V. Prasad's, the transition was rather dramatic. Financial distress even among well-off cultivators in the Krishna–Godavari districts during the Depression proved a catalyst in NTR's migration out of the countryside. He grew up with his maternal aunt's family, which moved to Vijayawada with the teenaged NTR. His father lost most of his land during the Depression, his uncle worked as a bus conductor. The boy sold milk and attended high school (Lakshmi Parvathi 2004a; Venkat Narayan 1983; Venkata Rao 2003). It was as a college student in Vijayawada that NTR was drawn to amateur theatre that led him to the film industry (Lakshmi Parvathi 2004a; Venkat Narayan 1983).

The rise to prominence of descendants of peasants in the later decades marks a shift away from zamindar dominance of the industry in the 1930s. Ironically, this was an indirect outcome of the collaboration between the Kamma zamindar of Challapalli (Krishna district), Yarlagadda Sivaramaprasad, who had earlier invested in Vel Pictures, and Gudavalli Ramabrahmam, an intellectual and business manager of the same caste. Ramabrahmam, the key facilitator of the transition, was a reputed editor and public intellectual long before he became a film-maker. He directed the reformist Gandhian melodramas *Malapilla* (1938, Image 6) and *Raitu Bidda* (1939, Image 7), arguably the most significant and influential Telugu films made in the 1930s.[5]

[5] I discuss these films at some length in chapter 3 to foreground their importance for Telugu cinema.

Image 6: Songbook of *Malapilla*, indexed by an anonymous latter-day collector as the "First revolutionary social." The text of the advertisement says that it is the chastity of the housewife (*grihalakshmi*) that is important and not her caste. Source: Manasu Collection, M.V. Rayudu.

Sivaramaprasad, a zamindar who distanced himself from the Justice Party (perceived to be a party of zamindars), nurtured political ambitions. Ramabrahmam, his close associate, was commissioned to establish a journal, apparently to launch the zamindar's political career.[6] The result was the weekly *Prajamitra*, established in 1932

[6] *Srimantu Raja Yarlagadda Sivaramaprasad Bahadur Challapalli Rajavari Shastyabdapoorti Sammana Sanchika* (1966) and Jaganmohan (2011).

Image 7: *Raitu Bidda*, indexed by an anonymous collector as the "First banned film in Telugu." Source: Manasu Collection, M.V. Rayudu.

and named after a political party started by the Raja. Apparently, the zamindar of Challapalli anticipated a bitter political contest with his counterpart from Mirzapuram of the Justice Party (Jaganmohan 2011: 45). So, *Prajamitra* soon became a forum for strident non-Brahmin nationalism. Its office in Madras was a regular meeting place of Presidency Telugu writers and intellectuals, and it was here that Ramabrahmam is believed to have first met B.N. Reddi in the mid-1930s. Ramabrahmam was also associated with a virulently anti-zamindari paper, *Zamin Ryot*, whose editor, Nellore Venkatarama Naidu, appears in the credits of *Raitu Bidda* as one of the film's lyricists. Ramabrahmam's standing as a public figure was so well established that he was called a "veteran Telugu director" by *Cinema Samachar* (July 1938: 14), even before he finished making *Malapilla* (Image 8).

This "Ramabrahmam moment," characterized by the forming of networks of first-generation urban immigrants from peasant backgrounds, initially centred around the printing press, magazines, and newspapers, and later the cinema. Education was a necessary precondition for the formation of such networks. Caste, kinship, and village-level connections can be seen crisscrossing, with new friendships and partnerships transcending the familiar modes of networking. These new networks, while being formed in Madras, were often traceable to some of the smaller urban centres of the Presidency. Ramabrahmam established his own theatre group in 1929 in Masulipatnam (now Machilipatnam, Krishna district) and moved to Madras only in 1931 or 1932.[7] While editing *Prajamitra* he worked as

Image 8: Statue of Gudavalli Ramabrahmam in Gandhinagar, Vijayawada, unveiled by NTR in 1983.

[7] Details culled from various entries related to Ramabrahmam's career in Jaganmohan (2011), Rajadhyaksha and Willemen (1999), and Murari (n.d.).

a publicity advisor and production executive for Vel Pictures. In 1936 he went into partnership with two others to set up the Vijayawada-based production company Saraswati Talkies Limited (Images 9 & 10). This company produced a mythological hit, *Draupadi Vastrapaharanam* (H.V. Babu, 1936), which featured a number of well-known stage actors (Rajadhyaksha and Willemen 1999: 267; Murari n.d.: 14). Saraswati Talkies continued to produce films but Ramabrahmam exited the company around 1937, apparently because he lost interest in mythologicals (Jaganmohan 2011: 77; Images 11, 12, & 13). Telugu film commentators credit Ramabrahmam with co-directing the reformist film *Balayogini* alongside the noted Tamil producer and director K. Subramanyam (Jaganmohan 2011: 72–8).[8] At some point between 1936 and 1938 he established Sarathy Films Private Limited with Yarlagadda Sivaramaprasad as the chairman and himself as a director.[9] He continued to be a key figure in Sarathy till 1945 when he left the company for reasons that are not clear (Jaganmohan 2011: 135). In just a couple of years the productions of Sarathy Films lent a high degree of respectability to Telugu cinema. This was in part due to the Gandhian-nationalist thematic concerns of *Malapilla* and *Raitu Bidda* but also the association of famous literary figures (as scriptwriters and lyricists) with these films. For reasons of focus I will discuss Ramabrahmam's films in the next chapter.[10]

In the early talkie era most Telugu films were essentially filmed versions of company dramas, the plays being already well known. These plays were for the most part *padya natakalu*, i.e. musical plays revolving around mythological stories, and performed by professional

[8] Rajadhyaksha and Willemen (1999: 266) list *Balayogini* (1936) as a Tamil and Telugu bilingual production and credit K. Subramanyam as its sole director. The advertisement for the Telugu version of the film in the magazine *Andhra Bhoomi* (March 1938) credits both K. Subramanyam and Ramabrahmam as directors. It is possible that Ramabrahmam worked on the Telugu version alone.

[9] Rajadhyaksha and Willemen (1999: 187) trace the company's origins to 1936, Murari (n.d.: 20) and Jaganmohan (2011) to 1937, while Damodaran (2008: 99) says Sarathy was established in 1938.

[10] See also Srinivas (1999) for a detailed discussion of *Malapilla* and *Raitu Bidda* and their production and reception contexts.

Image 9: Songbook of *Draupadi Vastrapaharanam*. Source: B. Vijayvardhan.

theatre groups. Their highlights were sung verses (*padyalu*) in a high-sounding Telugu.[11] Hughes' observation on filmed stage dramas in Tamil is also applicable to Telugu: "Generally speaking the pattern was for the studio film companies in Bombay and Calcutta to contract Tamil dramatists, actors and musicians and transport them from south India along with their families and servants" (2010: 214). The quality

[11] This is discussed in chapter 4.

Image 10: Songbook of the Saraswati Talkies' production *Kanakatara* (H.V. Babu, 1937), among the early crop of Telugu mythologicals made in Madras.

of films apart, there was also a minimal involvement of capital and technicians from the regions where these films would be exhibited.

Sarathy's productions increased the scale of Telugu film production. For example, *Malapilla*, which used dozens of extras, is reported by Murari to have cost as much as Rs 110,000 (Murari n.d.: 21). With the establishment of Sarathy the era of the filmed *padya natakam* could be said to be fully over. Zamindar investments in production infrastructure and (by the standards of that time) efficiently run companies capable of making big-budget films had, in effect, put an

11

12

Images 11 & 12: Top: Advertisement in the film magazine *Roopavani* (April 1945: 6) for *Mayalokam* a.k.a. *Kambhojaraju* (G. Ramabrahmam, 1945). This folklore film featuring Akkineni Nageswara Rao was the last Ramabrahmam directed for Sarathy. Bottom: Songbook of *Mayalokam*. Source: B. Vijayvardhan.

Image 13: Advertisement in *Roopavani* (May 1945: inside front cover) for *Maya Machhindra* (P. Pulliah, 1945). The film was produced in a Kolhapur studio.

end to the practice of filming company dramas. In 1940 the cost of producing an *average* film was estimated by Ramabrahmam (1940: 97) at a staggering Rs 100,000. Even as the industry demonstrated a capacity to absorb large infusions of capital, film-makers began to debate aesthetic questions that were specific to the cinema.[12] And by the late 1930s zamindar investment contributed to the emergence of Madras as an important centre for talkie film production.

The Beginnings of Telugu Cinema as a "Peasant Industry"

The conclusive shift away from zamindar domination can be traced to B.N. Reddi, a theatre enthusiast who was by training an accountant.

[12] This is discussed in chapter 2.

Reddi's wealthy landowning family had migrated to Madras, from Kadapa district of Rayalaseema, to run an agricultural commodities business (Guy 1985: 8; Images 14 & 15). His friendship with

Image 14: B.N. Reddi on the pages of *Vijayachitra* (December 1968: 12). Source: Manasu Collection, M.V. Rayudu.

Image 15: B.N. Reddi's *Swargaseema* (1945), which set new aesthetic standards for Telugu cinema (*Roopavani*, October 1945: back cover).

Ramabrahmam brought him in touch with major Telugu writers of the period (Dakshina Murthy 2006: 19). It also led to Reddi's investment in the BNK Press (Image 16). The press initially printed *Prajamitra* and later film-publicity material and songbooks. This brought Reddi into contact with film personalities (Guy 1985: 9; Murari n.d.: 29). Reddi entered the film industry as a partner in H.M. Reddy's production company Rohini Pictures (Guy 1985: 10; Murari n.d.: 28). He fell out with H.M. Reddy, however, and in 1939 established Vauhini Pictures with Moola Narayana Swamy—a businessman who was one of the partners in Rohini Pictures—and some others. Reddi directed Vauhini's first film, *Vandemataram*, in the same year (Guy

Image 16: Songbook of *Drohi* (L.V. Prasad, 1948), printed by the BNK Press. Source: B. Vijayvardhan.

1985: 12). In 1945–6 a separate company, Vauhini Productions, was established to infuse new investments into production while the older Vauhini Pictures was confined to distribution (Murari n.d.: 29). In 1948 a studio, also called Vauhini Productions, was built (Rajadhyaksha and Willemen 1999: 231).

B.N. Reddi's contribution to film aesthetics and high-quality production is widely known. Less known is his importance in the transition to the post-zamindar phase of the film industry. He played a key role in upscaling both the aesthetic and economic worth of the cinema.[13] With the Vauhini affiliates the studio era can be said to have come of age in Telugu cinema.

Over the years Vauhini's studio was taken over by Vijaya Pictures, the production company established in 1950 by Reddi's brother Bommireddi Nagi Reddy (B. Nagi Reddy) and Aluri Venkata Subbarao (Chakrapani). The duo had by then jointly acquired the ownership of the BNK Press. Nagi Reddy had earlier invested in Vauhini Productions and worked as its manager (Rajadhyaksha and Willemen 1999: 234). At some point between 1951 and 1956, B.N. Reddi exited the studio (Guy 1985: 16). In 1955 Vauhini Pictures, already confined to distribution, was shut down altogether (Kodavatiganti Kutumbarao, cited in Dakshina Murthy 2006: 155). Under the management of Nagi Reddy and Chakrapani, Vijaya-Vauhini, as it later came to be known, was the most-sought-after studio for Telugu film production through the 1950s and 1960s. One historian says it was the biggest studio in Asia during this period: "Vauhini Studios had 11 floors, and Vijaya 2, thus the total of 13 floors, along with the expansive Vijaya Gardens made it unequalled in the 50s and 60s" (Pillai 2010: 194 n.222).

Chakrapani, the other key figure in Vijaya-Vauhini, was a Kamma

[13] Guy's comment on Reddi's contribution is interesting and in fact applies to Ramabrahmam too, although the latter was better known for infusing nationalist politics into the cinema than setting high aesthetic standards: "Through his fine films, his artistic celluloid creations, BN [as Reddi was known in industry circles] brought respectability to Telugu cinema at a time when it had none. He brought in several men of education, culture and discipline to an industry which needed them, and did not always get them" (1985: 19).

by caste. He too had been born into an agricultural family. His literary career began as a translator of Sarat Chandra's novels from Bengali to Telugu (Lakshminarayana 1997: 24–5). Unlike B.N. Reddi and Nagi Reddy, his capacity to raise capital was not what made him a key industry figure, but like them and Ramabrahmam his arrival in the industry was mediated by a long engagement with the world of letters and publishing. All four of these men had in common a passion for Bengali literature. Chakrapani's partnership with Nagi Reddy began in 1945, when he was made the editor of the monthly magazine *Andhra Jyothi* that Reddy had just acquired (Lakshminarayana 1997: 27). In 1947 the Nagi Reddy–Chakrapani duo jointly established an illustrated children's magazine, *Chandamama* in Telugu, and *Ambulimama* in Tamil (Pillai 2010: 198).

Between Ramabrahmam and B.N. Reddi we notice the shift away from the industry's earlier reliance on zamindar investment. Reddi, with his family's business connections and training as an accountant, was able to mobilize investments from his immediate family and circle of acquaintances. Late in his life he made an observation on what set him apart from the 1970s producers: "The producer often has no money of his own. He borrows it from some Marwari or Chettiar at a heavy interest. So, his main worry is to make a profit in the bargain. Under such conditions how can he think of art, quality and all that? That's that; *I never borrowed for my films from financiers. Of course, I have raised money from friends. But they were friends, not film financiers. I never worried about money for my films*" (cited in Guy 1985: 56, emphasis added).

Peasant Capital and Zamindari Resistance

B.N. Reddi was more than a trend-setter: even in the 1970s there were no major industrialists from the Reddy caste in Andhra Pradesh. Reddi is in fact the only industrialist that Damodaran locates in a caste that was otherwise confined to "mining and public works contracts: businesses built mainly around muscle power rather than enterprise" (2008: 114). Modest as his scale of achievement might seem in comparison with those of prominent Kamma industrialists of the period, by the standards of the time the funding Reddi raised from peer and kinship networks was substantial. In the process he demonstrated the capacity of relatively new players in business to pool their resources and not rely on zamindars and Banias. Reddi was the first important film-maker to have made a clean break from both these categories of film financiers, anticipating what would become an important feature of the Telugu film industry from the 1950s.

The role played by the cinema in determining the career of capitalism in this part of India becomes evident when we compare the Raja of Challapalli, the most prominent among early Kamma entrepreneurs, with B.N. Reddi. What is striking in spite of their differences is their contribution to the *mobility* of capital from agriculture, moneylending, and commodity trade to urban centres, as also new kinds of investments. There was one major difference between the Raja and Reddi. The former was essentially a financier looking for venues in which to invest his considerable surpluses. Like other zamindars and traditional businessmen of the early twentieth century, his point of entry into this modern industry was moneylending (Ananth 2007: 48). The bank and film studio were desirable locations because the Raja was parking his funds virtually everywhere. Reddi's investment, on the other hand, was not merely sourced from a new category of investor but also based on two principles that we can now identify as the foundations of the Telugu film industry: the *distribution of risk* and the *lowering of the entry load* on individual investors. Investors were arriving at the Presidency capital in increasing numbers, looking for investment opportunities. By the 1950s the model of syndicated film financing that Reddi pioneered had trickled down to the Coastal Andhra countryside.

S. Ananth's (2007) work on the history of the finance business in Coastal Andhra allows us to place in perspective the economic significance of the cinema in the 1940s and 1950s described above. This was the period of establishment and rise to prominence of Vijaya-Vauhini and coincides with the increased availability of capital for investment outside agriculture and allied activities, which were no longer adequate for absorbing surpluses generated therein, making it the moment when zamindars lost their social and economic prominence. When examining the post-Independence economic boom in the Coastal Andhra region Ananth rejects the view that this was a direct outcome of colonial irrigation projects (2007: 85). He summarizes the thesis that he sets out to disprove as follows:

> The [Krishna and Godavari] anicuts increased the area of cultivation . . . in a previously famine stricken region. The cultivation of two crops in the region and the increased production along with the improvement in the transport facilities generated large amount of surplus. This surplus could not be deployed in agriculture due to the lack of opportunities and therefore this capital sought out more profitable avenues. This in turn led to the growth of Vijayawada city (as the surplus capital from the surrounding rural areas came to be concentrated in the city). This surplus agrarian capital sought out profitable avenues in finance, cinemas and other speculative ventures that the region is famous for. *Importantly, according to this theory, these changes were already in place by the 1920s or latest by India's independence* (2007: 85, emphasis added).

Ananth asks when and why rural surpluses from the region began migrating. Drawing attention to high levels of rural indebtedness in the Presidency—including the relatively more prosperous Coastal Andhra region—he argues that till the 1930s there was no need for rich farmers, who doubled as moneylenders, to look beyond their neighbouring villages, the need of the peasant to borrow taking care of the need to invest. Further, "Till the Great Depression, it was common for relatively prosperous peasants (especially the early examples of 'commercial farmers') to reinvest their surplus by purchasing additional land" (ibid.: 117). From the 1930s, however, there was a perceptible shift away from these time-tested means of deploying surplus. Damodaran too makes this point: "Till around the early 1930s the affluent Kamma peasantry's locus of diversification was restricted to rural moneylending and trade or erecting small rice and oil mills. The turning point was the Great Depression, as the collapse of the rural credit system and falling commodity prices rendered these hitherto safe activities unviable" (2008: 98). Ananth says an important reason for the movement of capital was additionally that "educational opportunities in the towns such as Bezwada [which] may have proved [to be] an important reason for this movement of a part of capital" (2007: 54). Typically, a part of the family moved to towns that had high schools and colleges. However, there is no evidence of major investments by agriculturists and rural moneylenders in urban areas in the 1930s and 1940s. This point was made earlier by Upadhya (1988a and 1988b). Why was this so?

Ananth draws attention on the work of the economic historian V.V. Sayana, who points out that during the Depression and throughout the early 1940s moneylenders, including those from agricultural backgrounds, bought land when cultivators sold land to repay loans (Sayana 1949: 118–21).[14] The families of L.V. Prasad and NTR, it is worth remembering, had sold their land during the Depression. Through the 1930s and 1940s, Sayana says, the Presidency witnessed a concentration of land in the hands of Reddys and Kammas, at the expense of Brahmins on the one hand and a cross-section of peasant castes on the other, including various Kapu castes (1949: 127).[15] He also points out that land was now passing to owners who were not "residential" but either from a neighbouring village or the town

[14] According to Sayana, "Large tracts of land had already changed hands during the years of the [G]reat [D]epression of the nineteen thirties and in its wake from cultivating ryots to non-cultivating money-lenders, agricultural or professional. Again during the period of the Second World War, it is observed that considerable extents of land were acquired by the trading classes and big landowners, to whichever caste they may belong, the Vaishya, the Chettiar, the Brahmin, the Kamma or the Reddi [*sic*]" (Sayana 1949: 118).

[15] Analysing data on land sales from the 1930s, Sayana states, "The bulk of the transactions have taken place among the agriculturalists themselves. Lands held by agricultural labourers, the artisan classes and people holding petty employment are being lost to others . . . The sowcars, the trading and business people, who are found at present among many castes, are acquiring land at a rate which is found more than double the rate at which they are disposing of their lands" (1949: 127). He goes on to elaborate on the caste composition of the sellers and buyers: "Expressed in terms of caste, land has been rapidly passing from the *Brahmins*, the *Artisans* and the *Harijans* . . . The *Reddis* and *Telagas* are also losing land in the districts where their population is sparse, while the *Reddis* and *Gouds* in Nellore and Ceded Districts (where they are big landlords) are, however, acquiring more and more land. Among the *Kammas* and *Kapus* or *Telagas*, the latter are gradually losing their importance as landholders, and the *Kammas* are seen more and more enterprising in acquisition of land and of late in business enterprise" (ibid.: 127; emphases in the original).

(Sayana 1949: 128). This strengthens Ananth's view that in the 1930s and 1940s there was no significant movement of capital out of the countryside because it was usefully deployed right there.

In the 1930s zamindars were among the few who had cash to invest outside the village, in capital-intensive businesses or industry. We have noted the range of investments of the Raja of Challapalli. Others, like the North Andhra Rajas of Bobbili and Pithapuram, laments Sayana, made unwise investments in politics that ruined them financially (1949: 88). In short they went into every sphere of activity that required a substantial cash infusion. So it is not surprising that zamindars were a presence in the film industry in the 1930s.

By the late nineteenth century the majority of the Madras Presidency was under the ryotwari settlement (Maclean 1885: 103). This meant that ryots or cultivators paid taxes directly to the colonial government. Generally, landowners in ryotwari settlement areas paid less land revenue and other taxes than did their counterparts in the zamindari estates. In the late nineteenth century there were 2.5 million ryots with an average of 8 acres each in the Presidency (ibid.: 105). There were also 678 zamindars. Only a fifth of the total area was under these zamindars. In comparison with the Nizam's Dominions, "the principal tributary native state of India" (ibid.: 10), it would appear at first glance that the presence of colonial feudal authorities was limited in the Presidency region. Sayana draws attention to the uneven distribution of zamindaris within the Presidency and their immense importance for the Telugu-speaking areas: "About 40 per cent of the area of the Telugu districts is under the non-ryotwari system, while it is 26 per cent in the Tamil districts" (1949: 49). Most of the non-ryotwari land was under zamindars. Presidency zamindars were a significant presence in north Coastal Andhra, Chittoor, and East Godavari and Nellore districts, where they controlled between 90 per cent and 50 per cent of the area (it was close to 90 per cent in the then Vizagapatam district—now Visakhapatnam—as well as in Vizianagaram and Srikakulam districts: Sayana 1949: 92). In Krishna district, which would emerge as a major contributor of men and money to the film industry in the years to come, there were 143 zamindari estates (Raman Rao 1993: 223). As mentioned earlier, two of the zamindars, from Challapalli and Mirzapuram, were engaged in political contests even as they invested in the film industry. Even as the North Andhra and Krishna zamindars were investors in the film industry, powerful Nellore zamindars played a pivotal role in suppressing *Raitu Bidda*, a film—made by the Challapalli Raja's production company— critical of the zamindari system (Rajadhyaksha and Willemen 1999: 281). Appeals against the film to the colonial administration by the Venkatagiri zamindar and his supporters resulted in a suspension of the screening of *Raitu Bidda* by the District Magistrate of Nellore in 1940 (*vide* Rc. No. 274/Confdl/40 dated 10 February1940), who felt "the film is calculated to show zamindars in the worst possible light" (Jaganmohan 2011: 106). The supporters of the Venkatagiri zamindar are alleged to have burnt prints of the film in Nellore (Murari n.d.: 21; Jaganmohan 2011: 107). Baskaran (1981: 142) observes that the zamindars of Venkatagiri and Bobbili also "threatened to sue the producers of the film on the grounds that some of the characters could be identified with themselves."

Zamindars thus made an important contribution in a variety of ways to the film industry—as also to capitalism in the region—till the late 1940s. Simultaneously, and this becomes clear only with hindsight, they were a source of blockage—they prevented the generation of surpluses in the areas that they controlled. As Sayana argues, the zamindars also caused a considerable financial *loss* to the colonial administration. Typically, they collected five times more from cultivators by way of rent than what they in turn paid the government (1949: 90). They thus had the effect of deferring a critical moment in the economic history of the film industry, as also that of Andhra Pradesh. In some of the best irrigated and fertile areas of the Presidency, the zamindars sucked out the surplus, postponing any significant shift away from subsistence agriculture. This, coupled with land transfers resulting from the Depression, ensured that there was not, in the Depression's aftermath, much investment outside agriculture.

After the Zamindars: Modelling the "Peasant Industry"

Immediately after Independence, in fact coinciding with the establishment of Vauhini's studio in 1948, the passing of the Estates

Abolition Act ensured removal of the source of investment blockage to the film industry. The act abolished all zamindari and other feudal estates with immediate effect. This then ended the domination of the film industry by zamindars. In combination with other factors that came into play around the time, substantial investible surpluses now became available in both village and small town. Ananth draws attention to these other factors, such as a reduction in the land revenue (it was anywhere between 30 per cent and 50 per cent of the produce during the colonial era), a sharp rise in the prices of agricultural commodities, and large-scale irrigation projects (whose consequences could be felt only in the 1960s), all contributing to the accumulation of investible surpluses among the rich and middle "capitalist-farmers" of the Coastal Andhra region (2007: 107–8).

The consequences of the economic boom in Coastal Andhra are evident from the rise in film production and the growth in cinema halls after Independence. Film production figures increased from 6 features in 1947 to 27 in 1956 and 36 in 1957 (Rajadhyaksha and Willemen 1999: 30–1). Rama Rao (1942: 203–11) lists a total of 94 cinema halls (including touring cinemas) in the Telugu-speaking districts of the Presidency and another 9 in Bellary district (now in Karnataka), which has traditionally been a market for Telugu films. By 1964 there were 350 cinema halls in the erstwhile Presidency districts of the state and another 15 in Bellary. Of this, 272 cinema halls were in the coastal districts alone (*Andhra Film Chamber Journal* 1964b: 56).

By the late 1930s and early 1940s, the first signs of this movement of surplus were becoming noticeable. Sayana says in passing, with specific reference to the Kammas in the 1930s, that they "are seen more and more enterprising in acquisition of land and *of late* in business enterprise" (1949: 127, emphasis added). Though insignificant in comparison with the post-Independence period, the impact on the nascent film industry is discernible; the earliest evidence of the small-town rich acquiring stakes in films comes from an essay written by Gudavalli Ramabrahmam (1940), who reflects on 1939, an important year for the industry—the landmark film *Raitu Bidda* was completed and Vauhini Pictures established. Ramabrahmam says that the number of productions in Telugu had increased to 15 in 1939 (12 according to Rajadhyaksha and Willemen 1999: 30). Further, production companies were now being started across the Telugu-speaking areas of the Madras Presidency, "not just in cities but also in villages" (Ramabrahmam 1940: 95). Many towns had more than one cinema hall (ibid.: 96). The proliferation of production companies, which Ramabrahmam claims were being set up by people who "had not even seen the Companies' Act", and the cinema halls were all signs that even in this period surpluses were finding their way into the film industry. The caste origin of this capital—whether Kamma, Reddi, Velama and Raju, or Komati—is not of immediate importance for my argument. It suffices to note that the post-zamindari investor had begun looking at the film industry. Only a few years earlier another commentator, Kodavatiganti Kutumbarao (2000a: 11), a younger contemporary of Ramabrahmam, is to be found lamenting that one of the obstacles to the development of the film industry (*talkie parisrama*) was lack of investment: "*Ee parisramaku ardhabalam chaladu*" (this industry does not have adequate economic strength).

It was not as if the problem of insufficient investments was solved in three years. But by 1940 an industry model, built on modest retail investment at the periphery and large investments in infrastructure at the production centre, was emerging. With their big-budget productions, the zamindar-owned Sarathy on the one hand and Vauhini on the other were in the process of demonstrating the capacity of the film industry to absorb substantial infusions of capital at the centre. Two "Telugu" studios, Vel Pictures and Jaya Films (soon to be renamed Sobhanachala Studio) were already functional. Against this backdrop the small production company and cinema hall were emerging as an investment option for the local surplus. We get a glimpse of the peculiar economics of the film industry even at this early stage of its evolution from Ramabrahmam's warning that most films made in 1939 were unlikely to recover their costs. He estimates that only a couple among the fifteen made a profit, while the others, though not dead losses, *definitely* did not earn a profit (1940: 95). Further, he argues, there were more cinema halls than could be supported by the small film market, resulting in competition between and losses to exhibitors (ibid.: 99).

There is one final point to be made about the nature of the

investments flowing into the industry. Kodavatiganti Kutumbarao (known as KoKu in Telugu literary circles) was a fiction writer, essayist, public intellectual, and occasional scriptwriter who later became a founding member of the Naxalite-affiliated Revolutionary Writers' Association (VIRASAM). KoKu's writings are among the few sources currently available on the early decades of Telugu cinema and offer valuable insights into what the 1940s may have meant for the industry. He had much to say about the issues outlined by Ramabrahmam. In 1947 KoKu highlights the consequences of World War II black marketing and profiteering on film production.[16] He begins by pointing out that the Telugu people had few industries. Only one studio was owned by a Telugu (the zamindar of Mirzapuram: unfathomably, he does not include Vel Pictures). Unlike other industries, the film industry—likened to a tent lacking stability—existed without foundations (2000a: 64). From the 1930s it didn't have any of the features characteristic of other industries. In fact there wasn't a single studio able to keep its workers employed throughout the year or undertake continuous film production. The industry, he argues, was characterized by the gambler's mindset (*joodabudhi*): the producer-investor did not think he was investing in the building of an institution, and having no long run in mind, exited *whether or not his film made a profit* (ibid.: 64). Inexperienced speculators in the industry either could not complete films or produced films that no one wanted to watch. This had a cascading effect: the number of cinema halls remained far too low because there were simply not enough films to feed a theatre through the year (ibid.: 65). KoKu traces the root of the problem to "third class producers" (*moodotaragati producerlu*) who had appeared on the scene to gamble (ibid.: 66). There was thus a need for the establishment of companies capable of producing at least half-a-dozen films a year. A guaranteed supply of good films would result in the building of new cinema halls even in small towns. He concludes by saying that only when *industrialists*, willing to make long-term investment that returned as little as 6 per cent per annum, replaced the gamblers and respectable

[16] This would become the subject of the Government of India's *Report of the Film Enquiry Committee 1951*.

bandits (*gauravaneeyulaina bandipotlu*)—the enemies of the people, governed by interest calculations and commissions—would the cost of production come down and quality go up. Most importantly, films would become popular and workers in the industry would find stable employment (ibid.: 66).

KoKu's anger and frustration are familiar from other commentaries on Indian film since the 1940s. His description of typical film industry investors suggests they were migrants, fresh arrivals from elsewhere. Their capital was perpetually on the move, exploring possibilities and shifting from one speculative investment to another. There is no evidence to suggest that these war-time investors were of peasant origin. According to Ananth (2007), the peasant-turned-entrepreneur had not yet emerged. Nevertheless, an industry model was taking shape.

From Ramabrahmam's assessment that the film business was one in which everyone stood to lose money, and KoKu's observation that the investor always moved on, emerge the outlines of a model that was not founded on the guarantee of profits but on the facilitation of the mobility of capital. While these features may have been shared by other emerging film industries across the subcontinent, the manner in which the Telugu film industry was becoming inextricably linked with local investment networks and practices is distinctive. The trajectory of these investors in the cinema would soon extend from village and agriculture, etc., to the small town and lead all the way to the Madras studios. Losses were likely to ruin individuals, yet as a learning experience for a social segment the industry's significance cannot be overstated.

The formation of Andhra Pradesh coincided with the arrival—literally and figuratively—of the post-zamindar investors from Coastal Andhra. In 1956, Presidency peasants did not immediately realize the potential of Telangana and Hyderabad as investment destinations. As a result, the well-established channels of migration of men and money terminated in Madras in the late 1950s and early 1960s. The "Movie Mogul" Daggubati Ramanaidu is a good example of the category of investor whose entry into the industry coincided with post-Independence developments, including the abolition of zamindari estates and the linguistic reorganization of states.

To conclude my argument about the industry's socio-economic origins, I would like to outline one man's career—that of Ramanaidu. In 1954, Ramanaidu's rich agricultural family was part of a syndicate that invested Rs 10,000 in *Nammina Bantu* (Adurthi Subba Rao), a film partly shot in their village, Karamchedu, in what is now Prakasam district (*Andhra Jyothi* 2009: 8). B.N. Reddi's model of syndicated investments in production appears to have trickled down to the Coastal Andhra countryside by this time. After spending some years as a typical rich farmer—engaged in agriculture while running a rice mill and a transport business—Ramanaidu shifted to Madras to establish a brick business but settled for real estate instead (*Andhra Jyothi* 2009: 8). His official biographer, Prakasam (2006), says Ramanaidu began his film career by investing in *Anuragam* (G. Ramineedu, 1963) and establishing Suresh Productions the same year. His first film as producer was the NTR starrer *Ramudu Bheemudu* (Tapi Chanakya, 1964).[17] Unlike most migrant investors, he stayed in the film business and, over the next four and a half decades produced over 100 films in Telugu, Tamil, Hindi, and other Indian languages (Prakasam 2006). This achievement earned him a place in the *Guinness Book of World Records* as the most prolific film producer. His family now owns a distribution company that has offices across the state, a film-processing laboratory, and studios in Hyderabad as well as (anticipating the reorganization of Andhra Pradesh?) Visakhapatnam (Image 17).[18] Their distribution company partnered Columbia Pictures (*circa* 2001–3) to distribute Hollywood films in the state (Srinivas 2003). More recently, the company acquired long-term leases for dozens of cinema halls across the state (Times News Network 2008: 3). In the 1980s Ramanaidu's son Venkatesh was launched as an actor and remains one of the major stars of the industry. In 2009 his grandson Rana (short for Ramanaidu) was launched as an actor.

[17] The film turned out to be hugely successful and was remade in Tamil as *Enga Veetu Pillai* in 1965 and Hindi as *Ram aur Shyam* in 1967 by Vijaya Productions. For a discussion of the film's different versions, see Narasaraju (2006: 39–56).

[18] Ramanaidu Studio, Hyderabad, was inaugurated in 1988 (Prakasam 2006: 81) while the Visakhapatnam studio became operational in August 2008 (*The Hindu Business Line* 2008).

Image 17: Ramanaidu Studio, Hyderabad, 2008.

Post-1956, it is safe to conclude, there was a consolidation of the position of surplus money from areas of the peasantry within the film industry. Over the decades, both exhibition and distribution became destinations of local investment, these being directly traceable to the activities of farmer-capitalists now located in urban areas and cities. Distribution became decentralized in the late 1970s with the breaking up of distribution territories into smaller units that were, at times, only as large as a single district, and the setting up of distribution offices in smaller cities. In 1964, as a direct consequence of state government incentives in the form of loans and subsidies, the Telugu film industry began the process of relocating to Hyderabad. The process was officially completed only in 1997 (*Jyothi Chitra*, 18 September 1998: 22). However, even as the first tentative steps began to be taken in 1964, there could have been no doubt that the industry was now owned, in more senses than one, by peasant-caste entrepreneurs who were also one generation removed from the erstwhile Presidency villages and agriculture.

All but one of the zamindari institutions failed to make it to Hyderabad. The Vijaya-Vauhini institutions didn't make it there. From the late 1930s the question of the industry's Teluguness became prominent: how could the industry ensure the Teluguness of films made in the Telugu language? The resolution to this question sought to create a cinema that lived up to its cultural and political mandate and, by committing itself to doing so, returned profits.

2

The Telugu Country and the Film Market: 1956 and After

However numerous the difficult problems which India has to solve, the language problem clearly is not one of them. It already is well on the way to solution.—**Jawaharlal Nehru, "The Unity of India," 1938**

Around the time that the cinema began to attract investments from Presidency towns, aesthetic and representational questions about its relationship with the Telugu language began to be raised. My attempt to understand this cinema–language relationship steers clear of the assumption that linguistic identity has an a priori existence *vis-à-vis* modern cultural and political forms. With reference to modern Telugu culture and politics, Lisa Mitchell challenges this assumption, pointing out that "the acquisition of a linguistic identity is indeed a historical process, rather than any sort of primordial natural identification" (2009: 98). The question before me, therefore, is not how films were shaped by a linguistic identity that pre-existed, but the particular contribution of the cinema to shaping a Telugu linguistic identity.

To begin with, the founding economic and political concerns of the film industry, and how these defined the notion of cinema's Teluguness, need to be seen. Subsequently, the formation of Andhra Pradesh changed the equations between economic, aesthetic, and cultural-political concerns, as also the very terms of the debate on Teluguness, by opening up new possibilities for the industry. These possibilities, in turn, impacted and overdetermined the careers of the two superstars, ANR and NTR, who came to represent two distinct aesthetic and economic responses to the opportunities and challenges thrown up after 1956.

In the early 1940s the speculative nature of the film business—exhibition included—was already a matter of concern to commentators and entrepreneurs alike, this being apparent in KoKu's writings on the problem. Neither KoKu nor Ramabrahmam were isolated in their concern. Of the twelve films made in 1940, a commentator noted a year after Ramabrahmam's observation, only three could be seen as having made a profit, or breaking even, or hoping to break even in the months to come. Most cinema halls in the Andhra region too made a loss over this year (Raraju 1941). This scenario was unfolding against the backdrop of Madras becoming the obvious choice for producers of Telugu films.

Founding Concerns: Representing the Telugu Country in Films

Ramabrahmam's essay of 1940 is centrally concerned with the profitability of the film business in general, and how Madras as the production centre of the nascent Telugu talkie directly affected matters.[1] His argument is counterintuitive because it did, after all, make financial sense for producers to use the Madras studios, where production facilities were improving. Every district of Coastal Andhra and large parts of Rayalaseema were already well connected to the Presidency capital by the railway network. Ramabrahmam identifies three reasons for the declining profitability of films: (1) increased competition among cinema halls—larger towns had more than one hall; (2) a dearth of films that matched up to audience taste (*prajabhiruchi*); and (3) the absence of *pratyekata* (speciality), *visishtata* (distinctiveness), and *jateeyata* (national character) (1940: 99). The second and third reasons, he says, were particularly important, the third perhaps the most important: Madras studios, he says, *do not support the production of* jateeyata *on screen.*

[1] At some point in his film career Ramabrahmam is reported to have been elected President of the South Indian Film Chamber of Commerce and also as having prepared a document titled "A Plan for the [Film] Industry" (Murthi Sri 1993: 57). I have not been able to locate this document.

Ramabrahmam makes a sarcastic passing reference to the claim of Presidency Telugus over Madras and cites an amusing example to show how the city did not support the production of on-screen Teluguness. During the making of his *Raitu Bidda*, which he points out was shot in a studio that he himself managed (Vel Pictures), the Madras extras did not know how to tie their dhotis like the Telugu peasants they were supposed to be playing on screen. Surely, he remarks, he was not spending hundreds of rupees a day to hire extras and feed them too in order to teach them to tie their *gocheelu* (loincloth)! It was pointless arguing about *pratyekata* and *visishtata* when the day was spent adjusting loincloths (ibid.). Telugus therefore needed their own studio on their land ("*Telugunata swanta studio*"). His advice to the film industry was to produce films that combined aesthetic and business sense with the *fragrance of Teluguness* ("*kaladrushtini, vyaparadrushtini melavinchi, Telugudanamto parimalinche Telugu filmulini tayarucheyali*", ibid.: 99, emphasis added). Pooling resources to construct a studio modelled on Prabhat, instead of setting up new production companies, was the need of the day. Prabhat Film Company had been established in Kolhapur in 1929 and relocated to Pune in 1933 (Rajadhyaksha and Willemen 1999: 178). It was a studio with impeccable nationalist credentials and closely identified with the director Shantaram's nationalist classics.

The larger issue that had to be resolved by sound/talkie films, especially those in southern India, was how film could be the bearer of a linguistic culture. A crucial point here is when Ramabrahmam uses *jateeyata* primarily to signal the distinctiveness of a linguistic culture: *jateeyata* is synonymous with *Telugutanam*, literally Teluguness. However, there is no hint that *jateeyata* as Teluguness is in conflict with *Indian* nationalism. This is all the more clear from his films, where Teluguness and Gandhian nationalism are seamlessly interwoven, the "regional" and "national" not in opposition. It is worth keeping in mind that, not just in Ramabrahmam and KoKu's work but in the Telugu cinema of the 1940s and 1950s as a whole, there is no indication that the pan-Indian exists in contradistinction with the regional or linguistic.

Ramabrahmam's problem with the early Telugu talkie had parallels with one that had surfaced in discussions of Tamil cinema some years earlier and been faced by Indian film-makers in the silent era. Hughes notes that the so-called first talkie (*Kalidas*, H.M. Reddy, 1931) was in fact multilingual and was advertised as a "Tamil-Telugu Talkie." He argues that location of production and identity of film-maker were considered important factors in the Tamilness of Tamil films in the early talkie period, when films in South Indian languages were being made in Bombay and Calcutta. In the early 1930s "the question being asked was how could a film be Tamil if a Bengali made it?" (2010: 217). For those engaged with the setting up of what went on to become the Telugu film industry, this problem was enmeshed with the aspirations of a class–caste constellation that grew with the cinema and gravitated to the Presidency capital after the establishment of talkie film-production facilities there in the second half of the 1930s.

As has been suggested by Rajadhyaksha (1993a), film-making in colonial India was founded on a swadeshi idiom that indigenized an imported technological form. Discussing what he calls the "Phalke/*Bhakta Vidur*" idiom, Rajadhyaksha says this idiom "went along with the line that a whole technology, to say nothing of a major culture industry, could now designate itself as *swadeshi* which itself sought cultural legitimation through the act of making and showing so-called 'Indian' images" (ibid.: 62). Once the images began to speak, the issue of linguistic specificity could only have complicated any claims that were made about the indigenousness of cinema. The representation of the nation, its places, people, and stories, which till this point had been achieved by showing "Indian" images, was in the talkie mediated by language. By the end of the 1930s, as we shall see, Telugu film-makers and commentators alike had identified a mandate for talkie films. In order for films to be Indian, they had to of course speak in Telugu, Tamil, etc.; but films had to do much more than speak in Telugu—they had to *be* Telugu.

As such, this distinction between speaking Telugu and being Telugu was not a new one discovered by film-makers. Mitchell's (2009) work on the changing status of Telugu in the nineteenth and twentieth centuries, and indeed the early-twentieth-century reification of the distinction between language as *medium* and language as explicit *marker of identity*, allows us to conceive of the problem as a feature of colonial modernity. Mitchell argues: "There is little evidence during most of the past millennium that language choice was ever considered one of these distinguishing practices of collective imagination. Instead, contestations over the necessity and validity of the above-mentioned practices were carried out in a variety of linguistic mediums, Telugu being only one of these mediums. It was not until the early twentieth century that language choice began to be deployed and claimed as a marker of identity rather than simply a medium for contestation over other sorts of non-linguistic identities" (ibid.: 50). Her work tracks the changes over a 150-year period of modern history and ends at the point when literary articulations of identity became available for wider circulation, feeding into mass mobilizations that eventually resulted in the formation of the Andhra state (1953) and, later, Andhra Pradesh with the linguistic reorganization of the states of the Indian union (1956).[2]

The evolution of criteria for the cinema to become a *Telugu* cultural form occurred against the backdrop of developments affirming that people and cultural forms now had a political relationship with language (as shown by Mitchell). However, the cinema did not merely inherit a fully formed equation from the world of letters and politics: the criteria by which the cinema could qualify to be a bearer of Teluguness had to be assembled anew by the industry. These criteria would change in response to economic and other challenges faced by the film industry in the five decades between the arrival of the talkie and the formation of the TDP.

The talkie-era version of the famous Phalke challenge of producing Indian images was, to recall Ramabrahmam, the creation of images

[2] In her discussion of the protests and police firing that followed the fast-unto-death of the Gandhian Potti Sriramulu in December 1952 in support of the demand for a separate Andhra state, Mitchell notes that while literary articulations of the early twentieth century had acquired a resonance in politics and crystallized into the demand for a separate linguistic state for the Presidency Telugus, the death of Sriramulu triggered off hitherto unprecedented and largely spontaneous agitations centred on railway stations (2009: chapter 6,189–212). The historian Ramachandra Guha argues that Sriramulu "had a more than minor impact on the history, as well as geography, of this country. For his fast and its aftermath were to spark off a wholesale redrawing of the map of India according to linguistic lines" (2007: 200).

that *smelt* Telugu. That project was, as seen, beset by obstacles encountered in Madras. Ramabrahmam makes a clear distinction between the language in which the films were made (Telugu) and their ability to contain or embody the cultural essence that he referred to as *jateeyata*. He also equates *pratyekata*, *visishtata*, and *jateeyata* when he shows that their lack plagued contemporary films. A second and more important equation he makes—or rather hopes will become possible in the future—is between business and the aesthetic sense. In fact, the founding problem for the Telugu film industry in its formative years, it is possible to suggest after Ramabrahmam, was to ensure that economic, aesthetic and cultural-political objectives were not separated from or opposed to each other. It made business sense to shoot with extras who could tie their loincloths because films were failing commercially due to the lack of *pratyekata*, *visishtata*, and *jateeyata*. Film-makers had to be committed to films that smelt Telugu because that was what their viewers wanted. An economic agenda was being layered with a radical vision. Telugu film producers were being asked to abandon Madras and invest in an entirely new production centre not only to make money but for the sake of what amounted to an agenda of economic regionalism deriving from nationalism. Neither the zamindars nor the other entrepreneurs were up to this challenge. Nevertheless, Ramabrahmam's vision and its links with *Telugunadu*—home, nation—as the natural location of the production centre would etch itself into the industry's consciousness.

Hughes (2010) allows us to note the parallels between Ramabrahmam's essay and a landmark intervention by Bharatidasan, an important figure in the Dravidian movement, in his late 1930s poem whose title translates as "The Cinema of Tamil Nadu." Hughes points out that "Like many of the other critics of the 1930s Bharatidasan condemned the borrowing of foreign elements; but . . . the improved Tamil content he advocated was aligned with a politics of mass empowerment. Bharatidasan echoed other critics in arguing that the Tamil-ness of Tamil films was being sacrificed by a crude capitalist drive for maximum profit. But he differed from other critics in that he argued that Tamil cinema would be more properly Tamil as a vehicle of social reform for the Tamil Masses" (Hughes 2010: 226). So the concerns of Ramabrahmam were not limited to the

Telugu cinema—for Bharatidasan, too, the problem was one of the equivalence between the aesthetic (borrowed elements), the economic (crude capitalism), and the cultural-political objectives (social reform of the Tamil masses) of post-silent cinema.

KoKu too had much to say on the language question through the 1940s and 1950s. His contribution to the discussion was to locate Teluguness in *film form*, implicating realism in the process. In an essay of 1940 he states that around this time there was a demand for social films (*sanghika chitralu*), which resulted in their increased production and, consequently, a shift away from mythologicals (2000a: 23).[3] Much of the output in 1940, he says, was accounted for by film-makers who had earlier made mythologicals badly—so there was in any case little likelihood of their making socials of high quality. Moreover—and this is important for our discussion—the crop of socials did not have "naturalness" (*sahajatvam*) and failed to provide a social atmosphere (*sanghika vatavaranam*). KoKu's notion of social atmosphere denotes at once realism and the generic distinctiveness of the social. Such films, he insists, cannot reflect *Telugutanam* (Teluguness); indeed, for the most part film-makers were struggling to prevent the saturation of social films with the "odour of the mythological" (*pauranika vasana*) (ibid.: 23).

In a 1953 essay he asks what implications the formation of the Andhra state, whose capital was not going to be Madras, would have for film production (2000b: 142–5). This essay was written when a number of commentators had been lamenting that the Telugus had "lost" Madras, which, contrary to the demand of the Presidency's Telugus, became the capital of the Tamil-speaking areas of the Presidency. The opposition of Nehru as well as that of the chief minister of Madras, C. Rajagopalachari, to the formation of Andhra and to making Madras a part of such a state, has been noted: it "enraged the Andhras, who had a strong demographic and economic presence in the city [Madras] and who believed that they had as good a claim on it as the Tamils" (Guha 2007: 187).

[3] In a later essay (1950) he explains that the reason for this shift, which he traces to 1937–8, was the Depression (*aardhika kaatakam*). He elaborates that mythologicals required expensive sets and props while socials were cheaper to make (2000a: 94).

In the talkie era the Madras-based film industry too was experiencing a linguistic reorganization of sorts, although this didn't have to do with political passions. Hughes notes that Indian silent films had a pan-Indian market, and "silent filmmakers in India anticipated the largest possible audiences over the widest possible geographic market. For the circulation of silent films linguistic boundaries were commonly addressed by the use of intertitles in as many as four different languages. In contrast to the fluid and overlapping multilingualism of silent film, sound forced Indian film producers to address new and still uncertain market conditions, which were simultaneously enabled and restricted by linguistic factors" (Hughes 2010: 214).

It was not as if the accessibility of sound films was totally dependent on the language used in the film because, well into the 1950s, cinema halls employed a narrator, known in Telugu as *dubashi* (translator), for Hindi and Tamil films.[4] Barnouw and Krishnamurthy assume that "the Indian narrators largely disappeared with the coming of sound" (1980: 46, n19). Repeated references and objections to the translator in the Telugu film magazine *Roopavani* in the late 1940s and early 1950s leave no doubt that the practice continued well into the sound era. Whereas in the silent era the narrator's task was to tell the story to an illiterate audience that could not read intertitles, in the talkie era he would offer a freewheeling translation of the soundtrack. At no point of time did the narrator limit himself to providing an accurate translation of either intertitles or soundtrack. It was noted in the *Report of the Indian Cinematograph Committee 1927–28* that the translators did much more than read out or translate intertitles.

[4] A *Roopavani* reader complained that the translator stood before the screen "like a pole" obstructing the view; moreover, he and his friends were more interested in passing comments on women than telling the story (Jeevan 1948: 61). A report on translators stated that they were incompetent in both Telugu and Hindi/Tamil and were not beyond providing comic translations of tragic scenes ("Ushasree" 1949: 45). Such was the popularity of the practice that doing away with translations of sound films was the one issue which a film viewers' association formed in Tenali town failed to convince the local cinema hall managements to implement (Subbarao 1951: 41–2). For a more detailed discussion of the translator in what is now Andhra Pradesh during the talkie era, see Srinivas 2000.

A high court lawyer from Ellore (now Eluru), Diwan Bahadur M. Ramachandra Rao Pantulu, when examined by the committee, said, "He [the translator] is a very clever fellow. He knows all about the story. Then as soon as one scene is on, he explains the whole thing in Telugu because everyone cannot read what is on the film" (*Report of the Indian Cinematograph Committee 1927–28*, III: 251). The chairman of the Indian Cinematograph Committee said of the translator: "We were told that such a man is a nuisance" (ibid.). Although Pantulu disagreed with him, the chairman had obviously heard complaints against the translator from other witnesses.[5] Murari notes in passing that Kasturi Sivarao, a stage actor who worked as a narrator in Vijayawada's Maruthi cinema before going on to becoming a film actor, made a variety of sounds (*vividha dhvanulu*) in addition to commenting on the scenes during the screening of silent films (Murari n.d.: 198).

In the early 1950s KoKu (2000b: 142–5) noted that as against the two past decades during which films were watched even by those who did not speak the language of the film, the increase in film production in the World War II period resulted in a reduced circulation of Tamil films in Telugu-speaking parts of the Presidency, and vice versa (Image 18). In other words, as the industry grew, the film's language could turn out to be a barrier for its circulation. The problem had its genesis in the origin of sound films. As Hughes points out with respect to the 1930s, "While the possibility of producing linguistically identified films was a tremendous marketing opportunity for Indian filmmakers, it also created the new problems and limitations that were already apparent at the outset" (2010: 215). He adds that, as early as 1933, an observer remarked on language determining the viewers' choice of films, as also their ability to appreciate the film. Sound film had, thus, effectively created and delimited markets. Against this backdrop—evidently to expand their market and to underwrite the increased cost of production—producers were shooting films in both Telugu and Tamil, or, as KoKu would put it, making two versions of the same film. The Telugu and Tamil industries were inseparably linked and in the early 1950s it was difficult to come across films made exclusively in only one of these languages (Kutumbarao 2000b: 143).

[5] Baskaran (1996) and Hughes (1996) discuss translators in the silent era.

Image 18: Before the emergence of the "Telugu" film market. Advertisement for the Tamil film *Rajarajeswari* in *Roopavani* (April 1944: 3). This Modern Theatres production, featuring the actress K.V.L. Vasanta (other details unknown), was distributed in the Presidency and Nizam's Dominions.

The entries in Rajadhyaksha and Willemen (1999) for the corresponding period allow us to see how prevalent this tendency was in Madras. Among the notable early 1950s films made in both Telugu and Tamil were *Patala Bhairavi* (K.V. Reddy, 1951), *Pellichesi Choodu/Kalyanam Panni Paar* (L.V. Prasad, 1952), *Prema/Kaathal* (P.S. Ramakrishna Rao, 1952), *Chandirani* (Bhanumathi, 1953), and *Devadasu/Devadas* (Vedantam Ragavaiah, 1953). *Patala Bhairavi* and *Chandirani* were folklore films.

In such a situation, KoKu argues, *jateeyata* (notice the recurrence of Ramabrahmam's term) was bound to be missing. Drawing attention to the close connection between film form/genre and *jateeyata*, he adds that the language issue did not arise in multilingual productions as long as the cinema in question comprised mythologicals and folklore films (2000b: 143–5). These didn't really need *jateeyata* because they were not set in any particular time and place. But socials, especially those attempting a degree of realist presentation, had to be shot on location (ibid.: 145). KoKu distances himself from the call by a section of the industry for relocating film production from Madras to Andhra, pointing out that the location of the industry did not matter to the Telugu and Tamil markets as long as they continued to make folklore films.

A few months later KoKu returned to the question of a film industry for the new Andhra state. Now he was strident about the need for the film industry to relocate from Madras. His reason for advocating relocation was not, as some observers had apparently argued, the possible economic loss or threat to the safety of industry property in Madras. Recalling Ramabrahmam he attempts a fusion of aesthetic and political concerns. The problem, he states, was discovered by Ramabrahmam while shooting *Raitu Bidda*. As we now know, in 1939 the director had had trouble finding props and extras appropriate for the story's setting. KoKu elaborates on this in his 1953 essay: in Madras and its surrounding areas, "the fields were different, the carts and bullocks, the whip, and the plough were different—*everything was different*" (2000b: 231, emphasis added). So Telugu socials made in Madras lacked a Telugu atmosphere (*Telugu desam vatavaranam*, 2000b: 233). He attributes this lack to conditions in the Madras industry: "In Madras productions non-Andhras work as art directors. Our films fail to show Telugu peasants, middle class Telugus and their houses . . ." (ibid.: 234). In other words, peasants and others were *speaking* Telugu on screen but not *being* Telugu. KoKu was responding here to the cosmopolitanism of the Madras industry which, by late 1930, included not only speakers of the different South Indian languages but also technicians who had earlier worked in studios within Bombay and abroad (Hughes 2010: 222). Interestingly, in relation to the Tamil end of things, Hughes points out that commentators on the Tamil cinema did not question the composition of the workforce and instead made the contentious issue the Tamilness of the songs in their talkies.

KoKu says, further, that it was not as if the talent required for making the screen adequately Telugu was lacking, but that this was just not to be found in Madras: "The Telugu country has many capable actors but they cannot come to the film industry in Madras. If studios are built in Bezwada, Rajahmundry or Visakhapatnam, these actors will materialize and also work for modest salaries. They will provide true/authentic Teluguness [*asalaina Telugutanam andistaru*]. Films can then be made quickly and cheaply" (2000b: 234). His response to the relocation issue was an acknowledgement, as also an attempt to address, the problem of the disconnect between quality, Teluguness, and profitability. Ramabrahmam's prognosis and diagnosis were being repeated by KoKu even as the Andhra state was being created.

In spite of the apparent similarities—the reappearance of olfactory metaphors and the repetition of the call for establishing studios in the Telugu country—a major shift had in fact occurred in the intervening period. For Ramabrahmam, the taste among viewers for films with *jateeyata* was not in doubt; indeed, films were failing because film-makers had failed to adequately realize the audience's interest in *jateeyata*, etc. But over the next decade it became clear to industry observers like KoKu that the grand unification—projected into the future by Ramabrahmam—of aesthetic, economic, and political interests under the aegis of *jateeyata* was not imminent. It now made economic sense to produce bilingual mythologicals or folklore films, as, in any case, viewers couldn't care less for quality. He had come to the conclusion that film production would begin on Telugu soil (*Telugugadda*) only in an era when viewers developed the taste to watch films with Telugu *jateeyata* (2000b: 145). Relocation was thus being proffered by him as an insufficient means of addressing difficult problems. His adherence to Ramabrahmam's formulation notwithstanding, his writings alert us to a wider context within which there was a displacement of Teluguness as primarily an aesthetic consideration to Teluguness as an attribute of geographical location because of the industry's changed production centre. While location (of shooting, production) was a key factor for Ramabrahmam and KoKu, from 1956 the mapping of Teluguness quite literally on to the map of Andhra Pradesh would increasingly determine discussions of what it meant for films to be Telugu.

The state capital, Hyderabad, as new home for the Telugu film industry, did not solve any of the problems attributed to Madras. It had little production infrastructure, and moreover was not at this point a part of the cultural universe of Telugu films. In Hyderabad "everything was different" from the Telugu country shown in films because the city, and the Telangana region as a whole, belonged to a distinctive cultural and geographical landscape. At Hyderabad the language widely spoken in public was Urdu, and the Telangana dialect of Telugu sounded very different from the "standard" dialect adopted for both print and screen. The distinctiveness appears in the accounts of Presidency immigrants into the city as the signifier of a palpable absence. Presidency Telugus who migrated to Hyderabad in 1956 were, in the words of one observer, struck by the "lack of Teluguness" in the city. The situation changed somewhat in later years, he added, which he saw as evidence of the positive role Telugu films had on Hyderabad society (Subba Rao 1964: 91). So, moving to Hyderabad would not have resolved the issues raised by Ramabrahmam and KoKu.

State Formation: Arguing for Andhra Pradesh and Telangana

The renewed demand for Telangana state since the 1990s, and the mobilization in its support since *circa* 2001, after the establishment of the Telangana Rashtra Samiti (TRS), provides an immediate context for re-examining the link between language, identity, and political geography. Mitchell notes that language was always associated with a territory: Telugu *desa* was the land where people spoke Telugu. By the early twentieth century, however, there was a shift "from understanding language as a feature of a territory—*desa bhasa,* 'language of the land'—to the acceptance of language as a personal attribute attached to particular people, viewed both as individuals and as members of a shared community defined in relation to that language" (2009: 36). The three regions—Coastal Andhra, Rayalaseema, and Telangana—that had been merged to form Andhra Pradesh in 1956 had never been part of a single kingdom or state. Yamada Keiko points out that "Even the medieval Kakatiyas, who covered relatively the territory closest to

Andhra Pradesh, ruled not more than two-thirds of Andhra Pradesh. In that sense, today's Andhra Pradesh is a rare political unit demarcated overall by language boundaries, and the origin of such an idea cannot be traced back to the pre-British period" (2010: 58). He also argues that there was an extremely shallow foundation for early-twentieth-century arguments on Telugu identity even in Coastal Andhra: they had their origin in the competition between Telugu-speaking Niyogi Brahmins and Tamil Brahmins who were in competition with each other for jobs and other benefits in the Presidency administration (ibid.: 61–2). This does not, however, mean that other castes and communities did not own Telugu identity, regardless of its origins in the quarrel between two groups of Brahmins.

The problem posed by Andhra Pradesh state is not that it is historically a recent invention but what constitutes it. The discourse on Telugu identity that Mitchell demonstrates as emerging only in the early twentieth century may have morphed into a demand for a linguistic state after Independence, but the merger with Telangana did not figure prominently in the demand for the creation of a linguistic state of Andhra from the Telugu-speaking Presidency. In the 1940s and 1950s the Communist Party of India (CPI) was a key player in the suturing of separate and non-converging articulations of Telugu identity in the Presidency and Telangana regions, respectively. The Andhra Mahasabha (AMS) was formed in 1928 in the Telangana region. P. Sundarayya, arguably the most important Communist leader of the Presidency region in the 1950s, recalls that, initially, the major demands of the AMS were neither radical nor focused on the unification of the Telugu-speaking regions. Instead, he notes disapprovingly, "it passed resolutions in conferences demanding certain reforms in the administrative structure, for more schools, for certain concessions for the landed gentry and for certain civil liberties" (Sundarayya 1973a: 13). This is corroborated by a history of the Nizam's Dominions which reports Ramabrahmam's speech at the second meeting of the Mahasabha in 1931. Deputed in all likelihood by the Presidency chapter of the AMS, he is reported to have been shocked by the ill treatment of "Nizamandhrulu" (Telugus from the state) by the police and warmly appreciated resolutions against bonded labour (*vetti chakiri*). He also called upon Presidency

Telugus (*Britishandhrulu*) to support their counterparts in the Nizam's state (cited in Jaganmohan 2011: 104). Nothing in this report, brief as it is, suggests that unification of the regions was on the agenda of either of the Andhra Mahasabhas. In 1940–2, Sundarayya goes on to add, a section of the AMS joined the communist movement and "transformed the AMS from a liberal organization into an anti-Nizam united mass militant organization—a united front against the Nizam leading the youth, peasants, traders, manufacturers and the middle classes" (1973a: 14). The demand for the creation of "Vishalandhra" (Greater Andhra), consisting of the Telugu-speaking regions of both the Madras Presidency and the Hyderabad state, was made by the Communist Party and taken up by the AMS.

Vishalandhra was premised on the Stalinist resolution of the nationality question in the Soviet Union. The CPI argued that the Telugus, including those in Hyderabad state, were a nationality. In his summary of the achievements of the Communist-led Telangana armed struggle (1946–51), which was initially against the Nizam and later against the Indian state, Sundarayya credits it with the linguistic reorganization of the Indian union:

> It must not also be forgotten that not a small share of credit goes to the Telangana struggle for forcing the pace of states reorganization on a linguistic basis, enabling the several disunited and dismembered nationalities to resolve their long cherished democratic demand for separate statehood. The powerful blows that this struggle delivered to the princely regime of Hyderabad inspired the struggle which won the Andhra State after the martyrdom of Potti Sriramulu in 1952; this, in turn, paved the way for the formation of linguistic states throughout India in 1956, forcing the Congress leadership to demolish the unprincipled and arbitrary division of the country made by the former British rulers. (ibid.: 5)

Potti Sriramulu's "martyrdom" was not, in fact, in support of Vishalandhra: the integration of Presidency Andhra and Telangana did not figure in his agenda. After Independence, Madras state witnessed a series of political actions (ranging from petitioning to the resignation of Tanguturi Prakasam from the Congress) as well as mobilizations in favour of the creation of a separate state from the Telugu-speaking regions of the erstwhile Presidency, with Madras as the capital (Guha

2007: 186). Mitchell notes: "Members of the local Communist Party [in Nellore] were also centrally involved in the Andhra movement" (2009: 197). However, Sriramulu's conception of an Andhra state remained Presidency-centred and his key demand was that Madras be its capital. The Communists' idea of Vishalandhra was much more ambitious, geographically and politically. It was also far more contentious.

Pro-Telangana intellectuals have suggested that invocations of the Telugu nation, including the Communist conception of Vishalandhra, appealed only to the people in the Presidency districts and were lost on the people of Telangana. For example, I. Thirumali notes that political parties thrust unification on the people of Telangana who had no clue what it meant:

> The Communist Party, having enough strength in the Andhra Assembly and Hyderabad state Assembly, brought enormous pressure on the central leadership. P. Sundarayya and C. Rajeswar Rao worked hard in Andhra and Delhi immediately after Fazl Ali recommendations were found to be against Vishalandhra . . . Every political party claimed that it had mass support, and [unification] was in accordance with the wishes of Telangana people. The masses did not even know what Vishalandhra was. Border village people felt joining "company" was Vishalandhra, but did not understand what it was. *Central Telangana people thought Vishalandhra was a religion*. (1997: 23, emphasis added)

It is questionable whether *any* ideological formulation percolates to the level of participants in a mass movement without significant "transmission losses" or resignification, depending on how we look at it. We need go no further than Gandhi's peasant loyalists in the Gorakhpur region to realize that there is normally a significant gap between the formulation of a political programme and its (mis) interpretation by the masses.[6] Further, there is no reason to believe that the idea of Andhra Pradesh was any less bewildering for the people of Presidency Andhra. Nevertheless, Thirumali's observation makes it clear that there was at best indifference to state formation among the populace in Telangana. The political scientist Duncan Forrester argues that there was also, in fact, opposition to linguistic reorganization in the Hyderabad state, as also the timing of it:

[6] See Amin (1984).

> After the police action [when the state was made a part of the Indian Union] Hyderabad remained as a separate political entity, and indeed there was a certain amount of public feeling against the division of the state on a linguistic basis: *on June 16, 1952, a motion in the Hyderabad Legislative Assembly for the dismemberment of the state* [along linguistic lines] *was defeated by 79 votes to 63 . . . Telangana played no part in the agitation which resulted in the setting up of the state of Andhra Pradesh in 1953* [*sic*], *composed of the Telugu districts formerly in Madras.* The national leadership of the Congress seemed to flirt with the idea that Hyderabad might be retained as a multilingual state, a kind of bastion against linguistic feelings. In addition, it was suggested that the Urdu tradition in Hyderabad made it an ideal centre from which Hindi could be propagated throughout the South. A large section of the Muslims and many professional people and bureaucrats were against disintegration, while all the political parties were at least formally committed to breaking up the state among the surrounding linguistic states. Most of the dispute was concerned with the question of whether disintegration should be immediate or delayed. (1970: 11, emphasis added)

The States Reorganisation Commission (also known as the Fazl Ali Committee),[7] constituted by the Government of India in December 1953, *did not* recommend the unification of Telangana and the Presidency Telugu districts. It also rejected the Presidency Telugus' claim over Madras all over again (Guha 2007: 194). The Commission concluded that "it will be in the interests of Andhra as well as Telangana, if for the present, the Telangana area is to be constituted into a separate State, which may be known as the Hyderabad State with provision for its unification with Andhra after the general elections likely to be held in or about 1961 if by a two-thirds majority the legislature of the residual Hyderabad State expresses itself in favour of such unification" (*Report of the States Reorganisation Commission* 1955: para 386). Pingle (2010), like Forrester before him, points out there was neither a popular movement nor unanimity among Congress factions on the unification of the regions along the lines that the Communists demanded. The Andhra Pradesh state was nevertheless created for a variety of political and economic reasons,

[7] Excerpts of the Commission's report, including the sections cited here, are available on: http://en.wikisource.org/wiki/India_States_Reorganisation_Commission_Report_Telangana_Andhra (visited on 17 May 2011).

including the possibility of the emergence of a stronger Congress party post-unification as well as the merger of the industrially developed Telangana region and the agriculturally developed Coastal region (Pingle 2010: 64).

The States Reorganisation Commission made an important observation on the advantages of unifying the Telugu speaking regions before recommending otherwise: "The advantages of a larger Andhra state including Telangana are that it will bring into existence a State of about 32 millions with a *considerable hinterland*, with large water and power resources, adequate mineral wealth and valuable raw materials. This will also solve the difficult and vexing problem of finding a permanent capital for Andhra; the twin cities of Hyderabad and Secunderabad are very well suited to be the capital of Vishalandhra" (*Report of the States Reorganisation Commission* 1955: para 371). After state formation, the "considerable hinterland" became not merely the destination of surpluses generated by agriculture and allied activities but also an important market for cultural commodities that Coastal Andhra capital produced. This, in turn, would have important political consequences in the years to come. My interest, more specifically, is the pioneering role of the film industry in creating an integrated market for the circulation of film—the first of the cultural commodities to find a market across the state.

After 1956: The Andhra Pradesh Map and the Market for Telugu Films

With the formation of Andhra Pradesh the two nodes in the circuit of capital flows in the film industry—Madras at one end and the Krishna–Godavari delta districts of Coastal Andhra at the other—were extended to include Hyderabad as a critical third. This did not occur overnight but it is necessary to anticipate the arrival of Hyderabad on the scene to understand post-1956 events.

By inaugurating two entirely new developments, state formation changed the very basis on which the industry had been organized. First, it opened up the underexploited market in Telangana. Second, soon enough the government of Andhra Pradesh became a key player in framing the discussions on the Teluguness of the Telugu cinema.

As a result of both, there was a further displacement of aesthetics in the conception of how film could be Telugu.

To begin with the film market in 1956, there was a striking mismatch between the map of the newly formed state of Andhra Pradesh and the contours of the market for Telugu films.

Till the 1950s Telangana—or the distribution territory of the Nizam (Naijam in Telugu)—marked a frontier not particularly hospitable to Telugu cinema. This region was otherwise a part of a distribution territory comprising the erstwhile undivided state of Hyderabad. Officially known as the Hyderabad Film Circuit, it continues in existence to this day as a distribution territory for Hindi and English films (Image 19). Before the 1950s, the territory had as a whole far fewer cinema halls than the Telugu-speaking areas of the Madras Presidency, and very few distributors for Telugu films. Rama Rao (1942) lists a total of 46 permanent cinema halls (including 4

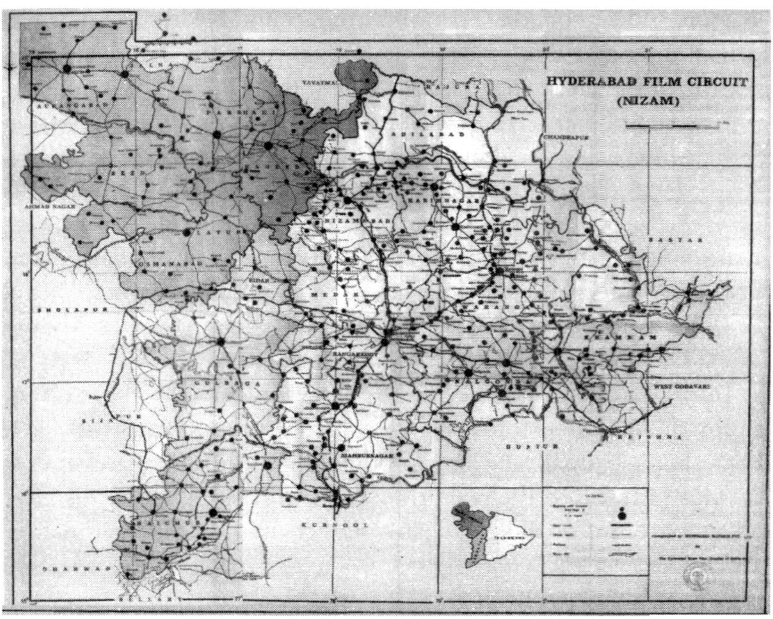

Image 19: The Hyderabad Film Circuit, which to this day includes regions now in Karnataka and Maharashtra. Published by the Hyderabad State Film Chamber of Commerce in *Hyderabad Film Diary 2007*.

"English Houses" in Secunderabad) and 11 touring cinemas in the whole of the Nizam's dominions. This includes cinema halls in towns which are now a part of Karnataka and Maharashtra (ibid.: 210–11). By comparison, the Telugu-speaking districts of the Presidency had 112 cinemas (85 permanent and 27 touring), without including Bellary (ibid.: 203–9). That Hyderabad (with Secunderabad, the twin cities) and the Telangana region in general were largely unavailable to the Telugu film industry for commercial exploitation before 1956 is borne out by Rama Rao, who mentions only one distributor in Hyderabad for Telugu and Tamil films: Deccan Films, which also distributed Hindi and Urdu films (ibid.: 111). The market share of the region for Telugu films, which was estimated at 10 per cent of box office collections, was disproportionately small in comparison to its size and population. By comparison, 50 per cent of the collections came from Coastal Andhra ("Circars and Nellore"), 15 per cent from Rayalaseema ("Ceded Districts and Chittoor"), 12.5 per cent from "Mysore and Coorg", 12.5 per cent from "Tamil Nadu" (the state was formed only in 1956, presumably this refers to the Tamil-speaking districts of the Presidency), 6.25 per cent from Burma, and 6.25 per cent from all other territories (ibid.: 76). An interesting illustration of these figures is offered by the advertisement of *Swargaseema* (B.N. Reddi, 1946, Image 20), which mentions only Secunderabad in its list of the towns and cities where the film was running. Other places mentioned are Bezwada, Kakinada, Rajahmundry, Vizianagaram, Guntur, Nellore, Machilipatnam and Visakhapatnam (Coastal Andhra), Kurnool (Rayalaseema), and Bangalore (then in Mysore state). The film was also due for release in Bellary.

To make matters worse, in 1941 the Hyderabad government imposed a steep customs duty on films imported into the state. There being virtually no film production within the state, almost all films screened in the region would be affected.[8] The relative size and importance of the Telangana market did not change much in

[8] The Hyderabad State Film Chamber of Commerce was formed in response to the Nizam government's announcement when alarmed exhibitors convened a meeting under the chairmanship of H.M. Reddy, who happened to be in Hyderabad city (Andhra Pradesh Film Chamber of Commerce 1981: 69).

Image 20: Advertisement for B.N. Reddi's *Swargaseema* listing cinema halls where it was being released (*Roopavani*, February 1946: back cover).

the 1940s, although Telugu film advertisements from the mid-1940s frequently (but not always) mentioned the distributor for Naijam. Distribution companies that find mention in the 1940s include Mallikarjuna Pictures (*Roopavani*, May 1946), Royal Film Exchange (for "Nizam and Deccan"; *Roopavani*, October 1946) and also Chamaria, which was among the major distributors of Telugu films in all the regions. As for film production in Hyderabad, a notable attempt was made in the 1920s when Dhirendranath Ganguly established a film studio and also the Lotus Film Company (1922–4), reportedly with financial support from the Nizam himself. During this period Ganguly also either owned or leased two cinema halls in the city (Barnouw and Krishnaswamy 1980: 27; Rajadhyaksha and Willemen 1999: 98; Mikkilineni 1975: 64). Barnouw and Krishnaswamy note that Ganguly was ordered to leave Hyderabad for screening the controversial *Razia Begum* (Nanubhai Desai and B.P. Mishra, 1924) in one of his theatres (1980: 28).

In 1946 there was an unsuccessful attempt by a Hyderabad-based businessman and film producer, Mahadeva Singh, to set up a studio in collaboration with Adavi Bapiraju, the art director and editor of a newspaper, *Mizaan* (Mikkilineni 1975: 64). I have not found evidence for the production of Telugu films in the region before 1956. Even in the early 1960s production companies from the region appear to be few and far between. There is a fleeting reference in the newspaper *Krishna Patrika* to the Hyderabad-based production company Manjeera Films Private Limited, established by "youngsters from Telangana" ("*Telangana yuvakulu stapinchina Manjeera Films*"), which was about to begin its second film (*Krishna Patrika* 1962a: 22). The company's first film *Chivariku Migiledi* (G. Ramineedu, 1960) was not shot in Hyderabad after all but in Narasu Studio, Madras, the new name for Vel Pictures.[9]

Hyderabad no doubt had a distinct film culture, characterized by a preference for Hindi and Urdu features. Reminiscing about the 1930s, an observer says that while a number of cinemas in the city showed English, Hindi, and Urdu films, only one cinema hall regularly showed Telugu films (Damodaraswamy 1986: 58). Another says, not without exaggeration, that in the 1930s and 1940s Telugu films were limited to a single screening per day, the morning or matinee show (Subba Rao 1964: 91). Advertisements in the Hyderabad-based newspaper *Golconda Patrika* from the late 1930s suggest that new Telugu releases were relatively rare as compared to Hindi films. For example, on 8 March 1937 there was a half-page advertisement for *Sarangadhara* (P. Pullaiah, 1937) in *Golconda Patrika* (p. 7), whereas five Hindi/Urdu films were advertised on the same day (p. 9). Well into the 1940s,

[9] The film is a remake of the Bengali *Deep Jweley Jai* (Asit Sen, 1959). The Telugu remake features Savitri in the lead role of a nurse in a mental asylum. She gets romantically involved with a patient, cures him, and in the end loses her sanity. Rajadhyaksha and Willemen (1999: 358) point out that the Bengali original was later remade in Hindi as *Khamoshi* (Asit Sen, 1969), featuring Waheeda Rehman in the female lead, played by Suchitra Sen in the original. They do not mention *Chivariki Migiledi*. I am grateful to B. Vijayvardhan, a film enthusiast based in Bangalore, for lending me the DVD of the film that he himself digitized from a VHS copy.

Kannada and Marathi too were frequently advertised in the paper.[10] We notice a significant increase in the advertisements for Telugu films during the 1940s. However, the larger point, that they had a rather modest presence in the city's exhibition circuit, is well taken. Even after 1956, Hindi films outperformed their Telugu counterparts at the box office. Film advertisements from the early 1950s suggest that some Telugu films may not even have been released in the Telangana region.[11]

The coverage of Telugu cinema in Telugu periodicals published in the Telangana region was limited and intermittent, according to the film journalist Bommakanti Subba Rao, who says that the very first regular newspaper column on Telugu cinema began to be published only in 1946 in *Mizaan*. It is not as if reports on Telugu films were earlier non-existent. The comparison he makes is with the Presidency region, where full-fledged film journals were apparently published in Madras, Vijayawada, and Machilipatnam from about 1937 (Bommakanti 1991: 43–4).

There can be no doubt that state formation had a direct and immediate impact on the growth of the Telugu film industry, which expanded impressively over the next four decades. This is reflected in the rise in film production and expansion of distribution-exhibition.

The annual production of films went up from 27 in 1956, to 36 in 1957, to 47 in 1959 (Rajadhyaksha and Willemen, 1999: 31–2; the figures are 33 in 1957 and 46 in 1962 according to the *Andhra Film Chamber Journal* 1964a: 41). In 1967 the figure stood at 62 and since 1976 there have always been more than 90 productions per year, matching (and at times exceeding) the production levels of Hindi films (Rajadhyaksha and Willemen, 1999: 31–2).

The boom in production was partly due to the rapid expansion of the exhibition and distribution sectors (Table 2). The number of cinema halls increased across all the regions of the state from 402 in

[10] There is a front page advertisement for a Kannada and Marathi film in *Golconda Patrika*'s 5 July 1943 issue.

[11] For example, no distributor is mentioned for the Nizam territory for *Perantalu* (Gopichand, 1951) in the advertisement (inside back cover, *Roopavani*, April 1951).

Table 1. Film Production

1939	1940	1953	1956	1957	1959	1962	1967	1976	1977	1978	1979	1980
12/15	14/12	29/29	27	36/33	47	48/46	62	90	99	94	131	152

Between 1956 and 1977, the selected years represent new peaks in production. Notice that in 1978 there is a temporary reversal of the general trend of the late 1970s and 1980s.

Sources: Rajadhyaksha and Willemen (1999: 30–2) for all years; Ramabrahmam (1940) for 1939; Raraju (1941) for 1940; *Andhra Film Chamber Journal* (1964a) for 1953, 1957, and 1962. Rajadhyaksha and Willemen's figures appear first, when more than one source is referred to.

Table 2. Cinema Halls

	1942	1953	1957	1962	1975	1980	1995
Coastal Andhra	85 (18 touring)			272 (permanent)	473 (129 touring)		1545 (413 touring)
Rayalaseema	27 (9 touring)			78 (permanent)	191 (99 touring)		713 (338 touring)
Hyderabad State (1942) or Telangana (post-1956)	57 (11 touring)			134 (permanent)	28 (33 touring)		799 (264 touring)
Hyderabad-Secunderabad	18			43 (permanent)	74		121
Bellary (Mysore/Karnataka)	11 (2 touring)			15 (permanent)			
Andhra Pradesh total	169 (40)	402	575	484 (permanent)	892 (261 touring)	1904 (751 temporary	3057 (1015 touring)

Sources: Rama Rao (1942) for 1942; *Andhra Film Chamber Journal* (1964a) for 1953 and 1957; *Andhra Film Chamber Journal* (1964b) for 1962; Mikkilineni 1975: 78–9) for 1975; Andhra Pradesh Film Chamber of Commerce (1981a: 131) for 1980; Andhra Pradesh Film Chamber of Commerce (1995: 23) for 1995. [12]

[12] There are inconsistencies and addition mistakes in the figures put out by all the sources from the *Andhra Film Chamber Journal* (1964b). Andhra Pradesh Film Chamber of Commerce (1995: 23) skips an entire district (Ranga Reddy, whose cinema halls are listed individually elsewhere in the same book) and also has a list of "additional theatres" (1995: 24) adding up to 27. Nevertheless, this is the most accurate and authentic of the computations available.

1953 to 575 in 1957 and 668 in 1962 (*Andhra Film Chamber Journal* 1964a: 41).[13] In 1962 the region-wise break-up of cinema halls was 350 in the erstwhile Presidency districts (272 in the coastal districts and alone) and 134 in the Telangana region (*Andhra Film Chamber Journal* 1964b: 56). Between 1962 (*Andhra Film Chamber Journal* 1964b) and 1975 (Mikkilineni 1975: 78–9), permanent cinema halls in the Telangana region, excluding Hyderabad and Secunderabad, grew from 91 to 121. Bellary district, which became a part of Karnataka in 1956 and was considered an important market for Telugu cinema, makes for an interesting comparison. Rama Rao (1942: 203–11) mentions 11 cinema halls in Bellary. Although the Telugu film industry continued to acknowledge the importance of this district, there was only a marginal increase of cinema halls here—to 15 over the next two decades (*Andhra Film Chamber Journal* 1964b: 56).

Mikkilineni, citing unnamed government sources, draws attention to the expansion that was already under way but was not reflected in the available tabulations: 100 cinema halls were under construction in different parts of the state. Narasaiah (1981: 146) notes that huge investments were made in the exhibition sector in the state capital: 10 cinema halls cost a crore (ten million) of rupees to build. Table 2 shows that, between 1975 and 1995, whereas Coastal Andhra's cinema halls grew by an impressive 3.26 times, those in Telangana grew slightly faster and increased by 3.5 times. Growth in the Rayalaseema region was even more impressive (3.73 times). Distributors in the state increased from 57 in 1953 to 357 in 1957 (*Andhra Film Chamber Journal* 1964a: 41), primarily because of the inclusion of distributors in Hyderabad–Secunderabad. Most of them did not in fact distribute Telugu films before 1956 and it is unlikely that they suddenly changed their specialization. But this vastly expanded network was potentially available for Telugu cinema.

The extent of growth of film consumption in the state is evident from increased entertainment tax collection, which rose from Rs 5,153,991 in 1957 to Rs 9,00,000 in 1962 (*Andhra Film Chamber*

[13] In all likelihood these included tent and touring cinemas because the district-wise breakdown provided elsewhere in the same issue of the journal (1964b) adds up to 484 theatres.

Journal 1964a: 41). Prior to state formation, box office collections in Hyderabad for Telugu films were less than those of Vijayawada. In less than a decade the Hyderabad box office grew six times and was twice as large as Vijayawada's (*Andhra Film Chamber Journal* 1964c: 83).

While the correlation between this impressive growth and the increased access to the Telangana market in general and Hyderabad city in particular is not in doubt, it is important to note that this was coeval with significant developments in Coastal Andhra, which in turn impacted the flow of investments into the industry. If the Telangana region and Hyderabad city proved to be a "pull" factor, the "push" factor was the increased availability of the surplus generated by the peasant economies of Coastal Andhra. Nagarjuna Sagar dam on the river Krishna was completed in 1966. It was estimated to have an irrigation potential of 150,000 hectares (one hectare is 2.4711 acres) in the Krishna river basin of Coastal Andhra (Ananth 2007: 104–5). Citing district gazetteers, Ananth points out that by 1966 there was an increase of land under cultivation to the extent of 172,119 acres (69,653 hectares) in Krishna district alone. There was a 10 per cent increase in the area under cash-generating paddy and sugarcane cultivation. Better irrigation in the 1960s was accompanied by low levels of tax on agricultural land and a sharp rise in agricultural commodity prices after Independence, especially in the 1960s when the farm harvest price of paddy rose from Rs 30.98 per quintal in 1960–1 to Rs 40 in 1965–6 (Ananth 2007: 106). According to the geographer S. Simhadri, while the dam itself was in Telangana, it was mostly the Coastal Andhra part of the river basin that benefited: "Nagarjuna Sagar is located in Nalgonda across river Krishna at an altitude of about 100 to 150 m at the south-eastern border. Therefore the small portions of low lands in the south-east margin get water leaving large areas of high elevation dry. In fact if it were to be constructed a few kilometres upstream the waters from the project could have been made use of for not only large tracts of Nalgonda but also for a few more semi-arid districts like Warangal, Karimnagar, and Khammam of Telangana. In fact the coastal politicians and engineering bureaucracy have conspired and denied water to the drought district of Telangana" (1997: 2315).

The steep rise in the number of films produced in the post-

Independence period in general and from the late 1960s in particular is a definite indication that the industry was benefiting from the boom in agriculture in the Coastal Andhra region. Indeed, so intimate was the link between Coastal Andhra economies and film production that the cyclone which destroyed crops in large parts of the region in November 1977 temporarily arrested the general trend of increased film production (see Table 1). Production fell from 99 in 1977 to 94 in 1978 and rose to 131 in 1979 and 152 in 1980 (figures in Rajadhyaksha and Willemen 1999).

Contrary to the stereotypical image of the rich farmer arriving in Madras with a sack full of cash to produce a film, the movement of surplus away from agriculture and into film (or other businesses for that matter) was a rather more complex process. Ananth's work offers valuable insights into this process, which was characterized by a two-way movement of surpluses between village and town. The rise in agricultural surpluses was bettered by the growth in trade in urban centres like Vijayawada, Ananth suggests, by interpreting the rise in sales tax collections from Independence (Ananth 2007: 108). Further, the amount realized by the government through the Motor Vehicle Tax in Krishna district more than quadrupled between 1962–3 and 1966–7, from Rs 21.63 to Rs 90.03 lakh (ibid.: 108–9), while the number of goods vehicles increased by over 1100 (ibid.: 110). Ananth goes on to explain that agricultural surpluses were deployed to set up leasing and finance companies which specialized in financing the purchase of goods vehicles and buses, making Vijayawada a major hub of the road-transport sector. Among the factors triggering the transportation boom was the export of iron ore to Japan from a now defunct mine in the district and, more importantly, the transport of materials to the Nagarjuna Sagar project (ibid.: 109). Surpluses generated by trade, finance, transport, and other businesses, as well as the savings of salaried professionals, argues Ananth, were used to acquire agricultural land in Coastal Andhra villages.

Interestingly, an overwhelming majority of Vijayawada city's current (rupee) billionaires "started their careers as lorry cleaners, drivers, small time clerks or small time commission agents who slowly climbed the economic ladder . . . A large number of them are migrants from the surrounding villages who came to the town in search of livelihood" (ibid.: 201). In other words these entrepreneurs were born in peasant families of modest means. There is also a close correlation between the growth of agricultural and other surpluses generated by the activities of the peasant caste–class constellation and the expansion of the film industry. Some of this surplus found its way into film production, although the flow was mediated by other businesses preceding its entry into the film industry: recall D. Ramanaidu,[14] who was already in the business of selling bricks. The point of entry could also be exhibition, with the cinema hall becoming one of the investment avenues for a successful peasant-entrepreneur. Ananth's discussion of the new entrepreneurs from the Kamma caste in Vijayawada draws attention to an interesting *pattern of investment*: surplus is ploughed back into the expansion of business but also into the acquisition of agricultural land and real estate, investments that "provide rent on a regular basis. This rent-seeking attitude seems to be widely prevalent in nearly all sections of the business class" (ibid.: 200). It is likely that the exhibition sector benefited from rent-seeking entrepreneurs because cinema halls are, after all, rent-earning urban assets. There was, however, a stronger and less incidental connection between the film industry's development and the investment preferences of entrepreneurs from peasant backgrounds. In order to appreciate this, it is necessary to move to Hyderabad, where a chain reaction—albeit one whose results were not immediately apparent—was set off with the formation of the state.

It is not clear to me who or what was contributing to the growth in cinema halls of the Telangana region. G. Haragopal advances the claim that "The capital thrown up by the agrarian surplus in [C]oastal Andhra could not be ploughed back into the agrarian sector partly on account of the inelastic nature of the agricultural sector and partly because of the failure to engender quick and attractive returns. Consequently the capital was in search of new avenues and green pastures" (1985: 69–70). These "pastures" included "skyscrapers [*sic*], hotels and cinema theatres," while a "part of this capital went into film production itself" (ibid.: 71). Haragopal's observation is useful because it alerts us to the links between the two regions, as also to agricultural surpluses and non-agricultural investments, real estate in particular. Much though this claim strengthens my argument about

[14] See the discussion on him in chapter 1.

Presidency peasants and the Telugu film industry, there is as of now no definitive evidence to suggest that the expansion of the exhibition sector in Telangana was due to the inflow of agricultural surpluses. As we shall see, Coastal Andhra entrepreneurs of peasant origin began to invest in Hyderabad from the 1960s, but it was not an unmediated movement of "agricultural surplus" being witnessed.

It is likely that the growth of the exhibition sector in Telangana, too, was due to investments by local entrepreneurs. Ironically Haragopal's attribution of the growth of film exhibition in Hyderabad and production in general to capital from Coastal Andhra was made at a time when the most-sought-after cinema hall in the twin cities, Sandhya 70mm, was built and owned by one Chandrayya, a Telangana Dalit entrepreneur from Nalgonda district, who went on to become the owner of eight cinema halls in the capital ("Naa Peru Kankara Chandrayya", 2011). Chandrayya is an exception, but other evidence points to the formation of locally generated surpluses. G. Parthasarathy says that the four Telangana districts—Karimnagar, Warangal, Nalgonda, and Khammam—recorded the highest rates of growth in agriculture throughout the state between 1955–6 and 1977–8 (1984: A-75). Vamsi Vakulabharanam (2004) argues that from 1970 the Telangana region saw substantial growth in the agricultural sector on account of the tapping of groundwater resources. Some of the surpluses thus generated may, as in Coastal Andhra, have been invested in the construction of cinema halls.

What is important for our purposes is that, by the 1960s, the expansion of the market for Telugu films in the Telangana region was coeval with other post-state formation developments that drew Coastal Andhra peasant entrepreneurs of the Madras film industry, even as other entrepreneurs of the region gravitated to Hyderabad. With specific reference to the cinema, the state government became an active player in channelling these flows by creating a new link between economics and cultural politics.

Investing in the Telugu Land: Loans, Subsidies, and Real Estate

In the 1950s, as noted, Madras saw the rise to prominence of the Vijaya-Vauhini institutions. Mikkilineni (1975: 61–4) states that there were four "Telugu" studios in Madras in the 1950s. These included the older Vauhini and Sobhanachala (renamed Venus in 1955), and two new ones: Bharani, which was established in 1950 and owned by the actress Bhanumathi and her husband P.S. Ramakrishna Rao (Image 21); and Prakash, which was established around 1952 by K.S. Prakash Rao.

In 1954 Vel Pictures had been acquired by one D.L. Narasu (Murari n.d.: 104). Either by oversight or the "mother tongue" of the new owner, this studio lost its status as one of the "Telugu" studios in Mikkilineni's account. In 1951 L.V. Prasad, a director of commercially successful and critically acclaimed social films, set up the production company Prasad Art Pictures in partnership with some investors from

Image 21: Songbook of *Prema* (*Kathal* in Tamil, P.S. Ramakrishna Rao, 1952), a Bharani production featuring Bhanumathi and ANR.

his village ("Film Vartalu," *Roopavani* 1951: 17–18). It is possible that his partners were rich peasants looking for investment opportunities beyond their village. Prasad then went on to build a studio in Madras in 1965 (Murari n.d.: 116; Pillai 2010: 7). The construction of new studios well into the 1960s, alongside the increase in the number of films produced in Madras through the 1950s and 1960s, leaves little doubt that the film industry had settled down comfortably in the city. The formation of Andhra Pradesh did nothing to destabilize the production centre in Madras.

Nevertheless, almost immediately after the state came into being the government of Andhra Pradesh initiated a process of which the consequences for the language question were only felt some years later. Its intervention was such that from the late 1950s the state emerged as something of a patron of Presidency peasants in the industry. More importantly, the intervention shifted the equilibrium between aesthetic, economic, and political concerns further from aesthetic considerations than ever before.

In the years between Independence and the formation of Andhra Pradesh the growing prominence of Vijaya-Vauhini was coeval with the expansion of the post-zamindari base of the film industry. ANR, who began his acting career in 1940, played an important role in the consolidation of the industry's peasant base. In 1949 he partnered a major female star of the period, Anjali Devi, among other investors, to set up the production company Aswini Pictures (Rajadhyaksha and Willemen 1999: 86). Aswini's first film was, according to Murari (n.d.: 83), the Telugu and Tamil bilingual production *Mayalamari/ Mayakkari* (P. Sridhar, 1951). Anjali Devi and her musician husband Adi Narayana Rao went on to establish the studio Anjali Pictures in 1951 (Rajadhyaksha and Willemen 1999: 86; Mikkilineni 1975 does not mention this in his list of Telugu studios of the 1950s, Image 22). ANR did not invest in the studio.

However, he became the founding chairman of Annapurna Pictures Private Limited, which was established in the same year (Prabhu 1993: 70). Annapurna's first film, *Donga Ramudu*, was released only four years later in 1955 due to the board's decision to work with the director K.V. Reddy, of *Patala Bhairavi* fame, who was busy with other projects (ibid.: 11, Image 23).

Image 22: Songbook of *Paradesi* (*Poongothai* in Tamil, L.V. Prasad, 1953), an Anjali Pictures production featuring Anjali Devi and ANR.

Image 23: Songbook of *Donga Ramudu*, the first film produced by Annapurna.

Annapurna Pictures Private Limited was the first major institution established by Krishna district Kammas of peasant origin *without* zamindar support. It remained in business from the 1950s till the end of the 1980s, its last production being released in 1987 (ibid.: 274). ANR apart, there were two other prominent Kammas from the district among the company's founders: first, Annapurna's managing director, Dukkipati Madhusudhana Rao, who had earlier "discovered" ANR as a stage actor, worked with him in the amateur theatre (*parishath natakam*), and then put the actor in touch with key industry figures who offered him film roles (Murari n.d.: 107; Ramachandra Murthy 1996: 48); and second, Katragadda Srinivasa Rao, the other important director from the district, who was the managing partner of the distribution company Navayuga Films (Prabhu 1993: 70). Navayuga was established in Vijayawada by Kamma entrepreneurs with communist sympathies in 1947 and acquired a reputation for promoting "progressive" films: indeed, it was inaugurated by the communist leader P. Sundarayya himself (Murari n.d.: 57). Navayuga began distributing Telugu films in 1950, having distributed Hindi films till then (Images 24 & 25). In 1956, anticipating an expansion of the market in Telangana, it opened its Secunderabad branch. It had had a branch in Guntakal from 1952. By 1981 it had distributed over 400 films (Andhra Pradesh Film Chamber of Commerce 1981b: 163).

The establishment of Annapurna flags the increasing prominence in the industry of male stars who are now seen acquiring stakes in production. Till this point it had been the female stars, such as Krishnaveni (who married the Raja of Mirzapuram: Murari n.d.: 63), Lakshmirajyam (ibid.: 85), Bhanumathi (ibid.: 56), and Anjali Devi, working in partnership with their husbands, who had set up studios and production companies. Among the major male stars, "Chittoor" V. Nagaiah had been involved in film production before ANR (Images 26 and 27). He had acted in over 300 films and was at the height of his career paid up to Rs 100,000 per film, yet he ended up losing his substantial wealth and was deeply in debt towards the end of his life (ibid.: 48). So it was not as if there was already a model of the male star-as-producer to emulate in the early 1950s.

Annapurna's success is an indication that in the 1950s the production sector could detach itself from the ownership of studios and infrastructure, and focus instead on, first, integrating the (male) star into the production process by making him a key stakeholder in

24

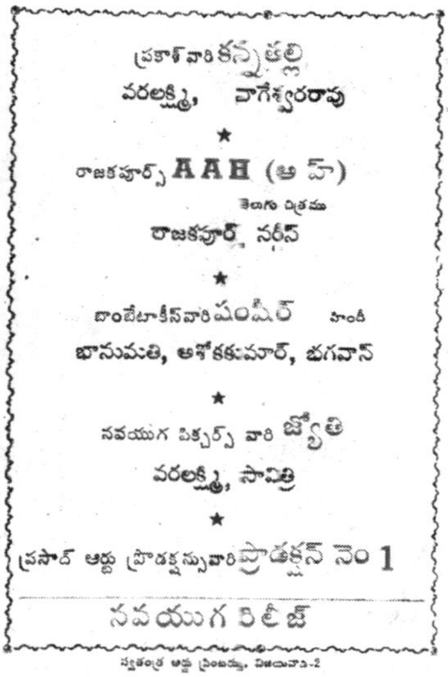

25

Images 24 & 25: Navayuga before 1956. Front and back covers of Telugu songbook of the Hindi film *Aan* (Mehboob Khan, 1952). The back cover lists both Hindi and Telugu films distributed by the company. *Aah* (Raju Nawathe, 1953), which figures in this list, was released in Telugu as *Premalekhalu*, but here the Hindi title is used.

the sector; and second, fostering close ties between film production and the growing distribution sector.

A further point of interest is that the establishment of Annapurna coincides with Vijaya-Vauhini's attempt to build NTR into a star. The actor was in 1950 contracted by Vijaya Pictures to act in four films over two years (Venkat Narayan 1985: 206). Vijaya-Vauhini continued to thrive even as NTR went on to work with other producers as well as produce his own films. Vijaya Pictures cast both NTR and ANR, after they were well established as stars, to make the hit films *Missamma* (L.V. Prasad, 1955), *Maya Bazaar* (K.V. Reddy, 1957), and *Gundamma Katha* (K. Kameswara Rao, 1962). The absence of any conflict of interest between rising male stars and the institution—and indeed the reason why Vijaya-Vauhini survived much longer than the other Telugu studios in Madras—was on account of its significant rent-based revenue under the management of Nagi Reddy and Chakrapani. Through the 1950s and early 1960s the studio expanded well beyond

26

27

Images 26 & 27: Songbook of *Thyagayya* (1946), "Chittoor" V. Nagaiah's directed and produced classic. The back cover (right) has an advertisement of HMV's gramophone records of the same film.

the needs of its home productions. In the 1970s it had 12 floors, 10 cameras, and 6 projection rooms, and could support the simultaneous shooting of 6 films on any given day (Mikkilineni 1975: 61).

In a manner of speaking, Annapurna came closest to actualizing Ramabrahmam's proposed unification of aesthetics, economics, and politics. The company was widely praised for its quality socials, which had a good run at the box office too. Among its distinguishing features was, as one reporter charmingly put it, the "Bengali type delicate film" (*Bengali typu sunnita chitram*: Bommakanti 1964a). Annapurna's socials were in fact widely perceived as its mark of distinction. As KoKu had argued, unlike mythologicals and folklore films the social was closely associated with *Telugutanam*. Although both NTR and ANR acted in films of all genres, they became strongly identified with distinct aesthetic, and by extension political, trends within the industry. Annapurna, and by implication ANR, became rapidly and closely associated with both high quality socials and Teluguness. An instance of this is apparent from 1962, when the film director C. Pullaiah stated that there was wild enthusiasm (*verri jastiga undedi*) for mythological and folklore films among audiences of Telugu cinema. This was moderated primarily by the efforts of Annapurna and Prasad Art Pictures (L.V. Prasad's company), which had made socials more acceptable to audiences. Pullaiah made this comment in the light of his observation that Telugu film audiences, unlike their Tamil counterparts, continued nonetheless to patronize mythologicals and folklore films (*Krishna Patrika* 1962b: 30). One film critic, who nostalgically compared the company to (H.M. Reddy's) Rohini, Vauhini, and Sarathy, bemoaned the closure of the first two and the declining standards of the third which, he claimed, was making money by remaking non-Telugu films. He then commended Annapurna for its ability to deliver five consecutive hit films—these, it seems had a 100-day run each—adding that this Telugu institution was a ray of light in the otherwise disappointing world of Telugu cinema (*Krishna Patrika* 1962a: 16).

Soon, ANR's superstar status, as also the company's growing reputation, brought it to the notice of the political leadership in Andhra Pradesh. Shortly after the state's formation its chief minister, Neelam Sanjeeva Reddy, reportedly gave a call to ANR and other industry figures, asking them to relocate to Hyderabad (Bhageeratha 1980). Throughout the 1960s it was ANR who was the epitome of the Teluguness that was an attribute of the social. If anything it was his "cultural authenticity", which Prasad (1999) draws attention to, that was enhanced by his association with what I term the "Hyderabad faction" in the industry.[15] In the 1960s ANR and Annapurna were the centre of the discussion on relocation. Chronologically, however, it was another Madras-based Kamma enterprise that made the first move.

In response to the interest shown by the state government, Mikkilineni states, Sarathy Studio was launched in 1956 by Yarlagadda Ramakrishnaprasad of Sarathy Films Private Limited (of *Malapilla*

[15] Madhava Prasad (1999: 48) notes that ANR in Telugu, Sivaji Ganesan and Gemini Ganesan in Tamil, and Kalyan Kumar in Kannada, "tend to be invested with a sense of *cultural authenticity*".

and *Raitu Bidda* fame). Ramakrishnaprasad was a younger brother of Yarlagadda Sivaramaprasad, the Raja of Challapalli, and was involved in the activities of Sarathy since *Grihapravesam* (L.V. Prasad, 1946). He had taken over the management of Sarathy after Ramabrahmam left the company in 1945. Meanwhile, the Raja had become busy advancing his political career (Murari n.d.: 101). Sarathy Studio, built with a loan of Rs 225,000 from the Andhra Pradesh State Finance Corporation (APSFC), was completed in 1958 (Mikkilineni 1975: 65–7). Ramakrishnaprasad was its managing director (Andhra Pradesh Film Chamber of Commerce 1981c: 53).

Annapurna's establishment coincided with the making of the Sarathy production *Rojulu Marayi* (Tapi Chanakya, 1955), a film critically acclaimed by KoKu (2000a: 471–3).[16] It shows the struggle of the peasantry against a rich landlord, Sagaraiah (C.S.R. Anjaneeyulu). While continuing many of *Raitu Bidda*'s aesthetic and thematic concerns, *Rojulu Marayi* makes the strongest link yet between representation of the countryside, peasant life, and realism. It features ANR in the lead as Venu, the defiant son of a submissive sharecropper who organizes the rich and poor peasants of the village against Sagaraiah. Unlike *Raitu Bidda*,[17] the film leaves no room for reconciliation between the peasants and landlord, and ends with the latter's arrest. Although shot mostly in the studio, it makes effective use of outdoor locations, especially during its song sequences, which tend to be instructional and directly addressed to the camera in order to paint a detailed picture of village life and agricultural activity. Great care is taken, even in its studio settings, to re-create houses, yards, and even peasants' fields. In fact it begins with a studio song shot on farmers' harvesting paddy. We see large piles of paddy, haystacks, and oxen along with a dozen or so extras, all of them with their *gochees* in order! Reinforcing its authenticity is the film's use of folk tunes in songs written by Tapi Dharma Rao (who had also worked for *Raitu Bidda*). The film was a major commercial success and, as we shall see, played a critical role in determining the future course of the industry–Telugu connection.

[16] It was shot in Narasu Studio, formerly Vel Pictures.

[17] Discussed in detail in the ensuing chapter.

Sarathy Studio is the only establishment in Hyderabad which is directly traceable to Presidency zamindars (Image 28). Historically significant and high in symbolic value, it remained economically marginal to the film industry even as it became the catalyst for events that would shape Telugu cinema in the years to come. Ironically, developments that Sarathy indirectly facilitated are evidence of the definitive shift away from the industry's reliance on zamindari investments.

Before elaborating on how Sarathy and Annapurna came to become a part of the same story, brief mention is necessary of the growing intimacy between the film industry and the political establishment after 1956. The government's film policy in Andhra Pradesh was predicated on this intimacy. As such, of course, film–politician links in the Presidency region have a pre-Independence history. Baskaran

Image 28: *Bhyagya Devata* (*Bhagya Devathai* in Tamil, Tapi Chanakya, 1959), a Sarathy Studios production.

(1996: 70–1) points out that in the Madras Presidency Tamil film stars were associated with political campaigns since the 1930s. With specific reference to the Telugu cinema, political figures had occasionally expressed their support for or disapproval of individual films in the past, starting from the late 1930s. In the late 1930s Telugu film producers made repeated attempts to enlist the support of prominent political leaders and public figures through highly publicized special screenings. In Madras, B. Gopala Reddy, minister for local administration (reported in *Madras Mail,* 5 February 1938: 12), P. Subbaroyan, minister for education, K. Venkataswamy Nayudu, deputy president, Madras Legislative Council, and C.R. Reddy, vice chancellor of Andhra University (reported in *Madras Mail,* 2 April 1938: 12) attended such screenings, which inevitably included speeches by the dignitaries.

In the post-Independence period the political leadership was a willing participant in the industry's attempts to increase its visibility in the public domain and also earn respectability. For their part, Congress politicians actively cultivated film personalities and appeared in public with them even as intra-party feuds became more pronounced in the 1960s. Ministers regularly participated in public functions organized by film producers to celebrate the success of their films. Annapurna played an important role in establishing this trend. The practice of staging public celebrations of a film's success and making such events occasions for political propaganda was instituted in Tamil Nadu some years earlier: "When *Nadodi Mannan* [MGR, 1958], in which MGR starred, completed a successful 100-day run, the party organized a huge colourful procession in Madurai to celebrate the event. The public meeting that followed the procession was addressed by eminent leaders of the party, including C.N. Annadurai" (Pandian 1992: 34). In the official history of Annapurna (Prabhu 1993), public functions organized to celebrate the 100-day run of the company's films play a critical role in determining the course of the state's film policy. During these events ministers made public assurances of government support to the Telugu film industry, even as they tried to persuade film personalities to relocate to Hyderabad.

One of Annapurna's biggest hits in the early 1960s was *Iddaru Mitrulu* (Adurthi Subba Rao, 1961) which featured ANR in a double role.[18] It was reported to have been the very first Telugu film to have had a 100-day run in the Hyderabad–Secunderabad twin cities (Murthy 1962: 17). The success of the film in the state capital was a sign that the city was becoming increasingly important as a market for Telugu films. The celebration marking its 100-day run was held in Hyderabad. Earlier, such celebrations had usually been held in Madras or Coastal Andhra towns like Vijayawada. This particular event, Prabhu claims, was attended by most ministers of the state cabinet and was presided over by M. Chenna Reddy (Prabhu 1993: 131–40).[19] At the time, Chenna Reddy held the planning and panchayati raj portfolios and some years later went on to become an important leader of the movement for the formation of a separate Telangana state. The Hyderabad-based Telugu newspaper *Andhra Bhoomi* reported Reddy expressing his desire to see the film industry relocate to the state. Reddy also hoped that the state's finance minister (Brahmananda Reddy), also present at the meeting, would take steps to ensure government support to the industry. Chief minister Neelam Sanjeeva Reddy and his other cabinet colleagues did not attend the event but conveyed their regards (*Andhra Bhoomi* 1962: 5). Chenna Reddy's statements on the need for the film industry to relocate also received prominent coverage in *Golconda Patrika* (7 April 1962: 4).

The immediate trigger for what we can now see as a chain reaction was a strike in the Vijaya-Vauhini studios in 1962. This threatened to disrupt the shooting schedules of Annapurna's Telugu and Tamil bilingual production *Chaduvukunna Ammayilu* (Adurthi Subba Rao, 1962). The company thus decided to shoot in Sarathy Studios in Hyderabad instead. By this time Sarathy Studio, after only three years of existence, was virtually shut because of the meagreness of productions coming in to Hyderabad. Even the attempt at producing its own films had not made matters sustainable. Between 1959 and 1963, reportedly, only 14 films were produced in Sarathy Studio (*Andhra Film Journal* 1964d: 38). According to another report

[18] For a discussion of the film and its remake featuring Chiranjeevi, see Srinivas (2009: 144–7).

[19] These 100-day celebrations continued to be held in Madras for years to come.

L.V. Prasad, Tapi Chanakya (director), Katragadda Narasiah (Navayuga Films), and some others had formed a company called Nagarjuna Films and leased the studio. But they too failed to turn things round for the studio (Rao 1964: 99).

The decision to shoot *Chaduvukunna Ammayilu* in Hyderabad may have been a direct consequence of Chenna Reddy's intervention. The minister, who met Madhusudhana Rao and Adurthi Subba Rao (hired to direct *Chaduvukunna Ammayilu*) at the 100-day function of the latter's *Manchi Manasulu* (1962) in Hyderabad, reportedly suggested to them that they shoot the film in Hyderabad rather than wait out the strike. Chenna Reddy and his cabinet colleague K. Brahmananda Reddy (then finance minister) assured the director that the government would offset the additional cost incurred by the company in Hyderabad, where production was expected to be more expensive than in Madras (Prabhu 1993: 152). Within days the strike in Vijaya-Vauhini was called off, but Annapurna had by then decided to shoot in Hyderabad. Advance payments were made to Sarathy Studios, government assurances being the stated reasons for the company's decision (ibid.: 153). Coming in the wake of the successful run of *Iddaru Mitrulu* in the city, this decision was widely appreciated by commentators who wanted the industry to shift to Hyderabad. One reporter predicted that this was the beginning of a new era in the history of the Hyderabad industry (*Krishna Patrika* 1962c: 26).

The immediate fallout of Annapurna's decision to shoot in Hyderabad was the reopening of Sarathy Studios (Prabhu 1993; Rao 1964). The Sarathy management had well-established business links with Navayuga. Even before the studio was built Sarathy Films' *Rojulu Marayi* (Tapi Chanakya, 1955) had been distributed by Navayuga, and its success resulted in a long-term partnership between the two companies. This later extended to the studio's association with the distribution company. Soon after the studio reopened in 1962, Navayuga acquired a majority stake in it (Prabhu 1993: 193). By 1969 the management of the studio had passed on to Srinivasa Rao of Navayuga (Murari n.d.: 101). A government loan to Sarathy in 1964 was therefore not to a zamindari institution but to one under the effective control of peasant entrepreneurs.

Within months of Navayuga's acquisition of Sarathy Studios, ANR was considering relocating to Hyderabad (*Krishna Patrika* 1962d). Soon he did, becoming the first major Telugu actor of any standing to move to the city. ANR's decision to base himself in Hyderabad meant that his producers would have to shoot there rather than in Madras. For precisely this reason, the move was hailed by a section of the press. One commentator called it a selfless act reminiscent of stories from the puranas (Rao 1964: 99). ANR's erstwhile co-star and business partner Anjali Devi recalled, more recently, that his ability to convince his producers to shoot in Hyderabad was an important development for the industry (*Andhra Jyothi* 2008: iv). Presumably, ANR risked losing projects by insisting that his films be produced from Hyderabad. However, as one observer pointed out, his decision effectively meant that he was forcing his producers to use Sarathy Studios, the only facility available in Hyderabad in the 1960s; and the fact was that government subsidies for films produced in Hyderabad only benefited ANR starrers made in Sarathy (Sivaram 1964: 61). Even as ANR was passing on the cost of his commitment to the Telugu cause to his producers, he was ensuring a synergy between the different businesses that were being organized around him.

Unfortunately for him, ANR's attempt to fuse business strategy and cultural politics could not be long sustained. He backtracked on his decision to act only in Hyderabad productions and in 1964 returned to work in Madras. This decision too may have been part of an effort at promoting his business partners, because a report attributes it to an unnamed distribution company leasing Bharani Studio in Madras (*Krishna Patrika* 1964a: 14). Clearly, Hyderabad in the early 1960s was not working out either for ANR or his associates.

By 1962 NTR had overtaken ANR as the highest paid actor in the industry, and he had begun to act in over ten films per year (Venkat Rao 2003: 21). It is possible that ANR's self-fashioning as the representative of "Telugu" interests within the industry was, at least in part, an attempt at compensating for his diminishing stardom. NTR had no role to play in the events leading up to the announcement of the government's film policy in 1964. NTR's biographer Venkat Rao (2003) states that, around this time, the rivalry between the two big stars began to be spoken of in terms of the rivalry between the

Madras and Hyderabad factions in the film industry, NTR being identified with studios and other interests in Madras. There was also some public censure of NTR's (in)action, expressed in the form of dung being flung on posters of his films (Venkat Rao 2003: 20).[20] Even as ANR gained stature as the representative of Telugu interests, NTR participated in public functions showcasing his popularity and performed high-visibility charitable acts.[21]

In early January 1964, after a few rounds of discussion with industry representatives—including ANR and Madhusudhana Rao—the state government headed by Neelam Sanjeeva Reddy announced a new film policy. The highlights were a Rs 50,000 subsidy for films (in any language) produced in Hyderabad,[22] loans for the construction of industry infrastructure (such as studios and cinema halls), and the institution of (Nandi) awards for Telugu films. Loans of Rs 500,000 each for two proposed studios were approved, as was an interest-free loan of Rs 250,000 for the expansion of Sarathy Studios (Sivaram 1964: 60). The promptness of the government decision and the comprehensive nature of the new policy were greeted with pleasant surprise by industry and journalists alike.

Rajadhyaksha and Willemen (1999: 25) altogether miss this comprehensive policy of the Andhra Pradesh government and suggest that the Karnataka government's announcement in 1966 was the

[20] Well into the 1980s, dung-covered film posters and plywood cutouts of stars were a common sight in urban Andhra Pradesh. Dung was not a particularly accurate indicator of a star's (un)popularity because fan rivalries were often the main cause for such displays of disgust and contempt. In the 1960s, however, fans were not yet a significant presence in most parts of Andhra Pradesh, as we shall see in the next chapter.

[21] From the work of Robert Hardgrave, Jr., on films and politics in Tamil Nadu, it becomes possible for us to see how closely NTR's charitable and public work paralleled that of MGR and Sivaji Ganesan. To cite just one example, NTR collected Rs ten lakh for India's war effort in 1965 by touring the state performing plays (Venkat Rao 2003). Hardgrave, Jr. (1979: 98) notes that Sivaji Ganesan too did this in 1965. The point is not who emulated whom but the model of stardom that was emerging in the Madras-based film industries.

[22] This was at a time when big-budget films cost Rs 800,000 to Rs 1,000,000.

watershed event in relation to state government interventions in local film industries.[23] The larger point about the developments in both states, which followed each other in quick succession, is the respective state government *ratification* of these film industries' role as key players in language politics. In the case of Telugu cinema, the policy announcement came at a time when the industry was attempting to consolidate its market in the Telangana region. Although technically speaking film production was to be supported in all languages by the government as a part of its avowed policy to expand the industrial base of the state, it was clear that Telugu film production was the key focus. The implication was that the health of film industries with linguistically defined markets was the business of state governments. The relocation of film production, it was now officially declared, was part of the mandate of the linguistic state.

This government intervention facilitated the displacement of aesthetic questions from the discussion of language politics. Government policy did not distinguish between films on the basis of their aesthetics, commitment to depicting the Telugu country, or quality. It was, for obvious reasons, focused on bringing the industry "home," no matter what it produced. The state government thus inadvertently endorsed the reductionist view that Teluguness was an attribute of the geographical location of the production centre. The policy of loans and subsidies also financially compensated for the loss of the obvious advantages offered by the superior production facilities in Madras. This meant that the unification of political and economic concerns too was no longer predicated on Ramabrahmam's claim that viewers rewarded films with *jateeyata* or Teluguness. Good politics and economics could now, potentially, be fused but existed separately from aesthetic considerations as well as audience preference and approval.

In the 1960s this displacement of aesthetic considerations was not noticed, for two reasons: first, the most articulate position in the press was in any case the one demanding relocation of the industry on purely political grounds—the industry had to move to Hyderabad because it was the capital of the linguistic state. This Telugu nationalist

[23] See Venkatasubba Rao (2007: 6) for a brief but informative account of the Karnataka government's film policy in the 1960s.

line on the location of the industry, which KoKu would have found distressing in the early 1950s, continued to be taken in 1964 and was echoed by a commentator: "But the state [Madras] was divided. Our new state and capital were born. Everyone felt that along with other industries we needed our own film industry. Why say we lack the art which entertains and educates the populace? Don't we have our own industrialists? Do we lack exhibitors? Is affection for the industry lacking? We have everything . . . But the industry has to be shifted to the [new state's] capital" (Rao 1964: 98). Second, ANR, the hero of the relocation saga, was in any case identified with a Teluguness that was an attribute of quality social realist productions.

The extent to which the discussions on the need for making Telugu films in Hyderabad was insensitive to the demography of the city and its cultural specificity becomes clear from the statement of one Srivatsava (1964: 70). He believed Hyderabad had the potential to support film production in Hindi/Urdu but also any of the languages spoken by the inhabitants of Hyderabad—"Kannada, Marathi, Telugu, Urdu, Gujarati and Hindi," languages for which there already existed schools, knowledge centres, and entertainment providers. This view finds no resonance in discussions of the period within Telugu film journals.

The creation and acquisition of permanent assets, including real estate, became a feature of the new investments flowing into the film industry in Hyderabad. Peasant entrepreneurs of the Telugu film industry were seen reaffirming their faith in land as the most preferred investment. As such, this infusion of capital was part of a larger pattern of investment flows into Hyderabad. Baru (2007) argues that the development of Hyderabad is largely attributable to two factors: the strong presence of public sector units and the inflow of agricultural surpluses from coastal regions. State government film policy contributed directly to this pattern of investment by earmarking land—including residential land—in the capital at subsidized rates for the industry (Bhageeratha 1980). Among other incentives, 200 acres of land was set aside for housing personnel of the film industry in Hyderabad (Sivaram 1964: 60).

L.V. Prasad had applied for a loan of Rs 500,000 in response to the government's announcement. In the 1960s there were other loan applicants too: the Madras-based Shankar Reddy, producer of the mythological starring NTR, *Lava Kusa* (C. Pullaiah/C.S. Rao, 1963), Bombay film personalities Sohrab Modi, Kamal Amrohi, and A.K. Nadiadwala, and the little-known Hyderabad studio Southern Movietone owned by Kadapa-based businessmen (Bommakanti 1965: 16–17, 30).[24] Four studios, Annapurna, Bhagyanagar, Ramakrishna, and Southern Movietone, received loans (Bhageeratha 1980). Bhagyanagar Studio was reportedly inaugurated by the chief minister Jalagam Vengal Rao, in 1977. It was established by one Badam Ramaswamy, who also owned the Hotel Krishna and Sangam theatre (ibid.).

NTR's response to the developments in Hyderabad offers valuable insights into what the city meant for entrepreneurs within the film industry. In January 1964 construction began for the Ramakrishna twin theatre complex in Abids, then the heart of the "new city" of Hyderabad. Around this time news began to circulate of NTR's decision to construct a studio in the city. He was also reported to have expressed his willingness to spend two weeks every month in the city (Subba Rao 1964). The state government permitted the twin-theatre complex to be built on land where a school building stood. As per municipal rules, school buildings in Hyderabad could not be demolished. An exception was therefore made by the government. Starting with this project, NTR made so many investments in Hyderabad that Venkat Rao claims he put "all his hard earned money" into urban real estate here (2003: 39). Ramakrishna 70 mm was inaugurated in November 1968 and its 35 mm twin in December 1969 (Images 29, 30, and 31). By the early 1980s, film industry-related holdings of the NTR Estate (as it was in fact called) in Hyderabad included, in addition to the twin theatres, Ramakrishna Cine Studio (1976), Tarakarama Theatre (1978), and the Ramakrishna distribution company which began functioning in 1981 (Andhra Pradesh Film Chamber of Commerce 1981d: 160).[25]

[24] A Telugu movie website claims that Southern Movietone was established in 1966. It was later renamed Ajanta Studio. Posted by "Venkat" on www.teluguone.com, url: http://www.teluguone.com/cms/cinema/view/extraContentInnerC.jsp?ecId=CNT005585&eId=MEX000002&pno=4&lang=telugu. Visited on 4 July 2011.

[25] By the 1990s the twin theatre complex, once a tourist attraction, had run to seed and was screening pornographic films. A case filed against the theatre

29

30

Images 29 & 30: Photographs of the inauguration of the NTR Estate in Abids, Hyderabad. The multi-storeyed hotel (top) and Ramakrishna 70mm theatre (bottom) were constructed, but Ramakrishna 35mm had not yet been built. Source: Manasu Collection, M.V. Rayudu.

---

complex in Hyderabad High Court was widely covered by the local press. Liang (2011) discusses the High Court judgement against the management of the complex in some detail.

Image 31: MGR felicitated by NTR during the inauguration of the NTR Estate while Brahmananda Reddy (corner right) looks on. Source: Manasu Collection, M.V. Rayudu.

There is a noticeable time lag between the announcement of the government policy (or the rush of applications) and the actual construction of studios. In 1968 the state government inaugurated Brahmananda Chitrapuri (named after Brahmananda Reddy, who was chief minister), where land was earmarked for studio construction. Construction did not begin for years to come because of delayed loan sanctions till 1975. This in turn was due to the political situation in the state (Bhageeratha 1980). Indeed, the separate Telangana and Andhra agitations (1969–73) came soon after plans had been drawn up for major investments in Hyderabad.

In December 1968 students of Osmania University in Hyderabad went on strike. They were protesting against the systematic violation of *Mulki* rules for providing reservation in government jobs to those living in the region. *Mulki* rules were introduced by the Nizam in the 1930s in response to popular discontent against the appointment of Muslims from outside Hyderabad state in government jobs. The student strike was supported by faculty and the administration of the university. Over the next six months the movement for a separate state spread across the region. Forrester said that the "Imbalance in economic development is surely the greatest single cause for the 1969 troubles" (1970: 17). Notable, for our purposes, among the causes he identifies for resentment against the merger of Telangana and the Presidency districts was "the migration of farmers from the [Krishna-Godavari] Delta to Telangana, where they bought land cheaply, developed it, and prospered . . ." (ibid.: 15). Once in Telangana, Presidency peasant entrepreneurs were in direct competition with well-entrenched financial interests controlled by non-Telugu-speaking *traditional trading communities*: "Non-mulkis from the Delta have also entered trade and moneylending and have become very influential in the business life of the twin cities, as well as in various rural areas. This has posed a challenge not only to Telangana businessmen but also to the Marwari and Gujarati communities which used to dominate commerce and business in Hyderabad State. It is notable that several prominent separatist leaders are non-Telugus, and there are many reports that the separatist agitation was liberally financed with Marwari money" (ibid.: 15–16).

The agitation was led by the Telangana Praja Samiti (TPS), formed by intellectuals with no known Congress affiliation. Much later former minister M. Chenna Reddy, whose election to parliament in 1967 was annulled by the high court, became associated with the TPS (Gray 1971: 467). Gray (ibid.: 468) also points out that N.G. Ranga, the most important leader of Coastal Andhra Kammas and key functionary of the Swatantra Party, supported the formation of Telangana state. He interprets this as support by the Kamma caste for a separate Andhra state in which the caste would be politically stronger. We can also read Ranga's support as an indication that, in spite of the emerging pattern, investment in Telangana was not yet on the immediate agenda of the agricultural castes of the Coastal Andhra region: they were thriving on account of post-Independence economic policies.

The agitation for a separate Andhra state began soon after a supreme court judgment on 3 October 1972 upholding *Mulki* rules. Political observers point out that there was already resentment in the Andhra region to the channelling of government funding into the Telangana region. Further, it has been argued that because of the freezing of all land transactions by chief minister P.V. Narasimha Rao in 1972, and the subsequent passage of a Farm Ceiling Act some months later, "The Kamma landlords of the coastal districts were among the dominant agricultural castes incensed by PV Narasimha Rao's reformist zeal" (Gray 1974: 339). What began as a student agitation spread to other sections and was soon supported by most political parties (with the exception of the CPI and CPI-M). On 18 January 1973, after numerous general strikes which had paralysed the administration, President's Rule was imposed on the state. Many months of President's Rule went by before a compromise was reached between Congress factions on either side of the regional divide (Jan Sangh, Swatantra, as well as the TPS rejected it). The proposed solution included the setting up of a central university in Hyderabad. In December 1973 President's Rule was lifted and Jalagam Vengal Rao, a Telangana Velama who was said to be close to the Coastal Andhra Kammas, was appointed chief minister (ibid.: 346–9).

The state government's film policy as well as the plans drawn up by Madras-based Telugu film personalities to invest in Hyderabad in the years to come were closely linked to emerging patterns of migration among people and capital across the regions of Andhra Pradesh. The large-scale serial unrest in both regions temporarily halted the move by film personalities to invest in Hyderabad. With the return to the integrationist model of statehood, there was now no fear of "losing" Telangana or much chance of "returning" to Andhra, for that matter. Hyderabad was re-established as the sole eligible site for housing the Telugu industry.

Moment of Integration: Consolidating the Telugu Film Market

Remarkably, there is almost no trace of the Telangana and Andhra agitations in the films of the period.[26] However, the film industry did assemble an integrationist model from the 1970s. This was founded on the inclusion of the Telangana region into a consolidated film market

[26] Notable exceptions are *Talla Pellama?* (NTR, 1970) and *Telugunadu* (Lakshmi Deepak, 1982). I discuss these films in chapters 4 and 5, respectively.

that, finally, resembled the map of Andhra Pradesh. Investments in studios and other projects were resumed in the late 1970s, even as major changes in the distribution system resulted from the increased inflow of investments into the industry. The male star was pivotal to the model, which remained incapable of generating surpluses.

Marking the moment of integration, the Andhra Pradesh Film Chamber of Commerce was formed by the merger of the Andhra Film Chamber and exhibitors and distributors who were a part of the Hyderabad Film Circuit. It was formally inaugurated by chief minister M. Chenna Reddy in January 1979 in Hyderabad (Andhra Pradesh Film Chamber of Commerce 1981e: 59). By 1981 the Andhra Pradesh State Film Development Corporation Limited had sanctioned Rs 2.62 crores (26.2 million) for the construction of cinema halls in towns with a population of less than 50,000; 83 such halls had already become functional; 5 film studios/laboratories (in Hyderabad) had received loans adding up to Rs 75.09 lakhs (Andhra Pradesh Film Chamber of Commerce 1981f: 158).

Soon after they were completed, it became clear to observers that the Hyderabad studios were, on the whole, loss-making enterprises. Nevertheless, new investments continued to flow into this sector of the industry even after the rush of inaugurations in the 1970s, notably by the film stars Krishna and D. Ramanaidu who built their own studios in the years to come. As early as 1980 NTR's Ramakrishna Studio was confined to home productions (Bhageeratha 1980). Evidently, there was never a plan to make this studio a stand-alone profit-making venture. By 1985 Bhagyanagar Studio was virtually defunct in spite of its attempt to get into film production. The studio owner's lack of understanding of the film business and limited contacts with the industry were cited as the reason.

But surely these were not the only reasons for the poor performance of the other studios in the city. Venkat Akkineni, ANR's son who managed Annapurna Studio, was quoted as saying that it had accumulated losses of Rs 70 lakh (7 million) since inception. Annapurna had also gone to court against the state government in an attempt to defend the conversion of studio land to commercial uses (i.e. property housing commercial establishments other than the studio). In the 1980s a committee was constituted by the legislative assembly to examine alleged violations of land-use regulations by

Padmalaya (Bhageeratha 1986: 71–4). Southern Movietone does not find mention in accounts of the industry in the 1980s. Sarathy, located some distance away from the emerging film industrial hub in Jubilee Hills, became the venue of more art house film screenings than film shootings. With hindsight it is possible to suggest that these infrastructure projects were long-term investments, rent seeking "side-businesses" whose value grew with the appreciation of real estate prices, offsetting their failure to collect rent.

Returning to the 1970s, the film critic and distributor K. Narasaiah noted that the growth of box office collections in the Telangana districts (not just the twin cities) in the decade resulted in the increase of market share of the region from 20 per cent to 30 per cent, while that of Coastal Andhra declined from 60 per cent to 50 per cent (1981: 145). He was writing about a period when there was an exponential growth in film consumption as a whole across the state. This means Telangana had grown at a much faster rate than the other two regions. Telangana's share of box office collections had thus risen from 10 per cent (Rama Rao 1942) to 30 per cent and most of this increase had occurred in the two decades since the state's formation. Today Telangana, including Hyderabad–Secunderabad, accounts for 50 per cent of the box office collections (Sushil Rao 2011: 2).

Narasaiah argues that the watershed development in the 1970s was what he calls the decentralization (*vikendrikarana*) of the film industry, especially the distribution sector (1981: 145). Companies with state-wide distribution networks yielded ground to a new kind of distributor, known as the "buyer," who made high and risky bids for the outright purchase of under-production films in smaller distribution territories.

As we saw earlier, distribution territories for Telugu cinema had in

Table 3. Share of Box Office Collections

	Coastal Andhra	Rayalaseema	Nizam	Others
1942	50%	15%	10%	25%
1981	50%	20%	30%	NA
2011	NA	NA	50%	NA

Sources: Rama Rao (1942); Narasaiah (1981); Sushil Rao (2011).

the past corresponded with vast political-geographical areas (Andhra, Ceded, Nizam, Mysore, and North Andhra which included southern Orissa). By the late 1970s distribution territories grew—not by the inclusion of new geographical areas but by the subdivision of existing territories into smaller units. The growth of the market from the 1970s was really an implosion, or intensive exploitation, made possible by the increase in cinema halls rather than the spread of Telugu films into areas where they were not earlier a presence (like Telangana in the 1950s). Films now began to be sold districtwise in regions where there were a substantial number of cinema halls: East and West Godavari, Krishna, and Guntur, to begin with. It may be noted in passing that by far the most successful distributor to have emerged in the wake of the sector's fragmentation was Usha Pictures, established in Eluru (West Godavari) in 1974. In the first two decades of its existence the company reportedly claimed to have distributed 1017 films (*Super Hit*, 28 February 2003). Krishna is reported to have said that the very first film to have been sold "outright" district-wise was *Bhale Dongalu* (KSR Doss, 1976) featuring him in the lead (*Super Hit*, 4 July 2003).

The control over exhibition began slipping out of the hands of distributors with the fragmentation of territories and the emergence of a district-wise "buyer system" in which these smaller distributors or "buyers" made outright purchases of films. In the face of increasing competition among buyers for exhibition venues, cinema-hall owners could now demand weekly rentals at flat rates regardless of gate collections, instead of sharing the income on a "percentage basis" as in the past (Madhusudhana Rao 1981: 150). Rao traces the origins of the buyer system to Tamil Nadu of the late 1970s. Its spread into Andhra Pradesh in a relatively short period indicates that there continued to be strong ties among the Telugu and Tamil industries, and that regional (not just state-centred) industrial reorganization was happening around this time.

With the buyer system, distribution was becoming more localized than ever before. Fragmentation resulted in the growth of the Telugu film industry by bringing local and even *retail* investments into it (Srinivas 2009: 194–7). Between them, buyers increased the price of films and ensured there was a far more efficient exploitation of films within the geographical area in which they had exhibition rights. These investments were sourced locally, from activities unrelated to the cinema, creating a system of tributaries that eventually flowed into film production, including the production of films dubbed from other languages. It was largely on the strength of the vastly expanded but fragmented distribution sector that a loss-making production sector made increasing numbers of films for close to two decades—till the late 1990s, when production slowed down.

As discussed in the previous chapter, B.N. Reddi laid the foundation of the industry's business model centred on the distribution of risk and the lowering of entry load for investors. This model reached something of a high point with the buyer system, where a new regime of risk management was instituted by distributing losses—of which there would be plenty—to a number of relatively small players. In 1986 D.V.S. Raju, chairman of the Andhra Pradesh Film Development Corporation, said that unlike a decade earlier, when the producer alone had to face the consequences of a film's commercial failure, "with the district-wide buyer system, all [parties involved] are able to share this risk" (Raju 1986: 141).

If films failed to recover costs, as was often the case, each distributor or buyer stood to lose money. There was a high attrition rate among distributors. But then there were also a number of fresh entrants maintaining the equilibrium. Often, distributors would hedge their bets by finding sub-distributors within their territory. Or a number of small investors would form a syndicate and bid for a territory. Distributors of major stars' vehicles collected advances from exhibitors who were keen to screen big-budget productions. At the lowest end there were those who would bid for a single print of a film. Yet others specialized in supplying to second-run cinema halls.[27] Older distribution companies like Poorna Pictures and Navayuga exited from the distribution of Telugu films and focused on Hindi and English, even as they refrained from any outright purchase of rights. All this did not happen overnight in the late 1970s but the foundations were laid during the latter part of the decade.

It soon became clear that the male star was the most critical player

[27] Observations about distribution are based on fieldwork conducted among distributors in Tirupathi, Hyderabad, and Vijayawada in 2001–2, and interviews with industry representatives in Hyderabad and Vijayawada in 2008. Some of the findings have been published in Srinivas (2003).

in the emerging order. The star's importance for the buyer system lay in lending his body to projects worthy of investment. Only a certain kind of producer, the maker of big-budget star vehicles, was able to profitably engage in pre-sale of films. A number of smaller producers found no buyers for their films even after they were completed. Madhusudhana Rao (1981: 149), among others, draws attention to the fact that dozens of films were lying in cans by the end of the 1970s for this reason. Yet other producers were forced to release their films on terms that were far from profitable. Narasaiah makes the interesting comment that stars were deployed by producers to sell the film—not to viewers but to distributors (1981: 146)![28]

There was a regional dimension to the expansion of the distribution sector too. The breaking up of territories did not impact Rayalaseema or Telangana beyond the emergence of the Hyderabad–Secunderabad twin cities as a separate territory—and that was much later, in the 1990s. Notably, there were no distribution offices in the smaller cities in Telangana even in the early years of the twenty-first century. The entire Telangana region (minus the twin cities) remains a single distribution territory to this day, although the larger distributors including Mayuri Film Distributors and Suresh Film Distributors have had offices in most of the district headquarters.[29] Narasaiah points out that Vijayawada, which was the traditional centre for film distribution and remained the largest distribution centre for Telugu films after Madras even in the 1960s, actually witnessed a decline in relative importance. The distribution offices in the city came down from 100 to 77. In the corresponding period the figure for Hyderabad–Secunderabad reached 125. Distribution companies also sprang up in the district headquarters of those districts which had become standalone territories (ibid.: 145–6).

[28] In a tongue-in-cheek account of the film business by scriptwriter D.V. Narasaraju, a producer approaches him with a proposal—to write a script and get a leading star to agree to do the film. The producer tells him that he plans to complete the pre-sale of the film on the strength of a star's call-sheets and hopes to make a profit of Rs 10 lakh without investing a single rupee (Narasaraju 1986: 186–8). Such was the importance of the star to the buyer system.

[29] Interveiw with R. Gopal, Manager, Telangana Telugu Film Distributors' Association, 31 January 2008, in Secunderabad.

How then was the question of Teluguness resolved by the industry that remained centred on Madras? As we have seen, the problem was intractable enough in the 1950s and was further complicated by state formation when Telangana's specificity had to be contended with. In the 1960s it appeared the problem would be solved by relocating to Hyderabad. Over the years the supporters of this idea grew incrementally. At the representational level, location shooting retained its pride of place as a major source of the cultural authenticity of films. Curiously, the production sector did not relocate for decades to come. When it finally began doing so in the 1980s, it was very gradual.

Why did place-of-production as a determining feature of Teluguness lose some of its charge after the mid 1960s? Why did the demand for relocation lose its sense of immediacy? The political situation in the late 1960s delayed the construction of studios and other facilities, but it cannot be said to have been the most important reason for the delay since, in the long run, it did not affect the overall pattern of investments by film personalities in the state capital. The key players did not appear to be in doubt that it was merely a matter of time before the actual relocation took place. With the exception of L.V. Prasad (whose Madras studio was completed in 1965), none of the Telugu film personalities invested in the creation of industry infrastructure in Madras after 1956. Moreover, Prasad had also invested in the Bombay film industry and had applied to the state government for a loan, so it was not as if he chose Madras over Hyderabad. The sense of inevitability was partly due to the currency of arguments in favour of relocation for political reasons, soon strengthened by the economics of loans, subsidies, and real estate investments. The other important factor was the growing importance of the Telangana market for the industry. But what of the loss of charge within the relocation demand?

Even as efforts to build studios in Hyderabad suffered a temporary setback due to political movements for reorganization of the state, the problem of the Teluguness of Telugu cinema found a new and more permanent resolution. As a result there was no longer any immediate *need* for the industry to relocate on cultural-political grounds. Territorial expansion of the film market compensated for the industry's inability to unify aesthetic-cultural-political concerns around Teluguness. We notice that in the late 1960s, when the social gradually began to overtake the mythological and folklore film in number and economic importance, it did so without paying attention to what were earlier considered the defining features of the form—realism and *jateeyata*. These remained important concerns for a section of film-makers, from Adurthi Subba Rao to K. Vishwanath and Bapu, for decades to come. Such film-makers were widely respected and seen as makers of culturally authentic films. But it was now possible for the social to stage Teluguness on a new ground.

The popular appeal of Telugu cinema in all the three regions implied that Teluguness resided in the "universal" viewership of Telugu films. With the spread of Telugu cinema across the state, there was a far more accurate fit between the map of the state and the film market than ever before. This fit facilitated the equation of the viewership of the cinema with the Telugu nation. Under these conditions it became possible for NTR to emerge as a representative of the Telugus, in spite of his inauthenticity by the standards of the earlier paradigm.

While sound films resulted in the gradual delimitation of the market along linguistic lines, linguistic reorganization facilitated the integration of various "territories" (literally distribution territories but also political-geographical ones) into a common market. Post-1956, the Telugu film industry created, for the very first time, a market for cultural commodities that extended across all the regions Andhra Pradesh. With the opportunity to integrate the vast "hinterland," as the States Reorganisation Commission would have it, came a new political possibility which rested on the cinema's claims of inclusivity. This in turn transformed the very terms of the debate on Teluguness of Telugu films.

In the next two chapters I examine how NTR's star persona came to embody a specific kind of Teluguness that had no precedents in the Ramabrahmam–KoKu discussions, but which was instead made possible by the expansion of the film market.

3

The Star and Mobilization: 1951–1980

We now shift attention to evidence from films and other textual sources in order to understand the political possibilities opened up by the changed aesthetics of, and expanded market for, Telugu cinema. Tracking these changes allows us to situate the rather surprising claim NTR made in 1982 to being a representative of the Telugu nation within the context of film history and his own acting career.

In the previous chapter we saw that cinema's Teluguness was displaced from the aesthetic domain to the place of film production. The demand for relocation to Hyderabad lost some of its charge on account of a further displacement of Teluguness to the political geography of the film market. Once the consumer base of Telugu cinema expanded in the Telangana region, the equivalence between popularity of films and Teluguness became a possibility: films were popular among Telugu people and *therefore* Telugu. This in part makes it necessary to look at the period from the 1950s to the early 1980s, during which NTR was launched as a star and elected chief minister of Andhra Pradesh. During these decades the film industry experienced rapid and all-round growth, even as its peasant foundations were strengthened by inflows from agricultural and related surpluses.

Against the backdrop of diegetic crowds as a constant presence and the recurrence of mobilization as a story-level concern, Telugu films of this period threw up and resolved the question of who would speak to and for the masses. Mobilization, a key concern for Indian film-makers since the silent era, came to be inextricably linked to the emergence of the male star as the narrative pivot and object of spectatorial investment. By the late 1970s the male star, who had become the centrepiece of the loss-making film industry's business model, was routinely cast in the role of mobilizer of the masses and their natural representative. Later I examine how the star who had mastered the ability to speak for the masses came to embody Teluguness, and how the addressee of his vehicles was misrecognized as a member of the Telugu nation. And that will then enable us to see how this relationship between star and mobilized linguistic nation was carried over to the domain of electoral politics.

Assembling the Nation

In Indian cinema the link between the consumption of films and mass mobilization can be traced to the silent films of D.G. Phalke. His *Shri Krishna Janma* (1918) ends with a sequence in which we see the teenaged Krishna facing the camera while devotees of each of the four varnas enter the frame separately from the side and pray to him. They are appropriately dressed to match the description of the intertitles which name them as "The Brahmin Devotee," "The Kshatriya Devotee," "The Vaisya Devotee," and "The Shudra Devotee." This, we are to understand, is the reality of India. After the four varnas make their separate appearances, there is a shot of all the varnas crowding around Krishna, who blesses them all (Images 32–40).

Images 32–40: *Shri Krishna Janma* (1918)—assembling the nation before the screen.

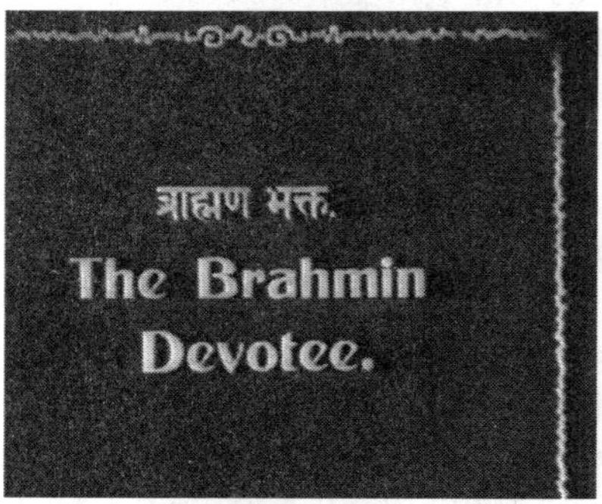

32

33

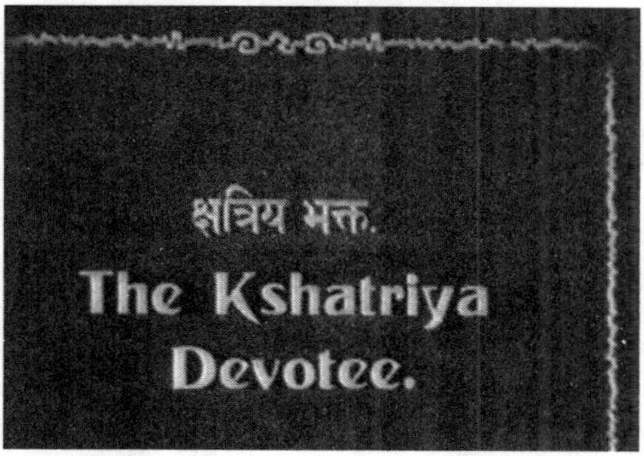

34

35

36

37

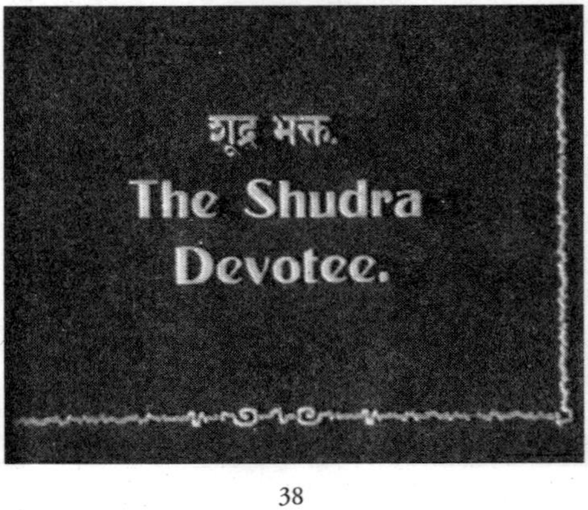

38

39

40

The cobbling together of a community, the mobilization of separate groups into the formation of an entity that could be named "the nation," is presented in the film as something that happens around the figure of Krishna. But, of course, the glue is the cinema itself, bringing before the moving image diverse or antagonistic groups that have hitherto existed separately. What we see in *Janma* is the on-screen rendering of the process which K. Sivathamby (1981) attributed to the cinema hall in Tamil Nadu—the performance centre where all castes came together, under the same roof.[1] In the very act of consumption (of the film), the social domain is produced as a unified whole, and the viewer, marked by his or her varna, constituted as a member of a larger community—of Krishna devotees and the Indian people alike.

A similar attempt at assembling the nation from groups marked by their particularities is made in some of the most influential early talkie films in Telugu. To begin with, there is *Malapilla* (Gudavalli Ramabrahmam, 1938), the film that announces the arrival of the social as the form committed to nationalism. The larger film-industrial context was one in which the setting up of production facilities locally came to be linked with ideological as well as formal concerns that would shape both Telugu and Tamil industries. Rajadhyaksha draws attention to this backdrop: "Until the mid-1930s most films in [Tamil and Telugu] were made in Calcutta [and other cities as we have seen], and the setting up of a local film industry had in itself acquired a political dimension. After the 1930s, moving concurrently with the project of establishing a local infrastructure that could compete with the Hindi cinema, Tamil and Telugu saw the biggest and most elaborately scripted melodramas in the history of Indian cinema, made with unusual awareness of the politics of both nationalist (later subnationalist) allegories, as well as of manufacturing indigenous film stars" (1993b: 68).

We have seen *Malapilla*'s director in his role as an industry pioneer who had an articulate position on the Telugu question. Recall here that *Malapilla* was the first production of the zamindari establishment, Sarathy. The explicitness of this film's political commitment and the stridency with which it advocates the abolition of untouchability are remarkable. There were protests against the film by Brahmin organizations in Vijayawada, as also strong support from a cross-section of commentators and the educated public. *Madras Mail* reported it had received "vigorous protests from Brahmins against the film," and there was the report of the view of one Pandrangi Kesava

[1] In Sivathamby's words, "The Cinema Hall was the first performance centre in which all Tamils sat under the same roof. The basis of the seating is not on the hierarchic position of the patron but essentially on his purchasing power" (1981: 18).

Rao who had been nominated to review the film in a meeting of Brahmins in Bezwada (now Vijayawada): "He [Kesava Rao] thinks the film will create an impression on the public far different to that which the producers may have had in view . . . The film deals with the love of a Brahmin youth for a Harijan girl, but, says Mr Kesava Rao, the romance degenerates into immoral suggestions. Mr Kesava Rao warns the Government that 'the so-called non-Brahmin movement has crystallized into a Kamma versus Brahmin movement in *Andhradesa*'" (1 October 1938: 12). Another opponent of the film said "anti-Brahmin feeling is visible everywhere in the villages." Presumably the film contributed in no small measure to this state of affairs. One N. Pattabi Ramayya replied to the Brahmin groups' accusations by calling the film's alleged anti-Brahminism

> a figment of the imagination . . . I have witnessed the picture myself and I can, without fear of contradiction, assert that far from creating communal disharmony, "Malapilla" is a great picture of recent times which is calculated to solve the burning problem of untouchability . . . The picture has already earned the encomiums of the public and the critics alike. It is becoming more and more popular day by day in every centre where it has been released, as evidenced from the great crowds attending each show. Leaders of public thought of all shades of opinion—Congress and non-Congress, officials and non-officials, Ministers and Parliamentary Secretaries—have showered praise on the production and felicitated the producers. (*Madras Mail*, 8 October 1938: 12)

In the film Congress activists inspired by Gandhi enter a Dalit hamlet, organize the "Harijans," and agitate for the latter's right to enter the village temple and use its pond. Early in the film two Congress leaders, Chaudhuraiah (Suribabu) and Radhabayamma (Hemalata Devi), repeatedly invoke Gandhi. We also see Gandhi's portrait with an accompanying caption that translates as: "Hindu society cannot let go of seven crore Harijans." To retain them within "Hindu society," the film advocates reform among both Dalits and Brahmins. In addition to being "backward" in their own different ways, these communities are also seen as being on the verge of a violent confrontation. As the antagonism between the Congress Dalits and the village Brahmins grows, Nagaraju (Venkateswara Rao), the son of the temple priest Mallikarjuna Sarma (V.V. Subbaiah), and Sampalata (Kanchanamala) the Dalit elder Munaiah's (Raghavan) daughter, fall in love. Their growing intimacy is contrasted with the increasing tension and threat of violence between the two castes. The lovers are soon discovered by Munaiah. After a brief separation accompanied by a major misunderstanding, the lovers elope to Calcutta, taking Anasuya, Sampalata's younger sister, with them. Meanwhile, the anti-untouchability agitation enters a critical stage with the Brahmins preventing the Dalits from using the village water sources. More than a highly successful and non-violent strike supported by the Kamma farmers of the village, it is the rescue of Mallikarjuna Sarma's wife from a fire by the Dalits that results in the priest's decision to open the temple to Dalits. Upon hearing this news on the radio, Sampalata and Nagaraju return from Calcutta. Dalits enter the temple and the parents of the couple ratify their inter-caste marriage.

At the thematic level, the film is avowedly about incorporating Dalit castes into Hindu society, which is gearing itself up for the formation of the Indian nation.[2] Gandhian ideas of caste reform are named as such and are central to the story.[3] There are elaborate sequences depicting mobilized masses, as also scenes showing mobs of both Dalits and Brahmins preparing for violent confrontations prevented only by the intervention of a Gandhian, Chaudhuraiah. Also notable is the manner in which this film—as also Ramabrahmam's next film *Raitu Bidda*—addresses its spectators as objects of mobilization. Those who are gathered before the screen, these films suggest, share the political purpose of being mobilized: they are like the masses they see in the film.

[2] For an overview of Telugu films (including *Malapilla*) which make explicit references to the problem of untouchability and caste differences in society, see Kusuma (2010).

[3] Theodore Baskaran makes this interesting point about the changed censorship regime which coincided with the making of *Malapilla*: "After 1935 Government of India Act, the Congress contested in the elections in 1937, assumed office in six provinces [including Madras] and ruled for two and a quarter years. In this period Indian cinema enjoyed a respite from the restrictive control of the British Government's censorship policy . . . filmmakers were free to propagate nationalistic and reformist ideas in their films" (1981: 143).

During *Malapilla*'s opening sequence the Gandhian Harijana Seva Sangham (Harijan/Dalit Service Society) enters the hamlet, walking in procession towards the camera and singing to the "heroic Dalit son" (*Harijana veera kumara*), asking him to "wake up" (*lera, lera*). The static time-space we see on screen is on the verge of being transformed by the arrival of history. Indeed, it is rendered visible by the agency—the Seva Sangham—that will transform it by mobilizing its inhabitants. The sequence of the Sangham in procession is intercut with documentary-style footage of half-naked people scattered across a rural setting. These people are presumably the inhabitants of the hamlet where the rest of the sequence is set. However, they stand out and do not appear to be a part of the fictional universe because they smile and stare at the camera. This "movie mistake" serves a crucial function as it presents the spectator with "real Dalits" off screen whom the film intends to mobilize into becoming a part of the nation. These people don't belong to the rest of the sequence in any immediate sense—the montage has to work towards creating the link. The cinema, as the apparatus of reform, quite literally brings these outcastes into the frame (Images 41–8).

Images 41–8: The arrival of the talkie. *Malapilla*'s opening sequence, preceded by the dedication, depicting the arrival of the Gandhians. Notice the crowds of people (46–7), whose relationship to the Dalits lining the procession is not established.

41

42

43

44

45

46

47

48

Against this larger backdrop, the film's story unfolds. It is one of Dalits and Brahmins overcoming their antagonisms and being eventually transformed into modern subjects. The modern subject is in turn imaged as one who has shed his or her excessive caste identity. This process of naming, mobilizing, and ultimately incorporating different population groups into the nation-in-formation (or the nascent nation, as the case might be) is the hallmark of the form that Rajadhyaksha calls "epic melodrama" (1993b), assembled across the subcontinent by various film industries from the 1930s to the 1950s. Mobilizing different population groups into performing actions that qualify them for membership in the emerging nation was the foundational raison d'être of the Telugu social film and the inaugural moment of the industry that produced it. This particular industry, as it turned out, was being established by zamindari investments in Madras.

Malapilla's mobilizer is an archetype that Telugu cinema continues to deploy well into the present. The political representative of the Dalits and the agent of their reform, as also that of the Brahmins, belongs to neither community. Chaudhuraiah (his name suggests that he is a Kamma) mediates between antagonistic caste groups, and such mediation is acceptable to both communities because he is himself "casteless:" he transcends particularity and indeed the excesses of each caste even as he calls himself a "Harijan."

Peasants, Nativity, and the Telugu Land

What makes Telugu cinema Telugu? Selvaraj Velayutham's discussion of Tamil cinema is a useful starting point:

> In cinema, the use of Tamil generates a symbolic, embodied and affective connection to "Tamilness" and Tamil identity. Movie dialogues and songs often glorify and celebrate (often nondiegetically) the Tamil language, people, culture and identity. This locates both the film and the audience within a particular national imaginary and ethno-linguistic space which is Tamil and Tamil only. For instance, frequent articulation of *Tamil Nadu* (Tamil country) or *Tamilakam* (*akam* means home or interior) which refers to the land of Tamil language, culture, and/or people is a powerful signifier and . . . it evokes the imagery of internal psychic/emotional unity of all Tamils against the "external other." (2008: 6)

Velayutham does not pay adequate attention to what might be specific to *screen* Tamilness, as distinct from, say, a literary or theatre-centred production of Tamilness. References to language, culture, and people are to be found in plays, poems, and novels too. Hughes (2010) allows us to note that the question of how films could be Tamil had exercised commentators from the early talkie period. In the absence of such a historical perspective, Tamilness and the Tamil identity to which cinema generates a "symbolic, embodied and affective connection" (Velayutham 2008: 6) appear to have ante-dated the cinema itself and merely been reflected or re-presented in films. While linguistic identity is periodically articulated in the public domain without regard to the cinema, the question before us is how and why cinema is linked to the production of identity. What, in other words, is cinematic about the production of "Teluguness" in cinema?

It is not uncommon for the cinema to lay claim to its context of production and reception, even as articulate sections of the viewing public demand that a film demonstrate or display its situatedness (for want of a better word). Film industries are often called upon to prove their Hong Kongness, Tamilness, Teluguness, or something-or-the-other-ness. Such demands and supply of somethingness are likely to be coeval with manifestations of identity politics (Hong Kong, Tamil, etc.) in other spheres of the public domain.[4] The phenomenon at hand cannot be reduced to a mere reflection of an a priori set of characteristics that exists independently of the cinema. It is pointless to turn our attention to films if they have so little to contribute to our understanding of the identity question or politics in general.

The Madras film industry term *nativity* is indicative of the kind of demands that were being made on the industry and individual films alike. Nativity, as readers of Telugu and Tamil film magazines know, has nothing to do with Christianity. This Indian English word has been used by the Madras film industry to refer to a variety of things, from the 1960s if not earlier. KoKu (1964: 6) places the term under erasure in an essay written in English, suggesting that he was aware of the term's Indian, or more specifically film-industrial, connotations. Nativity, meaning on-screen Teluguness ("nativeness"), has been something of a hold-all category for the South Indian film industry's creation of a diegetic or fictional space that is marked by its linguistic-cultural specificity. Nativity is closely associated with realism and has been a crucial site for the negotiation between linguistic identity, or the particularity of the local, and the larger Indian nation-state. Nativity has most often been produced by representing the countryside and its customs and festivals. Women in traditional costumes, expectedly, are embodiments of nativity (Images 49 and 50). Nativity finds mention in some of the essays in Sastry (1986), and in particular Kannala (1986). Such is the currency of the term in writings on the Telugu cinema that none of the authors in Sastry (1986) who use the term explains what it means. Sundar Kaali (2000), in his essay on the Tamil

[4] Linda Lai's (2001) essay on Hong Kong comedies allows us to note how in Hong Kong too the identity question is tagged on to particular genres and stars. See Srinivas 2005 for a discussion of how the Hong Kongness of Stephen Chow's films is predicated on cinematic techniques and spectatorial practices that are not in fact unique to that industry's productions.

49

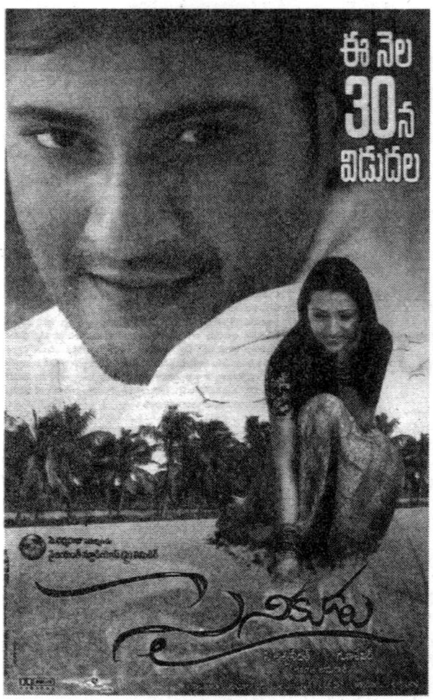

50

Images 49–50: Woman as embodiment of nativity: Advertisement for *Sundarakanda* (Bapu 2008) and *Sainikudu* (Gunasekhar 2006). Neither of the two female stars in question, Charmi and Trisha, are Telugu speakers. Source: *Andhra Jyothi*, Chitra Jyothi, 7 February 2008, p. iv; and *Andhra Jyothi*, 26 November 2006, p. 10.

cinema, draws attention to the term, and to the existence of a genre of films invested in rural settings, plots, and characters. Anand Pandian notes that the nativity film in Tamil is "shot extensively in rural locales, depicting peasant protagonists, staging dialogues in regional dialects and idioms, and introducing folk rhythms and instruments into cinematic soundtracks" (Pandian 2008: 125).

The existence of the concept is evidence that the Telugu film industry had internalized the call made by Ramabrahmam and later KoKu that films had to *be* demonstrably Telugu. Of late, in a clear manifestation of the tendency of centring identity politics on region rather than language, nativity has been used to refer to the regionally specific (not linguistically specific) content of cultural forms. For instance, there is now such a thing as "Telangana nativity," meaning that which is specific or unique to the region (Rajamani 2009: here too there is no attempt at defining the term). As the referent of nativity shifts from the linguistic to the regional domain, the concept continues to be politically loaded.

Let us revert here to the opening sequence of *Malapilla*, discussed earlier, for in it the means by which the early social represented the Telugu country becomes clear. Although the term itself may not have been in existence during Ramabrahmam's time, it is possible to suggest that *Malapilla* made a paradigm-setting attempt at producing nativity. Its outdoor locations are critical to the film's realism and to establishing its linguistic-cultural authenticity. Soon after the opening sequence, with its huts and half-naked bystanders, the film moves on to another outdoor location, to the Siva temple which is the site of the temple-entry agitation by Dalits. This place, possibly Kotappakonda in Guntur district, is not named in the narrative but the film depicts the temple festival at some length in a series of documentary-style shots which include performing folk artistes. Tableaux shots of the festival are intercut with the procession of the Dalits towards the temple. Owing to poor continuity editing, the shots of the temple festival stand out as a component not quite integrated with the narrative. Nevertheless, these shots facilitate the linking of the narrative to a "real" place. Although the spectator does not see the procession of Dalits passing through some of the spaces, the setting of the story is a place marked by its "Telugu" folk customs (Images 51–71).

Images 51–71: The procession of Dalits interspersed with images of worshippers, idols, priests, Congressmen, street performers, folk dancers, and beggars.

51

52

53

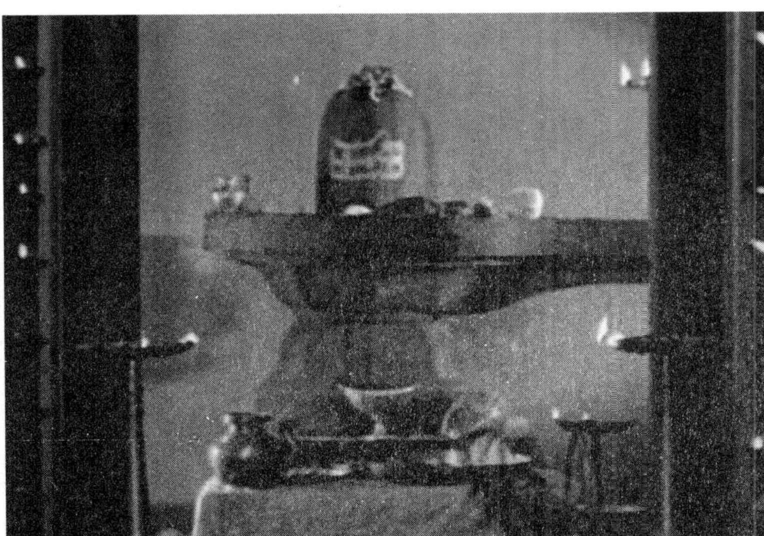

54

55

56

57

58

59

60

61

62

63

64

65

66

67

68

69

70

71

In Ramabrahmam's work nativity is textually manifest but not limited to location, props, or narrative. Authentication of the image is also achieved by the association of the film with people who already have the legitimacy to speak and stand in for the linguistic community which the film seeks to depict. *Malapilla* is dedicated to Kasinadhuni Nageswara Rao Pantulu, the founder of the newspaper *Andhra Patrika*, which was the voice of God as far as nationalist issues went. The association of nationalist and progressive literati with this film (as also *Raitu Bidda*) is a part of the process of underwriting the representational work of the film. Among the literary figures credited in the two films are Gudipati Venkatachalam (Chalam), and Tapi Dharma Rao who co-wrote the story of *Malapilla*. Rao, who was one of *Raitu Bidda*'s lyricists, had a zamindari connection in a manner of speaking because he worked as the secretary to the Raja of Bobbili in the early 1930s (Rajadhyaksha and Willemen 1999: 89–90). The other literary figures are Nellore Venkatarama Naidu (co-lyricist, *Raitu Bidda*), editor of the anti-zamindari newspaper *Zamin Ryot*, and the budding writers Tripuraneni Gopichand (dialogue writer, *Raitu Bidda*) and Kosaraju Raghavaiah Chaudhury (co-lyricist, *Raitu Bidda*).

Gopichand also wrote a column for *Prajamitra*, which Ramabrahmam edited (ibid.: 103).

The ur-nativity of *Malapilla* and *Raitu Bidda* alerts us to two crucial elements in the representation of cultural geography in Telugu cinema. First—and this has more specifically to do with the reformist socials of the pre-Independence period—the gaze of the camera is a transformative one. What appears on the screen will be reformed by the very act of rendering it visible. Oppressed groups will be organized and have their problems solved; the oppressors too will change for the better during the course of the film. The latter point needs some elaboration: the act of representation, which is also an act of naming (*this* is the Telugu country), is accomplished by drawing on sources and influences that are not necessarily indigenous. In *Malapilla* the shots of the Dalit hamlet and the temple festival draw rather directly on depictions of "native customs and manners" by colonial film-makers. The analysis of borrowings of the Telugu social from the British colonial archive is a project in itself.[5] Such is the generic nature of the depiction of the countryside in *Malapilla* that it could well have been found in footage shot by some visiting British or American film-maker.

Malapilla's transformative mandate extends to the representational domain where extant modes of depicting cultural geography that actually belong to a colonial project—the footage from that archive, in a manner of speaking—is re-labelled as both original and truthful and claimed for a nationalist project. This manoeuvre recalls Phalke's claim that the cinema was an indigenous cultural form. In colonial travelogues and propaganda films, the voiceover narrator anchors the visuals by offering a descriptive account. Sound works differently

[5] I was alerted to Ramabrahmam's borrowings by the discussion of British colonial films by the participants of the International Conference on Film Cultures: Historical Perspectives. Organized by the Department of Cultural Studies, English and Foreign Languages University, Hyderabad, 21–22 October 2011. A collection of synopses, analyses and even footage of some of the films is available on http://www.colonialfilm.org.uk. From Richard Osborne's analysis (http://www.colonialfilm.org.uk/node/4676), the film *Village in India* (John Hanau, 1938) promises to be an interesting point of comparison with Ramabrahmam's work.

in both the Ramabrahmam films. In *Malapilla* and *Raitu Bidda* depictions of the countryside are accompanied by songs which are not exactly commentaries on what is shown. The scenes in turn have little story-level significance. The function of sound in them is not explication of the visual but incorporation of the "found" footage into the films' narrative universe. Only when this work—of reclamation and naming—is done does the story proper begin.

With *Raitu Bidda* the peasant became the object of cinematic representation, replacing other categories of the "folk." A distinct regime of visual and thematic concerns was instituted around this figure. The film opens with a song ("*Nidra melukora tammuda*") by a beggar describing the difficulties of peasant cultivators in zamindari areas (*zamindari raitu*). The song strings together footage of rural life and festivals, but also of hills, streams, and valleys—the country, in short. As in *Malapilla*, we notice that the footage could well have come out of a colonial film archive. However, the beggar's song ensures that these scenes of native peasant life are recognized as belonging to the world of the oppressed *zamindari raitu*—whom the camera will render mobilized (Images 72–104).

Images 72–104: *Raitu Bidda's* opening sequence depicting scenes of the Telugu country, agricultural activities, and rural festivities. At the end of this sequence we are introduced to Narsi Reddy's household and, finally, the protagonist himself is seen against the backdrop of a wall with slogans in support of the Raitu Sangham (farmers' association).

72

73

74

75

76

77

78

79

80

81

82

83

84

85

86

87

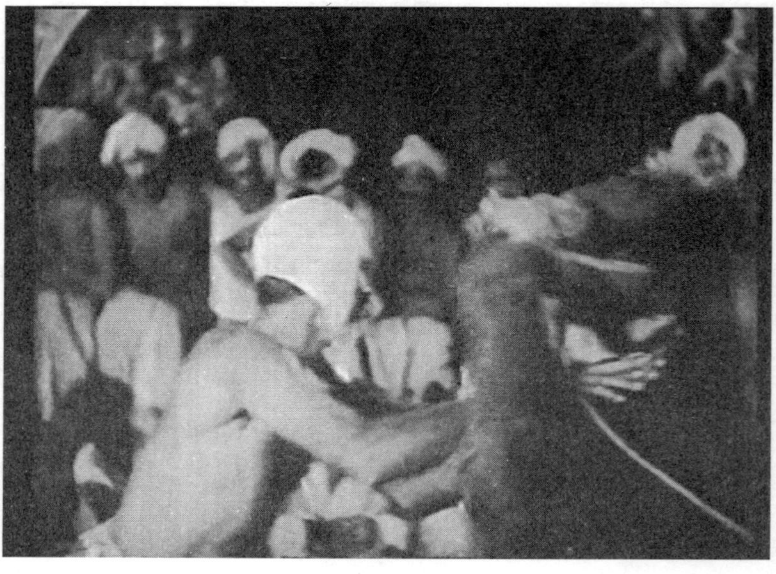

88

89

90

91

92

93

94

95

56

97

98

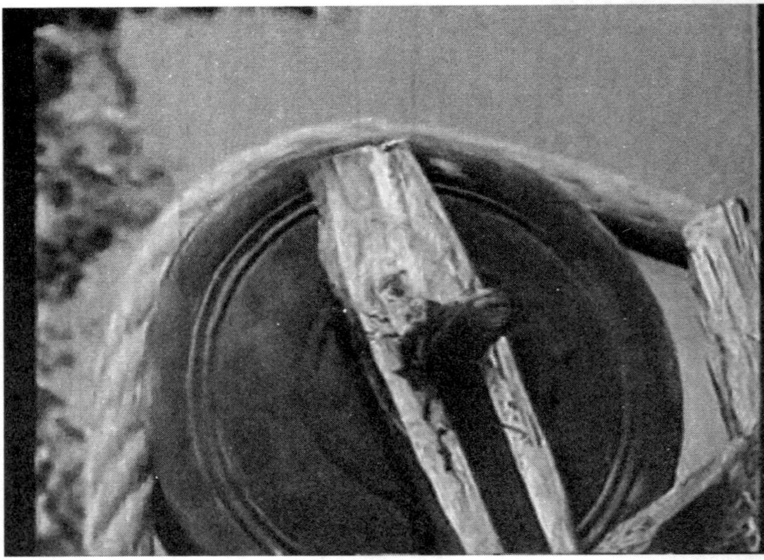

99

100

101

102

103

104

The film's characters are introduced, after the song is over, in a sequence showing them performing rituals in preparation for the new agricultural cycle. The story proper does not begin till after the village peasants are seen ploughing their fields, about sixteen minutes into the film (eleven minutes after the credits). The mode of linking the village and peasants with custom or festivity would, in the years to come, become the standard for filming rural life. More important for our purposes, such detailed depiction of peasant life is the means by which the fictional universe is named "Telugu."

Raitu Bidda revolves around the farmer Narsi Reddy (Bellari Raghava) and his confrontation with the local zamindar (Seetapati Rao). The film is in two parts, and each has a separate but related resolution. The first part deals with the electoral battle between the representative of the farmers' party (a thinly veiled reference to the Congress: we see the Congress tricolour, the *charkha*, as also pictures of Gandhi and Nehru), Rami Reddy (Kosaraju, co-lyricist of the film) and the nominee of the local zamindar—easily recognized as a member of the Justice Party, the party of the non-Brahmin landed elite (Images 105 and 106). The local moneylender (*shavukaru*) and the village writer (*karanam*), both allies of the zamindar, fail to muster support for the latter's candidate. Despite spending a large amount of money on this candidate, alongside attempting to bribe the electorate, threatening the opposition, and attempting to lock the farmers in the village temple on the eve of the election, the zamindar fails to prevent the victory of Rami Reddy. The farmers' electoral victory brings the first part to a close (the second part is separated by the film's interval). In addition to exposing the corrupt and undemocratic deeds of the zamindar, the first half of the film demonstrates the incorruptibility of Narsi Reddy: he remains unmoved by the threats of the *shavukaru* who has lent him money, the breaking of his daughter's marriage alliance, and the offer of a large bribe. We are also introduced to the zamindar's evil advisers who, it later turns out, are the real villains of the piece.

In the second part of the film we realize that the victory of Rami Reddy only deepens the crisis. The zamindar's evil younger brother (K.N. Simha), and the dismissed servant Subbanna (Narasimha Rao), come together to plot against the zamindar. Even as the zamindar's

105

106

Images 105 and106: Political meetings with Congress flags and images of Gandhi in *Malapilla* (top) and *Raitu Bidda* (bottom).

men punish the farmers, presumably without the landlord's knowledge, the *karanam*, *shavukaru*, and village *munsif* join the farmers. The zamindar's brother employs the scheming Subbanna to kidnap the zamindar's five-year-old son and blames Narsi Reddy for it. When Narsi Reddy approaches the zamindar with a charter of demands, the latter begs him to release his son. Narsi Reddy's denial of the allegation is immediately followed by the arrival of the police, who arrest the zamindar's brother for the kidnapping. The enlightened zamindar not only agrees to all the demands of the farmers but also gives away his *rajyam* (literally kingdom) to the Raitu Sangham (farmers' association), declaring he too is now a farmer. The film ends with the inauguration of an ashram named after Narsi Reddy's dead son (killed in an accident caused by the zamindar). The last shot of the film is of a Congress flag, with the declaration within a background song that there is no difference between farmer and king.

The film anticipates Independence, imaging the nation as a unified community. The zamindar's absolute reformation is achieved partly by transferring the responsibility for the oppressiveness of farmers to his servant and brother. Like Mallikarjuna Sarma in *Malapilla*, the zamindar can emerge smelling of roses largely because many of those around him are carefully shown to be unsavoury. Subbanna, presented as a comic figure in the early part of the film, grows increasingly dangerous and begins plotting against the zamindar in the later part of the film. The zamindar's wife, upon reading a newspaper report on Subbanna's misdeeds, warns her husband and he heeds her warning by dismissing the man. There is a discernible shift in the development of the zamindar in the second part; throughout the early part he has come across as a decadent autocrat who is mostly to be seen indoors talking to his dog in English, pampering his son, and dressing up. Gradually, however, his younger brother, a drunkard and womanizer, emerges as the true villain of the piece: unlike Subbanna, he is consistently presented as selfish and evil. Rather early in the film we become aware of his intention to kidnap the zamindar's son. The villain makes a speech against the law of primogeniture when arrested and, lacking all decency, is not even remorseful about his plan (though he apologizes to Narsi Reddy for accusing him falsely). While his resentment against unjust inheritance laws may be well founded, the fact of the matter is that on account of his moral degeneration he—unlike Narsi Reddy—has no credible qualification for mounting a challenge to the zamindar.

The naming of true villains is an integral part of the solution to the rupture in the social. It also facilitates the closure of the melodramatic narrative which piles upon Narsi Reddy's family one suffering after another.[6] These include the breaking of the marriage alliance of his daughter, the injury and subsequent death of his son, and financial hardship; the zamindar is directly or indirectly responsible for all of this. The transformation of the zamindar occurs in the wake of the kidnapping of his son. He is absolved of his misdeeds because he now suffers like Narsi Reddy. When accused of the kidnapping, Narsi Reddy tells the zamindar that he too is a parent and knows what it is to lose a child.

The build-up to this dramatic but peaceful resolution is gradual. It is anticipated by the individualization of the conflict between landlords and farmers as a confrontation between the zamindar and the representative of the peasants, Narsi Reddy. Early in the film Narsi Reddy, who has kept his family waiting, is introduced saying he has been held up trying to bring about a compromise between people in a dispute. A respected public figure to begin with, his stature increases with his suffering. Narsi Reddy's authenticity as the farmers' representative rests on his ability to face hardship on behalf of the farmers. It is as if his suffering qualifies him to be a leader of people. The film does not detail the difficulties faced by other members of the farming community. While the opening song frames the story as one about zamindari oppression, what we are presented with by way of evidence is Narsi Reddy's troubles, which are only inter alia economic. At crucial points the village beggar sings songs about the misery of the peasant community, generalizing Narsi Reddy's condition. Narsi Reddy, too, speaks frequently of his condition as typical of the entire community. For instance, when offered a bribe to support the

[6] This strategy for rescuing the object of reform is adopted in *Shavukaru* (discussed below), in which the moneylender's servant is held responsible for misleading him. Towards the end of the film the moneylender pays for his misdeeds when the servant tries to rob him.

zamindar's candidate in the election, he says, "You should realize that in civilized society [*sabhya samajam*] the farming community [*raitu jati*] is free of corruption." As the film progresses, the spectator's gaze begins to merge with that of the villagers watching Narsi Reddy suffer in full public view. When the zamindar's men confiscate Narsi Reddy's cow and injure his daughter over the confiscation, the villagers comment on the injustice and brutality of the act, verbalizing the spectator's response.

At the very end of the film the zamindar and Narsi Reddy come to an agreement on the farmers' charter of demands. The scene has the two filling up the entire frame. There is no indication of an audience for this interaction between the two till the zamindar raises a slogan, "*Raitu sanghaniki* . . ." An invisible crowd, presumably the villagers who accompanied Narsi Reddy, responds with "*Jai*." The unseen village community and the spectator share a field of vision, bearing witness to king and farmer becoming equals. The farmers have become a community of spectators. Their final chorus of approval of the resolution of the conflict erases the distinction between diegetic and extra-diegetic spectatorship. The formation of a unified village community is mirrored off screen, in the cinema hall.

The nation therefore is a community that has transcended its antagonisms. The peasant is the prototype of the nationalist subject and the village—marked by its Teluguness—is the site for housing the community. In this chain of signification, the strongest link is arguably between peasant and Telugu land. In post-*Raitu Bidda* Telugu cinema, being peasant meant being Telugu. Location shooting highlighting physical and cultural geography was inevitably associated with rural melodramas that centred on heroic and villainous peasants. Missing in most of the later films depicting the Telugu country is the figure of the zamindar.

Being Peasant and Telugu

In the 1950s' social, even as the film industry came under the control of its peasant entrepreneurs, the links between peasants and representations of the Telugu country were strengthened. Two landmark films, *Shavukaru* (L.V. Prasad, 1950) and *Palletooru* (T. Prakash

Rao, 1952), which are centrally concerned with peasant life, exemplify the post-Independence coupling of the peasantry and Teluguness. Both films feature NTR and, along with *Patala Bhairavi* (K.V. Reddy, 1951), contributed to making him a star.

In 1950, the production company Vijaya Pictures, established by B. Nagi Reddy and Chakrapani, was launched with the social film *Shavukaru*. By then L.V. Prasad had acquired a reputation as a director of socials. *Shavukaru* was commercially unsuccessful but critically acclaimed and was hailed by KoKu as "the forerunner of 'progressive pictures' in Telugu" (1964: 6). This was the first of the four films for which NTR was contracted by the company over a two-year period (Venkat Narayan 1985: 206). *Shavukaru* is centred on the peasantry and its problems, as is *Palletooru*, a film that KoKu argued was a paradigm-setting example of Teluguness. All its outdoor scenes were shot in a Coastal Andhra village (Kutumbarao 2000b: 145). This was no doubt because the makers of the film knew all too well that even bullock carts were different in the Telugu country.

Chengaiah (Govindarajulu Subba Rao) the village moneylender, and the farmer Ramaiah (Srivatsava), his brother-in-law, are neighbours. Subbulu (Janaki), Ramaiah's daughter and Satyam (NTR) fall in love. The neighbours fall out because of a problem created by Rangaiah (S.V. Ranga Rao), Chengaiah's servant, and the family of the local Komati trader. Later, Ramaiah's son Narayana is implicated in a crime he did not commit by Chengaiah and Rangaiah and sent to jail. Meanwhile, the city-based Satyam too is falsely implicated in a theft and sent to jail, where he meets his cousin and finds out about his father's misdeed. Chengaiah is shocked when his son refuses to defend himself against the charge and is sentenced. Chengaiah dismisses Rangaiah when he comes to know the latter has been extorting money from the villagers. Rangaiah, who is shown to be in league with a gang of robbers early in the film, plots to rob Chengaiah. The village washerwoman finds out about the plan and informs Subbulu. After some hesitation Subbulu, who has earlier unsuccessfully begged her uncle not to send her brother to jail, informs Chengaiah. Rangaiah and the robbers strike while she is in her uncle's house. Ramaiah and the villagers reach Chengaiah's house and capture the robbers. The families are reunited. Satyam and Narayana are released from prison. The film ends with the marriage of Subbulu and Satyam.

The film's credit sequence rolls out against the backdrop of panoramic shots of the countryside, recalling *Raitu Bidda*'s opening, but the film itself was entirely shot in the studio. Close attention is paid to the representation of social and familial relations in the village. Traditional performances and festivities are foregrounded. The film renders insignificant class antagonisms between the moneylender and the farmer, the latter being indebted to him. Early in the film it is revealed that Ramaiah is repaying a part of the loan to the *shavukaru* (moneylender), his brother-in-law, and there is much warmth between them. He even tells his nephew Satyam that Chengaiah's loan has allowed him to buy land and live in comfort. After they fall out, Chengaiah insists that the full loan amount and interest remains due, although Ramaiah has already repaid two-thirds of it. Narayana tells his father that he should not have trusted the moneylender to begin with and laments: "Who does not know about Chengaiah?" The matter does not end here. Ramaiah raises another loan to repay Chengaiah but the latter is easily persuaded by Rangaiah that the farmer's crop should be burnt. Narayana, forewarned of the plan by the moneylender's accountant, manages to protect the paddy by hitting Rangaiah (and is implicated in the criminal case that lands him in jail).

The film presents class antagonism as a deviation—as not the state of countryside normality. By featuring a family of traders distinguishable by their names and occupation as Komatis, and by distinguishing the traders from the *shavukaru*, the film clearly indicates that the moneylender is from an agricultural caste; he is a rich peasant, not a Komati. The anticipation of a cross-cousin marriage between Satyam and Subbulu from the very beginning of the film, their budding romance, and also the warmth between the neighbours, all ensure that the disruption that follows appears as aberration and not general condition. At heart, the problem is literally a quarrel between neighbours, nothing more serious. *Shavukaru* is in fact described as the story of neighbours (*Irugu porugula katha*) in its booklet (Images 107 and 108). Notice here the difference in the representation of conditions of the peasant in *Raitu Bidda*, where the story is framed by a general statement on the oppressive state of affairs. Post-Independence, *Shavukaru* suggests the village that has now been evacuated of the zamindar houses a community with shared customs and festivities.

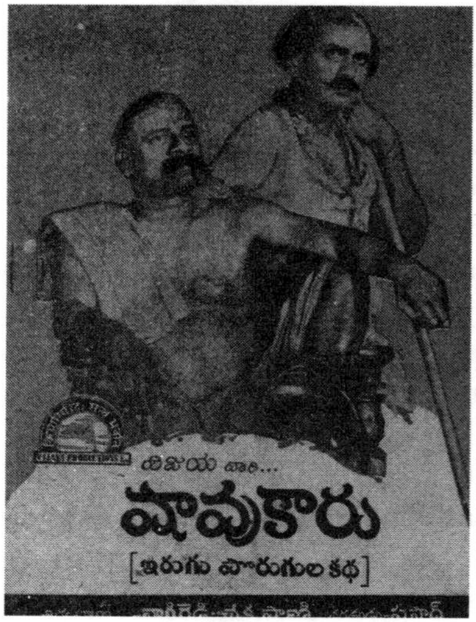

107

108

Images 107–8: Film booklet, outlining the plot of *Shavukaru*. The back cover (bottom) says that this is the first Telugu film to have been appreciated by people and the press. Source: Manasu Collection, M.V. Rayudu.

Indeed, the film begins with a performer singing about a miser, evidently introducing a *shavukaru* who has not yet entered the story. The performer gathers the entire village community before him, the sole exception being the moneylender. We learn later that he never leaves his house for fear of robbers. The problem therefore is not class or caste division but the voluntary abstention of a miserly moneylender from the enjoyment of community life. Later, while the entire village celebrates Deepavali, Chengaiah is seen sitting quietly with a bundle of crackers gifted him by the Komatis. It is only Subbulu's taunts that make him light a few crackers—and they turn out to be duds. Changed social relations in the villages are foregrounded in the two Deepavali songs. The first shows a happy village celebrating the festival while the second shows an inactive and gloomy village. This technique, of using the backdrop of a festival to show the deterioration of community life in the village, is also deployed in *Palletooru*. In *Shavukaru*, the representation of the Telugu country is accompanied by the production of a community that is by and large free of class-caste antagonisms to begin with. The narrative movement is circular in that it returns to the idyllic state after a period of disruption.

Broadly adhering to the official CPI line on linguistic reorganization of states, *Palletooru* makes a direct connection between the peasantry and the Telugu nation. The depiction of the countryside, the foregrounding of the problems of the peasantry—including their exploitation by the landlord, who doubles as the moneylender—and the demand for the formation of a separate Andhra state are fully integrated in the film's attempt to reproduce life in a typical "Telugu" village. The film opens with a quotation from Ramabrahmam's *Raitu Bidda*: as in the earlier film, the first shot is of a cock crowing on the roof of a hut. The next half hour is more or less exclusively dedicated to the production of nativity. To begin with, the villagers are shown celebrating Sankranti in a song ("*Vachchindoi Sankranti*"). We then see documentary-style footage of cockfights and battering rams, events associated with Sankranti festivities, followed by a *chedugudu* (a variant of kabaddi) match between the Vishalandhra and Youth League teams. Having thus gestured towards the overtly political, the film rapidly sets about tying together nativity, peasantry, and Telugu-nationalist agendas. The second nativity song of the film is occasioned by a *Bommala Koluvu* (where toys are arranged thematically). Suguna (Savitri) sings about a rebellion against an arrogant prince by peasants with the line "*raitu lenide rajyam ledu*"—no kingdom can exist without peasants. This is almost immediately followed by a "reactionary" *Hari Katha* performance sponsored by the landlord Ganapathi (S.V. Ranga Rao). The assembled villagers leave out of sheer boredom and gravitate towards the programme organized by Chandram (NTR), leader of the village youth. Chandram's programme begins with singing "*Cheyyethi jai kottu Telugoda*" (Raise your hand in victory, O Telugu) which, decades later, would become the anthem of sorts of the TDP. And then comes the highlight of the programme, a dance on peasants and workers that Chandram tells the audience is based on a poem by "Prajakavi" (People's Poet) Sri Sri (*Polalananni halaledunni*). Indeed, Sri Sri (Srirangam Srinivasa Rao) was referred to by this honorific title in left circles. The dance is choreographed in the agitprop style of the Communist Party's cultural wing, Praja Natya Mandali.

The landlord is as infuriated by the success of Chandram's programme as the failure of his own event. The story now begins. Ganapathi's attempt to appropriate the village library by planting a godman there is strongly resisted by Chandram and his friends. Ganapathi tries to rape his servant Kondaiah's (Nagabhushanam) wife Shanta (Kamala Devi). Seeing his wife distraught, Kondaiah thinks she is having an affair with her cousin, Chandram, and drives her away. Shanta returns to Chandram's house, where she had grown up, but soon leaves the village and becomes a maidservant in a town far away. Ganapathi then ensures that Chandram's sick mother is denied medical treatment. He also decides to marry Suguna, Chandram's lover. Soon it is established that, in addition to being a general-purpose villain, Ganapathi is also opposed to the formation of the state of Andhra. When Chandram points out that the newspapers are full of news of the agitation for Andhra (*Andhra rashtram godava*), Ganapathi says it is foolish to oppose the government. Chandram, drawing a parallel between Independence and the formation of Andhra state, remarks that people like him had said no to Independence earlier and were opposing statehood now (*appudu swarajyam vaddannaru, uppudu rashtram vaddantunnaru*). Ganapathi attempts to sell off his paddy to a hoarder. Chandram and the village youth ruin this plan by launching an attack on the loaded carts. The illiterate Kondaiah, who was earlier made to put his thumb impression on certain documents by his master, is arrested by the police. Ganapathi denies involvement in transporting the consignment and blames Kondaiah. By the next Sankranti the village is immersed in sadness. Friends and relatives are now estranged and no one celebrates the festival. Chandram's oxen are seized by the landlord as payment for a loan taken from Ganapathi a generation earlier. Another tragedy strikes Chandram—his mother dies. Ganapathi tries to rape Suguna but is hit on the head by an unidentified assailant. Chandram is accused of assaulting him and arrested. Shanta is discovered in the house of a lawyer who is approached by Chandram's relatives to plead his case. Chandram's associate—and Ganapathi's servant—Subbanna (Kutumbarao) accepts cash from his master's English-educated relative and sidekick Shankaram (Ramana Reddy) to lie in court. During the hearing of the case Kondaiah makes a dramatic appearance and confesses to the crime. Subbanna then shows the money paid to him by Shankaram to testify against Chandram. The court passes an order whereby Ganapathi is arrested and Chandram released. Back in the village, the villagers list his many crimes as the police come to arrest Ganapathi. The film ends with an inspirational song, "*Andhruda, levara*", exhorting Andhra to arise and bring glory to Mother India (*Bharatamata peru nilapara*).

This is among the few Telugu films to make direct references to local nationalism. However, although the film is faithful to the CPI's line on Telugu nationalism, there is no mention of Telangana. Like *Shavukaru*, this film is mostly shot in the studio but location shooting plays a critical role in the representation of the village as the site of traditional cultural practices. Some of the outdoor scenes, in particular those of the village fair that are seen just before the *chedugudu* match, recall *Malapilla*'s temple festival with the tableaux of rural exotica. With this film, nativity and the peasant, as also the peasant and Teluguness, are forever fused.

Folklore Film and its Male Star

A decade after the making of *Malapilla*, a curious development came to be noted by film journalists: the cinema seemed to have been successful in the actual mobilization of vast numbers of people. However, this mobilization was not along the lines that reformist film-makers had dreamed of. Instead, the mobilized were consumers who took their obsession with movies beyond the cinema hall. Understandably, stars became implicated in the process and it was not the social but the folklore film (*janapada chitram*, the locally produced Ruritanian fantasy) that was the centre of attention.

The folklore film was very popular in Telugu between the 1940s and the late 1960s, playing an important role in the careers of both ANR and NTR. The genre sometimes drew on plays, or on the vast volume of fantasies and romances already in print. Rajadhyaksha and Willemen (1999: 324) point out that the genre was strongly influenced by Hollywood's Orientalist fantasies, as well as the Douglas Fairbanks-style stunt films. Like the folklore film, much of the "folklore" in print is of modern origin and not directly traceable to actual folk tales, which are supposedly timeless, of indigenous origin and transmitted orally. Nagi Reddy and Chakrapani's children's magazine *Chandamama* (established in 1947) was an important vehicle of modern folklore.

The event flagging the public manifestation of cinephilia, which in the years to come would acquire the uniquely South Indian organizational form of fans' associations—dedicated mostly to promoting male film stars—was reported in the film journal *Roopavani*. Large crowds gathered in various towns to catch a glimpse of the stars of the hit folklore film *Balaraju* (G. Balaramaiah, 1948, Image 109), who were on a promotional tour. The size of the enthusiastic crowds exceeded the anticipation of the cinema hall owners hosting the stars, as also the police on duty. In many places the result was a police cane-charge on the crowds (Deshpande 1948: 68).[7]

Parachuri Gopalakrishna (2003: 11) says that with this film ANR was established as the "Telugu young women's dream prince" (*Telugu adapaducula kalalaraju*). Other observers too have drawn attention to ANR's youthful good looks in the film, which was a major commercial success. Interestingly, ANR does precious little in the film. The action

[7] The incident took place on 6 June 1948. Another *Roopavani* columnist argued in the same issue of the journal that though the incident was regrettable, it was a lesson of sorts to the audience and such cane-charges would result in the emergence of good films, actors, and directors (Murthy 1948: 7).

Image 109: Female star all the way, on the songbook of *Balaraju*. Source: Manasu Collection, M.V. Rayudu.

revolves around the heroine Sita (S. Varalakshmi) and not Balaraju (ANR)—who turns into a snake once and dies twice. On all three occasions he is revived by the heroine's efforts. Why then is the film named *Balaraju*? Referring to a Kannada film featuring Rajkumar, which casts him in a similarly passive role, Madhava Prasad points out that the male star's role in that film is purely symbolic: "From the point of view of narrative *movement*, however, he is a marginal figure" (1999: 44). In *Balaraju* the male lead, who is the husband of the heroine, is not required to perform heroic actions: it is the heroine who is crucial.

The seeming mismatch between ANR's role and the popular response it elicited raises interesting questions about the pleasures of and viewer investments in stardom. In later years two things happened: first, the star became the focus of the narrative in a manner not anticipated by *Balaraju*; and second, the emerging focus was the *male* star. Prasad argues that in all three South Indian cinemas produced from Madras (Telugu, Tamil, and Kannada), only in the late 1940 and early 1950s does the "trend towards male-centred narratives" begin (1999: 44, original emphasis). Female stars continued to be the focus of film narratives well into the early 1960s, but there is no denying the establishment of this trend, which was coeval with the emergence as stars of both ANR and NTR. They succeeded the singing stars Bellari Raghava and V. Nagaiah, who had already acquired a formidable reputation as stage actors before they began their film careers (Rajadhyaksha and Willemen 1999: 182, 157–8).

Eileen Bowser points out that in the USA both independent producers and licensed film-production companies initially resisted the star system, or rather refused to institute one for a variety of reasons, including the fear of losing players to competitors. For their part the actors, who had stage careers, were reluctant to be associated with the cinema (1990: 101–19). Biograph, for instance, was unwilling to supply the names of the players or other staff till 1913 (1990: 108). Bowser says: "It was the public who harangued the theatre managers with questions about their favourites, who wrote to studios, who asked for photographs, who sent in proposals of marriage and less proper invitations" (1990: 107–8). For viewers, recognizing players was exciting and pleasurable. On this count alone off-screen sightings of Varalakshmi, Nageswara Rao, and so on will have cheered the film's viewers. Producers could no longer escape acknowledging the importance of actor-recognition and therefore had to do something about it. Miriam Hansen's analysis (1991: 245–94) of the American silent-cinema star Rudolph Valentino, whose fans in the USA were sometimes riotous, suggests that the spill-over of the fascination for stars into the public domain was not unique to the Telugu cinema.

From the histories of other film industries, including Hollywood, it seems that the next important development in the emergence of a star system in a given film industrial context is the *narrativization of star recognition*, including the assembling of regimes of storytelling that harness the fact of spectatorial recognition of actors to produce pleasure and intelligibility. In the process, the star becomes central to the working out of what stories will be told, and how. Hansen's work on Valentino offers valuable insights into this aspect of stardom too.

Patala Bhairavi was the second of the four films that NTR acted in as a part of his contract with Vijaya Pictures. This film, while a major hit, also heralds the creation of a new kind of male star in the Telugu cinema. By the early 1950s the folklore film, like the mythological, was a discredited genre. Commentators spoke of the genre as a "menace" (see, for example, Bruhaspathi 1949). Moreover, notwithstanding the commercial success of *Balaraju* and *Keelugurram* (a.k.a. *Magic Horse*, Raja of Mirzapuram, 1949), the disastrous performance of *Tilottama* (Raja of Mirzapuram, 1951) at the box office made the industry nervous about the folklore film's prospects. An editorial in *Roopavani* (Editorial 1951: 8), while pointing this out, also noted: "These days people [audiences] are becoming smart and trick photography alone is not going to work [at the box office]." Evidently, the time had come for the genre to be scaled up from a serial compilation of attractions and special effects to something else. And at precisely this point, Vijaya made a top-of-the-line folklore film as a part of its attempt to launch a little-known actor as a star.

Patala Bhairavi, made simultaneously in Telugu and Tamil, depicts the adventures of a gardener who falls in love with the princess of the kingdom (Images 110 and 111).[8] He defeats an evil sorcerer twice over to marry her and they live happily ever after. Quite early in *Patala Bhairavi*, Thota Ramudu (literally "gardener Ramudu," played by NTR; notice the play with the actor's name) and his friend Anji (Balakrishnan) go to the city square and join a crowd of people watching a song-and-dance performance (*Itihasam vinnara, aa ati sahasule unnara*). The song is about heroism and says that every eon (*yugam*) has a hero (*kathanayakudu*, literally protagonist), who leads the populace into a state of well being: it adds, this is the lesson of history. When, towards the end of the song, the singer asks the crowd if the bravest of men is amongst the audience (*aa ati sahasule unnara?*), an

[8] See Pillai (2010: 198–221) for a detailed discussion of the Tamil version of the film. Among the points he makes is that the Tamil version uses Sanskrit words, shunned by scriptwriters associated with the DMK propaganda film. Furthermore, the setting of the action in the Central Indian kingdom of Ujjain (in present-day Madhya Pradesh) contrasts with the attempt by DMK scriptwriters to make explicit references to the antiquity of the Tamil race in the folklore film.

110

111

Images 110–11: *Patala Bhairavi's* songbook (top) and advertisement (*Telugu Cinema*, April 1951, back cover). Notice the relative (in)significance of NTR in these images: he is barely visible on the songbook. Source: Manasu Collection, M.V. Rayudu.

onlooker quickly shouts Ramudu's name, only to be mildly rebuked by an obviously pleased hero. The song ends with Ramudu confronting the queen's brother (Relangi), who arrives with soldiers and attempts to extort money from the crowd.[9] Ramudu organizes the crowd against the soldiers, beating up the king's brother-in-law in the process. The sequence ends with the crowd shouting the slogan "*Kathanayakudiki jai*" ("Long live the protagonist") after which Ramudu is decorated with a turban and wrapped in a shawl (Images 112–15).

The ceremonial nomination of the film's protagonist as a hero occurs in and by the public *before* the protagonist has any adventures, that is, before the story proper has even begun. Even before Ramudu stands up to the soldiers he is already *recognized* as a hero (by the crowd). The character Ramudu thus has a history of heroism which is not explained in the film. The narrative postpones the demonstration of his valour.

Images 112–15: The ceremonial nomination of Ramudu as the protagonist.

112

[9] In a tongue-in-cheek reference to film policy, the film has the Relangi character telling the crowd that he is collecting tax on entertainment (*vinodapu pannu*), robbing the performer and the audience in the process!

113

114

115

How is this time lag, between the naming of Ramudu as a hero of extraordinary proportions and the narrative's demonstration of his valour, to be understood? The film demands that the spectator defer judgement on the protagonist for a period of time and repose faith in the narrative. At this point of time (1951), nothing in the career of NTR could support expectations raised in the early part of the film. He was a relatively new actor who had not featured in folklore films earlier, and he was not yet a stunt/action hero. Paradoxically, it is precisely the relative insignificance of NTR's star status that allows us to see how the star is envisaged in the film. The narrative is organized around Ramudu/NTR, making him an object of spectatorial investment and *trust*. Underscoring the centrality of the NTR character to the film, Marcus Bartley's camerawork presents the actor with great care, foregrounding his solid physique and striking looks.

This film was made at a time when stars were becoming focal points in the unprecedented mobilization of a new category of film consumer who was taking *his* obsession with the cinema into public spaces beyond the cinema hall. *Patala Bhairavi* contributes significantly towards directing this obsession to the glamorous *male* star in an industry that had few prior models of male stardom—other than that of the theatre singing star—to work with. In doing so the film puts in place a new kind of narrative, even as it addresses the possibilities opened by mobilized consumers' cinephilia spilling onto the streets (something that *Balaraju* brought to the industry's notice). *Patala Bhairavi* was released with 13 prints and had a 100-day run in 10 cinema halls (Venkateswara Rao 2011: iv). Not surprisingly, it celebrated its long run by parading its actors. Once again, groups of film enthusiasts gathered in strength, only to be dispersed by cane-wielding policemen.[10]

Orders of Representation and Spectatorship

Patala Bhairavi's attempt to account for the star in narrative terms was not in itself remarkable. All film industries grapple with the issue of a star's role when organizing the film's narrative. In Madras, the evolution of stars—the emergence of first-generation male stars in South India and the reduced importance of the female star both industrially and narratively—facilitated what Prasad (1999) calls "cine-politics"—which is expandable thus: "A set of contingent factors led to a situation where cinema, a form of entertainment that was then [1950s] learning to speak, came to be chosen as the site of a strong political investment, where audiences responded with enthusiasm to an offer of leadership emanating from the screen and, through fans associations that emerged later, established a concrete set of everyday practices that re-affirmed the position of the star as leader" (ibid.: 49). Prasad's claim that the cinema was still "learning to speak" after two decades of the talkie is not convincing; however, his more substantial point about cinema and politics is. The specifically South Indian nature of cine-politics is the adulation of stars "based on the ascription to the star of the status of a representative. The star is taken to represent the *linguistic community* for whom his films were made" (ibid.: 41, original emphasis). The centrepiece of Prasad's argument

[10] According to Pandurangarao (1951: 40), eighty people were injured in the cane-charge by the police.

on cine-politics is substitution, when the community finds in an individual the capacity to stand in for itself: "[S]ometimes, political representation is not effected through acts of election or delegation, but through *substitution*, i.e., through the unexpected arrival of a figure who seems to be already endowed with the legitimacy to represent us" (ibid.: 46, original emphasis). Critical for our purposes is the collapse of two orders of representation—aesthetic and political—into one: depicting the community on-screen and speaking for it are merged within a single manoeuvre.

Among the questions that Prasad's argument leads us to is the manner in which the industry produces a convincing authority figure. A related question is how this figure came to represent a linguistic community.[11] The advantage Telugu cinema of the 1950s and 1960s offers is that this question can be de-coupled from the propagandist or political intention of the films in question. In the Tamil instance the strong presence of DMK ideologues in the industry tends to deflect critical attention away from the cinematic to party ideologies.

There is a commonsensical understanding to the effect that the authority figure emerges as a direct consequence of the viewer's inability to realize that stars are ordinary people and not gods or legendary heroes. Chidananda Das Gupta (1991) has the most clearly articulated position on this, summed up by the title of his book, *Seeing is Believing*. In such analyses we witness the positing of what Christian Metz would call the "credulous" spectator (1982: 72), who doesn't quite know that films are fictional. What is interesting about Metz's discussion of credulousness is that while no one will admit to being fooled by the fiction, it is necessary to be invested in the fiction in order to derive pleasure from the cinema. A degree of credulousness is a prerequisite for pleasurable film spectatorship. The spectator therefore disavows credulousness by projecting it on to others who are not sophisticated enough to distinguish between film and reality: children, women, peasants, etc. However, the credulous person is very much a part of us: "By a partial identification with this character, the spectators can sustain their credulousness in all incredulousness" (ibid.: 73). A significant body of literature on the cinema's social and political

[11] Discussed in the next chapter.

consequences is predicated on the critical conviction that someone out there is fooled by the cinema into believing what s/he sees on the screen is both real and worthy of imitation.[12]

Cinema's ability to produce another kind of spectator holds the key to understanding how post-1950s Telugu stars in general, and NTR in particular, work. I have termed this the "willing spectator," one who is deeply, wilfully, invested in the fiction and makes a series of demands on the film and its star (Srinivas 2009: 105–28). Were the spectator to be credulous, the mythological and folklore films would be the most important sources of a star's authority, for it is in these genres that the star plays figures of extraordinary authority such as gods and kings (cf. Das Gupta 1991). Prasad (1999) points out that whereas in the mythological film the star's authority is an attribute of the role he plays (as a god the character could perform superhuman tasks and also *speak* with authority), the social had to create a new/contemporary framework in which the figure of authority could be located. Without disagreeing I would add that the folklore film and mythologicals provided vital resources to the social in order that the on-screen male authority figure be created in the first place. Exactly what the contribution of *Patala Bhairavi* may have been becomes clear in the light of developments over subsequent years. Moreover, the timing of *Patala Bhairavi* is interesting: in Telugu cinema the emergence of the male star, as also his status as a representative of the masses, is both coeval and inextricably linked with entrepreneurs of peasant origin acquiring control over all branches of the film industry between 1947 and 1956.

Genre, Nativity, and the Star

Patala Bhairavi's star and the folklore film as a genre represented a tendency that was spoken of in contradistinction to nativity, which throughout the 1950s and 1960s was strongly identified with socials. On the other hand, folklore films (and mythologicals) were seen as

[12] I have examined at some length the centrality of the spectator's credulousness for discussions on cinema and agitations against specific films in the 1990s. See, in particular, "Fans, Families and Phantoms: *Alluda Majaka* Revisited" in Srinivas 2009: 157–88 .

forms that eroded nativity. KoKu, for example, argued that "Telugu films lost their 'National' character and nativity [in the 1950s] because of the success of 'folk-lore' pictures and revival of mythologicals . . . Because mythologicals and folk-lores [*sic*] had no use for 'nativity' such things did not tell upon the quality of those films" (1964: 6). It is necessary to add a caveat: notwithstanding the widespread critical condemnation of both genres, specific films within both genres were warmly praised. These include folklore films, including *Patala Bhairavi*, *Malleeswari* (B.N. Reddi, 1951), *Chandraharam* (K. Kameswara Rao, 1953), and the mythological *Maya Bazaar* (K.V. Reddy, 1957) produced by the Vijaya-Vauhini institutions.

As we have seen, both ANR and NTR acted in films of all genres in the 1950s. NTR had to his credit a number of critically acclaimed socials, and Rajadhyaksha and Willemen (1999: 339) note that he produced the realist film *Todu Dongalu* (D. Yoganand, 1954), in which he also acted.[13] By the 1960s, however, NTR, who acted in his first major mythological role as late as 1957 (*Maya Bazaar*), came to be associated with folklore and mythological films. The development assumes importance in the light of KoKu's argument that, apart from contributing to the erosion of nativity, there was in these genres (which he termed "culturally something of a retreat") "plenty of glamour—glamour in the stars, costumes, settings and photography. And the stars were the vital link between the film-hungry millions and an industry which was shaping into one of the nation's most vital industries. These stars were no longer the artistes who played this or that conspicuous role: *they made the roles conspicuous*. In short they were the roles. The audiences were ready to laugh or weep with them, or gloat in their romances and to feel elated by their triumphs, in short, to identify themselves with the stars" (1964: 5, emphasis added). NTR was scarcely capable of making the role conspicuous in *Patala Bhairavi* for he was not yet a star. But the film instituted what we may, in KoKu's honour, call the folklore star. KoKu also argued that the expansion of the film market over the 1930s–1950s was *made possible by folklore films*, whose stars had overtaken the social stature

[13] KoKu warmly praised this critically acclaimed but commercially unsuccessful film in his review (2000a: 444–6).

of political leaders and were being paid better than state governors (2000a: 175). The social had no use for such a star, at least not till some years later.

At this point, a brief discussion of the emergent models of stardom would be useful to understand the link being made between them, film form, and aesthetics. KoKu argued that the problem with stars was not limited to the folklore film. Without directly referring to any particular film or star, he suggested that major stars in general represented an aesthetic-economic-cultural tendency inimical to the production of realistic socials. In an essay dating to 1953 that called for relocating the industry to a town in Andhra, he stated such a move would enable the industry to gain access to actors who could create the required Telugu atmosphere (*vatavaranam*) on screen. Not the least important consequence of relocation, he argued, would be the replacement of the star's appeal with strong story lines (2000b: 234). In the year before he wrote this he stated that a film industry founded on stars had no chance of taking root in the country (ibid.: 82). Defining stardom as the quality which strongly attracts people to the cinema, regardless of the role played by the actor (ibid.: 80), he argues that Kanchanamala, the heroine in *Malapilla*), was the only (real/substantial) star the Telugu industry had ever had, and even she had retired a while back. In such a situation it was in the best interest of producers to move beyond stardom and focus on characterization and acting skills, introduce new actors, and stop trying to sell the *sahaja akarshana* or charisma ("natural appeal," as distinct from acting abilities, which were acquired) to viewers (ibid.: 82). No suggestion he made to the industry over four decades of film journalism was rejected as comprehensively as this.

KoKu's writings are evidence that, well into the 1950s, realism and the social were inseparable. The star was an obstacle to both. In the light of the strong association between the social and realism on the one hand and the opposition or incommensurability on the other between nativity and stardom, it is possible to suggest that NTR was *disqualified* many times over from making any kind of claim to being capable of representing Teluguness. Not only was he strongly identified with genres that represented a "cultural retreat" but also, in the 1960s, he was perceived to have sided with the industry faction opposed to relocating to Hyderabad.

The Social without Realism

Regardless of NTR's roles in socials that were praised for their realism, at a certain point he either became unavailable for the realist/nativity film or was seen as unsuitable by the industry. Around the time that NTR's distance from realism became obvious—the late 1960s to be more precise—the social itself began to be reconstituted as an extension of the mythological and folklore genres. The development worth tracking is the gradual shift away from both realism and representations of physical geography—of Telugu land (especially the village), peasants, women, and customs—as the means of achieving screen Teluguness, to the creation of a male star who would render that older paradigm for producing Teluguness insignificant. This is not to suggest that physical geography, etc. were no longer of interest to filmmakers, but that their relative importance diminished. Increasingly, realism and nativity came to be associated with distinctive, genre-like tendencies, whereas in the 1950 they were characteristic of the social as such. By the early 1970s even ANR's films were realist only on occasion.

In the 1960s ANR and NTR represented two approaches to the larger and much older problem of screening Teluguness. The first, associated with ANR, was aimed at extending realism into an organizing principle of the industry. This tendency held that Teluguness was achieved by realistic representation and needed certain kinds of locations, props, etc. The second, associated with NTR, was assembled as a reaction to the social as it existed in the early 1960s. It was made possible by the expansion of the film market after state formation and the increasing popularity of the major stars. The new social was an attempt at working around the blockages of the realist aesthetic of the social, which did not quite learn how to harness the increasing ability of stars to mobilize film-consuming collectives around themselves.

In NTR's films from the mid-1960s the star is produced as someone who stands above the narrative and is inserted into it to make the story happen. This is coeval with the (re)emergence of mass mobilization as a key concern of the Telugu cinema. The new social returns to mobilization—a central issue within the celebrated socials of earlier decades—even as it makes a clean break with the older social's realist aesthetics. There are striking parallels between NTR's films from the late 1960s and Amitabh Bachchan's films of the 1970s, which Prasad (1998) characterizes as the "re-formed social" where "[t]he star became a mobilizer, demonstrating superhuman qualities and assuming a power that transformed the others who occupied the same terrain into *spectators*" (ibid.: 134, original emphasis). Simultaneously, the narrative in these films institutionalizes the subaltern as a "mobilized subject" (ibid.: 142).

An incongruous moment in *Devata* (K. Hemambaradhara Rao, 1965) alerts us to the nature of the transition under way. This film is a domestic melodrama in which the action is centred on its female lead (Savitri) in a double role. In the first half, the wife's actions demonstrate that she is an angel (*devata*). Her transformation after a train accident into a rude and hysterical woman who systematically violates decorum to humiliate her family is followed by the discovery that the transformed "wife" is actually a lookalike. The wife died in the accident and the lookalike, who happened to be on the same train, was brought home by mistake, her protests being attributed to the shock of the accident. The storyline ensures that through much of the film the male star has very little to do by comparison with his female counterpart. As in *Balaraju* the male star is cast in a role more symbolic than agentive. However, towards the end of the film the focus of the narrative shifts to the male lead who, having discovered that his wife is dead, decides to find a husband for the lookalike. He is now the *devata*. His attempt fails and the film ends happily with the two deciding to marry.

About an hour into the film, Varahalu (Padmanabham), a film buff and aspiring actor who routinely worships the pictures of film stars, walks into the room of his cousin Prasad (NTR). As if seeing him for the first time, he expresses surprise and remarks that the latter looks like NTR in the film *Shavukaru*. Varahalu goes on to predict that Prasad will become a "great hero" (i.e. major star). Interestingly, one of the film-star pictures that Varahalu prays to is of NTR in a mythological role (Images 116 and 117).

The explicitness of the biographical allusion, in the shape of a reference within the fiction to its own star's life and work, while typical

116

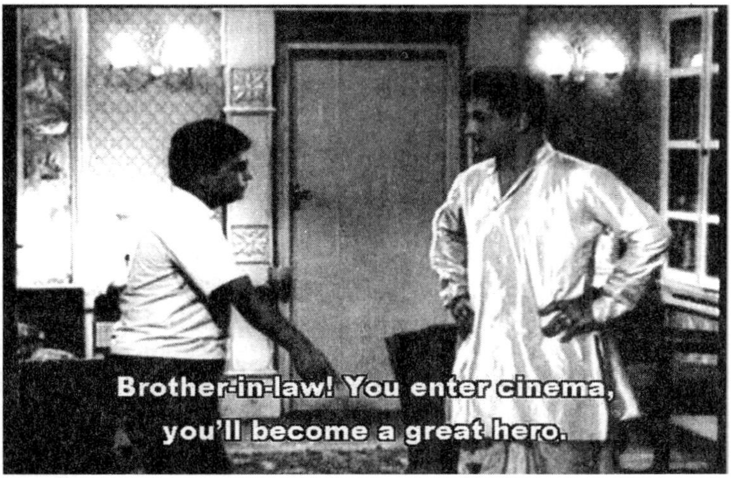

117

Images 116-17: Biographical references in *Devata*. Varahalu, who worships film actors (top), "discovers" that his cousin looks like NTR and predicts a bright future in the industry for him.

of 1980s films of both Telugu and Tamil stars, is unusual in the NTR films made over the 1970s.

About two years before the release of this film, a commentator noted that there were essentially two kinds of stories in the Telugu cinema, namely hero-oriented and heroine-oriented. The film industry now preferred hero-oriented subjects, implying that the shift of focus away from the female star was now complete. Furthermore, he says, casting one of the *hero dwayam*—our superstar twosome—was seen as being essential to the success of a film (*Krishna Patrika* 1963). *Devata* does not do much more with the male star than name him as such. Varahalu's comment is brushed aside as a joke by Prasad and the film goes on with its narrative as if innocent of NTR's presence. This is very like the other 1960s socials, in which there was at best passing mention of the star's status but for the most part the connection between the star and his role was worked out within the framework of the fiction. Another striking incongruity in the film appears in the form of a digression wherein Varahalu lands up in Madras and makes a round of its studios to meet his idols. We see him cheering at stars from the sidelines, grinning foolishly at them, and actually managing to meet them. The film, while gesturing towards the value of stars and their capacity to incite spectatorial obsession, does not quite figure out what else might be done with the male star put into a social.

Devata's release was preceded by the announcement of the state government's new film policy. ANR was also in the news for reasons other than his association with the announcement. He had returned from a much-publicized tour of the USA and, upon his arrival, his narration of experiences there was serialized in *Krishna Patrika* (1964b), the newspaper which took a pro-relocation stand in the 1960s. As if in response to the increased visibility of ANR in the public domain, a confederation of 125 associations announced they would felicitate NTR at a grand public function in Vijayawada. The town, a major centre for film exhibition as well as being a crucial node for channelling investments into the film industry, was apparently selected because NTR had studied there. Of course, there was a much closer link between the town and the star: he had begun his amateur acting career while in college there. Appropriately, NTR was to announce a scholarship scheme for students on this occasion (*Krishna Patrika*

1964c: 18). The event was to be presided over by the chief minister, K. Brahmananda Reddy, during whose term both ANR and NTR were awarded the Padma Shri. One of the reasons cited for organizing this tribute to NTR was the charitable work that he had performed—most notably for the victims of a fire accident in Vijayawada. The other reasons included the award of an All India Certificate of Merit for NTR's mythological *Nartanasala* (K. Kameshwara Rao, 1963), judged the second-best feature film of 1963, and an award for Best Telugu Film to his *Lava Kusa*.

The NTR felicitation had an unanticipated consequence. Weeks before the function it was reported that the organizers were encountering a strange problem (*chitra samasya*). Whereas there were already a few scattered fans' associations, including a prominent one in Kurnool, once news of the function got around many new associations began to sprout. "Piles of letters" were received from these associations from across the state, all wanting to be a part of the ceremony. Some admirers of the star even dashed off legal notices demanding a chance to participate in the event. The Kurnool association wrote to the organizers saying that their *daiva bhakti* and *papa bheeti* (devotion and fear of sin) had increased after watching NTR's mythologicals (Sudarsanam 1964: 18).

Devata came in the wake of the emergence of these fans' associations and the undeniable fact that the star had evolved into a mobilizer in his own right. In the Tamil-speaking Presidency region, the first fan club devoted to MGR was formed in 1953, the year of the star's admission into the DMK (Hardgrave, Jr. 1979: 121). That development coincided with the formation of Andhra state on 1 November 1953, resulting also in a new Madras state that was not yet a linguistic state though far more Tamil than during the Presidency era. The question we could well be asking is whether, even for the Tamil cinema and its stars, the formation of linguistic states was a watershed event in more ways than has been understood. Over a decade later, both ANR and NTR had grown in stature as public figures and were seen in the company of the most powerful men in the state. Fans' associations now became a noticeable presence in the province, demonstrating that these stars' constituencies extended beyond the cinema hall. This went hand in hand with the film industry extending its reach by increasing cinema halls across the state, and with the wider circulation of the Telugu cinema—in particular in the Telangana region.

Notwithstanding anything that Tamil cinema and its stars had achieved till this point, the social was not the primary vehicle of MGR or NTR even in the mid-1960s. The biggest 1960s hits of both stars were folklore films (and mythologicals in the case of the latter).[14] How then could the social work with the kind of superstar who was a public figure, the leader of an industry faction, the centre of fan mobilization? In the Tamil instance, the star was actively engaged in party politics too.

The logical next step was taken in *Kathanayakudu* (K. Hemambaradhara Rao, 1969), when the viewer's recognition of the star was integrated into the organization of the narrative. Incidentally, this film features two future chief ministers, NTR and Jayalalithaa. With *Kathanayakudu* the narrative of Telugu films began to exhibit an acute awareness of the star's special status; it went on to present him as existing within the fiction while simultaneously standing above it. As a result the star becomes *in the fiction* the figure "who seems to be already endowed with the legitimacy to represent" (Prasad 1999: 46). Unlike in the mythological and folklore film, the hero's authority is not traceable to a prior schema—godhood or fantasy setting, respectively—which usually accounted for his status in those genres.

The film virtually names the star NTR as the protagonist/*kathanayakudu* who arrives into the narrative to solve a crisis. The film's pre-credit sequence shows the villains killing the honest manager of an orphanage because he has threatened to expose their misdeeds. They then collect money from the public in the dead man's name. Towards the end of the sequence the villains laugh manically, having appropriated the money collected. As the camera pans over an unnamed city the voice-over narrator says this is the story of every village and town. "A hero [*kathanayakudu*] is needed to confront this [evil]," he says, just as the NTR character appears—his role in the film is yet to

[14] Hardgrave Jr. (1973: 299) makes a passing reference to the importance of the folklore films *Nadodi Mannan* (MGR, 1958) and *Adimai Penn* (K. Shankar, 1969) when discussing MGR's career.

established—walking on a road towards the camera. Mid-stride, there is a freeze frame and the film's title card appears, labelling the star the *kathanayakudu* and flagging his entry into the fiction. Immediately after—in the title sequence itself—the star-protagonist is seen doling out instant justice to the pettiest of offenders (street vendors selling fly-infested food to children, and the like) and performing minor altruistic acts (helping an old woman cross the street). The modest nature of the good work notwithstanding, the narrative logic leaves no room for questioning the legitimacy of the *kathanayakudu* or the naming of the would-be protagonist.

The process of labelling the NTR character (about whom we know nothing, not even his name) as the hero mandated to deal with the evil in "every village and town" ensures that the *star*—not a character—is offered as an object of spectatorial investment at the very moment of his introduction. The film provides no logical explanation for why this should be the case. Spectatorial investment is invited on the basis of an implicit trust in the narrative because of the strength of awareness of the character's star status: this man is going to resolve the story-level crisis and we can trust him to do so *because* he pre-exists the story—he is NTR, the star. In its remarkable credit sequence the film thus unravels the worst-kept secret in the history of filmgoing—after all, an important reason for our going the movies is our love of movie stars (Images 118, 119, and 120).

The story revolves around a confrontation between on the one hand Sarathy (NTR), a municipal clerk; and on the other a villainous troika comprising (1) Dayanandam (Nagabhushanam) the philanthropist, businessman, and politician; (2) Satyamurthy (Mikkilineni) the contractor; and (3) Appaladora (Allu Ramalingaiah) who runs a government fair-price shop. Sarathy prevents Satyamurthy from occupying a slum and ensures that the poor receive titles over the land they live on. He is dismissed from service by his corrupt superior and leaves home on account of a misunderstanding with his older brother. Dayanandam floats a fraudulent subsidized housing scheme, implicating Sarathy's brother, who works for him as an accountant.[15]

[15] The scheme recalls the *Janta Ghar* scam in *Shree 420* (Raj Kapoor, 1955), which promises the poor houses for a mere Rs 100.

118

119

Images 118–19: Advertisements for *Kathanayakudu* in *Vijayachitra* (February 1969: 24, 37). Source: Manasu Collection, M.V. Rayudu.

Image 120: Songbook of *Kathanayakudu* (back cover). Source: Manasu Collection, M.V. Rayudu.

Meanwhile, Sarathy is offered shelter by slum dwellers and persuaded by them to contest the municipal election. He defeats Dayanandam in the election and becomes chairman of the municipal council. He puts an end to the expropriation of government funds by Dayanandam and his men. Sarathy's brother discovers the fraud in the housing scheme and manages to hide the money collected from the poor. But he is captured by Dayanandam, who holds him in captivity and tells the public he has decamped with the money. Sarathy loses the chairmanship after being accused of fraud. He is then humiliated by the villains, beaten up, and thrown unconscious on the street. Jaya (Jayalalithaa), his fruit-seller girlfriend, brings him home. At this point, after his attempts to help the poor as a government servant and elected representative have failed, he declares there is no place for honesty in this world and decides to counter deceit with deceit. Sarathy and Jaya disguise themselves as a gold smuggler and his blonde moll, trap the villains, and have them arrested. They are aided by Simham (Padmanabham), Sarathy's friend and former clerk of the municipality, who is disguised as their driver. It turns out at the very end that Sarathy was in fact working for an officer (Dhoolipala) deputed by the central government to investigate Dayanandam's crimes.

With *Kathanayakudu* we witness a 180-degree turn from *Patala Bhairavi*. For here is a well-known actor whose star status is being recalled by the narrative at the very outset in order for the story to begin. *Kathanayakudu* was remade in colour in Tamil and Hindi by Vijaya as *Nam Nadu* (Jambulingam, 1969) and *Apna Desh* (Jambulingam, 1972). The Tamil version features MGR and the Hindi Rajesh Khanna, making for a total of four star politicians associated with the film's several versions.

A comparison of the film's Telugu and Tamil versions helps pinpoint how films and their stars might now be political in ways different from earlier attempts by the Madras film industry in their propaganda films. The Tamil version retains the essence of the opening sequence while making it more action packed and overtly political. The MGR character is introduced walking towards the camera engrossed in a book he is reading. As the camera zooms in we notice that the book has Gandhi and Annadurai on its front and back covers, respectively. The poor street vendor selling dirty food is compensated by the hero who, after tossing his basket into the air, offers him a fistful of currency notes. Robert Hardgrave, Jr., places *Nam Nadu* at the centre of an important shift in the DMK's approach to the cinema. He argues that the DMK's arrival in the domain of electoral politics (1957) resulted in a watering down of the propaganda content of its films: "Displacing content as the thrust of the DMK's use of the film media, the party now sought to emphasize star popularity as a vehicle for political mobilization. The DMK now hitched its political wagon to the stars of the silver screen" (1973: 294). Pandian (1992) offers a useful description of the DMK propaganda films which allows us to note the significance of Hardgrave's observation: "These films . . . propagated atheism, Tamil nationalism (which was often couched in anti-North and anti-Hindi rhetoric) and anti-Brahminism. The narratives of these films were peopled by womanizing temple priests/religious men, helpless deities, usurious north Indian money-lenders and villainous Brahmins" (ibid.: 34). And Hardgrave elaborates thus on the nature of the shift: "Early DMK films, like *Parasakthi*, were basically oriented to social reform, but as the 1957 elections neared, the party chose less obtrusive themes with more of a specifically political flavour" (1973: 299). Virulent speeches on the injustice of the Brahminical order were replaced by passing references to the DMK, invocations of its leaders, the use of party colours (red and black) and its symbol (rising sun), etc. The star-protagonist is seen performing a series of heroic and generous actions. The "ultimate in this genre" of films marking the move away from propaganda is *Nam Nadu*. Hardgrave goes on to highlight the film's numerous explicitly political references: "M.G.R. makes his first appearance wearing the party colors—a red shirt and black pants . . . Throughout the film, the black and red combination appears, Annadurai's portrait hangs on the wall of almost every scene, accompanied by pictures of Gandhi, and in one song, Anna is specifically called the 'South Indian Gandhi.' The huts of a slum fly the DMK flag . . . The film concludes with a self-respect marriage under a statue of Gandhi" (1973: 299–300).

It is widely held by commentators that *Nam Nadu* contributed to building MGR into a star with a definite political agenda. K. Sivathamby argues that "The entire film *Nam Nadu* was an indictment against the corrupt practice of the DMK administrators (1981: 45). Rajadhyaksha and Willemen's entry on the film says that "MGR, who would soon be expelled from DMK, here turned the DMK propaganda discourse against the Party" (1999: 400).[16] My interest is not so much topical references at the level of the story or the film's embeddedness in electoral politics and the DMK–MGR conflict, but the kind of star emerging in films of the period. The crucial difference between the Telugu and Tamil versions is that the "original" is devoid of any

[16] The following interpretation is even more strident about the film's politics: "He [MGR] fell out with the DMK chief Karunanidhi and used the DMK's propaganda idiom against the DMK itself in *Nam Nadu* (1969). In 1972 he set up the rival Anna-DMK party claiming allegiance to the DMK's founder, the late Annadurai" (http://www.upperstall.com/people/mgr.html, visited on 22nd June 2004).

overt references to linguistic identity politics and party ideologies, although both are films about corruption and feature an electoral contest involving the protagonist. Nonetheless, *Kathanayakudu* too is politically significant. The leftist Telugu film commentator Hari Purushotham Rao argued that this film marks the entry of autocratic populism into Telugu cinema. He traced this variety of populism to Indira Gandhi in the domain of politics (Interview, Hyderabad, 8 January 1995).[17]

Even Tamil cinema, already in the thick of electoral battles from the late 1950s, suggests that a fundamental transformation was occurring in the production of the star in the social post-*Kathanayakudu/Nam Nadu*. The possibilities opened up by these films are extended by *Rickshawkaran* (M. Krishnan, 1971), a Tamil film which is aware of the star MGR's presence in the diegesis and ensures that there is adequate enunciation of this awareness at the level of the narrative. In addition, there are of course the usual references to Tamil language and culture. In the opening sequence of *Rickshawkaran* we see MGR participating in a rickshaw race as hundreds of onlookers cheer. He wins the race and a crowd surrounds him as a woman garlands him. There is a flimsy story-level justification for the enthusiasm of the crowd—he is after all the winner of a race— but there is no doubting that the star is in a situation analogous to the world of fans' associations as well as electoral politics (Images 121 and 122). Mass adulation in the film requires no further explanation, although the remarkable ability of the star to gather the masses around him is not linked to electoral politics within the fiction. The scene of Selvan (MGR) being garlanded is intercut with those of a rickshaw-puller being shot dead (by the villain, as we learn later). Selvan *hears* the gunshot as he is garlanded at the crowded racecourse—a glaring "movie mistake" if we assume that conventional realist representation is being attempted by the film. He immediately rushes to the scene of the murder—to find a burning corpse. And the story proper begins.

It is as if MGR is entering the world of the fiction from another

[17] I will have more to say about the intersection of NTR's film career with Indira Gandhi's political career below. For the moment I limit myself to the making of a new kind of film star.

121

122

Images 121–2: Selvan/MGR in *Rickshawkaran* after winning the rickshaw race. The story begins at this point.

domain, one in which he is already popular with the masses, in order to deal with the problem (of injustice, failed patriarchy) posed by the fiction. As the film unfolds we are provided evidence of the story-level extraordinariness of the protagonist—he is a graduate and former soldier who is widely recognized as the leader of rickshaw-pullers and other common people. In short, the rest of the film justifies the behaviour of the crowds in the opening sequence by showing the goodness and nobility of the character. The narrative will demonstrate what the spectator is already aware of: MGR is a leader on and off screen.

Developments in Telugu cinema demonstrate that the loss of innocence, of the narrative to the star, is not merely because of the star's (say MGR's) involvement in electoral politics—or a party's (read DMK's) need for replacing propaganda with something else that could be used for mass mobilization—but because *stardom in Madras-based film industries was undergoing a fundamental transformation*. From the late 1960s, in the Telugu and Tamil film, there is almost a compulsion to acknowledge the star's status in order for the character he plays to come into being. The presence of the star is flagged in MGR and NTR films to ensure that there is at all times an awareness of the simultaneous existence of the star as star and character.[18] Hardgrave, Jr., notes that "The [MGR] films are filled with references which blur the role and the actor into one" (1973: 299), implying the technique was useful to garner votes, presumably by convincing potential voters that the star-politician was noble/heroic on and off screen. I would like to argue that the issue at hand is not the production of the credulous spectator at all. Cross-references between films and (often fabricated) biographical details is the stuff of stardom. There is no need to attribute a priori political intent to this technique. Richard Dyer argues that film stars exist simultaneously on and off screen and the star image is "authenticated as something more—truer, more real—than an image" by referring back to his/her existence in the "real world" (1991: 135). Gestures towards the "real person" and references to the star's life, which is in fact carefully fabricated by the industry, are features of stardom in general.

What was unfolding in popular Telugu and Tamil cinema alike was the assemblage of cinematic techniques for the production of

[18] For a detailed discussion of how popular film narratives work with the "double existence" of the star in post-NTR Telugu cinema, see Srinivas 2009: 143–52.

a spectator who was fully aware that the film was fictional and was *invested in this fiction*— in a new kind of star capable of offering a variety of pleasures. I will cite a few examples from the 1970s films of NTR to show how there is a further refinement and sophistication with respect to the deployment of the star. A focus on these allows us to highlight the emergence of the figure of authority in cinematic terms, rather than only thematic ones. The relative absence of overtly political themes that place the star in a clearly defined political/electoral context in NTR's films is a useful and necessary counterpoint to MGR's career, and for understanding what the cinema was doing in and to politics.

Populism and the Recovery of the Feudal

In the early 1970s NTR's onward march was halted by a workaday problem which had its origin in developments that began some years earlier. By the mid-1960s sections of the industry started investing in minor or unknown actors to make low-budget films distinguished by their aesthetic quality. Even as *Thene Manasulu* (Adurthi Subba Rao, 1965), which had a cast of newcomers including future "Super Star" Krishna, was being made, it was reported that many moneyed people (*dhanikulu*) were eagerly awaiting its release to figure out how much of the new talent would be useful (*paniki vastundi*) as an investment vehicle (Madras Representative 1964: 29). The surplus flowing from peasant economies was, in all likelihood, responsible for the lining up of would-be investors. Although *Thene Manasulu*, co-produced by Adurthi Subba Rao and ANR (Rajadhyaksha and Willemen 1999: 386) was not commercially successful, a new generation of stars was created in the next few years.[19] Some years after the *Thene Manasulu* experiment and other low-budget films, NTR, now close to 50, found himself underemployed.

Venkat Rao attributes this downturn in the star's career to the rise to prominence of younger actors who were cheaper and proving successful at the box office. The journalist-biographer states, somewhat

[19] The film critic Bommakanti (1965) hailed *Thene Manasulu* as the film that "rid the eyes of rust" (*kalla tuppu vadilinchina*).

dramatically, that after 1972 the star was "spending many days without painting his face" (2003: 23). Still, there is no doubting that for a star who had done two shooting shifts on most working days for close to twenty years, this was a lean period.

About a decade after he overtook ANR, the middle-aged superstar was facing difficulty contending with other models of stardom, with their attendant aesthetics and economics. From the filmographies of Krishna, ANR, and NTR compiled by Rajadhyaksha and Willemen (1999: 128, 189, 193) we learn that whereas Krishna acted in 12 films in 1971 and 18 films in 1972, NTR had to his credit 9 and 3 films, while ANR did only slightly better with 9 and 6 films. It was only in the 1990s that major South Indian stars began limiting their annual turnover to less than 6 films per year (sometimes less than 1 film per year, as has been the case with Rajnikant and Chiranjeevi over the past decade). In the 1970s, however, such a drastic reduction in the number of films featuring a major star could only mean that that star was on the wane. Krishna was closely identified with genre experiments. Early in his career he co-starred with Sobhan Babu, the other young actor who would go on to become a major star in the 1970s, in the spy film *Goodachari 116* (*CID 116* in Tamil, M. Mallikarjuna Rao, 1966). In the early 1970s this star had to his credit such diverse hits as the big-budget western *Mosagallaku Mosagadu* directed by B. Vittalacharya (1971, Image 123). Vittalacharya was well known in the Madras film industry for his special effects and came to be closely associated with the folklore film as it became a low-budget genre—indeed he was given the honorific title Janapada Brahma, the god of folklore films. He went on to act in more spy films, such as for example *James Bond 777* (K.S.R. Doss, 1971).

However, Krishna was not a "genre film" specialist—indeed, none of the major Telugu film stars have been—and also starred in commercially successful family dramas like *Pandanti Kapuram* (Lakshmi Deepak, 1972). In spite of stunt and other genre films earlier on (such as *CID*, Tapi Chanakya, 1965), for the most part NTR continued to be identified with folklore and mythological films, both of which were gradually declining in terms of their relative importance to the industry. For his part ANR, hitherto associated with middle-class taste, began dancing during the song sequences, starting with the film *Dasara Bullodu* (V.B. Rajendra Prasad, 1971),

Image 123: A preview of Krishna's *idli* western, *Mosagallaku Mosagadu* in *Vijayachitra* (August 1971: 63). Source: Manasu Collection, M.V. Rayudu.

in order to cope with the changing times. NTR had begun dancing with *Kathanayakudu*, but it was not till the mid 1970s that dances became regular features in both stars' films.

The lean season would end in a few years, when NTR became more popular and commercially successful than ever before. His return centre-stage was accompanied by a transformation in his star persona as well as in the narrative focus of his films. Basing himself on box office collections, Venkat Rao suggests that *Aradhana* (B.V. Prasad, 1976) was the turning point. However, regardless of its success, *Aradhana*, being a classic romance, is precisely the kind of film that NTR would not do from this point onwards.[20] Instead, he would build on *Kathanayakudu* and fashion himself as a figure of authority

[20] The film is a remake of the Hindi film *Geet* (Ramanand Sagar, 1970). A striking feature in the film is the passivity of the NTR character, whose lack of agency is also manifest through his loss of speech in the later part of the film.

whose primary concern was mobilization. Given the overall trajectory of NTR's career, the noted film director Dasari Narayana Rao's claim that the star's fortunes were revived with *Manushulanta Okkate* (Dasari Narayana Rao, 1976) is perhaps more accurate. In Dasari's view, not only did NTR not apply make-up for nine months, he even just sat at home (*intipattuney koorchuni unnaru*). NTR himself had apparently declared during the 100-day celebrations of *Manushulanta Okkate* that financiers and distributors had become wary of investing in his films (Prasad 1996: 63).

Interestingly, the process of reinventing an ageing star included an episode with Amitabh Bachchan's career. NTR acted in Telugu remakes of Bachchan films, notably *Nippulanti Manishi* (S.D. Lal, 1974) and *Yugandhar* (K.S.R. Doss, 1979), based on *Zanjeer* (Prakash Mehra, 1973) and *Don* (Chandra Barot, 1978), respectively. Also, unlike the past, there was now an increasing consistency and coherence to the kind of screen presence that NTR would cultivate. The star's mythologicals too would be affected. The most striking example of the new NTR in the mythological is *Dana Veera Sura Karna*, a film produced and directed in 1977 by the star himself.[21] The new NTR was in evidence as early as *Raitu Bidda* (B.A. Subba Rao, 1971, not to be confused with Ramabrahmam's film) but not fully in place till *Adavi Ramudu* (K. Raghavendra Rao, 1977) and *Yama Gola* (T. Rama Rao, 1977). While *Kathanayakudu* introduced the star as always and already endowed with the authority to represent—speak for—the populace and sort out society's problems, the focus of NTR's 1970s films lay in the distinction of the characters he played: feudal origins became the social basis for the character's authority within the fiction, to the extent that it might be said NTR ended up making a major contribution to the feudalization of Telugu cinema. The discursive production of feudal patriarchs on screen was carried over to the careers of Krishnam Raju, Chiranjeevi, Balakrishna, and Mohan Babu, from the 1980s to the present. In other words, Telugu cinema's "offer of leadership emanating from the screen" (Prasad 1999: 49) was fused with the cinematic production of a feudal authority.

In the post-Independence period the Telugu cinema rendered invisible the history of zamindari oppression. This aspect of colonial

[21] Discussed in the next chapter.

feudalism became more or less unavailable for the discursive production of rural life on film. While some films which challenge my claim may have escaped my attention, it is possible to make the generalization that Telugu cinema of the 1950s had little use for the zamindar except as an incidental figure of wealth or prestige or as the epitome of decadence. The zamindari order and its decadence were represented on occasion—in *Devadasu* (Vedantam Raghavaiah, 1953) the first Telugu version of *Devdas*, for example—but depictions of rural life more or less consistently avoided references to oppressive zamindars. As we have seen, the celebrated 1950s films on rural life, *Shavukaru* and *Palletooru*, feature oppressors who were peasants albeit much richer than the rest of the village. Whether it is the moneylender in *Shavukaru* or the landlord in *Palletooru*, the oppressor belongs to the same caste-kinship network as the oppressed. In both films the absence of the pillars of the colonial order, the zamindar and the Komati moneylender, respectively, (who figure prominently in Ramabrahmam's *Raitu Bidda*) is striking. In *Rojulu Marayi* the landlord, who is the source of oppression, is not named as a zamindar. This evacuation of the zamindar from cinema meant that rural life appeared to be effectively detached from feudal oppression. Consequently, the on-screen production of Teluguness too was disengaged from feudal figures—there was no investment in the zamindar as a figure of nostalgia in the 1950s either. In films, the Telugu rural universe was organized around the heroic and the villainous, rich and poor peasants.

It would be disingenuous to treat these films as evidence of post-Independence ideological regression or an upper-caste conspiracy to suppress evidence of zamindari oppression. Both *Shavukaru* and *Palletooru* were critically acclaimed by contemporary commentators and made by companies run by peasant entrepreneurs who had little use for zamindari investments. Arguably, feudal nostalgia was not a real possibility for the Telugu cinema of the period because "progressive" or reformist agendas were immanent to the social as a genre and were its raison d'être. So strong was the social's identification with reform that leftist film commentators assumed folklore films and mythological films were repositories of "feudal values."[22]

[22] Reiterating the accusation often made by leftist commentators, Krishnabai and Prasad (2000: vi) argue in their preface to KoKu's film writings that

The banning of *Raitu Bidda* in Nellore and Vizagapatam (now Visakhapatnam) districts in 1940 was an important reason why this sensitive political subject was avoided in the pre-Independence period.[23] The situation did not really change after Independence, in spite of the passage of the Abolition of Estates Act. The violent suppression of the Telangana uprising, and the crackdown in the coastal districts on communist sympathizers in the early 1950s, could well have worked as a disincentive for probing the more explicitly political aspects of peasant life, especially feudal oppression, because it figured prominently in communist articulations and agitations. Moreover, in the popular imagination feudalism was closely identified with the Telangana region. Accounts of the Telangana movement by communists like P. Sundarayya (1973a, 1973b, 1973c, 1973d), as also novels by supporters of the movement, notably Dasarathi Rangacharya (*Chillara Devullu*), foregrounded the feudal question in Telangana.[24]

The Return of the Zamindar

The NTR starrer *Raitu Bidda* reintroduced the zamindar to the Telugu cinema. The film returns to peasant–zamindar relations, the central concern of its distinguished namesake, exactly one generation later. The zamindar is now dead and is survived by his second wife and two sons, born of different wives. Rambabu (NTR), the older of the two, is not quite a farmer himself but is generous and pro-poor. Early in the film he is seen writing off the debts of peasants who

---

the Raja of Mirzapuram decided to arrest the growth of socials and made folklore films and mythologicals to protect feudal values (*feudal viluvalini samrakshinchadaniki*).

[23] The Madras government refused to revoke the ban despite the efforts of H.M. Reddy who was a member of the Madras Board of Film Censors (Home G.O. no. 3914, 24 September 1940).

[24] Interestingly, historical accounts of Telangana under the Nizam have cited novels such as *Chillara Devullu* as evidence of feudal oppression in the region. See, for example, I. Thirumali (1992: 482 n.30), who refers to official government records, non-fiction accounts, and novels in the same footnote.

have had a bad year and offering them financial help. He is a loyal son to his stepmother and loves his stepbrother Prasad (Jaggaiah). The villain, another zamindar-cum-village moneylender Bhushaiah (Satyanarayana), is a sworn enemy of this family. Their running feud intensifies when Rambabu prevents Bhushaiah from exploiting certain simple peasants. Rambabu falls in love with Shanta (Vanisri), a village volunteer (*grama sevika*) who is the educated daughter of a poor farmer. Under her influence he decides to establish a cooperative farm by pooling his family's land with that of all the peasants in the village. The turning point comes in the form of a proposal of marriage between Bhushaiah's daughter and Prasad. Bhushaiah agrees to the marriage grudgingly, but then learns to his horror that the dead zamindar bequeathed his entire estate to Rambabu because he didn't want the property partitioned; worse, Prasad's biological mother had been a willing party to this decision. The villain schemes to create a rift between the brothers but his plot fails when Rambabu transfers the property to his brother rather than partition it. When further objections are raised about the possibility of future litigation by his unborn children in the distant future, Rambabu, like Bhishma in the *Mahabharata*, vows to remain a bachelor, although his marriage with Shanta has been agreed upon. By now the cooperative farm has all but been established. The peasants invite Rambabu to lead the cooperative enterprise while the government, represented by an honest young Block Development Officer (Sridhar), offers loans and fertilizers. Bhushaiah meanwhile transfers the property of his son-in-law, Prasad, to himself when the latter is drunk.

A point is soon reached when everyone, including his stepmother whom he holds in high esteem, doubts Rambabu's intentions and accuses him, among other things, of stealing money from the cooperative. Rambabu then leaves the village and is found wandering the streets by Pullaiah (Rajanala), who is married to Shanta's older sister but has been disowned by her: he too has been a victim of Bhushaiah's schemes and is now a pickpocket and petty crook. He nominates Rambabu to become the leader of his gang. Prasad learns of the true intentions of his father-in-law but is a helpless witness to the villain's attempt to auction the family property. Rambabu and Pullaiah, with some help from an employee (Rajababu) of Bhushaiah's ally Seshaiah (Allu Ramalingaiah), recover the family property and also prevent the villain from forcing Shanta to marry him. The film ends with all the major characters becoming a part of the village's cooperative.

The *Raitu Bidda* of 1971 is usefully situated in the immediate political context. Ramachandra Guha points out that the general election was advanced by over a year to 1971 because Indira Gandhi sought a fresh mandate after the supreme court struck down a presidential order derecognizing princes, an order passed in the wake of the failure of the government to pass a bill in the Rajya Sabha abolishing princely privileges (Guha 2007: 440–1). Events leading to the election, Guha argues, are among the signs that around this time the Congress led by Indira Gandhi was characterized by a left-leaning populism. For state politics too, 1971 was an important year. The Telangana Praja Samithi (TPS) led by M. Chenna Reddy, a former Congress minister and future chief minister who played a key role in initiating the migration of the film industry from Madras to Hyderabad, won 10 of the 14 seats it contested in the parliamentary election. The TPS, which became the most recognizable face of the agitation for a separate Telangana, had gone ill prepared into the electoral contest. After his victory Chenna Reddy reached an agreement with Indira Gandhi and returned to the Congress fold, resulting in the replacement of Brahmananda Reddy with P.V. Narasimha Rao (who was from the Telangana region) as chief minister (Innaiah 1986: 120–2). Soon after this the Jai Andhra agitation, demanding the formation of a separate Andhra state, broke out.

The Telugu cinema of the period remained resolutely silent about regional conflict and instead went about assembling a screen authority by unfreezing the feudal lord. *Raitu Bidda* makes multiple references to Congress policies and leaders—verbally, visually, and thematically. The film's overtly political anti-zamindari and pro-peasant messages and slogans faithfully echo Indira Gandhi's socialism, even as they gesture towards Soviet-style collectivization. The film also actively invokes Indira Gandhi with as much reverence as Gudavalli Ramabrahmam had once invoked Mahatma Gandhi. For example, when the Block Development Officer is approached by the villains, who offer a bribe to stop government support to the cooperative, he strongly rebukes them and the scene ends with his asking them to vamoose. At one point in this meeting the officer, framed against the backdrop of a portrait of Indira Gandhi, tells his visitors that he was appointed on the basis of a selection process and not the recommendation of some (corrupt) minister. The framing of the officer against the backdrop of the portrait is repeated when he refuses to be cowed by further villainous threats. His resolution is the voice of the developmental state backed by the authority of Mrs Gandhi. Some years later NTR himself would play the revolutionary bureaucrat.

Also interesting are scenes shot against the backdrop of a Gandhi statue in the village square where much action, including a panchayat hearing of the property dispute raked up by Bhushaiah, takes place. When Rambabu declares he will give away his property and stay unwed, the camera placement has NTR virtually backed up by the Gandhi statue in the background. Rambabu's association with the statue takes on an overtly political hue when he is, once again, seen in front of the same statue subsequent to the property dispute. This time he delivers a speech against zamindars, calling them idle exploiters and asking the peasants to rise up against oppression. On both occasions NTR (and he alone) is filmed soft focus, underscoring his iconicity.

The mobilization of peasants in support of the state's agenda is an important concern of the film (Images 124 and 125). Rambabu, and to an extent Shanta, are agents of mobilization, which is introduced as a key concern early in the film during the song "*Devudu srushtinchadu lokalu, manishey srushtinchadu bheydalu*" (God created the universe and man differences). Pictured against agricultural activities—like tilling the land—the song has Rambabu singing to the camera in an address to the spectator as much as to the peasant on the screen. Throughout the film the peasants reaffirm their faith in his leadership and repeatedly raise the slogan "*Rambabugariki jai*," recalling the act of nomination of Ramudu as protagonist in *Patala Bhairavi*.

The mobilizer's *distinction* is never in doubt—from the very opening shots of the film which show an as-yet-unnamed NTR character on horse cart in a sequence which, recalling *Kathayakudu*'s opening, presents the star first and only then has him enter the story. We soon learn the story-level manifestation of his distinction—he is the zamindar's sole heir. Having qualified him thus, the film goes on

124

125

Images 124–5: Advertisements for *Raitu Bidda* in *Vijayachitra* (April 1971: 4, and May 1971: 51, respectively). Large groups of farmers can be seen tilling land in both images. Source: Manasu Collection, M.V. Rayudu.

to show how good a leader he is of the peasants (and of course how good a son he is of his father).

Cinematic Populism Revisited

Cinema would be unworthy of critical attention if it was merely about how political ideologies, fully formed elsewhere, acquire a screen existence and a star advocate. Populism is a constant presence in Telugu socials from the early 1970s and some of its elements can be traced to *Patala Bhairavi*. I suggest that populism in the Telugu cinema can be located at two distinct levels. First, it is at the level of the diegesis: stories about common people, the presence of crowds, the hero's attempts at mobilizing the masses and in the process relegating them to the position of a diegetic audience, are the obvious signs of this level of the elaboration of populism. The second is at the level of spectatorial positioning. By deploying a variety of cinematic techniques, films constantly remind the spectator that the fictional world exists for his or her benefit and unfolds along anticipated lines. The positioning of the spectator and the organization of pleasurable expectations reinforce the thematic concerns of films to produce a set of linkages between populism and the cinema that is specifically, even uniquely, cinematic. I have proposed the notion of *cinematic populism* to understand the specificity of cinema's engagement with politics and argued that Telugu cinema is foundationally populist. This is because its populism is not merely a reflection of developments elsewhere, but is manifest in the fusion between thematic concerns and spectatorial positioning (Srinivas 2009: 73–128). Considering that people pay to watch films because they derive pleasure from them, and not because they are eager to be instructed or told whom they should be voting for, the question before us is not how political agendas were worked into the NTR film but what spectatorial pleasures came to be associated with the elaboration of politics, and how.

Both *Kathanayakudu* and (NTR's) *Raitu Bidda* are early instances, if not the earliest, of a cinematic populism that continues to animate Telugu cinema (cf. Chiranjeevi's 1990s films, discussed in ibid.). In these NTR films the two levels of populism are elaborated *separately* and sequentially, which makes them particularly useful as objects of analysis. In *Kathanayakudu* Sarathy loses the battle against the villains twice over: as clerk and elected representative. After he loses the second round, the film makes an interesting transition, anticipated by the two comic characters, namely Puliraju (Rajababu), fair price shop-owner Appaladora's son-in-law, and his neighbour Simham (Padmanabham) who is a colleague of Sarathy's and who resigns in protest when his friend is dismissed. Both are married into well-to-do families and live in their in-laws' houses (the practice is known as *illarikam*; *ghar jamai* in Hindi) and is often the butt of jokes in popular culture. At one point in the film Puliraju is heard singing a song from the film titled *Illarikam* (T. Prakash Rao, 1959). These young men, who are ironically named after the ferocious tiger (*Puli*raju) and lion (Nara*simham*), spend their days doing "women's work" at home. The turning point comes when they decide to play an elaborate hoax to normalize gender relations. In a hilarious sequence, Puliraju turns up in drag, disguised as Simham's rich grandmother, and fools the parents-in-law into transferring all their property to the "grandson." Both young men then thrash their respective wives and in-laws as part of their education in patriarchy. This incident occurs just before Sarathy is beaten up and thrown unconscious on the street, its significance becoming clear a little later. Immediately after Sarathy decides to counter deceit with deceit, there is a cut to an auction in which Sarathy, transformed into a pipe-smoking and bearded man and introduced by his "driver" (Simham in disguise) as a Singapore-based businessman, outbids Satyamurthy. Simham later tells the villains that his boss is on the lookout for local agents to expand his smuggling operations. Of course they believe him.

In the latter half of the film, when characters begin to masquerade as grandmothers, gold smugglers, and the like, there is a transition to a different register of plausibility. The disguises fool the in-laws and villains but not the spectator, who knows all along that they are only play-acting. Further, the narrative no longer hinges on references to political corruption and mobilization against it. A similar shift of registers, as also narrative focus, is witnessed in (NTR's) *Raitu Bidda*, where again political mobilization hits a dead end.

In *Raitu Bidda* the happy circumstances of aristocratic revolutionary working with the backing of benevolent state comes to an abrupt end when Rambabu is accused of stealing from the cooperative. The state, the mobilized peasant, and his mother alike disown our hero. The desirable and the state-authorized resolution of conflict through cooperative farming is no longer a possibility. Rambabu has to rescue the cooperative—and solve the multiple crises of the film—without the aid of family, peasants, or state. That he does so with the help of a pickpocket is interesting and the manner in which he achieves his objective fascinating. Rambabu and the rest of the gang assembled by Pullaiah trick the villain by disguising themselves on four different occasions, all in quick succession, to undo the damage caused by Bhushaiah's schemes. On the first two occasions Rambabu and gang are disguised as folk performers who fool the villain into believing that they have come to entertain him and his guests on the occasion of his marriage. In the second of their performances they run away with his bride. They then return, this time with Rambabu playing a Tamil merchant who wishes to buy Prasad's property. While the "merchant" engages Bhushaiah in conversation, Pullaiah empties the latter's safe. The next day, dressed as an old zamindar of colonial vintage, Rambabu buys the property with Bhushaiah's money.

Why is the first register of plausibility, relatively more realist and replete with topical references or actual political leaders, abandoned for the more overtly performative one? What do we make of the disguises? Evidently, spectatorial trust placed in the star early in the film is rewarded by the series of see-through disguises and performances that are presented as such—as attempts to please the spectator. In *Kathanayakudu*, for instance, the only colour reel in the otherwise black-and-white film features is the song "*Intenaya, telusukovaya*" which has NTR performing directly to the camera. Sung presumably to entertain the villains, the song also features Jayalalithaa in the get-up of a screen vamp (what with her blond wig), but she is only a little more prominent than the dozen or so extras.

The technique of having the star don disguises was not invented in NTR films. In her discussion of Rudolph Valentino, Hansen notes that his films often featured him "in a series of disguises and anonymous identities." The point is that "The spectator-fan recognizes her star in all his masks and disguises—unlike the female protagonist whose trial of love consists of 'knowing' him regardless of narrative misfortune or social status." She goes on to make the interesting point that "The emphasis on costumes and disguises . . . implicitly acknowledges the spectator as part of the scenario" (1991: 282).

The turn to overtly political themes and concerns in NTR's films was one in which a particular kind of stardom and spectatorship was instituted. As the star became the focus of the spectatorial expectations of the cinema and its pleasures, films began to acknowledge the presence of the spectator for whose benefit the star performed. Take the instance of *Raitu Bidda*, among the most overtly political films NTR ever made. Its political messages are inadequate to account for the kind of star being constructed. The mobilizer of the masses becomes a *veshadhari*—one who is in guise—within the fiction, to directly address the spectator with his role-playing. Spectatorial recognition (of his stardom; the character's ability) is the foundational premise for these films' manoeuvre towards a political-performative idiom. Not surprisingly, from the 1970s NTR films have the star indulging in a variety of vulgar or melodramatic excesses with the feeblest of story-level justification. The star will literally do anything to please the spectator invested in the fiction.

The Mobilized Peasant: Feudalism and Revolution in a "Naxalite" Film

The recovery of the zamindar in popular Telugu cinema is coeval with the Naxalite movement's critique of feudalism. Telugu cinema's uptake on the feudal question in the 1970s is influenced by the landmark film *Bhoomikosam* (K. Balagangadhar Tilak, 1974), which deals with a number of issues raised by the Naxalite movement in the state.[25] The manner in which this film—known as the first "Naxalite film" in Telugu (Murari n.d.: 118)—contributes to NTR's career cautions us against making easy equations between intention and consequence in cinema.

Bhoomikosam's director was an established figure in the film industry. His *MLA* (1957), now unavailable, was a critically acclaimed

[25] I am grateful to M.V. Rayudu for making the VCD version of the film available to me. There has been no official release of the film's VCD/DVD versions.

critique of post-Independence politics. Tilak, like many Presidency Telugus born in the first half of the twentieth century, was named after the nationalist leader. He went on to take an active interest in politics and was arrested in 1942 for destroying railway tracks and other such disruptive activities. After his release he worked with communist cultural activists in Bombay before reaching Madras with his uncle, L.V. Prasad, in 1946. There he assisted Prasad and trained as an editor. He became director with the Navayuga production *Jyothi* (1954) when the film's original director walked out over differences with the producers (Murari n.d.: 116–17). *Bhoomikosam* is dedicated to Tilak's younger brother, K. Ramanarasimha Rao, and other "martyrs" of the Naxalite movement. The poet Sri Sri (Srirangam Srinivasa Rao), founding member of VIRASAM (Viplava Rachayitala Sangham, Revolutionary Writers' Association), wrote two of the songs and was co-story as well as co-screenplay writer of the film. The poet says he gave the film its title (Sri Sri 2010: 265). Murari (n.d.: 118) says the Naxalite leader Satyamurthy wrote the lyrics of one of the songs of the film ("*Chinnari chilakamma chellalu Chandramma*"). Satyamurthy went on to become a key leader of the CPI (ML-People's War) in the early 1980s.

The film features the Bombay star Ashok Kumar in a guest role and marks actress-turned-politician Jayaprada's screen debut. The historical significance of the film lies not merely in its references to the Naxalite movement but also the complex connections it makes between the presence of feudal authorities in the countryside and the need for mass mobilization.

Its undisguised Naxalite sympathies are evident from its dedication. During the credit sequence the spectator is offered a lesson in the history of anti-landlord struggles in the state, including the Telangana movement (Images 126–8). The film proper opens with a procession of workers belonging to the Raitu Sangham (farmers' association) holding the national tricolour and red flags (Image 129). They are led by Rajasekharam (Jaggaiah), the son of the zamindar Bhupathi Rao (Ashok Kumar). When the peasants reach the zamindar's house, an altercation between father and son results in the latter walking out of the house. He returns with his daughter Susheela (Prabha) from Calcutta twenty-five years later, long after his father's death, to

Images 126–8: The opening of *Bhoomikosam*: the dedication to martyrs (126), the title card (127) and images of colonial brutality (128).

126

127

128

Images 129–31: Masses on the move at different points in the film. Procession of peasants and workers in the beginning (129), Rajasekharam addressing the villagers just before his arrest (130), and the end with the card reading "not the end but the beginning" (131).

129

130

131

find that his sister Rajeswari (Jamuna) has remained single, taking care of the old zamindar. His arrival in the village coincides with the rebellious peasant Suryam (Chalam) breaking into the other local zamindar Bhupala Rao's (Tyagaraju) yard to release a cow stolen by the latter's men. We learn later that there is a history of enmity between two zamindar families. An injured Suryam is sheltered by Rajeswari's servant and treated by Susheela, a doctor. Soon, Suryam returns with Jagannatham, the "mad teacher" dismissed from service by Bhupala Rao for siding with the poor. Jagannatham narrates Suryam's story: he and his father were initially deprived of their fertile land and given a barren tract by the zamindar. When their hard work made the land fertile they were again deprived of it. Rajeswari is moved by his story and offers him some of her land, but Suryam says he only wants what was his, not charity. Susheela and Suryam fall in love, even as agricultural labourers (among the most important constituencies of the Naxalites in Andhra Pradesh), led by Rajasekharam and Jagannatham, agitate for better wages. The zamindar forms an alliance with a moneylender (who rapes schoolgirls), a rich "model" farmer (who exploits child labourers), and the local organizers of liquor and gambling dens. Susheela and Suryam marry with wholehearted support from Rajasekharam and Rajeswari. There is a direct reference to the Telangana armed struggle during which, as Sundarayya (1973b: 21) points out, landlords were socially boycotted and all manner of labour and services were denied them by the rural poor—including domestic help, barbers, washermen, etc. The film's reference to this has Rajasekharam calling for a social boycott of the villains when they begin to harass the peasants. Bhupathi Rao's driver Govindu (Prabhakar Reddy) tries to break the strike but is thrashed by Suryam and sent back. Suryam and Rajasekharam are falsely accused of Govindu's murder and arrested. Suryam escapes from prison and discovers that Govindu is not dead but hiding. A homesick Govindu tries to return to his wife and is prevented from doing so. He turns against the zamindar. He is rescued by Suryam and joins the rebellion against the zamindar. Bhupathi Rao's men steal the sharecroppers' harvest and the villagers, now supported by the better-off farmers too, retaliate by stealing the zamindar's paddy. The village is attacked and the huts of the poor burnt. Suryam acquires a gun and goes underground.

Rajasekharam is arrested when he calls for yet another social boycott (Image 130). The villagers who gather to protest the arrest are beaten by the police. One of the villains leaves the village along with the police escorting Rajasekharam. Rajeswari now joins the struggle and tends to the injured. She loses her property when the moneylender she had taken loans from attaches her house. Suryam and Govindu are now seen in khaki, wielding guns, suggesting that they have joined the Naxalites. Their armed squad captures the moneylender and destroys all his records. The women he raped in the past set him on fire. Soon after, all the lesser villains are captured and punished. The zamindar's men launch an attack on the armed squad. In the ensuing battle Suryam kills Bhupathi Rao and dies. Susheela gives birth to a boy, symbolizing the regeneration of the revolution despite the destruction. In a mammoth meeting of the poor, Rajasekharam calls for a continuation of the struggle and the destruction of landlordism. The film ends with shots of a procession of people superimposed by a card reading "*Antamkadidi Arambham*" (this is not the end but the beginning, Image 131).

The film is mostly shot outdoors on location and has some stunningly beautiful scenes of the countryside. Much attention is paid to nativity, with a detailed depiction of the village and its practices, including agricultural. Folk tunes are used to authenticate the political message of songs and represent the erotic. Suryam and Susheela consummate their marriage on a platform erected in the middle of fields while a song embedded in a folk tune ("*Kondagali veechindi*") is heard in the background. Chandramma's story (Images 132–4) has some striking nativity scenes and, more importantly, presents the feudal lord's actions as disrupting the otherwise idyllic life in the countryside.

Liberally sprinkled with Naxalite slogans and speeches on exploitation, the film depicts a peasantry which is, from the very outset, defiant and rebellious (Image 135). In a picture-perfect rendering of class struggle, the entire village rallies together even as the oppressor's mistress elopes with the lower-caste sub-inspector of the local police station. The action is framed by scenes of mobilized masses, seen in procession at the beginning and end.

Bhoomikosam (meaning for land's sake) is a paradigm-setting film. The twenty-five-year period of Rajasekharam's exile roughly

Images 132–4: Chandramma's story in *Bhoomikosam*. The performers (132), a picture-perfect nativity image of Chandramma (133), and Kasi Reddy the obscene feudal lord (134).The film is remarkable for the manner in which the revolutionary undergoes a generational change, from the aristocratic rebel to the poor peasant.

132

133

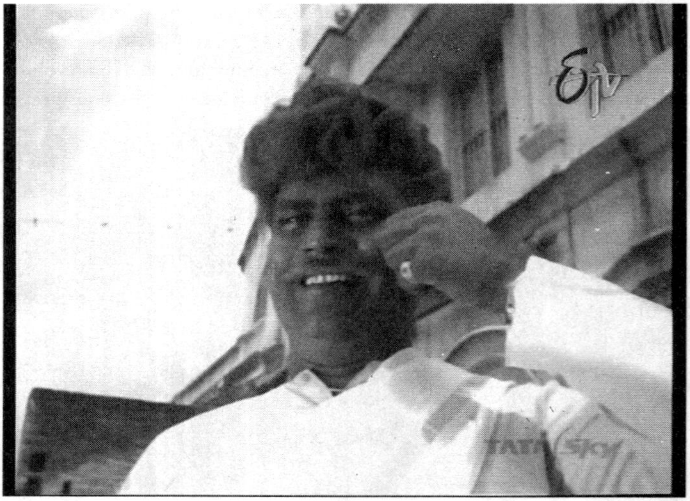

134

Image 135: Naxalites on the screen. Jamuna (left), Chalam (centre), and Prabha (right) in a photo feature on the film in *Vijayachitra* (April 1974, p. 52). Source: Manasu Collection, M.V. Rayudu.

corresponds with the elapsed time between the Independence struggle and the beginning of the Naxalite movement in the late 1960s. Arguably, this is the first post-Independence Telugu film to reopen the question of feudal oppression and exploitative colonial elites that survive into the present and thrive under the protection of the state. Feudal oppressors and the justness of the struggle against them would figure repeatedly in popular Telugu cinema in the years to come. In retrospect, the absence of the male star-protagonist leading the masses in *Bhoomikosam* is glaring because, over the next few years, films about feudal oppression and the mobilization against it became increasingly centred on the male star.

Legitimizing the Mobilizer's Authority: Two Emergency Films

Telugu cinema's gesture towards the left-leaning populism of Indira Gandhi was accompanied—even facilitated—by substantial changes in the deployment of the male star. At the story level the hero, engaged in acts of mobilization, is discovered or revealed with a feudal lineage. The connection between the star and the recovery of the feudal past is not limited to the story. There is a further equivalence: *stardom is to the role what a feudal lineage is to the character*. Both sources of distinction have to do with qualities or attributes that are passed on or inherited, literally and metaphorically, from earlier films of the star, and from another generation within the fiction. Inaugurating the last and most successful phase of NTR's acting career, when his films frequently returned to the how and why of the transition from feudal to post-feudal authority, is *Manushulanta Okkate*, whose director, as we have seen, claimed NTR's career revived with this film. From this point on a steady trickle of NTR vehicles revolve around the problems and possibilities of the feudal legacy. *Manushulanta Okkate* and other NTR films made during and immediately after the Emergency allude to the immediate political context; worth examining alongside is *Bangaru Manishi* (A. Bhimsingh, 1976), which also exemplifies this tendency. My purpose in drawing attention to these films is not to elaborate on representations of the Emergency, or whether there was support or opposition to it, but to show how Indira Gandhi's populism became a point of reference—a resource—for the construction of mobilizer of the masses in NTR films.

These films also make an interesting political manoeuvre—Communist and Naxalite political agendas and slogans are integrated into conventional narratives that are politically conservative. *Manushulanta Okkate* makes perfect sense as a remake of *Bhoomikosam*: retaining the setting of the earlier film and some of its concerns, it transforms its model into an ideal star vehicle, making the NTR character the leader of a revolutionary struggle against feudal oppression. *Manushulanta Okkate* is explicit in its criticism of the feudal order, which is presented as a legacy of the colonial past. Simultaneously, the hero's lineage—he is a direct descendant of the very feudal authority he takes on—distinguishes him from those he leads into rebellion.

The movie begins with a shot of the Union Jack while a voiceover narrator "introduces" the problem of zamindari oppression. We then see an enormous palace as the narrator continues the story of colonial history. The title of this quintessentially Emergency film translates as "all humans are equal." Apart from its saturation in populist slogans associated with this period, the film makes explicit reference to Indira Gandhi on two occasions. The story highlights the prevalence of the zamindari order after Independence and calls for its destruction. How this is done and who does so are of interest.

Rajendra (NTR), the son of the zamindar Sarvarayudu (Satyanarayana), is introduced while on a hunt. He rides a horse cart—an intertextual reference to the NTR character in *Raitu Bidda*. But Rajendra is a decadent and arrogant man whose motto is aptly summarized by the lyrics of the song he sings upon introduction: *anubhavinchu* (enjoy) *raja*, for we know not why we are born. There is a detailed if exaggerated elaboration of zamindari expropriation and violence on the peasantry which owes much to New Indian Cinema's concerns about feudalism. The zamindar himself is implicated but it is his assistant Chalamaiah (Allu Ramalingaiah) who is the main culprit. Rajendra is attracted to Radha (Jamuna), the daughter of a lower-caste man and a maidservant in the zamindar's palace. He falls in love for her after she refuses to give in to his aggressive sexual advances. When her father is killed by the zamindar's men, Rajendra visits the slum and is moved by the plight of the poor. She however believes Rajendra is responsible for the murder. Learning of the murder, Rajendra confronts his father and condemns his action. Their argument recalls the conflict between father and son in *Bhoomikosam*. Rajendra leaves home and begins living in the slum. When Sarvarayudu goes to London to receive an award from the British government, Rajendra marries Radha. Upon his return the zamindar is furious with his son's marriage to a woman from a "race of slaves." He concludes that this is an insult to his dynasty (*vamsam*) and orders his men to kill Radha. The pregnant Radha is rescued by Rajendra and is sent away unconscious on a boat, but he himself is killed by the attackers. The action then moves to the post-Independence period. Rajendra's son Ramu (also NTR) is a tourist guide. He is unaware of his family's past and falls in love with Shanti (Manjula), Sarvarayudu's niece. When Radha discovers that Shanti is related to Sarvarayudu, she objects to their marriage. Ramu learns about the zamindar from his mother and sets out to avenge his father's death. He meets his grandfather and informs him of his decision to seek revenge. He soon takes on the zamindar's thugs and also aids Dalits denied entry into the temple by Chalamaiah. Injured in a fight with the zamindar's men, he is discovered by the villagers who immediately *recognize* him as their leader's son. Ramu now takes up his father's mission of organizing the poor. Soon, Radha too returns to the village. She is fielded as a candidate in the election against the zamindar. However, she withdraws when Chalamaiah threatens to kill Ramu. Fearing for his safety, she forbids Ramu from supporting the villagers. When the zamindar's men beat up the villagers, Ramu pleads with his mother to release him from his vow. She relents and Ramu resumes his leadership. Following many rounds of confrontation, Ramu leads an attack on the palace. Chased by a mob of villagers, the zamindar runs for his life—like Vishwam (Naseeruddin Shah) and Susheela (Shabana Azmi) in Shyam Benegal's *Nishant* (1975)—and is about to be lynched when Radha intervenes to save his life. The contrite zamindar asks that he be punished. Shots of Gandhi and Indira Gandhi are accompanied by a voiceover commentary by the film's director asking for revolutionary changes among the people, bringing the film to a close.

The film's depiction of the transition to Independence from British rule is noteworthy. The influence of *Bhoomikosam* is discernible from its depiction of the persistence of the zamindari order into present time. In yet another borrowing from the earlier anti-feudal film, the sequence in which Rajendra defends Radha from his father's servants is intercut with scenes of a *burra katha* on the Abhimanyu story from the *Mahabharata*. *Burra katha* is a folk form, but also one with a considerable history of association with anti-colonial and communist insurgencies in the state. In *Bhoomikosam* a folk performance based on the life of a local legend, Chandramma, who killed the feudal lord responsible for her lover's death, becomes the means by which Susheela (Prabha) inspires villagers whose huts have been destroyed by the zamindar's men. She calls on them to rise like Chandramma. As pointed out, the lyrics of the song were written by the Naxalite leader Satyamurthy. Shots of the performance—watched by hundreds of villagers—are intercut with a reconstruction of Chandramma's life. The reconstruction is a story within the story, complete with a whole set of characters who do not appear in the rest of the film. In spite of obvious differences, both films invoke legend in order to comment on present injustice.

The *burra katha* in *Manushulanta Okkate* is written by the reputed poet and film lyricist C. Narayana Reddy; the performance is credited to "Burra Katha Samrat" P. Banerjee, based in Hyderabad (the film was made in Madras), suggesting that considerable effort had been made to authenticate the *burra katha* by involving a professional artiste from outside the industry.[26] In this film the parallels between the epic and the action are so close that the *burra katha* lyrics accurately describe to the last detail the action unfolding in the present. Like Abhimanyu, Rajendra is injured by a blow struck from behind; he picks up a cart wheel and fights to the death. The *burra katha* however continues on

[26] Dasari Narayana Rao would go on to use *burra katha* and other folk theatrical performances intermittently in his films to make comparisons between protagonists and historical or epic characters. In the next chapter I discuss the *burra katha* performance in *Sardar Paparayudu*, another NTR film directed by Dasari. By far the most memorable invocation of folk theatre in Dasari's work is to be found in *Osey Ramulamma* (1997), where the heroine kills the feudal lord's son (her half-brother) when he attempts to have sex with her. During this sequence scenes of a folk threatrical performance are intercut with scenes of the feudal lord's house as the song from the stage performance is heard in the background.

the soundtrack, making a comparison between the Kurukshetra war in the epic and the Independence struggle. We are told, as we catch a glimpse of Radha's infant son, that heroes like Abhimanyu are reborn in our time. Archival footage of anti-British protests is followed by images of nationalist and post-Independence leaders, making for a neat transition to the present. After the rollcall of great leaders—including Gandhi, Bose, Nehru, and Lal Bahadur Shastri—the song ends with a shot of Indira Gandhi. As the camera zooms in on Mrs Gandhi making a speech, the lyrics hail her as the new force which wishes to build an egalitarian society (*samasamaja nirmanamkore naveenasakti*). The very next shot is of a close-up photograph of NTR (the dead Rajendra). The camera zooms out and we find ourselves in the present.

The praise lavished on Indira Gandhi, and the comparison between her and the NTR character, indicate the nature of cinematic populism attempted by the film. To begin with, the equivalence between the prime minister and NTR frames the propagandist content of the film: its socialist slogans, even Communist and Naxalite ones, such as, for example, *dunnevadidey bhoomi* ("land to the tiller"), songs, and speeches. Like the NTR *Raitu Bidda*, this film embeds the authority figure created by *Kathanayakudu* in a socio-political context where the feudal order is to be replaced by a modern one. The key question is who or what will replace the malevolent feudal lord. In *Bhoomikosam* it is the revolutionary movement, personified as the newborn son of Suryam and Susheela. In *Manushulanta Okkate* it is the man of distinction approved by the masses. This role will be played by an actor whose star status the film will ensure the spectator is aware of. The latter half of the film presents Ramu's vigilante interventions against the zamindar's men in a tableaux format reminiscent of the sequence introducing the hero in *Kathanayakudu*. Extending the invitation of *Kathanayakudu* to spectatorial investment in the star-protagonist, the film has a song whose lyrics are a stringing of the titles of NTR's films.[27] In yet another obvious reference to the "real" NTR, Shanti,

[27] Paidipaala draws our attention to this remarkable song (1992: 76). The lyrics include various titles which used Ramudu, the good old diminutive of Rama Rao that can be traced to *Patala Bhairavi*. Drawing on a well-established practice in NTR films referring to the star's real name in the fiction, one of the NTR characters in this film too is called Ramu.

Ramu's girlfriend, is seen dancing on stage to collect money for a flood relief fund, recalling the star's charitable activities.

In genre terms, the assembly of NTR's star persona in the early 1970s involved his socials borrowing elements from the folklore film. The most striking of these is the practice of marking the pro-poor hero's distinction by providing him with a royal or feudal lineage. In the 1970s such "genre mixing" coincided with the decline of the folklore film: fewer such films were being produced, and with relatively small stars (Kanta Rao and Ramakrishna, for example). A song in *Manushulanta Okkate* alerts us to the decline, degeneration even, of the folklore film: "*Mutyalu, vastava, adigindi istava?*" (the opening line roughly translates as, Mutyalu, will you come and give me what I want?), set to the tune of the Hindi hit "*Roop tera, mastana . . .*" (from *Aradhana*, Shakti Samanta, 1969). Picturized on Chalamaiah/Allu Ramalingaiah and Mutyalu/Rama Prabha, one of the segments has Allu Ramalingaiah, well known for his roles as the comic sidekick of the villain, in the get-up of the genre's hero. As the folklore film's aristocratic rebel is incorporated into this film in a reinforcement of the *Raitu Bidda* model of heroism, the genre itself becomes a source of parody. It is as if there is virtually nothing left of the genre once its star-protagonist migrates to the social.

Simultaneous with the increased investment in the feudal, we notice that in the later 1970s mass mobilization is a key function of the star-protagonist, as can be seen in *Bangaru Manishi* (Image 136). Here, criticism of the establishment begins with the opening song: "*Ekkadikelutondi desam, emaipotondi?*" (Where is the country going, what has become of it?). Although the song ends in disavowal by attributing the problems foregrounded to British rule, there really is little doubt about the contemporary relevance of the criticism. Having established that the country has nowhere left to go, the film introduces Venu (NTR) as the agent of reform. Like the revolutionary bureaucrat who is the protagonist of Shyam Benegal's *Manthan* (1976), Venu, the son of the district collector's peon, mobilizes the masses against their oppressors. He endears himself to the people with his pro-poor activism. When he intervenes to prevent the demolition of a slum, grateful slum-dwellers raise a slogan that is repeated at the end of the film: "*Collector Babuki Jai.*" As the film progresses, Venu's efforts to

Image 136: Songbook of *Bangaru Manishi*.

help the poor pit him against the industrialist Bhanoji Rao (Prabhakar Reddy). The workers at Bhanoji Rao's factory are misled into believing that Venu is responsible for its closure. The film's climax has a crowd of workers launching an attack on the collectorate. Venu is stoned but prevents the police from firing at the mob. Instead, he makes a speech to the agitated workers, explaining he is not responsible for their woes. Realizing that they have been duped by Bhanoji Rao, the workers decide to attack the villain but are prevented from doing so by Venu. The film ends with the arrest of Bhanoji Rao in the presence of a large crowd which chants long live the collector and long live the *bangaru manishi* (golden man).

Bangaru Manishi stresses the importance of popular approval as a means of legitimizing authority, even when the source of this authority is the state. The slum demolition sequence is striking in this context: in spite of the film's overall adherence to Emergency slogans and themes (eliminating political corruption, for example), this sequence makes a risky reference to the unpopular slum-demolition drive in Delhi, suggesting it was wrong.[28]

In 1977, a year over which NTR had a string of hits, *Adavi Ramudu* and *Yama Gola* consolidated the star's popularity as a mobilizer of the masses. The NTR character rallies tribals and village folk against those who exploit the populace. In *Adavi Ramudu* he is a friend of the indigenous people; he turns out to be a forest officer working under cover to investigate the misdeeds of Dharma Raju (Nagabhushanam) and Nagaraju (Satyanarayana). This evil father–son duo smuggles timber and wildlife and exploits tribals. He is *not* a member of the tribal community whose interests he fights for (Image 137). On the contrary, as it is revealed towards the end, he is the lost son of the estate owner Rajasekharam (Gummadi), rescued from the villains by a maidservant who raises him.

Ramu (NTR), introducing himself as "Adavi Ramudu" (Ramudu/protector of the forest), saves an elderly tribal man and his niece Chilaka (Jayasudha) from poachers who are intent on punishing the old man for refusing to trap animals. In addition to protecting forest-dwellers and wildlife, Ramu persuades the tribals to acquire an education. This

Image 137: The mobilizer and the mobilized in *Adavi Ramudu.*

[28] Ramachandra Guha (2007: 514) writes that anywhere between 10 and 200 people died in the fighting that broke out in April 1976 when the Delhi Development Authority, under instructions from its vice-chairman and Sanjay Gandhi's bureaucrat-associate Jagmohan, attempted to clear houses in the Turkman Gate area of Old Delhi.

he does by singing to them ("*Krushi vunte manushulu rushulautaru*") of the greatness of Valmiki and Ekalavya, mythological figures believed to be of tribal origin. His attempts to help the community stokes the wrath of the villains, who manage to send him out of the forest by threatening to kill tribal children. Ramu then returns as the division's forest officer, to the delight of the tribals, and announces a variety of schemes for their development. The film's climax has Ramu, in disguise as an Arab sheikh, entering the villains' camp deep in the forest to rescue his parents, sister, and the film's two heroines. He is assisted in his mission by the forest department's cook and his girlfriend, also in disguise. A herd of elephants, led by the mother of a calf rescued from poachers by Ramu early in the film, destroys the camp. Dharma Raju is killed by the mother elephant and Nagaraju arrested. Ramu is reunited with his father—blinded earlier in the film in a failed murder attempt by the villains—and sister.

The film's director K. Raghavendra Rao, like Dasari Narayana Rao, made some of NTR's most successful films, including two major hits released after NTR made public his interest in politics. Scriptwriter Parachuri Gopalakrishna (2003: 18) makes the interesting observation that *Adavi Ramudu* created a new trend in the film industry by demonstrating that a film did not require a "story" to succeed, but could instead be based on a combination of male-star's glamour (he uses the English term), good music (meaning song-and-dance sequences), and comic sequences. The hero's glamour quotient in

Image 138: Birth of the story-less wonder: exotic locations, multiple heroines, and other attractions. NTR, Jayaprada (left), and Jayasudha (right) in *Adavi Ramudu*.

the film is considerably enhanced by the presence of two heroines, Jayaprada and Jayasudha, then very young (both went on to become politicians). Only one of the heroines, Jayaprada—who plays the daughter of a forest officer killed by the villains—has a relationship with the hero, but this does not prevent the director from featuring all three in song-and-dance sequences (Image 138).

As Rajadhyaksha and Willemen (1999) note in their entry on *Vetagadu* (K. Raghavendra Rao, 1979), from the late 1970s NTR was frequently featured in sexually charged song sequences with one or more heroines and/or cabaret specialists. *Vetagadu*, in which Sridevi played the female lead, became the subject of a joke: NTR's heroines had to begin their careers playing his granddaughters and grow up into his screen lovers. Indeed, Sridevi had played the NTR character's granddaughter in *Badi Panthulu* (P. Chandrasekhar Reddy, 1972), shortly before the older star's makeover. Pandian (1992) notes that MGR's heroines became progressively younger as the star grew older. Prasad makes this interesting point about MGR, NTR, and Rajkumar, who dominated their respective industries: "At the height of their career as star representatives of the linguistic community, these stars cannot indulge in romance without maintaining, as a supplementary feature of their subjectivity, a paternal function which extends to all characters in the film, including the heroine" (1999: 45). This is not to suggest that a paternal function undermines the libidinal economy of the films. The virile and vulgar hero was among the major attractions of the NTR film from the late 1970s.

The "*Adavi Ramudu* moment" in the late 1970s, when Telugu cinema transcended the *need to have a story*, as Parachuri Gopalakrishna would have it, is coeval, as discussed, with two key developments in the industry: the integration of Telangana into the film market and the fragmentation of the distribution system in Coastal Andhra into smaller territories. Both, in their own different ways, facilitated a greater circulation of Telugu films than ever before.

Yama Gola, the other NTR hit of 1977, is a socio-fantasy, a genre hybrid in which characters from epics or the puranas (and dressed in costumes associated with those genres) appear in stories set within the present. Satyam (NTR) is a popular village president who organizes young men against his wealthy and corrupt maternal uncle. He is killed by an assassin hired by the villain and finds himself in Yamalokam (kingdom of Yama where the dead are punished for their misdeeds). Much hilarity results from the dead hero's successful attempt to organize Yama's workforce, which is struggling to cope with the rush of sinners in modern times.[29] The production of the hero as mobilizer happens here in spite of the comic framing of the workers' agitation in Yamalokam. In NTR's films from the late 1970s, the star's distinction and leadership qualities are never lost sight of, regardless of experiments in genre.

Feudalism at Large: Telugu Films of the 1970s

There are convergences and divergences between NTR's career from the 1970s and Amitabh Bachchan vehicles made a few years later. As pointed out, NTR was featured in remakes of the Bombay star's films and, like him, was engaged in on-screen mobilization. Prasad argues in his discussion of Amitabh Bachchan: "The star's function is mobilization, the rallying of forces behind a narrative exposition. This elevation compensates for the loss of the hero's traditional authority, and enacts a transition from feudal to populist power. Through the production of a supplemental charisma, the industry overcomes the problems posed by a shift of narrative focus to the realm of the ordinary" (1998: 158). Prasad acknowledges that the film star was already engaged in mobilization in the Tamil and Telugu cinemas. The key difference between NTR and Bachchan films in the 1970s is that in the former (from *Raitu Bidda* onwards) lineage is *introduced*, rather than supplanted, as a source of distinction. It is not the revival of the extant or surfacing of the residual that we witness in *Raitu Bidda*, but the systematic assembly of traditional authority figures (the zamindar, the patriarch of the extended family) who had no precedents in the Telugu cinema. Simultaneously, the question of inheritance—of wealth, charisma, leadership qualities, and the values of an earlier period—gains increasing prominence. Take the example of *Adrushta Jathakudu* (K. Hemambaradhara Rao, 1971), a relatively

[29] I examine this film in the next chapter alongside NTR's late mythologicals.

minor NTR starrer which revolves around the problem of finding a man capable of and qualified to inherit a zamindari. In this film the NTR character is nominated as the successor of a wealthy zamindar played by Nagabhushanam. The succession is preceded by a series of tests of the hero, carried out by the zamindar. The latter, disguised as a madman, observes him facing various challenges. It turns out that the zamindar is responsible for the death of a poor man whose son, he decides, will be named his own successor. That poor man was the father of the hero. Although the film's title suggests that it is his *jatakam* (horoscope) that results in the inheritance, the NTR character has to literally earn his inheritance by demonstrating that he is worthy of it. By the end of the film it is proved that, despite his humble origins, the hero is a true zamindar.

The two notable points about the surfacing of the feudal question in the 1970s Telugu cinema are, first, that traditional authority figures were fabricated even as feudal authority in society was gradually undermined by post-Independence political and economic developments. Paradoxically, the growth of the film industry was itself evidence of the rise of a non-feudal elite in Andhra Pradesh. Second, cinema's increased investment in populism and reinvention of the feudal are a part of the same manoeuvre. We have seen that the inheritor of the feudal legacy is the leader of the masses, the voice of the reformist state—the revolutionary even. The new authority figure is firmly grounded on popular choice and approval but, unlike the populace which nominates him, he is endowed with an undeniable and inherent superiority.

Having discovered the feudal question, the Telugu cinema found several different uses for the new authority figure. Soon after *Manushulanta Okkate* the feudal lord appeared across genre tendencies of the Telugu social. In a spate of films inspired by the New Indian Cinema, he was a malevolent authority that had to be replaced by violent means.[30] At other times the feudal patriarch was the fountainhead of endangered values. NTR's own career was critically dependent on this figure. In his 1980s films, the benevolent authority figure grew older and was also split into an ageing patriarch and his young son.

[30] Examples are discussed in chapter 5.

Both roles were played by NTR, naturally. NTR's contribution to the introduction of the full-fledged feudal lord on the Telugu screen is best appreciated when we look at *Chanda Sasanudu* (rigid disciplinarian; NTR, 1983), produced by the star and completed after he became chief minister.

Chanda Sasanudu was promoted as a sweet masterpiece that ripened in the actor's sixtieth year (*nindina arvayyava natiki pandina prabhandam*). The film's publicity featured a brooding (or angry) patriarch, overlooking rebellious peasants with sickles held high (Image 139). The advertisements, evidently echoing NTR election rhetoric, also named the star as the *Telugu kathanayakudu* (Image 140). The film begins with a reference to *Dana Veera Sura Karna*, in which the younger NTR character is seen in the role of Duryodhana (in a stage performance) and making political statements. The story revolves around a village headman, Harischandra Prasad (NTR), whose traditional role is to sit on judgement over crimes committed in the village. As the film's title indicates, he is inflexible and authoritarian. He makes an error of judgement, incorrectly punishing his sister's husband Satyam (Jaggaiah). His sister Bhuvaneswari (Sarada) engages in public confrontations with him even as she secretly leads the rebellion started by her husband. Bhuvaneswari's son Raja (NTR) grows up in another village, not knowing who his real parents are. His foster-mother sends him to meet Harischandra Prasad and Bhuvaneswari. Once in the village, he sides with Bhuvaneswari and challenges Harischandra Prasad's authority. Soon, Raja discovers that the rebels and Bhuvaneswari are being misled by villains (Rao Gopal Rao and Satyanarayana). During the film's climax, both Harischandra Prasad and Bhuvaneswari are killed. The headman in *Chanda Sasanudu* is a tragic figure, doomed to fail in his attempt to hold together a crumbling moral and social order. Unlike the screen patriarchs played by NTR around this time, here there is little doubt that he is in the wrong.

This is among the earliest, if not the first, of the feudal nostalgia films, a genre that has been made and remade at regular intervals ever since across South India, as also in Bombay. Striking about the genre in Telugu is that its benevolent feudal authorities are only occasionally representatives of the zamindari order. The patriarch is a rich peasant

139

140

Images 139–40: Advertisements for *Chanda Sasanudu* in *Andhra Jyothi* (26 May 1983: 4, and 28 May 1983: 4).

and respected village headman who inherits his responsibilities. For example, in *Pedarayudu* (Ravi Raja Pinisetty, 1995) the headman is pitted against the decadent zamindar who is married to his sister. In this context, one landmark post-NTR film of the 1980s foregrounds the range of issues that the new feudal authority figure brings into sharp focus. *Bobbili Brahmanna* (K. Raghavendra Rao, 1984), the film in question, was a home production of the younger-generation star Krishnam Raju (Image 141). It was remade in Hindi as *Dharam Adhikari* (K. Raghavendra Rao, 1986). *Bobbili Brahmanna* borrows a part of its title from the NTR film *Bobbili Puli* (Dasari Narayana Rao, 1982).[31] Bobbili, now in Vizianagaram district, happens to be closely identified with pre-colonial authority as well as aristocratic patriots in the popular imagination. The kingdom's legends had been the subject of an earlier Telugu film (*Bobbili Yuddham*, C. Seetaram 1964). In the more recent past, however, the Raja of Bobbili was associated with Andhra Cinetone, the Visakhapatnam studio which shut down within years of its establishment in the 1930s. Recall that the Raja had threatened to sue Ramabrahmam for defamation and, as Sayana lamented, lost money in politics too (1949: 88). Steering clear of any possible identification with the erstwhile zamindars of the princely state, the film invokes Bobbili but not any Raja.

Bobbili Brahmanna's rehabilitation of the anachronistic feudal authority figure as awe-inspiring and admirable is obviously inspired by *Chanda Sasanudu*. The village headman Brahmanna (Krishnam Raju) has the power to judge and even behead criminals. He is a descendant of a heroic rebel of the same name who, we are told in a *burra katha*, saved the village from pillage and rape by British soldiers in 1857 and was put to death for that reason. The hero's sword—the symbol of justice—lies embedded in the stump of the tree to which the rebel was tied and hanged.

The film opens with a disclaimer borrowed from *Manushulanta Okkate* stating that the story is set in the colonial period—presumably the film-maker had anticipated objections from the censors to the depiction of a village where the police had no jurisdiction. That this was an afterthought is evident from the fact that the film makes no

[31] Discussed in the ensuing chapter.

141

142

Images 141–2: Advertisements for *Bobbili Brahmanna* stating that it created an all-time record by collecting 54-odd lakh rupees (*Andhra Jyothi*, 3 June 1984: 8); and *Gona Gannareddy* (*Andhra Jyothi*, 4 May 1982: 15), prominently featuring the Kakatiya dynasty monument, *Kala Toranam*. Some months earlier, photographs of NTR standing before this monument and addressing an election rally were published in newspapers (see chapter 5).

attempt at providing historical detail. On the contrary, it opens with modern-day policemen trying to enter the village in pursuit of a suspect. Villagers prevent them from doing so and Brahmanna defends the village's judicial system by pointing out that the newspapers were full of the misdeeds of elected governments.

The film's crisis does not result from external threats but enemies within the village: the rich farmer Venkata Rayudu (Rao Gopal Rao) and his son Bullabbai (Satyanarayana), resenting Brahmanna's authority. The villains, whose misdeeds are strongly opposed by the city-educated younger brother of the headman, Ravi (also played by Krishnam Raju), mislead Brahmanna into passing a judgement to the effect that his own daughter, Rajeswari (Aruna), should marry a poor man accidentally blinded by her. Ravi challenges the judgement and is excommunicated from the village alongside Rajeswari. Soon, Brahmanna is completely isolated from the rest of the family but does not relent. In the end, the truth of the villains' plot is revealed—the accident victim is neither poor nor blind and the accident itself was staged to implicate Rajeswari and thereby put Brahmanna in a spot. Brahmanna kills Rayudu when he tries to run away from the village. He then hands over the sword to his brother and leaves the village to surrender to the police awaiting him at the village boundary.

The feudal figure created by incorporating political authority, old wealth, and traditional values was among the lasting contributions of NTR to Telugu cinema of the 1980s and 1990s. At the same time, Dasari Narayana Rao's contribution to this tendency, as director of NTR vehicles but also those of other stars, cannot be understated. Even before NTR's *Bobbili Puli* was released, Dasari (the film's director) became associated with a project featuring Krishnam Raju titled *Gona Gannareddy* (*Andhra Jyothi*, Special Supplement, 4 May 1982, Image 142), named after the general of the Kakatiya dynasty queen, Rudrama Devi. The publicity material of this historical film, which seems to have been abandoned later, promised to situate the authority figure in the Telangana region (there is no mention of the film in Rajadhyaksha and Willemen 1999). Dasari went on to make a historical film centred on the eighteenth-century Bobbili hero *Tandra Paparayudu* (1986), with Krishnam Raju in the lead.

What then can we say about popular Telugu cinema's feudal

obsession? The nostalgic mode of representing feudal lords coexisted and dovetailed into demonizations of landlords and zamindars from the late 1970s. The latter trend drew heavily on Communist and Naxalite slogans of the period. We must note in passing that Parachuri Venkateswara Rao and Gopalakrishna, the "Parachuri Brothers," scripted both kinds of films from the 1980s. Among their major early 1980s hits was *Khaidi* (A. Kodandarami Reddy, 1983), which established Chiranjeevi as a major post-NTR star, and *Bobbili Brahmanna*. Gopalakrishna wrote the story of *Chanda Sasanudu*.

In conclusion, post-*Kathanayakudu* the male star, whose role in attracting investors, assembling the film, and determining its fate at the box office was critical, was narratively accounted as the mobilizer of the masses. When NTR's position in the industry—as also that of the very model of stardom built around him—was challenged, the narrative was reconfigured around the mobilizer of feudal lineage. This was part of the process of consolidation of the star-protagonist as someone always and already endowed with leadership qualities and, paradoxically, Telugu cinema's decisive turn towards populism that required the popular approval of authority.

From his biographers we learn that NTR's beginnings were relatively modest. His paternal grandfather, Peda Ramaswamy Chaudhury was a respected village elder and the richest landholder (*motubari raitu*) of his village (Lakshmi Parvathi 2004a: 14). The family had no known connections with the zamindari elite. We saw earlier that the family lost much of its wealth and that NTR's uncle relocated to Vijayawada in the 1930s, working as a bus conductor while the teenager helped raise buffaloes and sold milk. His sons, grandsons, and fans have nevertheless constantly made references to the Nandamuri *vamsam* (dynasty) to distinguish themselves from rival star families in the industry (Image 143). Notwithstanding the dubiousness of the claims made in family and fan propaganda, the feudalization of NTR is an interesting development. It is a sign that equivalence created by the 1970s Telugu cinema between stardom and lineage has gained currency outside the domain of fiction, indexing a important political development. As Prasad says of South Indian stars, the feudal figures we see on screen are, even in the fiction, appointed or approved by the masses: "These are kings chosen and anointed by the people: kings of

Image 143: The Nandamuri dynasty as imagined by Balakrishna fans. NTR, his son Balakrishna, and the latter's son Mokshaghna are seen in the picture, along with members of the Yuvasarvabhauma (Young Emperor) Balakrishna Fans Town Wide Association. Source: *Super Hit*, 27 June 2003.

democracy!" (Prasad 2009: 73). The appearance of the feudal figure is therefore not necessarily a sign of "regression" or a return to pre-modern loyalties but, paradoxically, evidence of populism at work.

4

Mythological Speech

Films in a Political Campaign

The post-1960s Telugu social, we have seen, was disengaged from realism and nativity, its focus having shifted to the production of cinematic pleasures and spectatorial expectations centred on the male star. The star-protagonist who thus emerged was engaged in mass mobilization. He was a populist figure whose distinction was inherited but nevertheless subjected to the approval of the people. The puzzle however is that nothing in NTR's career even up to the late 1970s, when he was re-established as the most-sought-after star of the film industry, suggests he was qualified to make a Telugu nationalist claim. So we need to examine what NTR carried over from his film career to his election campaign, and how it added up, or didn't, to making him representative of the Telugus.

The 1970s and 1980s films of NTR allow us to pose the question of South Indian stardom in broader terms than in relation only to the thematic concerns of star vehicles. In the light of NTR's career, as well as subsequent developments in the Telugu cinema, it is possible to argue for a substantial reworking of the commonsensical understanding of the links between cinema and linguistic identity politics in the region. Further, the particular variant of stardom that thrived and continues to thrive in South Indian film industries forces us to make distinctions between the general trend to import charisma into the domain of electoral politics, which can be traced to the late 1930s in the Madras Presidency, and the specific contribution, if any, of the cinema to this aspect of our public life.[1] In what follows I first look at NTR's "campaign films," namely, *Sardar Paparayudu* (Dasari Narayana Rao, 1980), *Kondaveeti Simham* (K. Raghavendra Rao, 1981), *Justice Chaudhury* (K. Raghavendra Rao, 1982), and *Bobbili Puli* (Dasari Narayana Rao, 1982), released after the announcement of his decision to enter politics. I subsequently focus on NTR's mythological films and their contribution to the election campaign, and conclude by proposing a conceptual framework for understanding the links between NTR's films and political career.

NTR's Campaign Films

Although the phrase "campaign films" has not been used by commentators, the consensus among Telugu film critics is that NTR's work of the early 1980s had political value and contributed to his nine-month-long election campaign in 1982–3. *Sardar Paparayudu* is claimed by NTR's biographers as the film which occasioned the announcement of his decision to enter public life. Dasari Narayana Rao credits his own films with making NTR a politician: "While *Sardar Paparayudu* inspired him to enter politics, *Bobbili Puli* is like a manifesto to his party" (cited in Prasad 1996: 64). The director himself went on to become a minister in the central government. A film critic points out that *Justice Chaudhury* was released on 28 May 1982, to coincide with NTR's birthday and also the first meeting (*Mahanadu*) of the TDP (Manigopal 2007: 4). An NTR biographer notes that in Tirupathi, at the venue of the Mahanadu, crowds greeted NTR with shouts of "Kondaveeti Simham, zindabad" (Narayana Naidu 1995: 40). Lakshmi Parvathi, describing a rally in Hyderabad, says that people shouted, "Sardar Paparayudu NTR, retaliate and fight . . . Bobbili Puli, we are with you" (2004b: 24).

While it is undeniable that NTR acted in these films when he was either contemplating a crossover to politics or was in the thick of the

[1] S. Theodore Baskaran (1996) states in the course of his discussion of the Tamil Congressman S. Satyamurthi: "When the Congress contested the [provincial] elections in 1937 he led the party's election campaign in the Madras province. In an astute move, Satyamurthi harnessed the talents of stage and screen artistes in support of the campaign" (71–2).

election campaign, the explanations offered for what and how these films contributed to his campaign are unconvincing. For example, a newspaper article lists the four landmark films made in this period and goes on to say that they advocated the creation of an egalitarian society and propagated *desa bhakti* or patriotism (*Andhra Jyothi* 2007: iv). In a way, this is true; the problems is that this can be said of virtually every Telugu film made since *Malapilla* (1938), if not earlier. What, then, do the star's films in general and these four films in particular have to do with his politics?

If any one film is to be pinpointed as the starting point for a definitive political turn in NTR's career, it is *Sardar Paparayudu*.[2] This film revolves around an anti-colonial rebel, Sardar Paparayudu. He is discredited and jailed by the villains—British collaborators who become powerful political figures in the post-Independence period—but decides to continue the rebellion upon his release. The film ends with a rather direct political statement in the form of a voiceover comment by the film's director. On a freeze frame of a tight close-up of the rebel, who dies fighting the villain, we hear the narrator say there should be more heroes like Sardar Paparayudu to weed out those who have betrayed the promise of Independence. My reason for re-nominating this film is not its stated political message. With *Sardar Paparayudu* we notice the convergence of various strands within NTR's oeuvre in the production of the authority figure and the fusion of this figure with a notion of "Teluguness" no longer tied to a realist presentation of the land and customs of the Telugus.

In the campaign films NTR is a figure of authority who is distinguished on account of his age and by being identifiable with a bygone era. In *Sardar Paparayudu*, *Kondaveeti Simham*, and *Justice Chaudhury* we see the star performing double roles centring on old and young characters. Initially, they occupy separate spaces and are both endowed with the authority to speak for a larger collective. The older NTR represents values (honour, patriotism, etc.) identifiably those of a past era; and he is burdened by enormous official, political, and familial responsibilities. The youth, meanwhile, is initially busy fighting petty

[2] Venkat Narayan (1983), Venkat Rao (2003), and Lakshmi Parvathi (2004b) have already made this claim.

criminals and taming the heroine. *Sardar Paparayudu* begins with the younger NTR character sending the heroine (Sridevi) into a dirt-water ditch as punishment for her rash driving. In *Kondaveeti Simham*, where too Sridevi is paired with the young NTR, she lands up in an irrigation canal at the end of their first meeting. The stories revolve around the two NTRs either discovering their relationship (since they have been separated) and/or the young man growing into his father's shoes. The state does not account for the older NTR's authority but merely ratifies it. NTR the father is a representative of the state—and famously, in *Kondaveeti Simham* and *Justice Chaudhury*. But he can also be a rebel, a discredited one at that, as in *Sardar Paparayudu*. There are also moments of conflict between the demands of the state and the responsibilities of the protagonist as parent, as guardian of a value system, and so on. In spite of the 1970s identification of NTR characters with old wealth and zamindari origins, the early 1980s films do not always offer this as the story-level justification of the character's distinction. However, the patriarch consistently embodied values threatened with extinction (the characters die).

Once the connection between authority and a bygone order as well as value system was established in NTR's films, it became possible for the later ones to do away with the father–son routine and yet raise the legacy question. In *Bobbili Puli* there is a negation of the father–son routine in order to pose the question of inheritance. NTR plays Major Chakradhar, a much decorated army officer whose biological father (Satyanarayana) is a spy turned army deserter turned fake *swamiji* (godman) indulging in a variety of criminal activities. He also kills Chakradhar's mother. Chakradhar becomes a rebel after his attempts to bring criminals to justice in a court are frustrated by his father and the other villains. When he loses his temper in court, he is jailed. While he is in jail his sister is raped (she dies later) and her husband murdered. Chakradhar escapes from prison and is believed to have perished but emerges as the rebel known as Bobbili Puli, the Tiger of Bobbili, and begins to put to death the criminal and corrupt that the courts failed to punish. At one point he also kidnaps the judge (Jaggaiah) and offers him instruction on justice. Finally he kills his biological father and is arrested by the police. The court awards him a death sentence.

The title of this film makes an obvious allusion via the protagonist to legendary "Telugu" heroes identified with the Bobbili kingdom. However, beyond the reference to Bobbili, the film makes no overt reference to language or linguistic nationalism. Instead, the hero is seen representing values of an older period that the heroine (Sridevi) at one point says are lost in an age threatened by deep-rooted corruption and public complacency.

Telugu with Hindsight: Fan Spectators and the Cultural "Insiderism" of Campaign Films

What is the relationship between the protagonist of a film like *Bobbili Puli* and Teluguness? Mitchell (2009) suggests that NTR's political appeal is traceable to the manner in which people related to (in this case the Telugu) language from the early twentieth century. In the course of her argument she tracks the changing meanings of a concept of interest to the study of cinema as well: *abhimanam* (love, pride). The meaning of *abhimanam* changed in the twentieth century:

> During the early twentieth century *abhimanam* began to assume important new connotations, leading to its most widespread use today in two new senses. The first is that of patriotism or political loyalty, not only in relation to language, but also in relation to one's nation or region (*desa*). The second contemporary use of *abhimanam* in the Telugu language is in relation to icons of popular culture, particularly movie actors. In some cases, these two meanings have coalesced around a single figure in the form of a film actor turned politician. The actor and former chief minister of the state of Andhra Pradesh, N.T. Rama Rao . . . inspired just such an intensity of affect-laden following, merging fan devotion with political loyalty among his followers. (Ibid.: 12)

The *bhashabhimani* of the early twentieth century, whose contribution to the formation of a political relationship with the Telugu language Mitchell tracks, had by the 1950s been displaced from debates on literature, etc. to agitational politics. Mitchell draws attention to how the Gandhian Potti Sriramulu's fast-unto-death resulted in the hitherto unprecedented mobilization of urban youth—including illiterate teenaged boys—in support of the formation of Andhra state (ibid.: 28). As language become available as a crucial axis of mass mobilization, the *bhashabbhimani* was less likely to be the connoisseur of the arts than the street agitator demanding justice for a very anthropomorphic language, complete with statues.[3]

There is a close correspondence between on the one hand the absence of overt reference to language and linguistic identity in NTR's career and Telugu cinema in general, and on the other the absence in post-1956 Andhra Pradesh of observable displays of what have been called "passions of the tongue".[4] Ramaswamy (1997) allows us to see a world of difference between the two contexts when she draws attention to extreme acts of devotion to *Tamilttay* (Mother Tamil), such as self-immolation, in the anti-Hindi agitation of 1964–5. How and why did "fandom" (*abhimanam*) or "devotion" attach itself to the Telugu language? Complicating the issue is the fact that in both Tamil Nadu and Karnataka there is a historical link between language politics and fandom which is not to be found in Andhra Pradesh—not even among NTR fans. The first fan club devoted to MGR was formed in the year he joined the DMK (1953). In Bangalore city fans of Kannada film stars have been in the forefront of mobilizations around language and linguistic identity. The notion of "linguistic masculinity" has been proposed to show complex connections between attachment to the Kannada language and masculinity (Niranjana 2000), and attention has been drawn to the involvement of Rajkumar fans in violent Bangalore agitations in the name of the Kannada language (Nair 2005: 234–70). A less disturbing but ubiquitous sign of overlaps between language and star fandom is the use of yellow and red colours—of the Karnataka flag—in fan promotions of films. But this is not all: images of film stars are often used in activities dedicated to the celebration and promotion of the Kannada language, and literary figures are invoked in street memorials of film stars. In other words the flag-waving language fan is very much a presence (Images 144, 145, and 146).

[3] Mitchell has much to say about what she calls the "personification of language" and the installation of statues of Telugu Talli (Mother Telugu) during the Telugu Desam regime. See "Making a Subject of Language," in Mitchell 2010 (68–99).

[4] A phrase coined by the historian Sumathi Ramaswamy (1997) in her study of the Tamil-speaking regions of South India.

Image 144: "Auto Raja," a Bangalore-based Kannada-language fan holds newspapers showing his charitable acts, which include free rides to people travelling to hospitals.

Image 145: Medals, awarded by an assortment of cultural organizations to Auto Raja in recognition of his good work, on display behind the passenger seat of the vehicle. The vehicle itself is decorated with images of film and literary personalities.

Overt reference to flags and language-mothers (Bhuvaneswari, the earth goddess is also the goddess of Kannada) in Kannada films is an interesting manifestation of the phenomenon but not a necessary condition for its production. The question that arises even in Bangalore, in light of the undeniable links between fans of film stars and language lovers, is that of the cinema's role in the emergence of a new kind of *bhashabhimanam*. How does one go about tracking this?

A perceptive observation on historiography pinpoints the methodological problem confronting analyses of visual materials which are unmindful of the *materiality* of the image: "The critical focus on these images [by historians], while enormously stimulating and raising issues of vital political importance, is nevertheless frequently a victim of a textual historiography that establishes its evidence 'by other means.' Because it has decided in advance that these images are

Image 146: Street signs of *bhashabhimanam* in Bangalore: bust of film star Rajkumar installed by the Karnataka Rakshana Vedike (Forum for the Protection of Karnataka). A lamp post in the background too is painted yellow and red, the colours of the Karnataka flag.

a visual manifestation of an ideological force, it is unable to catch hold of the ways in which the materiality of representation creates its own force field" (Pinney 2004: 204). Pinney goes on to make the crucial point that "images are not simply, always, a reflection of something happening elsewhere. They are part of an aesthetic, figural, domain that can constitute history" (Pinney 2004: 205). He could well have been referring to the late-twentieth-century Telugu cinema.

With reference to Telugu and other South Indian cinemas, fandom throws up a new set of challenges related to the socio-political life of images. Neither Film Studies nor the mainstream social sciences have ready-made answers to address these challenges. The question before us is one of NTR's Teluguness, as also the cinema's possible links with political mobilization. The film industry's attempt to infuse films with Teluguness in the 1940s and 1950s is part of the larger shift of *bhashabhimanam* away from the literary to the popular-political domain. We have seen that the demands for Teluguness in films, which began to be made around 1940, coincided with the Independence struggle and, later, mobilizations in support of a linguistic state. However, what we see in the NTR campaign films is an utter disregard for Teluguness as the industry had defined it. This is all the more striking because these films coincided with the emergence of the "class film" (post *Sankarabharanam*, K. Vishwanath, 1979), a genre critically acclaimed for its investment in Teluguness of the classic kind.[5] Moreover, the NTR campaign film, unlike the films of his Tamil and Kannada counterparts, seldom made overt references to the Telugu language.

A Singular Instance of Flag Waving: *Talla Pellama*?

To bring into sharp focus my argument on NTR's Teluguness, I digress now to discuss an unusual NTR film. The overlap between peasant mobilization and the demand for a separate Andhra state in *Palletooru* have been made clear, as also the fact that such overt references are

[5] I discuss the class film and its significance for 1980s Telugu cinema in Srinivas 2009 (201–9).

rare in NTR's career. Among the few obviously political statements on language in his later films is perhaps the song "*Telugu jati manadi*" (literally, We are the Telugu race) in *Talla Pellama?* (NTR, 1970; produced by his brother Trivikrama Rao). The scriptwriter Parachuri Gopalakrishna (2003: 16) notes (in a book which he dedicated to NTR) that the song courageously confronted the Telangana agitation.[6] The film is a domestic melodrama centred on the hero's suffering mother (Shantakumari), whose elder son abandons her upon getting a job in Madras. NTR plays Sudhakar, the younger and more responsible of the brothers—he pulls a rickshaw to earn enough money to join college and thus fulfil his dead father's wish that his sons be educated. In college Padma (Chandrakala), the sole heir of a wealthy politician, Rao Bahadur (Relangi), falls in love with Sudhakar after he makes a moving speech about the Telugu race. She marries Sudhakar against her father's wishes and begins to live in his modest house in the village. Soon the relationship between the couple begins to deteriorate and the mother forces them to leave to prevent the marriage breaking down. Rao Bahadur takes them to his home but begins to ill-treat Sudhakar. Retaliating, Sudhakar torments his wife. Even as he becomes increasingly sadistic, his brother Prabhakar (Nagabhushanam), who is in the habit of living beyond his means, gets into trouble with his creditors. Prabhakar's teenage son Krishna (Harikrishna, NTR's older actor son) leaves home to search for his grandmother. The family is eventually reunited by Krishna's efforts, while Padma is "reformed" after Sudhakar prevents her from seeing her newborn infant to give her a lesson in motherhood. Remarkable about the film, whose second half is mostly devoted to showcasing Harikrishna's acting and fighting skills, is Sudhakar's sadism, which causes endless suffering to both Padma and her father. However, the spectator is aware all through that Sudhakar is acting in her interest—husbanding her into responsible womanhood, as it were.

Where, in a film like this, does the song in question fit? Rendering the question all the more difficult is a powerful speech made by the

[6] Gopalakrishna uses the phrase *atisahasamuga* to describe NTR's courage, referring to the lyrics of the song in *Patala Bhairavi* which ends with Ramudu being hailed as the *kathanayakudu*.

NTR character in support of unified Andhra and against the "selfish elements" that have plotted the division of the state. The sequence of events leading up to the song-speech is as follows: Sudhakar, with his savings from rickshaw-pulling and his mother's salary as domestic worker, joins a college in Hyderabad and wins a scholarship that funds his hostel accommodation. The hostel administration invites for its annual day function the politician Rao Bahadur, who is introduced announcing proudly to his student acolyte (Satyanarayana) that he has changed his loyalties from the Justice Party to Mahatma Gandhi and is now a supporter of state and regional causes. At the hostel function, just as the politician is about to speak, Sudhakar is granted permission to say a few words. He then makes his speech, as though aware of the politician's intention to whip up "regional" sentiments.

Sudhakar's speech asserts that for 300 years the Telugus have been enslaved and split into regions. They have finally been reunited after Independence but in less than fifteen years since reunification selfish elements, jealous of the unity of the Telugu race and fearful of its capabilities, have created divisions. He then makes a surprising and almost direct reference to the threat to investments in the Telangana region: "For any state to progress, businessmen from all regions should be welcomed and encouraged. Their investments and knowledge should be properly used to our advantage." He goes on to list the past achievements of the Telugus and laments the community's decline in a present within which brothers view each other with suspicion. As his speech becomes more emotional, the camera tilts from side to side, visually reproducing the agitated state of minds in the audience. The speech ends with a slogan, *Telugu Talli ki jai* (Hail Mother Telugu). The entire gathering is now standing, while Rao Bahadur and his lackey make a quiet exit.

At the level of plot, the significance of the sequence is that upon witnessing his performance Padma (Rao Bahadur's daughter) falls in love with Sudhakar. The primary focus of the story is on familial disintegration. In very broad brushstrokes, it draws a parallel between the demand for the division of the state and the breakdown of the extended family. The hero punishes those responsible for both: the politician and his daughter, respectively. The references to the Telangana agitation early in the film continue to resonate as the mother's health declines. With one son lost to Madras and another to Hyderabad, she is taken care of by the village *haridasu*, a folk artiste and beggar whom she fed in better days. Let me add that the film does not quite work as an allegory, although the melodramatic structure allows for equivalences to be made between the familial and the larger political context. Rao Bahadur is not heard or seen supporting any cause remotely related to Telangana. The resolution to the narrative crisis does not make overt references to the political context.

Talla Pellama? is unusual for the explicitness of its references to Telugu language politics. But it is an exception which reinforces my contention that the shift we are tracking—of *bhashabhimanam* further away from the literary domain—may not be manifest in overt references to linguistic identity at all.

The Cultural Insider: NTR and Cinephilia

The late 1970s and early 1980s NTR films are interesting because of their sheer *inauthenticity* as epitomes of Teluguness. They were often remakes, or loosely based on non-Telugu films already released locally—their status as imitations was no secret. *Superman* (V. Madhusudhana Rao, 1980), in which the NTR character gets his superpowers from Lord Hanuman just before the interval, is unashamedly inspired by the eponymous Hollywood hit. In a defiant demonstration of the star's versatility, *Yugapurushudu* (K. Bapaiah, 1978) gestures towards Bruce Lee's work by casting NTR in the role of a martial arts (karate) champion. And then there are the Bachchan remakes.

In NTR films of this period, rather than any recognizable *bhasha*- or *desabhimani*, we notice the discursive production of an *abhimani*, the fan-spectator who is marked by her cinephilia. The film theoretical concept of cinephilia refers to excessive love or obsession with the cinema. Discussions of cinephilia revolve around intensely pleasurable moments in the cinema that defy explanation, as with Paul Willemen (1994) and Christian Keathley (2000), or with a heightened capacity for immersion in the screen and mobilization of cineliteracy, as with Lalitha Gopalan (2003). What is useful about the concept is that it alerts us to obsessive engagement as a common, if inexplicable, response to the cinema. Organized fans of the South Indian variety are marked by their tendency to make their cinephilia public, to display it and indeed house it in the public domain (Srinivas 2009: 27–36). Such displays of cinephilia, or its dovetailing into politics—as is evident from Bangalore's street memorials to film stars who double as icons of linguistic identity—have never been the subject of film theoretical reflections on the concept. For this reason I do not wish to elaborate on the literature on cinephilia here. Instead, I propose, NTR films from the late 1970s need to be situated in the larger context of the expansion of fan organizations where collective displays of cinephilia were already in evidence. The films themselves alert us to another instance, and one more directly connected to film spectatorship, where cinephilia and politics find a meeting point. However, this connection between the pleasures of filmic texts and politics was not immediately apparent; and nor was the political usefulness of these NTR starrers self-evident. Only much later, and only with hindsight, was the *abhimani*—regaled routinely with undisguised imitations of Hindi, Hollywood, and Hong Kong films, as also such scintillating numbers as "1, 2, 3, I am free, love me, love me, love me, me, me, me . . ." (*Aggiravva,* K. Bapaiah, 1981)—hailed as a political subject invested in a language-related political cause.

This is not to suggest that Mitchell is incorrect in suggesting that fan devotion and political loyalty merged in NTR's campaign, or that the notion of the *bhashabhimani* is irrelevant to a discussion of contemporary politics. What remains to be established is the nature of the three-way relationship between the star, his fans, and Teluguness. In a context where fans become language lovers, what is the work of the cinema? In relation to NTR's campaign films I will show how these became the site for a very contemporary *cultural insiderism* that did not pre-exist the cinema and, instead, had everything to do with cinephilia. The use of biographical references in Telugu films suggests, as we saw, that this is one of the techniques commonly used to address the spectator as a fan, ensuring awareness of the star status of the character on the screen. Taking this a step further, I suggest that NTR films created the conditions for the *misrecognition of the fan-spectator as a cultural insider*. And it was only after NTR decided to contest elections that this cultural insider acquired political valency as a member of the Telugu nation.

An obvious starting point for cultural insiderism of the cinematic variety is *Sardar Paparayudu*, which features NTR in a double role, as a discredited anti-colonial rebel as well as a police officer (the rebel's son). The film makes a polemical reference to Alluri Sitarama Raju, who led an armed insurrection of adivasis against the British in the early twentieth century in the Rampa and Gudem blocks of the Agency in Godavari and Visakhapatnam districts. At one point in the film Paparayudu (NTR) is watching a *burra katha* about heroic rebels. The song, "*Vinara sodara*", is written by Sri Sri and narrates the story of Sitarama Raju. The stage performance is intercut with sequences from the life of Sitarama Raju, in which Paparayudu/NTR appears in the get-up of the rebel (Images 147–55). Presumably this is the story that Paparayudu recreates in his mind.

In *Adavi Ramudu* NTR had appeared in the get-up of important historical and mythological figures in the course of a song ("*Krushi vunte*," where he plays Valmiki, Ekalavya, and Lord Rama, the figures the lyrics refer to). In *Sardar Paparayudu* the reference to Sitarama Raju is a not-so-subtle intertextual reference to the film *Alluri Sitarama Raju* (V. Ramachandra Rao, 1974), starring Krishna (Image 156). It has

Images 147–155: *Burra katha* on Alluri intercut with scenes of the rebel's death. NTR plays Saradar Paparayudu, imaging reconstructing Alluri's death in his mind.

147

148

149

150

151

152

153

154

155

Image 156: Krishna as Alluri in the eponymous film (*Vijayachitra*, April 1974: 14). Source: Manasu Collection, M.V. Rayudu.

been pointed out that Sitarama Raju's rebellion "served as an example and source of inspiration in the Andhra *desa* during subsequent phases of the nationalist movement" (Arnold 1985: 48). Such post-facto lionization of this rebel has also been seen in the two leading nationalist Telugu newspapers of the Madras Presidency, *Andhra Patrika* and *Krishna Patrika*, which condemned the rebellion (Murali 1984: 29–30). The heroism of Sitarama Raju became the subject of a popular play by the late 1940s (ibid.: 29n151). Murali mentions in passing that this film "is the best available account based on both historical and folk tradition mixed in a balanced way" (ibid.).

An important breakthrough made by the Krishna starrer is its production of Sitarama Raju's rebellion as an exemplary instance of *Telugu* heroism. This link, reiterated during NTR's election campaign, is missed by Murali. There is no understating the political significance of the film, made a few years after the agitations for separate Telangana and Andhra states. Alluri Sitarama Raju was a major icon of the Naxalite movement and Sri Sri was one of the film's lyricists. He needs to be credited with foregrounding the significance of the rebel for contemporary Telugu nationalist mobilization by literally naming him a Telugu hero in the song "*Telugu veera levara*" (which translates as "Rise, Telugu hero" and resonates with *Malapilla*'s "*Lera, lera, Harijana veera kumara*"). The song also calls Sitarama Raju "*Swatantra veeruda, swarajya bhanuda*" (Hero of Independence and Sun of Self-rule). Murari (n.d.: 206) notes that this was the first Telugu song to have won the prestigious national award for best lyrics.

Of immediate relevance to *Sardar Paparayudu* is not so much the rebel's identification with Telugu but the fact that Krishna, NTR's closest competitor in the 1970s, had played the role. It was rumoured that NTR had been planning to make a film based on Sitarama Raju but was beaten to it by the younger actor, whose production company made the film. Krishna is said to have ghost-directed most of the film after the original director died in the early stages of production (ibid.: 182). An elaborate intertextual reference embedded in the *burra katha* sequence draws direct parallels between NTR's role as a rebel and Sitarama Raju. Those aware of the back story of star rivalries and competition will recognize that *Sardar Paparayudu* gives us a glimpse, a teaser, of a film NTR was in fact planning to make but which he never did. The *burra katha* serves to emphasize the authenticity of NTR's portrayal of Sitarama Raju and the *version* of the rebel's story seen here. There are striking differences in the film's reconstruction of the events leading to the hero's death when compared with *Alluri Sitarama Raju*. How the star becomes central to the production of cultural insiderism is most noticeable. Whether most actual viewers are able to get into the polemics on Sitarama Raju's capture and death or not, the film's spectator is produced as someone grounded in a cultural and film-historical context that can become available for labelling as "Telugu." The film makes it possible to claim with hindsight that those who know their Sitarama Raju and Telugu cinema are Telugu.

Coincidentally, it was during the making of this film that NTR expressed a hitherto unknown interest in public life. Venkat Narayan

(1983: 6) and Venkat Rao (2003: 24) say that during a routine press meet in Ooty, while shooting for *Sardar Paparayudu*, the press was given the first hint of NTR's future plans. NTR had not expected the question from journalists asking him if he had any plans to "do anything by way of service to the people who have patronised [him] all these years." A "dumbstruck" NTR soon recovered and said he would like to spend "15 days every month to do social service" (Venkat Narayan 1983: 6). Lakshmi Parvathi begins the second volume of her two-volume biography of the star, which deals with his political life, with the shooting of the Sitarama Raju sequences. She has the star in the get-up of rebel wondering aloud what he would have to do if he were to be remembered—like Sitarama Raju—after he was long dead. She reports Dasari, the film's director, casually saying he would have to serve the people (perform *praja seva*). That very day NTR announced he would act fifteen days a month and perform *praja seva* the other fifteen (2004b: 1–2). All his biographers agree that NTR himself did not equate *praja seva* with electoral politics; clearly, he left the possibility open and was interpreted by the press as hinting at it. Parvathi adds that three sacks of letters asking him to enter politics were awaiting him when he returned to Madras from Ooty. And, as the cliché goes, the rest is history.

But not quite. The political significance of NTR's announcement was not immediately apparent—not least because the star was somewhat non-committal. Venkat Narayan claims that NTR announced the formation of his party almost immediately after the press statement,[7] but the star did not do much in the coming months and continued acting in films even as he was assessing his chances of success by sounding out friends and political figures. An article in the film magazine *Vijayachitra*, whose reporter was among the journalists invited to Ooty by the producer of *Sardar Paparayudu* to cover the shooting, does not so much as mention NTR's hints at entering public life but merely notes that the actor had decided to take on new responsibilities from 1982, when he turned 60. These included producing films based on Alluri Sitarama Raju and the saint

[7] This biographer is incorrect in attributing the date of the press statement to 1981 because the film was released in 1980.

Veerabrahmam (*Vijayachitra* 1980: 47). *Andhra Patrika* briefly reported NTR's intention to produce films based on the lives of *mahaniiyulu*, i.e. great people (1980: 13). And in any case the name of NTR's party was announced only in 1982. In the intervening period, when NTR was no doubt contemplating a crossover to politics but reluctant to announce it unambiguously, there was no indication that he would enter the electoral contest as a representative of the Telugus. While the most spectacular and commercially successful film ever made on a "Telugu" hero was actually made with Krishna in the lead, NTR himself had preferred to call Sitarama Raju a *mahaniiyudu* rather than an eminent Telugu.

Instead of direct references to Telugus and Teluguness, in the campaign films we witness a decisive shift away from "nativity." This is evident from *Kondaveeti Simham*, which features NTR in the roles of a sincere police officer as well as his son, separated at birth. The sequence I want to draw attention to is the one introducing the son. It is set in the countryside and occurs immediately after the police officer, Ranjeet Kumar (NTR), brushes aside the threats of the villain Nagaraju (Satyanarayana) to eliminate his family. The dynasty (*vamsam*) is dedicated to upholding justice and can never be destroyed, says Ranjeet Kumar, suggesting that the state, whose interests he represents as a police officer, only supplements his authority, which is dynastic in origin. There is then a cut to a rural setting. The tranquillity of village life, established in the first shot panning the hills and the houses in the village, is disrupted by the loud complaints of Sitapathi (Nagesh), a Brahmin with a topknot. He runs to Ramu (the young NTR) complaining that a girl from the city (Sridevi) has insulted him by tugging at his topknot. The hero goes on to teach her a lesson—as heroes are required to do in the films of MGR and NTR.

In this sequence the heroine is named as a "city girl" (*basti pilla*) and identified as such by the deployment of a range of signifiers: she wears a skirt, sports a hat, and declares that villages are fine for short trips but impossible to live in. She also uses English words and swearwords. Foregrounding her distinctive city ways, her friends are dressed in "traditional" clothes (half-saris). Unlike the village girls, NTR, who is presumably a village youth, is not identifiably a villager—he is neither dressed in a dhoti like Sitapathi nor does he bear any markers of rural life. Why is he presented thus? Why do we not see him as a city dweller like the heroine? Evidently, NTR can inhabit the village and speak for insulted village folk despite the absence of specific signifiers indicating his country origins. The character's claim to the village need not be elaborated upon or demonstrated—it can be taken for granted by the narrative. The sequence works because an equivalence had been created between recognition of the star and his habitation of this space. There is also the substitution of star recognition and "the unexpected arrival of the figure of authority" (Prasad 1999). The absence of a villager-like visage is more than adequately compensated for by the fact of his stardom.

What *does* the hero inhabit and the star represent in this film? It is not merely the village; it is the rural to begin with, represented by stock signifiers identifiable with nativity, such as paddy fields. But Ramu soon moves to the city, inhabiting it with equal ease. Let us also not forget that the *other* NTR, Ranjeet Kumar, already lives in the city. Even as the son is introduced, the star is seen occupying both spaces. I propose to call the spaces inhabited by the star-protagonist the *local*—this is a familiar world because we have seen it before on screen and the star occupies it with ease. Unlike the well-established practice of representing the Telugu nation on screen, the local is now striking for the absence of any attention to geographical detail. Location is merely backdrop and tells us nothing about the kind of character the star-protagonist is.

The workings of star-centred cinephilia—the means by which the local is produced—are brilliantly illustrated by *Justice Chaudhury*. In this film too NTR plays a double role, and the patriarch Chaudhury (NTR) is a judge. Villains attempt to blackmail him—to save his daughter's marriage he must give a wrong judgment. Elaborating on his predicament, he sings the song "*Chattaniki nyayaniki jarige ee samaramlo . . .*" (In this the battle between law and justice), drawing attention to the similarity between his situation and that of the mythological characters Rama, Harischandra, and Karna. The mythological allusion is by way of inserting short clips in the sequence from older films featuring the star himself: *Lava Kusa*, *Satya Harischandra* (K.V. Reddy 1965), and *Kathanayakudu Katha* (B.R. Panthulu, 1965), a social in which NTR acts as Karna in the course of a play. Is the film trying to present the NTR character in godlike terms? The answer, I believe, is decidedly "No." What the film is *not* trying to do is put in place a credulous spectator who believes NTR is God. Instead, it posits a spectator whose civilizational past is thoroughly mediated by the cinema. It is a cinema with NTR at its centre.

In her discussion of films made in Hong Kong around the time of the handover of the territory in 1997, Linda Lai (2001) alerts us to a similar attempt at community formation through cinematic techniques rather than via reference to overtly political themes. She argues that the Hong Kong films in question "constitute a shared textual horizon that addresses anxiety over the potential degeneration of Hong Kong's self-sufficient cultural identity beyond 1997. Such a shared horizon comes into place in the actual moments of viewing, as well as in the very act of remembering, invoking a history that is also the history of popular culture" (ibid.: 232). She coins the term "enigmatization" to refer to "the selection and reorganization of existing images from popular culture and in order to distinctly select the local audience as a privileged hermeneutic community . . . distinguishing those within from the 'outsiders' by marking who partakes in a shared history of popular culture" (ibid.). This formulation of the local is problematic because it presumes that the hermeneutic community pre-exists the cinema (in this instance Hong Kong cinema). It is possible—even likely—that there were viewers in Hong Kong whose low level of film literacy prevented them from accessing the "textual horizon." Simultaneously, it is possible that "non-native" viewers are able to access these films because of their familiarity with the language and cinema in question. Indeed, Lai argues that the "nostalgia film" addresses the local viewer with "quotations of popular stereotypes, stock characters, recognizable plot lines, and other conventions" (ibid.). Notably, these are *cinematic conventions* from "classical Cantonese and Mandarin films." The local that is of relevance for our discussion then is not merely a physical place but also a context which is shared by a viewing collective formed by encounter with the cinema. Although individual members of this collective might have a prior community identity (linguistic, national, etc.), a sense of shared history is created by the deployment of cinematic techniques. The production of the local is founded on *a shared history of pleasure of the cinema*. In the

Telugu cinema of the early 1980s we therefore witness the enmeshing of references to the past with references to cinematic history and the centrality of the star in the business of remembering. NTR characters bring to mind epics, which bring to mind mythological films, which bring to mind NTR.

Earlier we saw the recurrence of mobilization as a thematic concern in *Kathanayakudu*. This is increasingly prominent from the late 1970s, with the depiction of various groups of people as NTR's followers or the constituency on whose behalf he acts (*Adavi Ramudu* and *Yama Gola*). In the climax of *Naa Desam* (K. Bapaiah, 1983), the last NTR film released before the 1983 election, the NTR character parades the villains in the streets with a large number of people witnessing the spectacle. Such preoccupations are inseparable from NTR's emergence as a special kind of star, one who embodies a past history and future promise of cinematic pleasure. The star's strong identification with cinematic pleasure is evident from the box office success of his campaign films, each phenomenally successful and each bettering its predecessor. Unlike MGR, whose best work was behind him by the time he was elected chief minister, NTR remained the most commercially successful star of the Telugu film industry at the time of the election in January 1983. *Justice Chaudhury* had a 100-day run in 31 theatres and a 200-day run in 5 (Manigopal 2007: 4). After being held up for three months by censor troubles, *Bobbili Puli* was released on 9 July 1982 with an unprecedented 70 prints and in around 100 cinema halls. The film collected more in the first week than superhits of the period did in a hundred days. The enthusiasm was such that in some places the police had to fire in the air to disperse crowds (*Andhra Jyothi* 2007b: iv). Arguably, speculation about his political career and the actual crossover made a significant contribution to the commercial success of his films.

As legend has it, NTR's announcement that his party would be called the Telugu Desam Party, and that he would contest the 1983 election on the plank of Telugu self-respect, was spontaneous. He had apparently not thought through these questions when reporters asked him about his party and its agendas (Venkat Narayan 1983: 8). Nevertheless, it is unlikely that he was ignorant of the nature of his mass appeal. While there was nothing in the campaign films to suggest that language marked the local's specificity and held the community together, with hindsight a slippage between cinephiliac modes of film consumption and linguistic identity can be made. Cinematic pleasures were potentially identifiable as sources of linguistic identity because the Telugu cinema had, after all, emerged as the one cultural form that Telugus across Andhra Pradesh had in common. Moreover, as argued in relation to the national cinema in Germany, the textuality of films plays a critical role in the discursive production of national identity: "The national identity of a group of films . . . becomes, neither the realization of some hypothetical *Geist*, nor a trivial tautology (these films were made in Germany, therefore they are a part of a German national cinema), nor the catchwords of patriotic claptrap. National identity becomes an entity more or less realized precisely as a *readable coherence*" (Rosen: 2006: 26, emphasis added). Although the intentional naming of the local as the Telugu nation was either un(der)stated or absent till 1982, the mode of textual address that facilitated the misrecognition of the spectator, the *abhimani* who was invested in the star as a member of the Telugu nation, was well in place by 1980.

There was yet another aspect of his career that allowed NTR to make a unique claim to representing the Telugu language. This too was mediated by the cinema.

Cinema and the Language of the Gods

NTR played God to perfection in mythologicals for well over two decades before he launched his party. We cannot therefore ignore NTR's divine roles while trying to understand what he may have carried over from his screen career into politics. As Prasad notes, the initial explanation for NTR's electoral victory hinged on the impact of his divine roles: "Since he lacked MGR's political background, the experts quickly latched onto his mythological films as the basis of his popularity" (2006: 12). Chidananda Das Gupta argues that NTR had played the roles of "gods and god-like men" (1991: 222) and that the star was likely to have been mistaken for his screen roles because "Only in high-literacy areas subjected to Western thought structures, especially rationalism and Marxist materialism, such as the states of

Kerala and West Bengal, does the cinema audience have a ready ability to separate myth from fact" (1991: 41). Confirming the worst fears of high modernists like Das Gupta, NTR himself is reported to have drawn the attention of journalists to people's belief that he was god (Elder and Schmitthenner 1985: 383). K. Balagopal attributes NTR's populism to his belief in his own godhood: "Populism was always the weakness of Hindu gods. Witness how freely they have [*sic*] their boons and how often that magnanimity got them into trouble. And NTR, having played those gods too often on the screen during his film career, had *come to believe quite honestly that he was one of them*" (1984: 1902, emphasis added). In view of such assertions, it seems necessary to look at some of the literature on the relationship of film and television to religion and devotion in order to identify the issues worth foregrounding for an examination of a landmark mythological film made by NTR some years before he announced his decision to get into politics.

The Problem of Playing Gods on the Screen

The problem with screen gods is that they are often mistaken for actual deities—not just by gullible viewers but also by scholars. In her short but pioneering essay on *Jai Santoshi Maa* (Vijay Sharma, 1975), Veena Das makes what we can now see was the founding mistake about the film–religion relationship: the presumed unmediated access of film to the viewer. Das comes to the conclusion that the film is "directly accessible to the vast majority of illiterate people . . . Unlike the printed versions of a myth which might still need to be interpreted through the mediation of a priest, film as a medium does away with the necessity of all mediation" (1981: 55). It is as if film is to contemporary Hindu practice what the translations of the Bible were to Protestantism—the means of transcending priestly interference in religious matters. Das's use of the film as evidence of practices relating to popular religiosity is premised on the transparency of film as medium and its capacity to serve as a neutral carrier of content, which in this instance happens to be about a little-known religious cult. The focus of her study, naturally therefore, is not the cinema's work of re-presenting the cult but the cult itself. As a result, she makes a number of observations about religion on the basis of her reading of the film. Notice for example the claim that "Traditionally, a goddess who is not encompassed within a male principle can only appear in *shakti* form. All other forms of goddesses are encompassed within higher male principles. Now [from the reading of the film but with reference to the cult itself] it seems that direct, unveiled relations with benevolent goddesses, who are themselves unaccompanied by male gods, have become possible through the emergence of Santoshi Maa" (Das 1981: 54).

The blurring of film into cult in the literature on *Jai Santoshi Maa* (by Das but also other researchers) led to the diagnosis that "Although these authors provide a good deal of insight into the Santoshi Maa cult, I think it is fair to say that, broadly speaking, they are more interested in Hindu goddesses than in Hindi films, and show relatively little interest in the aesthetic narrative qualities that contributed to the film's success" (Lutgendorf 2002a: 15). While there can be no objection to the examination of film to understand contemporary devotional practice—this has been attempted with considerable success by Lutgendorf (1990) and Bhrugubanda (2011)—the question that arises is one of mediation: what the cinema or any other form does to the "mythic material" that it presumably transmits.[8] In Lutgendorf's view, this tracks the continuities and discontinuities of the movement from "*katha* [oral/written accounts of gods] to the camera" (2002b: 24). Ignoring this rather basic question leads to redundancy—clearly in evidence in studies of film's relationship to both religion and politics. This problem has been brought into sharp focus: "The Hindi film presents an enchanted world where gods are still present, and miracles are almost part of the everyday and their miraculous nature is barely noticed, a world not so far away from the real world where on some days the images of the gods drink milk they are offered" (Dwyer 2006: 160). There is no denying the truth of the statement. However, the question such a situation poses to the researcher is—why study films, let alone religious films, when we already know that in India the gods are everywhere?

In his study of Ramanand Sagar's *Ramayan* Lutgendorf (1990) makes the interesting claim that the television saga is not only

[8] "Mythic material" being Geeta Kapur's phrase: see Kapur 1987.

faithful to a long tradition of retelling the epic but is also a modern, electronically mediated *act of devotion*. He draws attention to the continuities between religious performances such as the Ramlila plays and the television serial. He also underscores the ways in which a variety of popular and contemporary religious practices spilt over to the viewing of the television serial: "Millions of Hindus did indeed feel a need to sacralise their TV screens each week in order to make them 'a frame for sacred events,' yet they apparently found no more difficulty in doing this than they do in sacralising their town squares for Ramlila plays each October, their kitchens for monthly 11th day ceremonies (*ekadasi*) or piles of cow dung for *govardhan puja*" (ibid.: 161).

He shows that the mediation of television makes sense only against the backdrop of a range of religious practices and performances of the epic. For the student of religion, therefore, the television epic is inadequate as an object of study. There is nothing that Sagar's *Ramayan* can reveal about Hinduism or the Ramayana that has not already been learnt from the study of other sources and forms. What it does reveal, however, is the transformation of the familiar epic into contemporary television: "The viewer's curiosity about the domestic aftermath of the banishment is more than satiated, and they are left with a feeling of intimate knowledge of the royal family. Female viewers are presented with a story in which women are more pervasively present and forcefully active than in most written versions. More than ever, this ultimate soap opera emerges as family saga, in which the members of the sundered royal clan are shown united in their emotions even though physically apart" (ibid.: 154).

A problem with Mankekar's landmark work (1999) on Indian television is the author's inadequate attention to the specificity of television epics and their (dis)continuities with other, pre-existing versions. As a result the response of her respondents to television epics leaves the reader wondering if it is television or the palimpsest of prior representations of a Sita or Draupadi that the viewer's comment illuminates. For example, when one of her respondents is asked what she liked most about Sita, she replies, "Her nature [*svabhav*] and humility, she spoke in a loving manner [*baton mein pyaar tha*], she respected her elders. The best thing was that she was very loyal to her husband. After all, who goes with her husband these days to roam in the forest? Only a woman like Sita could have gone [into the forest]" (ibid.: 213). One cannot but wonder if this is a response to Ramanand Sagar's Sita or to Valmiki's or to yet other versions of the epic. Where does a mass cultural form come into the picture in contexts where people are always already religious?

Lutgendorf (2002a, 2002b) applies the methodology he had tried out in his analysis of the television epic to his study of *Jai Santoshi Maa* and the cult. He focuses on the "inter-textual relationship" between the film and other versions of the story of the goddess (2002b: 25), discussing separately the non-filmic versions of the Santoshi Maa story and the film. He also draws attention to cinematic techniques used by the film to institute a "darshanic" relationship between the spectator and the screen-goddess, using fairly standard cinematic conventions like the group song performed before the statue of the goddess (ibid.: 28). His most significant breakthrough is the demonstration of how the film works to produce devotional *spectatorial response*: "within its aesthetic conventions of flatly-painted backdrops and gaudily costumed gods who appear and disappear with a clash of cymbals, the film presents a carefully-structured narrative abounding in references to folklore and mythology and offering trenchant commentary on social convention; it also develops a 'visual theology' that is particularly relevant to female viewers" (2002a: 16). The result of the film's "theo-visual argument" is the transformation of the spectator into a devotee. Viewing the film thus becomes one of the ways of performing a ritual devotional act. Returning to NTR via Lutgendorf's study, we can legitimately ask if NTR's oeuvre similarly reconstitutes the spectator as a devotee. Prasad (2006) notes that the star, like stage actors of an earlier generation, played not only the role of gods but also acted as Ravana and Duryodhana (the "villains" of the *Ramayana* and *Mahabharata*) as also Brihannala—the transgender dance teacher that Arjuna disguises himself as—in the hit film *Nartanasala* (Images 157 and 158).

By January 1983, when he became chief minister of Andhra Pradesh, NTR had acted in a total of 289 films. Only 42 of these were mythologicals as against 55 folklore films and 11 historicals. The rest were socials. He had played Duryodhana four times and

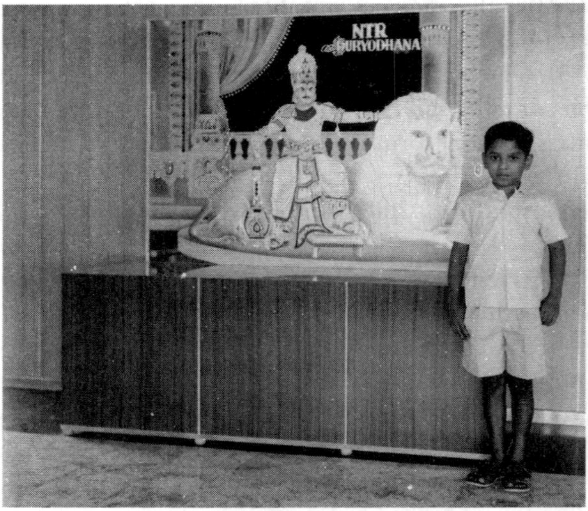

Image 157: A child poses by a glass engraving of NTR as Duryodhana during the inauguration of Ramakrishna 70mm. The engraving, from *Sri Krishna Pandayeevam*, was prominently displayed in the lobby of the theatre for decades to come. Source: Manasu Collection, M.V. Rayudu.

Image 158: NTR as Duryodhana in *Dana Veera Sura Karna*.

Ravana once. NTR acted in just three mythologicals between 1978 and 1983 (see Venkat Narayan 1983: 114–19). Arguments about the possible impact of his divine roles tend to ignore the (social) films he had made, denying them any role in the campaign—and this in spite of their timing and overwhelming number. What then was the contribution of the mythological to NTR's career as a whole and his crossover to politics in particular? T. Vishnu Vardhan proposes that the claim NTR made to representing—speaking for—the Telugu nation was founded on his close identification with mythologicals. Yet it was not godhood that was being attributed to NTR in the wake of his mythologicals but the capacity to speak in a timeless and "pure" Telugu, which was the hallmark of the genre (Vardhan 2007).

Stage versions as well as early sound adaptations of the genre were characterized by set-pieces of poetry (*padyalu*) in a high literary Telugu and these were sung with great flourish on stage. The poems were in fact the highlights of the genre, and stage audiences are known to have encored the actors for a particularly well-recited poem. Vardhan's argument is that early mythological films paid little attention to the spoken lines that were not a part of the set of poetic declamations around which the film/play was woven. As a result, when actors spoke to each other—as against sang poems to each other—they sometimes did so in "non-standard" dialects of Telugu.[9] This issue was not addressed by film-makers during the first decade of the talkie, when stage mythologicals were filmed with some changes in the script.[10]

It was only in the 1950s that the film industry began to systematically

[9] Mitchell has a useful description of "standard" Telugu: "In Andhra Pradesh today, 'standard' Telugu is a dialect associated with educated members of several dominant caste groups from the Krishna, East and West Godavari, and Guntur districts, representing the most agriculturally developed and prosperous region of coastal Andhra" (2009: 24).

[10] The songbook of *Draupadi Vastrapaharanam* (H.V. Babu, 1936)—the only available source of information about the film that I have been able to access—does not have a credit for the film's story. Instead it states that the film is an adaptation (*natakanuvadam*) of the eponymous play by Malladi Achyutaramasastry. However, the scenario as well as new songs and *padyalu* are credited to Pasumarthi Yagnanarayanasastry.

"clean up" the mythological as a part of its attempt to reposition the by now culturally and economically de-valued genre as a big-budget star-studded spectacle. While Vardhan builds his case on the evidence from the two versions of *Bhukailas* (Sundarrao Nadkarni, 1940; K. Shankar, 1958), it would be more accurate to say that the process was initiated in the Vijaya production *Maya Bazaar*, the film which cast NTR in his first significant mythological role, as Krishna.[11] *Maya Bazaar* is a romantic comedy centred on the marriage of Balarama's daughter Sasirekha with Arjuna's son Abhimanyu. While most of the important characters of the epic appear in this film, its relationship with the main *Mahabharata* story is incidental. Among the highlights of the film is magic and mischief by Bhima's son Ghatothkach.

The plot summary in the songbook of Vel Pictures' production of the same name (a.k.a. *Sasirekha Parinayam*, P.V. Dasu, 1936, Image 159) allows us to see that the 1957 film was based on the earlier version. Vijaya's *Maya Bazaar* was to the mythological what *Patala Bhairavi* was to the folklore film in terms of setting the industry benchmarks for the genre. K.V. Reddy directed both films, which, for their time, had high-quality special effects.

The new mythological was, among other things, rid of inconsistencies in the registers of Telugu between its poems and speech. Film commentators had argued in the past that it was inconceivable that gods *spoke* like commoners. The mythological was subjected to the standards of realism, which focused on its dialogues, now elevated to sound like the prose associated with literary production known as *grandhikam*. Meaning "Classical, poetical, peculiar to book" and "bookish" (Brown 1903: 244), *grandhikam* was at the centre of an acrimonious debate in the early twentieth century between those who insisted that all literary works be in this register of Telugu, and others who advocated the use of *vyavaharikam*, the language of daily use.[12] With specific reference to the mythological, the issue was not

[11] He had earlier played a supporting role as Nala in *Maya Rambha* (T.P. Sundaram, 1950).

[12] An evaluation of the literary figure Gidugu Venkataramamurthy, well known in literary circles for his contribution to the development of literary production in *vyavaharika bhasha*, offers this useful distinction between

Image 159: Songbook of *Maya Bazaar*, a.k.a. *Sasirekha Parinayam* (1936). Source: B. Vijayvardhan.

merely one of choosing between *grandhikam* and *vyavaharikam* but the fact that characters also spoke in *mandalikam*—"non-standard" regional dialects of Telugu. From the late 1950s, the dialogues (as distinct from the poems) of the mythological were meant to sound like *grandhikam* in the interest of creating a "Telugu atmosphere" in a genre whose stories, as well as theatrical ancestry, were not merely pan-Indian but also seen as inimical to regional and linguistic specificity. As a result of the elevation of the dialogues to *grandhikam*,

---

registers of Telugu: "The poetic Telugu language is *kavya bhasha*. The written language in prose is called *grandhika bhasha*. The spoken language is *vyavaharika*." *Mana Samskriti* (2004).

the mythological appeared to be consistently in high-sounding Telugu. The language of the mythological was meant to sound both timeless and distinctive, facilitating the identification between the genre and classical Telugu. Whereas in the 1940s and 1950s film critics and sections of the audience alike demanded that producers stop making mythologicals, the genre had by the late 1950s acquired a new cultural significance.

The grammatical correctness of NTR's (as also the genre's) gesture towards *grandhikam* was, on occasion, called into question. In his review of the mythological film *Brahmarishi Vishwamitra* (NTR, 1991), the eminent film critic Gudipoodi Srihari argues that the use of *grandhikam* in the film was inconsistent: "The dialogue is written mostly as free verse combining some chaste *Grandhikam* with *Sishta Vyavaharikam* [with commonly used words]. Sometimes, this combination created most awkward links of words" (n.d.: 70). The director Kamalakara Kameswara Rao, who was closely associated with the genre, claimed that the early Telugu mythological used a *grandhikam* which viewers could not understand. He does not raise the issue of consistency of register but makes the important point that the work of, among others, Samudrala Raghavacharya—whose oeuvre as scriptwriter includes *Bhukailas*, the film that Vardhan argues is a turning point in the genre's history—marks an important shift from incomprehensible Sanskritized language to *jaanu* Telugu (i.e. Telugu without Sanskrit words). This Telugu was easily understood but "classical" (he uses the English word) and not vulgar (*asabhya Tenugu*) like the language in contemporary films (Kameswara Rao, 1980). The question is not whether the post-1950s mythological was in *grandhikam* or the purer and more authentic *jaanu* Telugu, or if the post-*Maya Bazaar* mythological is in fact consistent in its use of *grandhikam*. What does the gesture towards the so-called "classical" have to do with politics? Recalling Mitchell's (2009) point,[13] I would like to note that the genre had evolved from merely speaking and singing in different registers of Telugu into *being* Telugu by gesturing towards *grandhikam*. The genre's connection with politics will be discussed after looking at NTR's contribution to the mythological.

[13] See chapter 2.

Returning to Vardhan's work on the genre, he notes that the transformation of the mythological was closely related to NTR's career. Over the years the industry was convinced that he alone had the command over Telugu, as also the physique, to play the roles of important mythological characters like Rama, Krishna, Karna, etc. (Vardhan 2006). NTR's strong identification with the genre is one of the consequences of the decline of singing stars, who were drawn from the stage. As Uma Bhrugubanda points out:

> [W]ith the arrival of playback singing in the 1940s, there was a split between the singing and speaking voices. While actors dubbed their own voices for the speaking portions of the film, when they sang, they sang with voices other than their own. In other words, while each actor dubbed the speaking portions for himself or herself, the playback singer sang the songs for them. In the mythological films, this was compounded by the singing of not only songs but also the singing of verse. Not always did the same singer sing both songs and verses (*padyalu*) for a single actor, sometimes not even the same singer sang all the songs for a particular actor in a film. Therefore, it was possible for the same actor to have different singing voices in the course of a film. (2011: 67)

Rather than sing like their counterparts in the 1940s, the mythological heroes and villains of the late 1950s were expected to possess a far greater command over refined Telugu prose than before. For they did not merely speak to each other but threw challenges and had monologues in more ornate, alliterative, and high-sounding Telugu than was ever heard on screen before. Pronunciation had to be *unaccented* and speech in non-standard dialects was not permitted even among menials depicted in the genre. With *Nartanasala* and *Lava Kusa* NTR became the master of the speech-centred mythological by the early 1960s. So much so that, Vardhan points out, it was virtually impossible to conceive of a mythological film without NTR playing the key role (Vardhan 2006). Vardhan's work allows us to make a clear and necessary distinction between playing god and acquiring mastery over a register of Telugu that gestured towards its purity and timelessness. The latter allowed NTR to stake a unique claim over embodying Teluguness.

High-sounding Telugu associated with the mythological underwent a major transformation in *Dana Veera Sura Karna* (1977), the film which NTR produced and directed to inaugurate his Ramakrishna Cine Studio in Hyderabad. A detailed analysis of the films shows the new political usefulness that NTR found for a genre on the verge of extinction; in fact this redeployment of the genre as a vehicle of political critique has few precedents in sound films. Unlike the silent era anti-colonial critique in *Bhakta Vidur* (Kanjibhai Rathod, 1921), which was advertised as a "*Swadeshi*" film (Rajadhyaksha and Willemen 1999: 244), the Telugu mythological was not associated with either political or reformist statements—or so it appears from the material currently available on the early talkie mythologicals in Telugu. In later decades there were occasional references to contemporary issues, like the song critiquing caste discrimination in the NTR starrer *Satya Harishchandra*. Social or political critique has, for the most part, been an attribute of the social in sound films.

In *Dana Veera Sura Karna* NTR plays the roles of Krishna and Arjuna, but also Duryodhana (called Suyodhana in the film). He had earlier played the role of Duryodhana as well as Krishna in the film *Sri Krishna Pandaveeyam* (NTR, 1966). Made at a time when NTR more or less consistently played mobilizer of the masses in the social, *Karna* is perhaps the most overtly political Telugu mythological ever. It is also the last commercially successful mythological produced by the industry (Bhrugubanda 2010: 42). Some months after its release, NTR's friend and Tamil superstar M.G. Ramachandran was sworn in as chief minister of Tamil Nadu.

Dana Veera Sura Karna: The Film

As we have seen, throughout the 1960s, even as nativity became less important as the defining characteristic of the social, state subsidies and the expansion of the market made it possible to lay claim to Teluguness on the basis of criteria that were other than aesthetic or formal. NTR digressed even further from the existing criteria for assessing cinema's commitment to the Telugu cause by returning to a genre that was gradually being phased out of the industry. The mythological has always been a studio genre, shot largely indoors and requiring elaborate sets and backdrops, innumerable costumes and props. As KoKu pointed out more than once, it could be made in a studio in any part of the country. NTR's decision to inaugurate his Ramakrishna Cine Studio in Hyderabad by making a mythological film was not founded on the usefulness of the location of production for realist representation of Telugu land and people. Notwithstanding how little use *Karna* had for geographical markers of realism and Teluguness, the film is the perfect example of how the post-*Maya Bazaar* mythological could make a claim to being Telugu in ways markedly different from those in the social of the 1950s vintage. This claim, as we shall see, is centred on the film's dialogues. I focus on how and why it digresses from the conventional modes of retelling the *Mahabharata* story in popular theatre and cinema. My purpose is not to demonstrate the incorrectness of the film's interpretation but to understand how *Karna* works as a *film*, and to analyse what is specific to its reinterpretation of the epic.

The film does not make sense unless we focus on what NTR, whose absolute centrality is never in doubt from the credit sequence, does in it. Like some of his earlier home productions, notably *Tatamma Kala* (NTR, 1974), the film features both his actor sons— Balakrishna (who went on to become a major star in the late 1980s and 1990s) and the less-well-known Harikrishna who we saw playing an important role in *Talla Pellama?* (Harikrishna became a minor but full-time politician after his father's death.) The film is dedicated to Lakshmaiah Chaudhury, NTR's father (Image 160). In the dedication slide we see a full-length photograph of the father flanked by an image of NTR as Krishna on the left and that of his son Harikrishna in the get-up of Arjuna on the right, leaving no room for doubt about the family's ownership of the film. In the film the two sons supplement the father's stardom, literally standing in for the older star during his brief absences—to ensure that someone from the family is seen at all times on screen.

Karna begins with the discovery of the infant Karna by Athiratha (Chalapathi Rao), supposedly a low-caste charioteer who is nevertheless seen on the river bank issuing orders to his servants like a rich landlord. With great economy the film shows Karna growing up under the loving care of his foster-parents during the course of a song ("*Ae talli ninu kannado* . . .") about his orphanhood and adoption. The story proper begins with Ekalavya (Jayabhaskar) offering his thumb to Dronacharya (Rajanala). The manner in which the familiar story of Ekalavya is reinterpreted and details and scenes interpolated are symptomatic of the film's repositioning of the mythological as an explicitly political genre. Arjuna (Harikrishna) is implicated in Drona's cruel demand for fees (*guru dakshina*) from the tribal youth by making a sign to his teacher, Drona, before the latter asks for Ekalavya's thumb. Even as Ekalavya is about to cut off his thumb, his sister Prabhavati (B. Saroja Devi) protests and tries to stop him. Ekalavya reminds her that it is not like tribal folk to go back on their word and cuts off his thumb. Karna enters the scene now to reprimand Drona and point out that he had in fact refused to teach Ekalavya because he was low caste ("*kulaheenudu*"). He then warns Drona, "The severed thumb is a symbol of your caste prejudice . . . do not forget that Karna will hunt down Arjuna, no matter where he goes."

This sequence, taking considerable liberties with more standard versions of the epic, frames the story of Karna as a struggle against caste prejudice and oppression. Karna's quest for the knowledge of the arts of war too is presented as a part of the struggle in the interest of justice. Karna introduces himself to the sage Bhargava (Gummadi), whom he approaches for training in archery, as a victim of upper-caste prejudice (*durahankaram*). Karna's ambitions are repeatedly thwarted by Indra, who tricks Bhargava, and also an unnamed Brahmin sage into cursing Karna. While stories of Karna's misfortunes are familiar enough, the manner in which the film relates them with upper-caste prejudice is striking. Among the novelties of the film's interpretation of the *Mahabharata* story is the romance between Karna and Ekalavya's sister. Their relationship too is presented as an extension of Karna's political agenda: Prabhavati tells him she fell in love with him because he always stands by the oppressed.

A mere nine minutes into the film, immediately after he is cursed by Bhoodevi (the Earth goddess), Karna arrives at the competition where he is discovered by Duryodhana (NTR). There is now a shift in narrative focus from Karna to Duryodhana—from one NTR to another. The introduction of Duryodhana anticipates the elaborate entries of the star-protagonist in 1980s Telugu cinema that the late 1970s social had not yet fully mastered. Before we see NTR's face in the Duryodhana get-up, a shot of his legs and another of his hand are interspersed with shots of women servants singing a song of welcome

("*Jayeebhava, digvijayeebhava*"). The entry of the character, as noted by Bhrugubanda (2011), recalls the introduction of Duryodhana in *Sri Krishna Pandaveeyam*. Duryodhana's popularity among the masses is established when the crowds that have gathered to watch the competitions cheer enthusiastically upon his arrival. The scene in which Karna is prevented from participating in the competition by Drona is presented as a continuation of the Ekalavya story. When Drona boasts that Arjuna is unbeatable, Karna challenges the claim. An angry Drona asks him who he is. Karna responds by asking, "Have you forgotten me already?" and reminds him of his cruelty towards Ekalavya. It is into this well-framed narrative of caste discrimination and injustice that Duryodhana—the popular prince—is inserted, quite literally as the voice of justice and dharma. As Karna turns to leave upon being told by Drona that this is a competition for *kshatriyas* and not a low-caste charioteer like him, Duryodhana calls out to him to wait. He then turns to the elders in the court and makes the first of his speeches. He argues that this is a competition among warriors and not *kshatriyas* (playing with *kshaatra* and *kshastriya*). Reminding them of their low-caste ancestors he asks them what, then, their caste might be. Bhishma intervenes to say that this is a competition among princes. Duryodhana immediately names Karna the king of Anga, passing a series of orders to courtiers that demonstrate his absolute mastery over procedures of the court. He then holds Karna by his shoulders and vows to destroy casteism for all time to come.

The film's focus now shifts to Duryodhana's romantic interest, Bhanumati (Prabha). We learn that her *swayamvaram* has been announced and that Duryodhana is in love with her. We then see Bhanumati completing a painting of Duryodhana while her servants tease her. *Karna* even has a duet between Bhanumati and Duryodhana ("*Chitram bhalare vichitram* . . ."). Presented as Bhanumati's dream of a romantic encounter with Duryodhana, the song calls to mind the sexually charged duets in NTR's socials of this period. At the story level, the song—and Bhanumati's love for Duryodhana in general—justifies her abduction by Duryodhana when she does not choose him at the *swayamvaram*. Making a fence of arrows, Karna prevents her father Jarasandha from pursuing Duryodhana. Jarasandha is so impressed with Karna's archery skills that he gifts him a city.

Duryodhana then persuades Karna that it is time that he too gets married to Prabhavati, and both couples marry at the same venue. The marriage is followed by a remarkable song ("*Telisenule priyarasika*") featuring the newly-wed couples. Halfway into the song Krishna, the third NTR character, is introduced. The song ends with a split screen image of all the three NTRs with their wives (Image 161).

By this point in the film, Duryodhana is established as the voice of justice; he is a generous friend and a master of the art of love—all these being traits seldom attributed to him in mythological films. The action now moves to the Pandava court, where Duryodhana arrives with much reluctance to participate in the ceremonial sacrifice (*yagam*). In Mayasabha, Pandavas' palace of illusions, Duryodhana is seen wondering at the brilliance of the architect. Among the illusions is a full-fledged song by a courtesan (Jayamalini, the most famous screen vamp of the late 1970s). As he begins to tire of the building's tricks, he steps into a small pond, which he mistakes for an illusion, and falls. He sees Draupadi (Sarada) laugh at his fall and is further infuriated by Bhima's (Satyanarayana) sarcasm when the latter offers him a change of clothing.[14]

At this point the film makes a brilliant attempt at depicting the agitated state of Duryodhana's mind. Recalling *Sri Krishna Pandaveeyam* but also the Kannada film-maker Puttanna Kanagal's use of colour lighting, loud non-diegetic voices, and jerky camera movements, the film shows Duryodhana haunted by Draupadi's laughter while multiple images of her laughing face trace dizzy circles.[15] The accompanying monologue, which went on to become one of the most popular "dialogues" (the word is used in Telugu to refer to monologues) by NTR, begins with "*Panchali, pancha bhatruka*" (Panchali/Draupadi, the woman with five husbands). Listing his achievements, he laments at how insulting it is for an emperor of his

[14] It may be noted in passing that Sarada and Satyanarayana went on to represent the TDP in parliament.

[15] Rajadhyaksha and Willemen (1999: 118) draw attention to the "very mobile, often highly subjective camera movements" in Puttanna Kanagal's work. A fine example of Kanagal's use of camera, light, and sound can be seen in the representation of the heroine's psychosis in *Sharapanjara* (1971). The film was remade in Telugu as *Krishnaveni* (V. Madhusudhana Rao, 1974), featuring Vanisri and Krishnam Raju.

160

161

Images 160–1: Film as property: *Karna*'s dedication (top) and the three NTRs.

stature to be laughed at by a woman, and one so low as to have several husbands. Parts of the monologue are addressed directly to the camera, as if presenting a case to the spectator (Images 162–8).

Duryodhana's monologue ends in the Kaurava palace with his brothers vowing to avenge the insult by destroying the Pandavas.[16] Karna offers to behead the Pandavas and make Panchali a slave. Shakuni (Dhulipala) suggests the game of dice, saying Dharma Raja (Yudhistara, played by Prabhakar Reddy) is addicted to gambling (*vyasanaparudu*).

The *vastrapaharanam* sequence—when the Kauravas attempt to disrobe Draupadi in view of the entire court—a regular attraction in most stage and screen renderings of the epic, is the turning point of the film. Draupadi comes across as a strong woman, contrasting with the weak and wavering Pandavas. Krishna now enters the story, performing the miracle of providing clothing to Draupadi. With this

Images 162–8: "*Panchali, pancha bhatruka . . .*"

162

[16] The transition is not noticeable in the DVD version and it is not clear to me if this is because some footage was edited out during digitization in order to limit the film to a single disc.

163

164

165

166

167

168

sequence the narrative focus shifts away from Duryodhana and Karna to Krishna as the agent of action. The shift is accompanied by a subtle but crucial change in the representation of Duryodhana, who, in spite of the elaborate justification he offers for ordering the disrobing of Draupadi, provides no explanation for the ethical objections raised by the latter to the game of dice and the attempt at disrobing her. The film skips narrating the Pandavas' exile and makes but one reference to the entire period by way of a scene devoted to revealing Draupadi's secret desire for Karna, and her hope that he too will become her husband.

The last of Duryodhana's speeches is made in the sequence when Krishna arrives at the Kaurava court as an emissary of the Pandavas. As such, the emphasis laid by *Karna* on this sequence is not in itself notable—numerous earlier films and plays had given it pride of place in their renderings of the epic. Bhrugubanda (2011: 58) points out that the second half of the film contains a number of *padyalu* sourced from the play *Pandava Udyoga Vijayalu* by Tirupati Venkata Kavulu. The first of the borrowed *padyalu*—which is also the very first poem in the film—is sung by Bhima when Draupadi is dragged into the court by Dussasana. In spite of the borrowings, Duryodhana's actions in general are presented as eminently defensible.

When the emissary Krishna enters the court, Karna is seen sharing the throne with Duryodhana. Krishna sings a *padyamu* to Drutarashtra, asking for five towns and warning him that war will destroy his dynasty. Karna objects to the tone of the message. All the elders present ask Duryodhana to agree to the offer. As Duryodhana listens on, Krishna sings another poem outlining the disasters that will strike him if the offer is not accepted. Duryodhana, refusing to be cowed down by Krishna's barely veiled threats, then responds. First, he points out that he cannot give away towns that are not directly under his rule (they have already been gifted away). Second, he argues, the Pandavas are not in fact his cousins because his paternal uncle Pandu was not their biological father. They do not share the same lineage at all. Moreover, he asks, if the empire were to be partitioned to each member of the extended family—the 100 Kauravas and the 5 Pandavas—how much would each one get? Surely such a partitioning was no good for the country (*desam*), which was *already divided along linguistic and cultural lines*. Therefore it was safer for people to remain united and be governed by a single ruler. Punctuating his speech with a brief *padyamu*, he concludes that he will give no land at all to the Pandavas.

The very next scene has Krishna hailing Karna as his cousin (*bava*) and revealing to him the secret of his birth. The revelation comes in the form of a flashback which ends with the box containing the infant Karna floating in the river (the point at which the film begins). In an exchange that is mostly in verse, Krishna offers Karna the highest place among the Pandavas and marriage with Draupadi. Karna refuses, stating that he has lived all his life as a low caste. He adds that he cannot accept his sister-in-law, who is like his own mother, as a wife.

During the Kurukshetra war the Pandavas, under Krishna's guidance, are seen resorting to unethical means to win over warriors on the Kaurava side. Abhimanyu (Balakrishna) is then introduced in a song with his wife Uttara (Deepa), who tries to dissuade him from going to the battlefield. The Abhimanyu sequences are among the few in the film when we do not see an NTR character on screen. When Drona proposes to Duryodhana that Karna attack Abhimanyu from the rear, Duryodhana hesitates for a moment before approaching Karna who, in turn, agrees with much reluctance to the violation of dharma. Karna breaks Abhimanyu's bow, and the youth is brutally killed by the Kauravas. That night Karna returns to the battlefield to search for Abhimanyu's body among the dead. Upon finding it he kisses it and says, "I should have blessed you as an uncle but caused your death instead." He then breaks down. Soon afterwards Subhadra (Kanchana) reaches the place with Uttara. Karna hides and watches Subhadra bemoan his violation of dharma. In a poignant scene she is shown in the background asking herself, unaware of his presence: "Karna, how could you have killed a child?" Karna is seen in the foreground of the frame, a focus light illuminating his face, weeping silently (Image 169). He then reveals himself and tells her: "Karna died on the battlefield today."

From this point, Karna's death becomes imminent; he becomes more and more tragic as the war progresses. As per Krishna's plan, Kunti meets Karna and asks him to spare the Pandavas. Karna refuses

Image 169: "Karna, how could you have killed a child?"

to accept her as his mother, but since he never turns away anyone he grants her a part of her wish: he will not harm any of the Pandavas except Arjuna. On the following day Karna spares all the other Pandavas, even as they slay his four sons. He says to himself, "Kunti, I have sacrificed my four sons to save yours." Prabhavati dies the next day and Karna sighs, saying he has lost everything while serving his master (Duryodhana). Soon after, he gives away his armour and earrings to Indra. On his final day on the battlefield his charioteer Selya (Mukkamala), instigated by Dharma Raja the previous night, insults Karna for his lowly origins and abandons the chariot when its wheel sinks on account of Bhoodevi's curse. When Arjuna critically injures Karna, Krishna says the guru, the Brahmin, Bhoodevi, Kunti, Indra, and Selya were responsible for his defeat—not Arjuna. Krishna then subjects Karna to a test to demonstrate to Arjuna the fallen hero's greatness. Disguised as poor Brahmins, they beg the dying Karna to make an offering of gold. He breaks loose a golden tooth with a stone, washing it clean with water from a spring that he draws out with his arrow. This is his last act of generosity. There is then a touching family union with the rest of the Pandavas and Kunti gathered around the dying Karna. The Pandavas now learn of their relationship with Karna who, finally, calls Kunti mother. Duryodhana then arrives and Karna once again demonstrates his love for him when he dies bidding him farewell. At this point Karna's story is over; the film continues.

The narrative focus once again shifts to Duryodhana, who is so saddened by Karna's death that he loses interest in the war. He does not *hide* in the pond, as the familiar story goes, but decides that he will perform penance underwater. He comes out of the water when unable to bear the insult of Dharma Raja offering to gift him half the kingdom. When he tells the Pandavas he will give up his claim to the empire, Krishna intervenes to say that he will have to fight one of the Pandavas. Duryodhana chooses Bhima. When he is about to slay Bhima, Krishna makes a sign that the latter should attack the thighs (against the rules of battle). Duryodhana falls and his reprimand to Krishna for violating dharma makes the latter flinch in shame. Duryodhana dies and his spirit is seen joining Karna's. The film ends.

Dana Veera Sura Karna and the Telugu Mythological

The film may be usefully compared with the box-office disaster *Kurukshetram* (1977), directed by Kamalakara Kameswara Rao, who had the reputation of being a master of the mythological genre. Produced by Krishna's Padmalaya Studio, *Kurukshetram* was a far more expensive production than *Karna*.[17] It is in many ways faithful to the conventions of the Telugu mythological film, as also the genre's interpretation of the epic. *Kurukshetram*'s narrative presumes audience foreknowledge of the story and focuses on highlighting particular moments without filling in the details or paying attention to transitions and plot-level connections between incidents. On the other hand *Karna*, which too works with spectatorial foreknowledge of mythology as interpreted by Telugu cinema, has a tightly-knit narrative

[17] Pulagam Chinarayana cited in http://www. telugucinema.com/c/publish/movieretrospect/retro dvskarna printer.php. Last visited on 2 December 2010.

and pays considerable attention to continuity between sequences and plot-level links between them. *Karna* also makes major digressions from the earlier screen interpretations of the Karna story and the *Mahabharata* in general.

In *Karna* it is Duryodhana/Suyodhana, and not Krishna or Karna, who has the best lines. Moreover, Suyodhana comes across as an advocate of caste reform as well as a forward-looking statesman who is worried about the territorial integrity of the empire. As we shall see, this interpretation of the epic is traceable to the influence of the early-twentieth-century non-Brahmin movement in Coastal Andhra. However, we also need to note that the mythological film has never been known for an *accurate* interpretation of the epics and puranas. On the contrary, the genre's primary sources are existing theatrical and filmed versions of mythologicals, not classical texts. Furthermore, as Prasad (n.d.) points out, the genre's representation of the mythological universe is thoroughly mediated by the social. He says in the course of his discussion of *Maya Bazaar* (1957 version):

> K.V. Reddy presents the *puranic* world as a consumerist utopia full of dazzling commodities and pleasures. Comedy, or the *hasya rasa*, remains the dominant mood of the film. The domestic scene is the setting for most of the action, away from the court, with its protocols and grandiloquence. Intimacy, domesticity, femininity, glamour, wonder, and sensuousness are the effects that the camera seeks to achieve. *Maya Bazaar* shows that the mythological as a genre develops in tandem with the other genres and is as often a social in costume as the social may be a mythological in modern dress. Reddy's version also shows how the exploitation of cinematic possibilities transforms a familiar narrative into a novel experience, affording a glimpse of the *puranic* world that is re-made in the image of the present. (Ibid.)

More recently Prasad (2011: 75) notes that *Maya Bazaar* inaugurated the trend in the Telugu mythological of borrowing elements from the social. The most notable among these was the comedy-track, which was already a standard feature of the 1950s social and now made an appearance in this film. Elsewhere, Prasad makes a more general argument about the affinities between the mythological and the social: "the genius of the Telugu mythologicals and the reason for their continued popularity lay in the adaptation of mythological content to the narrative form of the social. The mythological film was not only structured as a family melodrama, it also incorporated the standard features of the social, including the comedy track and the climactic fight scenes" (2006: 13). I should add that, even in the late 1950s, "mythological content" (Prasad's phrase) was thoroughly mediated by the innumerable filmed versions of the epics and puranas that were already in circulation. These in turn traced their origins to popular theatre.

Karna does not attempt to narrate the epic faithfully—as it was told and shown in the past. At the same time, it does not attempt to radically transform the mythological beyond recognition either. It is framed by spectatorial familiarity with the very generic conventions that it both relies on but also digresses from. Bhrugubanda notes: "The grand costume and jewellery worn by Duryodhana/Suyodhana along with a black train with figures of snakes embroidered on it and the giant sculpted sitting lion which serves as his chair in his ornate chamber were all first designed by art director, TVS Sarma in *Sri Krishna Pandaveeyam*. All of this was repeated in the 1977 film, *Dana Veera Sura Karna*. Much of the cast reprised their roles in the latter film and many scenes especially those involving Duryodhana's visit to the grand palace of wonders, Mayasabha commissioned by the Pandavas are reproduced almost frame by frame" (2011: 56n26).

In spite of its tight plot, the narrative of the film relies on viewers' familiarity with earlier screen mythologicals. Kunti (S. Varalakshmi), for example, is shown without any introduction whatsoever in the sequence when Karna is disqualified by Drona. She immediately recognizes him and weeps silently when he introduces himself as Radheyudu (the son of Radha) and a member of the Suta (charioteer) caste. *Karna* revisits the familiar and often highlighted sequences of the filmed versions of the Karna story, *inserting elements that facilitate a reinterpretation of those very sequences.* For example, in the Ekalavya sequence discussed above, the film inserts Karna and also has Arjuna gesturing to Drona, transforming the entire episode into a modern-day statement on the caste arrogance of the Pandavas and their teacher.

By the time *Karna* was made NTR was re-established as the leading star of the industry on the strength of the new social that was assembled to showcase his star persona. What then do we make of

NTR's choice to produce and direct a mythological film? What was left in and of the mythological that the social did not already offer a star of his stature? The film's explicit political statements—on caste oppression and governance as also the statist nationalism typical of the Emergency years—are at once striking and unusual for a 1970s mythological (Image 170). However, apart from flagging the influence of the non-Brahmin movement on NTR, there is little that can be claimed on behalf of the film's political critique: it tends to be conservative, like that of the star's socials.

The film's attack on casteism is a particularly interesting case in point, because it is traceable to a strand of (Kamma) non-Brahmin thought. Venkat Rao (2003) points out that NTR was influenced by the Dravidian movement and the mythologicals he produced tended to follow the interpretive framework of non-Brahmin intellectuals like Tripuraneni Ramaswamy Chaudhury and Narla Venkateswara Rao (both were Kamma by caste). For this reason, the biographer adds, the stories of mythologicals produced and directed by NTR have story lines which deviate from standard versions of the epics (2003: 26).

Non-Brahmin influences are borne out by *Karna*'s portrayal of Suyodhana and Karna, as also the film's critique of caste, which, as pointed out by Venkat Rao, is traceable to Tripuraneni's work. Known as Kaviraju (King of Poets), Tripuraneni was a major intellectual figure of the early twentieth century.[18] He was a rationalist and reformer whose influence is argued to have been an important factor in the spread of communism among the Kammas and Reddys of the Coastal Andhra region.[19] Uma Ramaswamy notes his rather provocative claim that his reinterpretations of the epics, being in fact revelations from the half-Kshatriya and half-Brahmin sage Suta, had the credibility of

[18] His son Tripuraneni Gopichand was a reputed leftist intellectual and short story writer whose contribution to Ramabrahmam's films we have noted. In the early 1950s Gopichand directed three films. The other important non-Brahmin intellectual to have been associated with the film industry was Tapi Dharma Rao, who too was credited in Ramabrahmam's *Raitu Bidda* and *Malapilla*.

[19] For a comparison between Tripuraneni and other major South Indian non-Brahmin intellectuals of the early twentieth century, namely "Periyar" Ramaswamy Naiker and Narayana Guru, see Hanuman Chaudhury (2011: 4).

Image 170: Karna speaks out against the treatment of Ekalavya.

other epics and puranas (Ramaswamy 1978: 294). She points out: "In *Kurukshetra Sangramam* . . . he argues that the Kauravas were in fact more upright than the Pandavas, and that the latter had no right to rule." Also relevant for understanding *Karna* is Tripuraneni's non-Brahminism, which was deeply problematic as a critique of caste: "He claimed that the Kammas, Reddis and Velamas were Kshatriyas and superior to [other] Sudra non-Brahmins such as Golla, Kummari, etc" (ibid.: 295).[20]

Given this lineage, the film's critique of caste is understandably inconsistent as an anti-caste statement. Duryodhana, in spite of his moving speech on casteism early in the film, refers to Krishna

[20] The extent of NTR's investment in the non-Brahminism of the Tripuraneni variety is also evident from the report that the marriage of his daughter, Bhuvaneswari, and N. Chandrababu Naidu (later chief minister of Andhra Pradesh) was performed by a Kamma-Brahmanudu, a Brahmin/priest of the Kamma caste (Online 2010: 23). Under Tripuraneni's influence, the Kammas of Coastal Andhra mastered marriage rituals and mantras and performed the marriages of non-Brahmins.

as a cowherd (*pasuvula kapari*) late in the film. Anti-caste rhetoric within it is also centred on a highly conservative sexual morality of colonial vintage; this is foregrounded in Duryodhana's *Panchali, panchabhatruka* monologue, as also Karna's comment against polyandry when he says the sister-in-law is like a mother. Emergency political sentiments—underscored in Duryodhana's refusal of Krishna's peace offer—were in any case liberally sprinkled in the NTR socials of the period. It is thus pointless to suggest that a mythological had to be made to propagate fairly commonplace nationalist slogans and arguments for a strong state.

The Language Question

The reason why we should be examining the film's representation of Duryodhana is not so much for the content of his speeches but their high-sounding Telugu. The language is meant to sound classical, timeless, and as distant from ordinary speech as ever attempted on film. *Karna* uses this register of Telugu with such consistency that even the most menial servants speak in it.

Bernard Bate's discussion of *medaitamil*, "platform Tamil" or "oration" which characterizes Dravidian parties' political campaigns, throws light on the register of Telugu that sets Duryodhana's speeches apart in this film:

> Though Tamil oratory (*medaitamil*) is relatively new in South India, the Dravidianist (or Tamil nationalist) style suggests an ancient mode of speaking by its use of archaic forms of Tamil modeled principally on the written word. During the first half of the twentieth century a first generation of political orators in Tamil addressed audiences in halls and streets in what Tamil people call "ordinary" (*nadaimuri*), "bent" (*kodun*), or "vulgar" (*kochai*) Tamil. With the advent of mass democratic politics in the 1940s, orators shifted from such common registers of spoken Tamil to a speech genre called "fine" or "beautiful" Tamil (*centamil*) in an elocutionary revolution: this new, archaic, and distinctly literary mode of speech distinguished the new democrats who deployed it from a previous generation of relatively plainspoken politicians. (2009: xv)

Bate points to the inherently paradoxical nature of the deployment of archaic Tamil for wholly modern forms of politics. The constituencies it addressed were likely to be less educated than those that were spoken to in vulgar Tamil by an earlier generation of politicians. But then, "When politicians spoke in a literary and archaic Tamil, they embodied ancient kings and gods addressing their people in heroic orations that had no historical antecedents" (ibid.: xvi). This mode of oratory was the means of making a claim on representing a linguistic culture, argues Bate: "To speak, then, in a highly stylized and literate genre on a populist stage was to embody an imagined past of a pure and ancient Tamil civilization" (ibid.). Bate says *medaitamil* was assembled by Dravidian politicians and did not pre-exist politics at all (ibid.: 31). Indeed, "The fateful move the Dravidian speakers made was to transform literary discourse into political propaganda" (ibid.: 34). Once it was in place, the refined Tamil of political oratory facilitated a range of distinctions:

> What we have called the *centamil* revolution embodied a "proper" distinction between leaders and the people, a political distinction between the DMK and the Congress Party, and a civilizational distinction between the Dravidian and the Indo-Aryan civilizations. A new, archaic, feminized, literary, and therefore "proper" mode of speech was markedly different from the ordinary speech of people in their everyday lives. It was distinguished from the plain speech of a previous generation of Congressmen and people like Periyar E.V. Ramaswamy of the DK (who was decisively not engaging in party politics). And Dravidianist orators became avatars of Tamil itself, of its purity, its virginity, and its antiquity. As far as the vast majority of Tamilians were concerned, the Dravidianist paradigm embodied Tamil tradition, and in so doing invented it. (Ibid.: 183)

In light of Bate's work it is possible to better appreciate the breakthrough achieved by *Karna*, as also note the crucial differences between equivalent forms of Telugu and Tamil. Political discourse in Telugu within and outside the cinema had no equivalent with *medaitamil*. While the Telugu of mythologicals was always easily recognized as "fine" and "refined," till *Karna* was made there was no association between such Telugu and political critique or propaganda. Whereas in the case of Tamil it was the domain of political mobilization that was the primary site for assembling a neoclassical variant of the language which was later deployed in films, in Telugu it was the cinema, drawing on the theatre, which was the site for the production of an archaic-sounding register of the language.

There is of course no denying the parallels between the Tamil of the DMK propaganda film and *Karna*. Compare, for instance, the famous courtroom speech by Gunasekharan, the Sivaji Ganesan character in *Parasakthi* (Krishnan-Panju, 1952). As in other DMK films, we notice here the deployment of rhetorical and elevated language—an aural treat even to those like me who cannot understand what is being said—to make a sweeping critique of the powers that be and the court itself.[21] As in *Parasakthi*, Duryodhana's speeches in *Karna* are in a register of language that is meant to stand out and draw attention to itself. The voice modulations, rhythms, and cadences of the utterance, the awesome ability of the actor to fluently speak interminable lines and impossibly difficult words are sources of spectatorial pleasure.

Karna creates a hierarchy between the *padyalu* it borrows from a well-known play and the speeches of Duryodhana in order to showcase the latter. Whereas *padyalu* were among the genre's highlights in the stage versions of mythologicals, as also most mythological films before *Karna*, in this film there is a noticeable shift of emphasis away from *padyalu*. This is particularly striking in the sequence when Krishna arrives at the Kaurava court to demand five towns. The film inverts the priority given by the mythological to *padyalu* and places Duryodhana's memorable speech after Krishna sings a number of verses. Duryodhana has only one verse in the entire film, while even Bhima has two.

T. Vishnu Vardhan (2006) notes that low camera angles enhance the prominence of the speaking star during Duryodhana's speeches. Each speech runs into multiple shots in which the camera angles are changed but the focus remains the star. There are moments when the star turns away from the camera, only to be seen facing it in the next shot. As pointed out earlier, the film continuously revolves around the multiple roles of NTR, often transiting from one sequence to the next by cutting from one NTR character to another. With the exception of a song and some scenes in the story of Abhimanyu, the only instance when the film does not feature an NTR role in the action is the

[21] See Pandian (1991) for a useful summary of this speech, as also a detailed discussion of the film and its contexts of reception.

cabaret-type song depicting the decadence of Selya (and starring the Bombay cabaret specialist Helen, known as Halam in Telugu). During the rest of the film, screen space is constantly occupied by NTR.[22] Spectatorial attention shifts from Karna to Duryodhana to Krishna and back to Karna and Duryodhana. As Bhrugubanda (2011) points out, the spectator is not allowed to forget that the speaking subject is NTR, the star. Just as NTR the star fully occupies the screen space, his *voice* too occupies pride of place on the soundtrack.

Drama Rao and his Mythological Speech

I propose the phrase *mythological speech* to describe the deployment of a non-colloquial, "classical"-sounding Telugu to authenticate public and political criticism, and discourse. Of utmost significance for our purposes is the theatricality of mythological speech—the fact that it is quite literally traceable to the theatre and sound film, and not to some ancient or traditional practice. Arguably, among the earliest instances, if not the very first, mythological speech is by the Duryodhana character in *Karna*. My notion of mythological speech does not merely underline the surprising—and unprecedented—surfacing of political criticism in the Telugu mythological. It is not even meant to underscore the dubious anti-Brahminism and nationalism of this film. Indeed, *mythological speech is not about the content of political discourse at all but its authentication by the deployment of a (pseudo/neo) classical Telugu that originates in the cinema itself.*

The deployment of mythological speech in *Karna* is evidence of a new node of convergence between film and (audio) recording industries, which had in any case been intimately related since early sound film.[23] In the late 1970s LP records of both songs and film dialogues were widely circulated in Andhra Pradesh. The increased

[22] According to the film critic Pulagam Chinanarayana, NTR is seen on the screen for 4 hours of the total running time of 4 hours and 17 minutes. Cited in http://www.telugucinema.com/c/publish/movieretrospect/retro_dvskarna_printer.php. Last visited on 2 December 2010.

[23] In the context of Tamil cinema, Hughes (2007) argues that the music recording industry mediated the relationship between film and drama in the first half of the twentieth century.

circulation of LP records—soon to be replaced by audio cassettes—coincides with the reduced importance of songbooks, which since the earliest days of the talkie were an important means of dispersing songs and *padyalu* beyond the cinema hall. The historical importance of the songbook for the Telugu talkie is indexed by the printrun of the booklet of the 1936 version of *Maya Bazaar*, whose back cover states that 75,000 copies were printed in Madras. I have come across an instance of the publication of NTR's speeches in the form of a booklet: his lines as Ravana in *Bhukailas* (1958) were printed in one such (details unknown). The success of *Karna*'s attempt to foreground the star's voice on the soundtrack is evident from the popularity of the film's dialogues: they had a phenomenal circulation on LP records and, some years later, audio cassettes. Mimicry artistes, both amateur and professional, recited Duryodhana's speeches for years to come. As we shall see in the next chapter, the audio cassette would become a ubiquitous presence during NTR's election campaign in 1982–3.

Karna was made at a time when elements of the mythological, a film form on the decline, began to be re-housed in the social. Mythological speech is located at the cusp of distinct but related migrations within the domain of cinema and between film and politics. With hindsight it is possible to suggest that an attendant consequence is the emptying out of the mythological film and its eventual extinction. The immediate use Telugu cinema found for mythological speech was as an object of parody in *Yama Gola* (T. Rama Rao, 1977), the hit film in which the NTR character (Satyam) finds himself in Yamalokam. In this film high-sounding language and political critique, the twin attributes of mythological speech, are associated with two different characters. Yama (Satyanarayana) is a character whose high-sounding speech recalls the mythological film while Satyam satirizes the deployment of a highly rhetorical Telugu for political critique. Bhrugubanda (2011: 64) notes how Yama in the film becomes a butt of the protagonist's jokes. Satyam himself, an honest and energetic village president while alive, sets about organizing the workers of Yama: they are, as we saw earlier, overworked on account of an increase in the numbers of sinners in *Kaliyugam*. Political speeches made by Satyam to Yama's workers parody Communist platform rhetoric in formal and stilted Telugu. Over hilarious sequences Satyam trains Yama's workers in agitational politics. When they elect him leader, he raises a slogan in his own praise: "*Viplava karmika nayakudu, veera comrade Satyam . . . zindabad.*" ("Long live the revolutionary workers' leader and heroic comrade Satyam;" Images 171 and 172). Interestingly, the film's parody of Communist parties does not dilute its direct and repeated criticism of the Emergency. First, Yama's rule is compared to the Emergency. While the workers march in protest Satyam sings: "*Yamudi niramkusa paalana vaddu/ Yama-urgency maakika vaddu*" (No more of Yama's anarchic rule/ no more Emergency for us; Image 173).[24] Later in the film there is a reference to the *yuva neta* (young leader, Sanjay Gandhi) and his mass sterilization programme.

While the character of Yama and the idea of Yamalokam are subjected to critical interpretation, there is nothing in *Yama Gola* to suggest that *Karna*'s deployment of classical language for political critique was anything but a one-off occurrence as far as the cinema was concerned.

Even outside the cinema, mythological speech found uses only much later. In 1982, as he kicked off his long election campaign,

Images 171–3: "Revolutionary leader and heroic comrade Satyam" mobilizes workers against "Yama-urgency" rule in Yamalokam. NTR's body language and gestures during the parody are strikingly similar to those of his platform speeches in 1982–3.

171

[24] This song, "*Samaraniki nede prarambham*", is by Sri Sri.

172

173

NTR gave the impression that he had walked out of the screen and into the electoral contest. He did not attempt to distance himself from the cinema or foreground his charitable activities (which were in any case rather modest in scale and achievement). Indeed, the electorate was never given a chance to forget his association with the cinema. His campaign was marked by his distinctive Telugu—of a kind that no one actually spoke off-screen and that he alone made famous on-screen. The language he deployed was rhetorical, alliterative, and spoken with pauses and modulations of voice that were glaringly theatrical. He had evidently discovered the utility of mythological speech as a political resource retrospectively, a good five years after *Karna*'s success. While his "classical" Telugu set him apart from everyone else, his critics were quick to trace the origins of his campaign style to the theatre—more accurately, to the stage mythological. NTR had not deployed some obscure classical variant of Telugu in the political arena but a method of language-use assembled by the film industry. This performative idiom, which marked his campaign, was strongly associated with acting style in mythologicals, a style shunned by the realist 1950s social. In short, the star-turned-politician carried over to the election campaign a mode of excessive performativity deriving from theatre and mediated by the cinema (Images 174 and 175). He was nicknamed Drama Rao (Venkat Rao 2003: 58), and the masses who gathered to participate in Drama Rao's rallies were dismissed as *cinema janam*—crowds of film viewers.[25]

NTR is known to have become completely immersed in his own histrionics. This was as true of his film career as of his speeches. Narayana Naidu, one of his biographers who accompanied him during some of his earliest political rallies, recalls NTR's first public meeting in Tirupathi when "He [NTR] was overwhelmed with joy at the love and affection of the crowd and spoke for one hour. He became more and more emotional when he saw the arrival of crowds from all directions" (1995: 40). The biographer has nothing to say about the content of the speech.

[25] The phrase *cinema janam* appeared frequently in press reports of statements of NTR's critics including the last Congress chief minister before the 1983 election, K. Vijayabhaskar Reddy (Newstoday 1982c: 1).

174

175

Images 174 and 175: Mythological speech: Duryodhana's gestures during the *Panchali pancha bhatruka* monologue (top) and a typical NTR gesture at an election rally.

Theodor Adorno's analysis of post-war fascist demagogues in the USA offers valuable insights into NTR's performance style, which combined theatrical speech and exaggerated bodily gestures on the electoral platform. A disclaimer is in order here: I am not suggesting NTR was a fascist. Although he was often called one by the radical left and by civil liberties activists, this is not an accurate description of his politics. In spite of the fact that he became increasingly authoritarian after his re-election in the 1985 mid-term poll, there are good reasons why the term fascist should not be loosely used to describe him. NTR was no rabble-rouser and his public speeches—in spite of his general disregard for democratic norms—were remarkably free of hatred for the out-group. Unlike the quintessential fascist, he did not depend on fear to mobilize people. His contempt was singularly focused on the Congress party. By referring to Adorno's argument when discussing NTR I wish to draw attention to the performative dimension, both on and off screen, as an object of critical-analytical attention. Although Adorno himself did not attempt to extend his analysis to include non-fascist political mobilizations, I suggest that his discussion illuminates electoral and other political mobilizations as well. What is not of immediate interest to my argument is Adorno's characterization of the demagogue as a hysterical or even paranoid type of personality, or even his point about the successful transference of the orator's own "neurosis and even mild lunacy" and other "psychological defects" to his listeners, whose personalities are structurally similar to their leader's (Adorno 1994: 223). Of immediate interest to me is Adorno's question: "what does [the] rapport between leader and followers in the propaganda situation consist of?" (ibid.: 224). Adorno revisits Freud's (1921; rpt 1985) argument about the role played by love in determining the relationship between the leader and the group that he leads by adding a new element—gratification to the listener by the leader's performance. Adorno's comparison between certain varieties of political propaganda and mass cultural forms such as soap opera is particularly interesting:

> . . . this type of propaganda functions as a gratification. We may compare it with the social phenomenon of the soap opera. Just as the housewife, who has enjoyed the sufferings and the good deeds of her favourite heroine for a quarter of an hour over the air, feels impelled to buy the soap sold

> by the sponsor, so the listener to the fascist propaganda act, after getting pleasure from it, accepts the ideology represented by the speaker out of gratitude for the show. "Show" is indeed the right word. The achievement of the self-styled leader is a performance reminiscent of the theatre, of sport and of so-called religious revivals . . . (Adorno 1994: 224)

His formulation of a relationship between the enjoyment of soap opera and the purchase of the soap is dubious, to say the least. However, whether or not soap is actually purchased does not dull the sharpness of his larger argument. His point is that soap opera, listener, and sponsor's product are linked in a circuit of exchange. The purchase of the soap is the means by which the listener is expected to express her satisfaction for the gratification offered via a good cry. Similarly, the fascist's speech sets up a trade-off or exchange between an entertaining performance and political support.

As with the fascist demagogue and the soap opera of Adorno's analysis, NTR's public meetings—obviously and deliberately centred on his skills as a performer—set up a direct connection between the emotionally charged performances of the star, the consequent gratification offered by the (political or theatrical) performance, and donation of political support by the spectator-participant. It is as if the gathered masses were being offered an entertaining performance in order to give them the chance of expressing their satisfaction and gratitude to the entertainer with their vote. Whether or not they went along and voted for him is immaterial for my argument—the issue is the exchange they were invited to be a part of.

The masses at NTR's political rallies are the mirror opposite of what Vasudevan terms "the melodramatic public," arguing: "If melodrama in Indian popular film constructed a subjectivity at once personalized and public, it also addressed its audiences in crucial ways as public rather than individuated" (2010: 43). Film thus addresses its audience as if it were a political community, a stand-in for it. Speech in the Indian popular film "suggests that it is aimed at an audience beyond the one presented within the fiction" (ibid.). As for the speaking subject, "The publicness of character derives from the idea that the subject is constituted in and through an address to the audience. This is relayed through 'public' modes of performance and *mise en scène* which the excess acting, acting conventions, and setting impart to a character's narrative functions" (ibid.: 44). In NTR's rallies the focus is not on transition from film spectatorship to political community (electorate/nation). Here the listener-participant is already part of a large group that has been assembled for explicitly political purposes. The political subject is addressed as if he were at the movies, or returned to the cinema, whose pleasures the biggest star of the industry recalls from the political platform.

What was the utility of NTR's campaign films for his campaign? Campaign films did not address their spectator as someone credulous who was likely to believe that the star was a saviour in real life. S/he was acutely aware that the hero, whose heroines were growing younger by the decade, was an old man with a painted face. No attempt was made at an image makeover to make NTR more presentable to the electorate. His sexually charged songs, including their risqué lyrics focused on heroines and cabaret specialists, were retained in his campaign films, even as his age and suffering were now foregounded via the roles of older men. These films did not contain propaganda; instead, they offered a variety of *cinematic pleasures* and the campaign itself carried over some of these pleasures into the domain of politics (Images 176 and 177).

There is a fusion of excessive performance of the here and now, and intertextual references to mythological films featuring the star himself in *Justice Chaudhury*. Unlike *Bobbili Puli*, which in the heat of the election campaign could be read as an attack on the government (and therefore the Congress party), *Justice Chaudhury* does not lend itself to being read as a critique of politics. During the song "*Chattaniki nyayiniki jarige ee samaramlo*" the insertion of clips from mythological films featuring the star is accompanied by another gesture towards the genre. There is a parallel between the acting and emoting styles of the mythological and this film. NTR's facial expressions, gestures, sudden movements of the body, and the camera angles recall the Duryodhana character during his speeches in *Karna*. Likewise, *Bobbili Puli*'s courtroom speech, an emotionally saturated performance during which political criticism is made in a rhetorical and elevated Telugu, is as close an approximation to mythological speech as is possible in the social's temporal frame. The mode of performance at issue here is not exclusive to the mythological film but is a feature of much

176

177

Images 176 and 177: NTR with Sridevi (above) and cabaret specialist Jayamalini (below) in *Vetagadu* (1979).

Indian popular cinema. Vasudevan (2010) terms this melodramatic and argues that the style is marked by hyperbolic facial expressions and coded gestures; the "character performs for us rather than *is* us" (ibid.: 261). NTR's mythological films are arguably among the finest examples of melodramatic acting style in Indian cinema and, moreover, our star had carried over this acting style to the social by the late 1970s.

Although campaign films featured a protagonist whose ability to deal with narrative crises was a foregone conclusion, these NTR films were increasingly marked by their emotional charge. In two of the campaign films I have discussed, the patriarch played by the star dies (*Sardar Paparayudu* and *Kondaveeti Simham*). In another he is awaiting death by hanging (*Bobbili Puli*). In a fourth he is forced to choose between saving his blind daughter's marriage and upholding the law (*Justice Chaudhury*). In these four films the protagonist's pain and suffering find expression in his tears. For example, *Sardar Paparayudu*'s rebel, jailed for crimes he did not commit, is taken in chains by the police to cremate his wife (killed by the villains). During the sequence the focus is entirely on Paparayudu's sorrow. This mode of establishing an emotional bond with the spectator, who vicariously feels his pain and cries with him, carries over to some of his later work, including *Chanda Sasanudu* and *Major Chandrakant* (K. Raghavendra Rao, 1993).

What kind of a community could be adequately represented by this film star? Weber's definition of the nation is usefully recalled to understand the nature of community formation that NTR's campaign films facilitated: "In so far as there is at all a common object lying behind the obviously ambiguous term 'nation,' it is apparently located in the field of politics. One might well define the concept of nation in the following way: a nation is a *community of sentiment* which would adequately manifest itself in a state of one's own; hence, a nation is a community which normally tends to produce a state of one's own" (Weber 1946: 176). Of interest to us is not state formation but the "community of sentiment." If one sociological consequence of NTR's stardom is the formation of fan associations, another is the formation of spectatorial collectives bonded by the sheer emotional and performative excess of his films. What NTR's election campaign did was, first, misrecognize and misname this community of sentiment before the screen, formed by its engagement with the cinema, as the Telugu nation. The second part of the crucial manoeuvre that transformed our film star into the linguistic nation's representative was to ensure the replication of an affective community—quite literally a collective formed by its emotional response to a set of issues presented before it—in the domain of politics. The two-step process of the leakage of his film career into his political career can thus be summarized as follows: in the cinema hall, "we" were formed by our response to his excessive/vulgar/gratifying on-screen performance. Some years later "we" were interpellated as members of a nation because we wept together and with our screen patriarch, *and* because the campaign itself was in some critical ways an extension of the experience of the cinema.[26]

Das Gupta indicates the foundational role of cinema to NTR's politics: "Asked about his policies as Chief Minister in 1983, NTR said: 'You have seen the film (*Bobbili Puli*). There is a man who always sides with the wronged sections of the people. So naturally there is sympathy for the hero. That is the style of role I perform. So that people expect good things to come of my service to them'" (1991: 225). No matter how limited the star's own understanding of politics may have been, we should not read this statement literally. Regardless of the actual campaign, which came later, the campaign films are about community formation around the cinema, not particular political issues or party agendas. As we saw, by the late 1970s the cinema had emerged as a cultural form potentially capable of addressing Telugus across regional divisions. The election was going to be won or lost on the basis of whether the electorate—addressed as the Telugu nation—could rise to the occasion and prove that it was indeed bonded by affect.

Mythological Film after the 1983 Election

The 1983 election had the effect of transforming the Telugu mythological film in unexpected ways. In 1984 NTR returned to a

[26] How the latter move was accomplished will be discussed at some length in the next chapter.

project that had been initiated in 1982 and timed the film's release to coincide with his second election campaign (the mid-term poll in 1985). This film, *Srimad Virat Veerabrahmendra Swami Charitra* (NTR, 1984), was based on the life of a backward caste saint, Potuluri Veerabrahmam. The subject matter of the film makes it an obvious candidate for classification as a "saint film"—a variant within the devotional genre (*bhakti chitram*)—which had a considerable history and prestige in Telugu but also Tamil and Marathi and was made intermittently in Telugu till the 1970s when it, too, faded in the wake of the social's dominance.[27]

NTR returned to *Karna*'s mode of deploying classicized Telugu for political critique in *Charitra*, which depicts the saint's life and times.

The genre hybrid that NTR assembled—and would have used in his 1982–3 election campaign had he managed to complete *Charitra* as originally planned, was at once saturated with mythological speech and devoid of *puranic* content. In *Charitra*, whose protagonist made predictions about the future, including some that NTR apparently interpreted as anticipating his own rise to political power, we are presented with a saint who is divinely endowed with the ability to see into the future.[28] His authority is underscored by his mastery of Telugu: not speech alone, but also the verses in which he made his predictions. By this time the Telugu mythological was otherwise

[27] See Kapur's (1987) discussion of the landmark saint film *Sant Tukaram* (V. Damle/S. Fattelal, 1936). This film was remade in Telugu as *Bhakta Tukaram* (V. Madhusudhana Rao, 1973), featuring ANR and Anjali Devi, and was among the last major Telugu saint films before *Charitra*. See Bhrugubanda (2011: 75–102) for a discussion of contemporary saint films in Telugu.

[28] Das Gupta sees a direct link between the making of this film and NTR's decision to enter politics: "Early 1982, the superstar of Telugu films was asked to play the role of this astrologer, Veera Brahmendra Swami, in a film about him. He was given a book of predictions to read, in preparation to playing the role of its author. Poring over it, superstar N.T. Rama Rao came across a line predicting that around that period, 'a man with a painted face will rule Andhra.' He sat up and exclaimed: 'But that is me!' Within a few weeks, he had formed a party, *Telugu Desam* (Telugu Country), named after the language of the state . . . " (1991: 221).

more or less dead. NTR alone revisited the genre in the 1990s with the express intention of producing campaign films. *Charitra* was the last commercially successful film NTR produced and directed. Post-*Charitra*, he acted in just one social, which he did not produce or direct (*Major Chandrakant*). In his own films he played the roles of historical figures, both Telugu and non-Telugu. For example, he played the lead in *Samrat Ashok* (NTR, 1992) and acted in his home production *Srinatha Kavisarvabhauma* (Bapu, 1993), based on the life of the fifteenth-century Telugu poet Srinathudu. He also played the role of the eponymous mythological character in *Brahmarishi Vishwamitra* (NTR, 1991).

As for his speeches, I will discuss their importance for the 1983 election in the next chapter; but here I draw attention to his very last political action: the production of an audio cassette whose title "*Jaamataa–Dasama Grahaha*" is a proverb that translates as "Son-in-law is the 10th planet," meaning he brings bad luck like the planets (the text of the speech is reproduced in Appendix 1, Lakshmi Parvathi 2004b). Shortly before his death, NTR was left with a minority splinter of the party that he had created in 1982. His isolation was the result of a revolt staged under the leadership of his son-in-law, N. Chandrababu Naidu, in August 1995, just a year after the star had led the TDP to a third electoral victory. In poor health and with few political allies standing by him, NTR recorded on audiotape the "act of betrayal" by Naidu and appealed to the people for their support. He died of a heart attack on 18 January 1996, before he could release this cassette. To the very end, his faith in the infallible power of his speech to move the masses remained unshaken.

5

The 1983 Election

Paper Tiger and Telugu Nation

Having seen the role played by the cinema in making NTR a politician, it is time to examine his election campaign in 1982–3 and ask how his film and political careers overlapped. NTR's campaign was a watershed event, one that is well worth re-examining in order to understand the transformation of Indian elections by the mediation of the media. The 1983 election to the Andhra Pradesh legislative assembly has been the subject of commentaries by social scientists, journalists, and political observers. I draw on this considerable body of literature, even as I foreground its major limitations in accounting for the role played by mass cultural forms—the cinema and newspapers, and to an extent audio cassettes—in creating equivalences between otherwise unrelated events, entities, and collectives.

What has never been in doubt is the importance of the 1983 election for politics in Andhra Pradesh, and for India as a whole. From 1983, the party that NTR established in 1982 was in power for sixteen years and to this day it continues to be a major player in Andhra politics. NTR also played a key role in the formation of the rainbow coalition that defeated the Congress (I) in the 1989 general elections. Almost immediately after the 1983 election, social scientists declared that the Andhra Pradesh and Karnataka assembly elections, held simultaneously in January 1983, marked a "shift in Indian politics" (contributors to Mathew, ed. 1984), one that resulted in the gradual decline of the Congress (I)'s domination of Indian politics. Balagopal argues that the election marked the rise to political power of the "provincial propertied class."[1] He traces NTR's origins to

> a class that is predominantly (but by no means exclusively) Kamma by caste and agrarian in its origins, which came of age in the period of the nationalist movement and the agrarian struggles against the Zamindars and the British Raj. These struggles that attended its birth have also given it the largest share of participation in radical movements: socialism, rationalism, atheism, communism, and Radical Humanism—you name the heterodoxy and they have seen it. Over the period, they have also grown substantially rich, and have multiplied their riches since the Green Revolution. But while wealth has come their way, they have been systematically kept out of the prime seats of power at Hyderabad. They lost it symbolically when they had to concede the name Visalandhra (in favour of the Hindi-ised Andhra Pradesh) for the state for which they fought the hardest, and had to simultaneously concede their demand for making Vijayawada the capital city; and they lost it substantially as part of the general "Congress culture" of keeping the economically dominant classes and communities in the states away from the seats of political power. (1984: 1901)

NTR's political ascendance needs to be situated against the background of the growing economic clout of the agricultural castes. As Guha notes:

> The commercialization of agriculture and milk production had benefited a significant section of farmers in rural India. Crucially, economic gains had converted themselves into political ambition. In the 1960s it was these rising rural castes who came to dominate the state governments in northern India. By the 1970s they had made their presence felt in national politics . . . After the 1977 Lok Sabha elections, 36 per cent of all members of Parliament came from farming backgrounds, up from 22 per cent in 1952. Their impact was felt in the rural orientation of the government's economic policies, as it was in the ever higher procurement price paid by the state for wheat and rice. (2007: 532–3)

It is apparent that the arrival of NTR the politician implicates the Telugu cinema and film industry quite directly in the ascendance of

[1] A class whose increased economic and political visibility had been noted earlier by Omvedt (1981).

erstwhile Presidency peasant-turned-entrepreneurs to the centrestage of politics.

The importance around NTR of caste and the rapid crystallization of Kamma interests, which were already substantial in the film industry, are both evident. Prominent Kamma supporters and members in the early days of the TDP included the former Congressman Nadendla Bhaskar Rao, credited with playing a critical role in the formation of the party; P. Upendra (later central minister); and Ch. Ramoji Rao, the editor-in-chief of *Eenadu*.[2] At the same time, Srinivas, *et al.* (1984) examined the candidates nominated by the TDP in the 1983 election and concluded that there was far *greater* social diversity in the party's list than Congress's. Although the number of Kamma candidates fielded by the TDP was higher than by the Congress, the former party also nominated an equally large number of Reddy candidates (see Table 6.1 in ibid.: 115). There were also a substantial number of backward caste candidates, which is interpreted as signalling a shift of the backward castes away from the Congress.

Where in this framework of caste calculations and class alliances do NTR's Telugu nationalism and stardom fit? George Mathew argues that whereas the Congress divided the people along ethnic lines, playing on their insecurities, in Andhra Pradesh and Karnataka intense "primordial sentiments" centred on linguistic affinities of the respective electorates were mobilized by the TDP and the Janata Party respectively (1984: 168–9).[3] Ratna Naidu, who too subscribes to the primordiality thesis, says: "Clearly NTR appealed in these speeches [where references are made to historical and literary figures] to the

[2] Whose role in the election I examine at length, below.

[3] Karnataka witnessed a major agitation in 1980–1 demanding the implementation of the recommendations of the Gokak Committee which included making Kannada compulsory in schools and the knowledge of the language an essential requirement for employment in the government service. Among the notable features of the Gokak agitation, as it was called, is the participation of the Kannada superstar Rajkumar which resulted in the expansion of the agitation and led to violent incidents, attributed to his fans. George Mathew (1984) points out that the Karnataka Kranti Ranga, formed by Devraj Urs who left Congress (I), had supported the Gokak agitation and also aligned with the Janata Party.

primordial instincts of the electorate" (1984: 133). She also discusses a pamphlet consisting of seven colour pictures of NTR in mythological and historical roles (Krishna, Karna, Bhishma, Veera Brahmendra Swamy [the film on the saint was under production], Sri Krishna Devaraya, Sri Rama, and Brahma Naidu (ibid.: 133). This pamphlet, we learn, highlights the characteristics of these figures and makes comparisons between them and the star. Elder and Schmitthenner (1985) similarly draw attention to this pamphlet, whose images they reproduce. Considering that the references to the linguistic-cultural domain during NTR's campaign were so thoroughly and obviously mediated by the star's acting career, I shall here reject the view that there was anything *primordial* about the invocation of mythological/historical/literary figures. What then was the nature of the Telugu nationalist claim being made by NTR? And how was it advanced?

Shifting the focus of the discussion on NTR's Telugu from primordiality to cinema, Uma Bhrugubanda argues that "NTR's screen image was able to provide the ingredients for legitimizing his representative claims and the forging of the Telugu identity. It was not as if a Telugu identity did not exist before—it did and had indeed provided the basis for the political struggle that led to the creation of the first linguistic state in 1953; however, in the eighties NTR revived it as an unfulfilled and pressing political demand and who was better suited to enunciate this demand than one who already embodied Telugu identity—NTR!"(2010: 61). Her suggestion that NTR's campaign shows continuities with the invocation of Telugu identity in political mobilizations of the 1950s is questionable. Balagopal argues rather more forcefully that there is nothing in common between NTR's Telugu nationalism and earlier articulations of it:

> We therefore have NTR proclaiming to the world about the "injury done to the Telugu pride," and everybody taking it for granted that such injury has indeed been done, and NTR represents the revival of Telugu nationalism against it. So much has been written about this revival that one is forced to stop and look around for it, and in vain does one do so. Telugu nationalism has had a rather long innings, from the first decade of this [twentieth] century till the end of the fifties, its dying embers were stoked by the agitation of the late sixties for a steel plant at Vishakhapatnam, but by the end of the sixties it had died a natural death

> and there has been no revival or reason for revival since no more injury has been done to the Telugus qua Telugus than to any other of the principal linguistic groups of India. (1984: 1901)

At issue for our purposes is not whether actual, empirically verifiable historical wrong or injury is an essential condition for the rise of nationalism. Even assuming that 1982–3 witnessed the revival of the passions of 1952–3 simply because during both these periods mass mobilizations happened in the name of Telugu, there is still no denying the discontinuities between them. It was earlier noticed that the inclusion of Telangana in 1956 resulted in a political-geographical entity that did not quite "map" with the demands articulated by Presidency Telugus, who conceived an Andhra state in relation and contradistinction to Presidency Tamils. The conditions for the articulation of a discourse on a Telugu country which included Telangana became available only in the late 1970s.

NTR's interpretation of Congress rule (especially its attempts at undermining federalism) as an affront to "Telugu pride," and therefore the basis for a Telugu nationalist political critique of the ruling party, is also puzzling. The political scientist K. Srinivasulu (1994) correctly notes that NTR defined Telugu nationalism as "anti-Congressism." The TDP itself is something of an exception among "regional" political parties, i.e. parties whose appeal is limited to linguistic or other constituencies within one particular state. The singularity of the TDP has been commented upon by another political scientist, K.C. Suri: "Unlike Shiromani Akali Dal, National Conference, Dravida Munnetra Kazhagam (DMK), Asom Gana Parishad, Shiv Sena, etc., the TDP did not emerge as a result of any long-drawn struggle or sustained social movement. When it was launched it had no leaders trained in any ideology or not many leaders who lived through the rough world of politics" (Suri 2004: 1481). Uma Bhrugubanda's reading of the NTR phenomenon via Ernesto Laclau's (2005) discussion of populism helps us understand the rise of the star-politician and his immaculately conceived party. As an instance of populism, notwithstanding its singularity, the TDP's rise is part of a truly global political phenomenon. Laclau says: "by 'populism' we do not understand a *type* of movement—identifiable with either a special social base or a particular ideological orientation—but a *political logic*" (2005: 117, original emphases). This logic creates equivalences between disparate sectorial demands to produce a unified front of the "people" or "race" or "nation." Compare, in our context, this with Balagopal's observation about the convergence of the interests and aspiration of the agrarian rich and the poor: the common people were apparently "utterly disgusted with the vulgar depravity of the Congress (I) leaders of the state and whose disgust . . . remained unfocused for a long time . . ." (1984: 1901).

Particularly useful about Laclau's notion of populism is his insistence that it *constitutes* identity through acts of representation: "the popular symbol or identity, being a surface of inscription, does not *passively express* what is inscribed in it, but actually *constitutes* what it expresses through the very process of its expression. In other words: the popular subject position does not simply *express* a unity of demands constituted outside and before itself, but is the decisive moment in establishing that unity" (ibid.: 99, original emphases). Bhrugubanda argues that NTR's artîculation of Telugu identity created a chain of equivalences between diverse groups:

> This contingent and historical mobilization of the Telugu identity helped to articulate a series of equivalential demands like the dissatisfaction with upper-caste Congress politics dominated by the party at the Centre; the political and economic aspirations of the *[K]amma* caste; demands for equality being made by the women's movement and other middle level and backward castes; all of these were forged together by a Telugu regional and cultural identity which could be posed against the north-Indian, Delhi-based Centre. (Bhrugubanda 2010: 61)

Laclau argues that popular identity constituted by populist reason has two important features. First, the demands made on its behalf are internally split between sectorial interests and universalist claims they spring from (2005: 95). To take the case of "the Telugu race" of NTR's campaign, his election speeches typically begin with sweeping statements on the betrayal of the Telugu race and end with very context-specific promises (such as better roads, or more jobs in a particular district). Second:

> The more extended the chain, the less these signifiers will be attached to their original particularistic demands. That is to say, the function of

> representing the relative "universality" of the chain will prevail over that of expressing the particular claim which is the material bearer of that function. In other words: popular identity becomes increasingly full from an extensional point of view; for it represents an ever-larger chain of demands; but it becomes intentionally poorer, for it has to dispossess itself of particularistic contents in order to embrace social demands which are quite heterogeneous. That is: a popular identity functions as a tendentially empty signifier. (2005: 96)

Thomas Blom Hansen's argument (2004) about political performativity has some parallels with Laclau's analysis of populist reason. Hansen too stresses the "here and now" of representation in his discussion of the local leader who "seeks to become a tangible embodiment of the 'community' or the locality he seeks to represent—or better still, he tries to express and create community and locality through the very act of representation" (ibid.: 22). In order to make the act of representation itself the object of study, he proposes the notion of *political performativity*, which comprises "the construction of images and spectacles, forms of speech, dress and public behaviour that promotes the identity of a movement or party, defines its members, and promotes its causes or worldview" (ibid.: 23). NTR had an extremely vague and all-encompassing notion of who the Telugus were; and Laclau notes that vagueness and imprecision of discourse are inherent within populist mobilization: "in a local struggle I can be relatively clear about both the nature of my demands and the force against which we are fighting. But when I am trying to constitute a wider popular identity and a more global enemy through an articulation of sectorial demands, the identity of both the popular forces and of the enemy becomes more difficult to determine" (Laclau 2005: 98–9).

Laclau's analysis also helps us to avoid the common mistake made by commentators that NTR's success had to do with populist welfare promises. Agendas that may be termed "welfarist," or even the promise of short-term economic relief, were necessary but not essential accompaniments of the campaign, which was empty of substance. In the initial stages of the campaign NTR had virtually no agenda, let alone even a welfarist plan, except a nebulous intent to cobble together the Telugu race. This comes across in the pamphlet issued at the time of the formation of the TDP (Rama Rao 1982). The pamphlet is in the form of a direct address by NTR to the Telugus and is titled "*Naa Manoratham*" (meaning: "my wish"). In it he lists the achievements of the race and juxtaposes past glory with the pathetic conditions in which Telugus now live: poverty everywhere, prices of agricultural commodities low while fertilizer prices rise (i.e. farmers are immiserized), essential commodities are adulterated, women are not safe in public places, and so on. Balagopal would have said none of these problems were specific to the Telugus. NTR's pamphlet then goes on to accuse the "Delhi *sarkar*" for this state of affairs and concludes that he is disturbed by this state of affairs and has decided to fulfil his responsibility to Mother Telugu (*Telugu Talli*). He will now dedicate his life to tell the world of the greatness of the race and give the Telugu people a new life of happiness and peace.[4] The pamphlet thus promises nothing and everything. The appeal to Telugu self-respect is easily translatable into a federalist critique of the Congress party. As for the substantial and material benefits on offer, the famous "two rupees rice scheme" which promised the poor subsidized rice was first made in June 1982, about two months after the party was formed (Parvathi 2000b: 33), possibly in response to the criticism that the party had no policies and programmes.

NTR's Switch to Politics: The Timeline

Although NTR did not make public his intention to enter politics till 1980, his political career shows some parallels with that of MGR. MGR joined the DMK in 1953 and his first fan club was established that same year (Hardgrave, Jr., 1979: 121). It is useful to recall here that the cast of *Patala Bhairavi* had toured various Andhra regions in 1951, when scores of people in the crowds that gathered to see them were injured in police cane-charges (Pandurangarao 1951: 40, see chapter 2 above). Venkat Narayan (1983: 6) notes that NTR was the first Telugu actor to take up charitable activities, which he began as early as 1952. Three instances show him raising money by staging plays featuring himself and his film industry co-stars. In 1952 he raised funds for drought relief in Rayalaseema, in 1965 for the National Defence Fund during India's war with Pakistan, and in 1977 for the

[4] I am grateful to Sekhar Yalamanchi for drawing my attention to this pamphlet.

Andhra Cyclone Relief Fund for victims of the cyclone that affected large parts of Coastal Andhra (ibid.: 6). The timing of the 1965 and 1977 fund-raisers is interesting. Venkat Narayan does not mention another well-publicized donation of Rs 10,000 made to Coastal Andhra flood victims in October 1964 (reported in *Visalandhra*, 6 October 1964: 5). As we have already seen, a major felicitation of the star was organized in Vijayawada in October 1964. The 1960s efforts were, at least in part, reactions to ANR's emergence as a champion of Telugu interests in the industry, as also to the criticism of what was then seen as NTR's pro-Madras stance. The last in Venkat Narayan's list occurred a few months after MGR became chief minister of Tamil Nadu. The cyclone in question was responsible for temporarily arresting the growth of the Telugu film industry.

MGR's election as chief minister was preceded by twenty-four years of involvement in politics, first as a DMK member, then as a member of the legislative council (MLC) and of the legislative assembly (MLA), and as founder of the ADMK (Hardgrave, 1979; Pandian 1992). Forrester's (1976) study of MGR, covering just the five-year period from his re-election as MLA in 1971 to 1976 (when the DMK government was dismissed and president's rule imposed in the state), shows how active the star was on the *political* front, and how much of a professional politician he was. By comparison, NTR's decision appears unpremeditated. He did not identify with causes that could be termed political and had no known association with any party. His biographers and political analysts alike point out that the announcement of the decision to form the TDP was preceded by some suspense. Although the air was thick with rumours, which NTR's comments triggered, there was a considerable gap between the press meet during the shooting of *Sardar Paparayudu* (1980) and the formal announcement of his arrival in politics on 21 March 1982 (the TDP's formation was announced on 29 March 1982). N. Innaiah claims that NTR's decision to enter politics coincided with the removal of Chenna Reddy as chief minister in 1980, and was a result of a suggestion by his son-in-law, the Congress MLA, N. Chandrababu Naidu (1986: 179). Sekhar Yalamanchi, who was NTR's press secretary during the election campaign, says the star had in fact planned to join politics when he retired from acting upon turning 60 in May 1983. However, he was persuaded by Nadendla Bhaskar Rao, the Kamma Congress MLA who went on to become a key NTR advisor in 1982–3, to advance the date of his political entry by a year in order to be able to contest the assembly election due in 1983 (Sekhar Yalamanchi, interviewed by the author, Hyderabad, 3 February 2008). All agree that the star had not openly expressed interest in a political career before 1980.

Between 1980 and March 1982 he was mostly in Madras, busy with the shooting of some of the most successful films of his career. While the election campaign can be said to have begun almost immediately after the party's formation, the real action began in June 1982, with his extensive tour of the state. Over the next six months, NTR was the centre of the largest mass mobilizations in post-Independence India in any of the regions that were now a part of the Andhra Pradesh state, and in possibly the rest of the country as well. In August 1982 a van owned by his Ramakrishna Cine Studio was refurbished and named Chaitanya Ratham (Chariot of Awakening). On this *ratham*, driven by his son Harikrishna, he toured the state by road many times over. According to Venkat Narayan, "Between June 14, when Rama Rao set out on the first phase of campaign tours and January 3, when he arrived at Tirupathi to make the last speech of the campaign, he had travelled for a total of 70 days, reaching every nook and corner of the state and covering a total distance of 35,000 km. He was seen and heard by an estimated three crore people, a record for the history books" (1983: 9). Lakshmi Parvathi (2004b: 46) claims that between October 1982 and January 1983 NTR travelled twenty-one hours a day. Venkat Rao (2003: 56) says he toured the state three to four times over and covered close to 40,000 kilometres. Lakshmi Parvathi also cites a BBC report aired on 21 December 1982 stating NTR had covered a greater distance and addressed more people in such a short period of time than anyone else in the world. His biographers note that in the years to come a number of "national-level" leaders—including L.K. Advani on his infamous *rath yatra*—adopted NTR's mode of mobilization and named their vehicles rath(am)s.

Situating NTR's First Campaign: "Decline of the Congress"

In order to appreciate the significance of NTR's election campaign, it is necessary to situate it in the context of political developments in the state. The political scientist Atul Kohli argues that "The rise of NTR is best understood as a 'negative' political phenomenon—i.e., as a consequence of the earlier decline of the Congress" (1988: 993). K.C. Suri agrees, albeit with some modifications:

> One thing is clear. NTR launched his party at the most opportune time. The Congress Party was in complete disarray. The Congress electoral support base had already shrunk to dangerous levels by the time of 1978 assembly election . . . People were extremely dissatisfied with Congress misrule, corruption, inefficiency, and rampant factionalism. But the non-Congress opposition was fragmented, their leaders were too mired in their own old thinking to inspire people, lacked the will to rule, and too exhausted to take on the Congress. It appeared as if the state was in search of an alternative new political formation. NTR fairly grasped the situation, immediately seized the opportunity and persuasively articulated the people's sentiment. (Suri 2004: 1483)

How "people's dissatisfaction" and "people's sentiment," as also the shortcomings of unnamed opposition leaders, can be spoken of with such certitude in academic discussions is not explained, but Suri's larger point is clear enough. N. Innaiah goes so far as to present the TDP victory as a foregone conclusion and titles his chapter on the formation of the TDP "Telugu Desam: Born to Win" (1986: 178–82). Venkat Narayan's description of the times is equally dramatic: "Things slumped into their nadir. This was precisely when Nandamuri Taraka Rama Rao jumped into the political fray. For 33 years, rattling his sword in film after film, the superstar of the Telugu cinema played the unsparing overdog who punished the guilty and rewarded the innocent. His people were in distress. Clearly, it was time to switch roles from a reel-life hero to a real-life hero" (1983: 51). NTR was not in fact to be found sword-rattling in his more recent films, but the exaggeration captures the star's lack of political experience. Venkat Narayan also has a chapter titled "A Procession of Faceless Men" (ibid.: 38–45) in which he discusses Congress chief ministers from 1978.

Kohli sums up the thesis on the TDP victory in the 1983 election that was echoed by journalists and political scientists before and after him: "Most observers of Andhra politics suggest a familiar story: Congress's decline was caused by repeated and increasing intervention from the centre. Between 1978 and 1982, for example, Indira Gandhi installed four different chief ministers in Andhra. None of these men had any significant, independent political base. Rather, they were all appointed because they had proven their 'loyalty' to Indira or Sanjay Gandhi" (1988: 993). How accurate is the "familiar story?" In spite of the neatness with which NTR arrives in these accounts to occupy his place as the agent of narrative and political progress, this story, of the rise of TDP against the backdrop of the Congress (I) on an auto-destruction mode, is of dubious worth as political analysis. M. Shatrugna (1984: 98) points out that it was not the Congress (I) alone that was routed in the 1983 election "but also the opposition parties like the Janata, BJP, Lok Dal and of course the CPI and CPI (M)." The claim that Congress (I)'s vote share had "shrunk to dangerous levels" (Suri 2004: 1483) is partly correct in that it came down from 52.3 per cent in 1972 to 39.2 per cent in 1978. But in 1967 Congress only had 45.1 per cent of the vote share (cited in Kohli 1988: 993). So in the decade from 1967 the overall decline is around 6 per cent. The reason for the fall in vote share in 1978 may not have had to do with state politics at all. Let us not forget that the 1978 election came in the wake of the Emergency. The ramifications of the Emergency were felt even in the state, although the Congress was returned to power in 1978. As Kohli notes, the Janata Party—formed as the direct fallout of the Emergency—won 60 of the 74 opposition seats and became the biggest opposition party in Andhra. Innaiah points out that a number of Congress (I) sitting MLAs and ministers were defeated (1986: 154). That the Congress retained power even in 1978, in spite of the Janata Party's challenge, is noteworthy, and can be read as a sign of the party's resilience.

The rapid change of chief ministers—among NTR's most repeated criticism of the Congress, reiterated by various observers—was an integral part of the party's strategy to manage the opposition as well as internal factions during Indira Gandhi's period. Without suggesting that Congress rule in Andhra Pradesh was unique in any respect, N. Innaiah's description of developments from 1978 to 1983, despite the author's subscription to the "decline of Congress" thesis, offers a valuable insight into what Congress rule meant at the state level. He points out that virtually all the major leaders who emerged from the 1950s were in and out of the Congress in the 1970s and 1980s, when Indira Gandhi consolidated her power over the party. These include the three former chief ministers K. Brahmananda Reddy, M. Chenna Reddy, and K. Vijayabhaskar Reddy (the last two were in office between 1978 and 1983). Typically, these leaders left the party after their replacement but subsequently returned to the Congress. Interestingly, K. Brahmananda Reddy, chief minister of the state 1963–71, is quoted by Kohli (1988: 994) making a damning criticism of the Congress party under Indira Gandhi—but he too returned to the Congress later.

Arguably, the Congress stayed in power by adopting a two-pronged strategy: ensuring that the states did not throw up charismatic leaders, and winning over opponents. The pattern remained unchanged from the late 1960s, and a textbook illustration of the strategy's success is Chenna Reddy's remarkable career. After his election to parliament had been nullified by the supreme court (Innaiah 1986: 114), he became an important leader of the movement for the formation of a separate Telangana state by joining the Telangana Praja Samiti (TPS) on 22 May 1969. Under his leadership the TPS became a political party in 1970, winning ten parliament seats out of seventeen in the Telangana region in the 1971 general election. Later the same year Chenna Reddy, his supporters in tow, returned to the Congress and became a union minister (ibid.: 119–21). In 1978 he became chief minister of the state and proved an exemplary Congressman: he brought over almost the entire opposition into the Congress fold. During Reddy's rule over seventy MLAs crossed over to the Congress, including the lone member of a Naxalite party. Chenna Reddy also bankrolled the party, which was voted out in most states (ibid.: 158). After the 1980 parliamentary election, when the Congress was back in power in Delhi, he was removed as chief minister because he was becoming too powerful. Two years later he resigned, once again from the Congress, formed his own party in 1984, and briefly aligned with NTR (ibid.: 168). In yet another turnaround, he returned to the Congress some years later and brought it back to power in 1989. The Congress (I) thus neutralized all rival centres of mobilization by incorporating them into its fold. It had no use for state-level leaders once they were in the party fold because the sole agent of mobilization and source of authority was Indira Gandhi. The so-called "vacuum" at the state level that Kohli and others claim NTR filled was not a result of mismanagement by Indira Gandhi but intrinsic to the model of managing the party in the regions. It worked well for years on end.

The Mobilized Masses of Andhra Pradesh

Why then did the Congress lose out? Mobilizations that were centred on political parties and electoral politics were a part of a problem that the Congress under Indira Gandhi had handled remarkably well from the late 1960s. I suggest that NTR in 1982–3 was part of another problem altogether: namely, the *entropy of the political subject* that was constantly displaying its propensity to form a mass in the course of multiple and (only) occasionally overlapping axes of mobilization. From the Srikakulam movement in 1967, Andhra Pradesh witnessed a series of agitations and mobilizations involving large numbers of people. In the post-Emergency period, Naxalite groups became increasingly important players in localized mobilizations of tribals, lower castes, unorganized workers, students, etc. New constituencies, such as Dalits, were assembled from older ones. The prominent axes—caste, occupation, region, and language—do not fully account for the tendency which was established even before NTR arrived on the scene and continued long after his election. But it is undeniable that there was a proliferation of mobilizable constituencies and of agents engaged in their mobilization.

In 1983 NTR appeared to benefit from this propensity of political subjects to gather into a mass. But soon enough he was engaged in a desperate attempt, one that was marked by increasing doses of state violence, to contain diverse mobilizations. Balagopal notes: "Instead of the single-minded Telugu nationalism that his promoters promised, what has resulted from five years of NTR's rule is a fractious and violent polity" (1989: 67). Early signs of the shape of things to come appeared almost immediately after NTR's election when the agrarian rich—not just the Kammas but the larger peasant class–caste constellation that the Kammas were a part of—began to launch attacks on the restive rural poor.[5] An important political watershed was the "Karamchedu massacre" in 1985, when a large group of Kammas attacked Dalits in the village of that name, killing six of them (Balagopal 1985; Murali 1995): coincidentally, this is the village from which D. Ramanaidu left for Chennai to start his brick business. The Dalit Mahasabha was formed in the aftermath of the Karamchedu massacre.[6] Dalits had thus emerged as a distinct political category (from the earlier category of "Scheduled Castes").[7] However, in almost exactly a decade the Dalit category came under severe strain on account of the Madiga Reservation Porata Samiti's (MRPS) demand for the classification of Dalit castes according to their socio-economic status for the purposes of reservation. Although this was often referred to as a "sub-caste" issue among the Dalits, the fact is that the Madigas are a caste while "Dalit" is a political category.[8] My point is that the proliferation of constituencies, and not the so-called return of caste, affected the Dalit movement too.[9]

In the years after his election in 1983, the NTR government

[5] On 5 January 1983 (election day) there was an attack on the Dalits of Padirikuppam village in Chittoor district. Eighty houses were set ablaze and four persons killed (Balagopal 1985: 1299). Three of the dead were non-Dalit Telugu Desam supporters captured by the Padirikuppam Dalits and killed in retaliation (Special Correspondent 1983: 215). Balagopal notes these attacks were neither restricted to any particular region of the state, nor were they perpetrated by any single dominant caste. Locally powerful dominant castes, including Kammas, Kapus, and Reddys, were responsible (1985: 1299).

[6] Balagopal observes: "Springing straight from the Karamchedu killing, the Dalit Mahasabha was formed, inaugurated formally at Chirala on September 1, 1985. Its first convention was held at Tenali on February 16 and 17, 1986 and today it is an active and growing movement" (1987c: 1378).

[7] For a history of Dalit literary and cultural assertion in the state, see Satyanarayana (1995).

[8] See Kumar (2001) for a discussion of "reservations within reservations" and the so-called "sub-caste" issue among the Dalits.

[9] See Balagopal (2000) for a discussion of the conflict between the Dalit Mala-Madiga castes in Andhra Pradesh and the mobilizations of both castes against and for the caste-wise subdivision of reservation quotas for Scheduled Castes.

came under attack from Naxalite groups, Dalit organizations, and also Kapunadu—the forum rallying members of the Kapu caste(s) against the TDP.[10] Andhra Pradesh also witnessed a major agitation by upper-caste students against the government's decision to extend reservations to backward castes (Balagopal 1986b: 1572–4). The anti-reservation movement was modelled on student agitations in Gujarat and anticipated the anti-Mandal agitation in 1990. NTR's long election campaign thus marks a moment of intensification in the post-Emergency era of mobilizations, when collectives were assembled by agents on the political Left, Right, and Centre. The question before us is: what did the cinema have to do with any of this, and how?

Convergence: Peasants, Cinema, and Print

The 1983 election was arguably the most "mediatized" to be held anywhere in India till that point. In a study of the audio cassette boom, Peter Manuel notes: "The 1989 general elections marked something of a watershed in Indian politics. For the first time since Independence, the Congress Party, which had hitherto dominated the central government (with the brief and aberrant exception of the Janata coalition period of 1977–80), suffered a decisive defeat, reflecting a fundamental and irreversible structural decline. Second, the 1989 elections can be said to have been the first in which the mass media—and especially audio- and video cassettes—played a

[10] "Kapu" is not a single caste. Balagopal points out that the term Kapu meant husbandsman and also meant hardworking cultivator (1989: 66). There are innumerable and distinct Kapu peasant castes, including the Balija, Telaga, Mudiraj, Tenuga, Toorupu Kapu, and Munnur Kapu. "A cinema hall and rice mill owner like Mudragada Padmanabham, a publisher and film-maker like Dasari Narayana Rao and a mafia gangster like Vangaveeti Mohana Ranga Rao, Cong(I) MLA from Vijayawada" were key figures in the mobilization of the Kapus of the Krishna and Godavari delta regions against NTR (Balagopal 1989: 66). Vangaveeti Mohana Ranga Rao, summarily dismissed by Balagopal as a gangster, was a charismatic Robin Hood figure engaged in assembling disparate Kapu castes into a single political constituency. He floated Kapunadu, whose name was derived in the TDP annual meeting or Mahanadu. His murder in December 1988, allegedly by TDP supporters, led to large-scale rioting and looting in Vijayawada and other Coastal Andhra towns.

significant partisan role" (1993: 243). Had Manuel's study not been entirely focused on North India, he would probably have said more or less the same thing about the 1983 assembly election in Andhra Pradesh, when the Congress lost the assembly elections in the state for the first time, and not least because it was an election in which the media—the newspapers and to an extent audio cassettes—truly arrived on the political scene.

NTR's campaign marks a qualitative shift: the election itself became a media event, a form of mass entertainment. It received saturation coverage in the Telugu newspapers and, for a state election, extraordinary national and international attention. The newsworthiness of the campaign was in part a consequence of NTR's performativity. But in Andhra Pradesh, in addition to every other contributing factor that can be identified, the election was at the cusp of a convergence between industrial cultural forms Overlapping investments and constituencies of the cinema and newspaper industries in the state were coming to the fore, even as the spread of a "cassette culture," as Manuel would have it, was leaving its mark in the public domain. Contemporary commentaries on this election alert us to the convergence of media forms and cinema, as also the ubiquitous presence of the audio cassette. From Ratna Naidu's essay (1984) we learn that cassettes recalled the work of early-twentieth-century literary figures like Gurajada Apparao and Kandukuri Veerasalingam, and that they retold, in *burra katha* format, the story of the peasant rebel Alluri Sitarama Raju: "Interspersed with such songs and *burrakatha* [*sic*], the cassettes recorded NTR's speeches in which he lamented that in the land where Gurajada had left his footprints, the land which is soaked in the blood of Alluri . . . and more recently Potti Sri Ramulu and Prakasam, a land which had produced such poets, social reformers, and heroes, now has leaders who are selling its pride and prestige and self-respect on the streets of Delhi" (1984: 132–3). Elder and Schmitthenner (1985), pointing out that NTR made excellent "use of the media" (ibid.: 381), add:

> One of his [NTR's] most frequent techniques was to prepare cassette recordings, with excerpts of his voice from the soundtracks of some of his approximately 300 films, interspersed with speeches from him indicating that he would implement those moral, ethical, and religious values which

> he had advocated when representing a deity or hero on the silver screen. *The cassettes were so produced that it was sometimes difficult to tell whether it was N.T. Rama Rao, the larger-than-life god or hero, who was speaking . . . or N.T. Rama Rao, the film-star running for political office, who was speaking.* These cassettes were distributed to villages, where they would be played over a loudspeaker mounted on a moving cycle rickshaw or scooter, displaying a large picture of N.T. Rama Rao, with Shaivite markings on his forehead. (Ibid.: 381, emphasis added)

The cinema was a constant referent during the campaign. The element of wonder in Elder and Schmitthenner's description is lost when we recall Hardgrave, Jr.'s observation on MGR that "The [star's] films are filled with references which blur the role and the actor into one" (1973: 299). From film theorist Richard Dyer's examination of Hollywood stars we can see that the play between what he calls "star-as-image: star-as-real-person" is a feature of stardom there as well (Dyer 1991: 135–6).

What then was the notable element in the campaign? Such was the popularity of NTR's speech-making style, which had already acquired a market beyond the cinema hall in the wake of *Karna*, that enterprising businessmen recorded his speeches at rallies and sold them as cassettes (Lakshmi Parvathi 2004b: 33). The pamphlet that Naidu and Elder and Schmitthenner discussed was in fact sold during the election, not distributed freely. Propaganda thus dovetailed into consumption in a rather immediate sense. There was a whole economy of films, cassettes, and publications around the election. We notice the spillover of the film star and the *cinematic*—as objects of consumption—beyond the spaces of film exhibition; so also the contiguous spaces of fan activity (street corners and other public spaces in the vicinity of cinema halls) blending into political mobilization. Such an expansion of the cinema's constituency and the dovetailing of the cinema with politics could not have been possible without the mediation of the audio cassette. But print, itself on the verge of becoming a key stakeholder in politics, was by far the more important player.

Historically, even before 1982 both cinema and print had been important spheres of investment by peasant entrepreneurs. The print industry in the state was not entirely controlled by peasant castes but had a sizeable presence of entrepreneurs of this constellation—since the days of Gudavalli Ramabrahmam and later the BNK Press controlled by Nagi Reddy and Chakrapani. From the 1970s print was transformed, the technological and economic foundations of its transformation being studied as a part of Robin Jeffrey's work on what he calls the "newspaper revolution" (1997 and 2010). As we shall see subsequently, the establishment of *Eenadu* in 1974 was a paradigm-changing development. However, the "revolution" was not limited to newspapers.

In the post-Emergency period, there was an explosion of low-priced periodicals, which included "yellow" journals that published shocking and sensational stories on public figures—politicians and film stars in particular. Soft pornography dovetailed into political activism in a rapidly expanding menu of publications which Balagopal (1987b)—in a crucial essay documenting their confrontation with the political establishment during NTR's regime in the late 1980s—termed the "yellow virus." The political fecundity of the post-Emergency period no doubt facilitated the growth of a whole cottage industry of sensationalist magazines; Balagopal estimates the number of such periodicals at two dozen since the early 1980s. In the years preceding the formation of the TDP, the legendary yellow journal *Encounter*, run by Pingali Dasaratharam from Vijayawada, emerged as the trendsetter of the yellow press. Dasaratharam, whose father Pingali Venkaiah designed the Indian national flag, was a rationalist, prolific writer of pamphlets, and a novelist (Images 178, 179, and 180).

Encounter set new standards in political journalism by carrying pictures of politicians on its cover and referring to them as pimps, bastards, eunuchs, and so on.[11] These would be accompanied by unsubstantiated reports on the corrupt activities of the public figures in question. The journal's editor was murdered during NTR's rule (Balagopal 1987b: 1022), it being widely rumoured that this was

[11] Balagopal offers the following sampling of what he terms the mass obscenity of popular political journalism: "For instance, a news item about a Congress leader trying to get a Telugu Desam ticket would run somewhat like this: 'That well known eunuch who pimped faithfully for the Nehru family all these years now wants to get into the brothel house [legislative assembly] at Hyderabad by licking NTR's behind" (1987b: 1022).

Images 178–80: Pingali Dasaratharam's novels and pamphlets. 178: *Chaavu* (Death), a novel based on the Padirikuppam incident (discussed earlier); 179: *Sexlo Moodhanammakalu* (Superstitions about Sex); and 180: *Vishasamskrutilo Stree* (Woman in Poisonous Culture), a "historical analysis, a shout from prison" written during his incarceration in the Emergency period.

178

179

180

a direct consequence of an article he had written on the sexual promiscuity of a powerful minister's daughter. There was, however, no shortage of candidates wanting to do him in, for Dasaratharam had to his credit dozens of other stories which had made him—to put it euphemistically—unpopular with political leaders even in the pre-TDP days.

Throughout the 1980s *Encounter* and its sister journals endorsed various political formations while also launching attacks on established political figures. *Encounter* was among the few periodicals (newspapers included) which openly sided with Dalits in the wake of the Karamchedu massacre. Other publications sided with Kapunadu and its chief organizer, Vangaveeti Mohana Ranga Rao. Balagopal attributes the growth of this sector of the print industry to the increasing numbers of urban neo-literates from the 1970s, and credits Ch. Ramoji Rao, the owner of *Eenadu*, with discovering this emerging market. He believes that the yellow virus was in fact traceable to *Eenadu*'s style of reporting, because "the paper is uncompromising in not distinguishing between facts, rumours, wishes, suggestions and innuendo" (ibid.: 1023). I will add, on a less stridently critical note, that the hallmark of *Eenadu*'s house style was arresting headlines in colloquial Telugu, which in the decades to come became characteristic of all Telugu newspapers.[12]

The thrust of the new journalism in Telugu—both mainstream and underground—was to show the political establishment as thoroughly corrupt, inefficient, and contemptible. This mode of representing the political leadership had by then found cinematic equivalents, most notably in the genre locally known as the red film, but even the films of major stars had villainous politicians. Between the cinema and print, therefore, there were convergences at the level of political economy, emerging markets, and thematic and representational concerns. It was during NTR's election campaign that the extent to which politics became the business of the culture industries became clear. Anticipating the shape of elections to come, the campaign was thoroughly mediated by the consumption of a range of media and cultural commodities, including newspapers, yellow journals, films, film magazines, and audio cassettes. I would therefore propose that the representational domain became the new front for waging the electoral battle *because media consumption was also the site of electoral mobilization*. We need to recognize that the election campaign had moved away from the propaganda model of finding instrumental uses for cultural forms. On the contrary, it was framed by the materiality of media forms and the pleasures they offered.

The public domain was saturated with NTR, and this was not entirely due to the effectiveness of the TDP's propaganda machine.

[12] The deployment of non-literary language was not unique to *Eenadu* or Andhra Pradesh. As Jeffrey points out, it was a technique adopted by newspapers across the country in their attempt to address newer constituencies (2010: 100).

Film magazines carried reports and pictures of NTR's new releases. Cinema halls, naturally, showed the latest NTR films, as also re-runs of the star's past hits as local distributors re-released old films to cash in. On the streets, audio recordings of his speeches and dialogues from his films played interminably. Newspapers—even those whose managements openly sided with the Congress (I)—were full of news and pictures of the campaign or what his opponents had to say about NTR.

The resilience of NTR's campaign against editorial censure comes across with much force in *Andhra Jyothi*'s coverage (Images 181

Images 181–2: Resilience against editorial censure on account of the newspaper's revenue model. Campaign film advertisements: *Justice Chaudhury*'s 150-day run (*Andhra Jyothi*, 24 October 1982: 8), and *Naa Desam*'s release, scheduled for 27 October (*Andhra Jyothi*, 10 October 1982: 8).

181

and 182). By the late 1970s film advertisements were an important source of *Andhra Jyothi*'s revenue, taking up entire pages on a daily basis. Apart from the paper's reliance on film advertising, which ensured that it was regularly plastered with images of NTR from his latest films, such was the consistency and regularity with which NTR made symbolic gestures that it was inevitable for at least some of their iconicity to be transmitted through the paper's reportage. Photographs proved to be a particularly important means for this "leakage." The star campaigner was eminently photogenic, in a manner of speaking, because of the performativity of his actions. For instance, he chose to address a meeting standing next to a Gandhi statue that he garlanded in a small town. And of course *Andhra Jyothi* carried a picture (26 October 1982: 6). While NTR's unique campaign style returned the electorate to the cinema, *Eenadu* in particular and other newspapers to an extent ensured that the election was *narrativized*, further underscoring the performative dimension that the star himself foregrounded. *Eenadu* systematically assembled an idiom of reportage that was at once blatantly partisan, captivating, clever, funny, and perfectly resonant with the theatrics of our star. It was, as we shall see, yet another level of the convergence between the cinema and print.

182

A Newspaper and the Telugu Nation: The *Eenadu* Story

Eenadu was established in 1974 by Ch. Ramoji Rao, a Kamma entrepreneur from Krishna district. It became the largest selling Telugu newspaper by 1979, published simultaneously from Visakhapatnam, Hyderabad, and Vijayawada. Jeffrey says: "*Eenadu*'s origins are popularly ascribed to chit funds (savings funds) and pickles" (1997: 193). Ramoji Rao began his career at the All India Radio, Delhi, and moved to advertising before starting Margadarsi Chit Funds in Hyderabad in 1962: "Margadarsi Chit Funds became the base for an array of other enterprises, including a pickle company, hotels and eventually *Eenadu*" (ibid.). Ramoji Rao's trajectory is remarkably similar to that of other Kammas of his generation who moved from the village to the city and from a primarily agricultural background to a variety of businesses, including films, within a short span of time. Recall here the career of D. Ramanaidu, who relocated from the village of Karamchedu to Madras, moving from agriculture to bricks and real estate to films in the 1960s.

The rise of *Eenadu* coincided with the fall of *Andhra Patrika*, the nationalist newspaper established in 1908 (ibid.: 192).[13] Among the factors that Jeffrey (1997 and 2010) and Uma Maheswari (1999) identify for the success of *Eenadu*, two were of relevance even in the early 1980s: an emphasis on local news and issues "seen as newsworthy for the first time," and "skilful business and marketing strategies" (ibid.: 73). Both authors draw attention to the strategy of establishing editions in places which had no prior history of newspaper publication. Ramoji Rao started the first edition of *Eenadu* in Visakhapatnam, where newspapers published from Vijayawada reached only in the afternoon. The initial print order of the Visakhapatnam edition was 4000 copies; by 1976 it had increased to 48,000 (Jeffrey 2010: 83). In 1980, the paper established its own news agency, called Newstoday, with as many as 1400 contributors (Maheswari 1999: 74). Most contributors were

[13] *Malapilla* is dedicated to the founder of *Andhra Patrika*, Kasinadhuni Nageswara Rao, a Brahmin Congressman who was a mentor to the journalists of Gudavalli Ramabrahmam's generation.

"stringers" or part-time employees paid by the column-inch, but the scale of its newsgathering network was impressive by any standards. By 1982 Ramoji Rao owned English and Telugu publications, including the largest circulated Telugu film magazine *Sitara*. By getting into film production (1984) and distribution he went on to become an important player in the entertainment business after NTR's electoral success. He produced about seventy films, mostly in Telugu but also in a number of other Indian languages (Murari n.d.: 265). Starting from the mid-1990s he also established satellite television channels in Telugu and other Indian languages. In the late 1990s Ramoji Film City, said to be the world's largest film studio, became operational.[14]

Ramoji Rao is widely believed to be one of the masterminds behind NTR's successful election campaign. Venkat Rao (2003: 58–9) says *Eenadu* was the first paper to have taken NTR seriously in the early days of the TDP's existence. Moreover, crucial meetings of the party were reportedly held in Ramoji Rao's residence (ibid.: 58). Ramoji Rao apparently used the newspaper's staff to gather information on local problems in each area that NTR toured and come up with a list of area-specific election promises that could be made there (ibid.: 59). *Eenadu*'s Newstoday network—this former journalist turned NTR biographer goes on to claim—was deployed to prepare a list of potential candidates and, upon NTR's request, it also carried out discreet enquiries on the claims being made by individual aspirants about their past record and worth. Innaiah too reiterates the widely-circulating rumour of the period that the newspaper vetted the list of candidates ("ticket aspirants") who applied to contest as the TDP's nominees (1986: 185).[15] He adds that *Eenadu* personnel even prepared NTR's speeches, including the one made at his victory rally in Hyderabad in January 1983 (ibid.: 195). Others, including Sekhar

[14] See also Shanti Kumar (2006) for a detailed discussion of the Film City.

[15] Narayana Naidu's hagiographic biography of NTR (1995) is the only account I have come across that is silent on the role played by *Eenadu* in the election campaign. Instead, the author credits himself for a survey in the Rayalaseema region and with the preparation of a list of potential winners in the constituencies of the region (ibid.: 64–74).

Yalamanchi (interview, op. cit.), stop at suggesting that NTR was given a list of local issues and problems by the *Eenadu* team so that he could mention them in his speeches.

Jeffrey makes an interesting connection between the TDP's election theme of Telugu dignity and the new and expanded market for print:

> *Eenadu* and its proprietor Ramoji Rao played a major role in *creating* the Telugu Desam Party (TDP) . . . It was not simply that the newspaper supported the film star N.T. Rama Rao and the TDP. Rather, the newspaper—and its rivals—*created the climate in which millions of Telugus came to share a sense that Telugu culture was suffering indignities that required a new political party to rectify*. The "Telugu dignity" theme on which the 1983 election was fought grew directly out of the surging interest in the printed word, which in turn stemmed from the competition among Telugu newspapers to reach new readers. (1997: 77, emphases added)

Although Jeffrey does not say it in so many words, there is no denying the fact that supporting the TDP was good business for *Eenadu*. The Audit Bureau of Circulation (ABC) figures Jeffrey cites show that *Eenadu*'s circulation reached a new high of 347,000 in the reporting period January–June 1983, when NTR was elected chief minister. Circulation then *fell* for the next decade (Jeffrey 2010: 85), suggesting that had it not been for the election *Eenadu*'s growth chart may have flattened out earlier.

Referring to the post-1956 period, Jeffrey notes the "close link between a state [government] apparatus and the rise of a capitalist-driven press." However, he does not provide evidence to substantiate this interesting claim. He merely states: "Only in the 1970s after Andhra Pradesh had existed for a generation did a Telugu language press begin to expand dramatically" (1997: 192). While his point about the link is eminently defensible, Jeffrey's exclusive focus on print prevents him from recognizing the true significance of 1956, not least because in the first two decades after linguistic reorganization the action was not in the realm of print: it was elsewhere. The crucial missing link in his argument is the cinema. The newspaper revolution in Andhra Pradesh resonates with the film industry's attempt at finding a fit between the market and the map of the state. In 1956 not a single

Telugu newspaper was published simultaneously from Telangana and the erstwhile Presidency. It was not till *Eenadu* established its Tirupathi office—as late as 1982—that a Telugu newspaper was published from all three regions of the state. By then the film industry had made considerable progress in tapping the new market thrown open by the formation of the state. *Eenadu*'s emergence as the state's largest circulating newspaper coincided with the integration of the Telugu film market, which in turn can be said to have been formally acknowledged by the industry with the formation of the Andhra Pradesh Film Chamber of Commerce in 1979—by merging the Andhra Film Chamber and its counterpart in Hyderabad (Andhra Pradesh Film Chamber of Commerce 1981a: 59). As for the size of the cinema's consumer base, citing figures put out by *India Today* (15 October 1982: 65), Joseph Elder and Peter L. Schmitthenner say that "in Andhra Pradesh, with a population of approximately sixty million, about twenty million people go to the cinema every week" (1985: 373). Arguably the "millions of Telugus," who Jeffrey refers to, were as likely to have been bonded by the Telugu cinema as newspapers in the period between 1956 and 1983. It would therefore be more accurate to say that the TDP was the political manifestation of the investment in a Telugu identity that was critically dependent on the existence of the state of Andhra Pradesh by both the culture industries, film and newspaper.

For its part, the TDP was attempting an ideological suture of the rupture that became all too visible in the wake of agitations demanding separate Telangana and Andhra states. Whether or not there was majority support for reorganizing the state in both Telangana and Presidency Andhra, the very existence of a Telugu identity on which statehood could be justified was called into question by these agitations. Regardless of the cynicism of the political leadership of these agitations—which led to their suppression—it could not be ignored that there was little emotional attachment to a unified Andhra Pradesh in either region. Whatever notions there may have been of the Telugu nation in different regions, these simply could not be mapped on to the boundaries of the state. The material conditions for an emotional investment in Andhra Pradesh became available only with the film market's expansion. NTR, being the most popular star, was an authentic claimant to being the representative of the Telugu *nation*, which was (notionally) unified by the cinema. The one thing that Telugus across regional as also class–caste divisions had in common was their cinema. By the late 1970s, even as NTR was re-established as the industry's biggest star, newspapers became the other platform from which the Telugu nation could be addressed.

It is now possible for us to see that the period of the newspaper revolution, as also the moment when the South Indian star-politician emerges, is one in which the consumption of cultural commodities created the material conditions for the articulation of a new kind of linguistic identity politics. The necessary condition for the articulation was the formation of Andhra Pradesh, which led to the creation of a territorially delimited market for *linguistically marked industrial-cultural commodities*. The spread of Ramoji Rao's business interests (from pickle to print publications to films and television) alerts us to the increasing economic importance of linguistically defined cultural commodities. The synergy between Ramoji Rao's businesses has been noted by Uma Maheswari: "On the one hand therefore, *Eenadu* is sustained by the capital generated by [the] other ventures and on the other, serve as a convenient medium for advertising these businesses. In fact *Eenadu* sells E.TV; E.TV sells *Eenadu*, Kalanjali [the handicrafts showroom] and Priya Pickles; *Eenadu* and E.TV sell Ushodaya Publications, Ushodaya Publications sell *Eenadu*, and so on. All are involved in a mutually beneficial, symbiotic relationship in ways that are obvious even to the occasional reader or viewer" (1999: 75). Notice that each of these enterprises—from Andhra/Telugu pickles to television—is predicated on the linguistic-cultural preferences of the consumer. Or, to put it differently, each interpellates the consumer as a member of a linguistic-cultural community. No doubt Rao also had his hotels and chit funds, but, regardless of their significance as sources of his wealth, they alone could not have made him the state's most famous entrepreneur.

Developments in Andhra Pradesh make it clear that cultural consumption—of films and newspapers in particular—was not fed by mobilizations elsewhere. There was also no equivalent of the Dravidian movement which could be claimed, albeit inaccurately, as the "original" reason for the desire for films or newspapers. In NTR's early 1980s films, as also in the election campaign, the very act of consumption—of films, cassettes, and newspapers—inserted the consumer into the circuit of political mobilization.

NTR's Election Campaign and Telugu Nationalism

NTR's interpretation of Telugu nationalism was unlike any that had been witnessed. It had a new socio-cultural foundation (film and newspaper consumption) and was centred on a film star. Ratna Naidu notes that, for all its rhetoric of Telugu pride and injury, "There [was] nothing regional [by which she means linguistic] in the symbolic imagery employed by the new-found Telugu Desam Party in the recent Andhra Pradesh Assembly elections" (Naidu 1984: 129). What she discovered instead was that the disparate images had one thing in common—NTR himself: "And NTR reminded the electorate that he had played these roles for their entertainment during the last so many decades, and that if elected he would like to activate these noble ideas, emotions and perspectives in the governance of the state" (ibid.: 132). Or, we might say, he introduced gratification as a political factor.

Kathanayakudu at Large

In commentaries on the 1983 election we notice a curious if unintended gesture to the cinematic genre that NTR helped the Telugu industry to assemble from 1969. Like the voice-over narrator in *Kathanayakudu*, in these writings the arrival of the protagonist is imminent even before he is sighted. Reconstruction of this moment has been overdetermined by *foreknowledge*: of both the author and reader, that NTR did win the election. What makes these accounts fascinating is the extent to which they are indebted to the *narrativization*—in real time—of the unfolding campaign by the local press in general and *Eenadu* in particular; indeed, the reporting of NTR's rise by various categories of commentators—from hagiographers to Telugu and English journalists to critical intellectuals and well-established academics—needs to be supplemented by looking at the contribution of *Eenadu* to the narrativization of the campaign, as well as in relation to the coverage of the election by *Andhra Jyothi*, *Eenadu*'s competitor, which supported the Congress (I).

NTR, with his rhetoric of Telugu pride, made a disarmingly simple claim. Congress had humiliated the Telugus and now the agent of change—he himself—had arrived. While NTR may have announced the name of the party and its main election plank without much thought (Venkat Narayan 1983: 8), the humiliation of the Telugus was a theme already available on account of the critical coverage of state politics by *Eenadu* from T. Anjaiah's time. The paper had presented the state-level Congress leadership as inefficient and the central leadership in Delhi as disrespectful of the wishes of the electorate. There had over a period of time been a representation of Congress failures and misrule, especially of the frequent change of chief ministers by the party's central leadership. These had been shown up as not merely undemocratic and political failures but insults and affronts to the Telugus. Reports on T. Anjaiah (chief minister 1980–2) are a particularly interesting example because he was frequently ridiculed in *Eenadu* as well as other periodicals—mainstream and yellow—not least because of his Telangana-accented Telugu (he was a member of the Telangana Praja Samiti led by Chenna Reddy: Innaiah 1986: 171). In fact so well established was the image of Anjaiah as a clown that Innaiah titles his chapter on Anjaiah's rule "Buffoonery in Politics" (ibid.: 169–73) without offering specific evidence of buffoonery by this popular trade unionist. Presumably, the examples seemed unnecessary because Innaiah's readers knew too many Anjaiah stories already.[16] Anjaiah's humiliation by Rajiv Gandhi at Hyderabad airport and subsequent replacement is worth detailing because it would figure prominently—though mostly with hindsight—as examples of the Congress leadership's "step-motherly treatment" of Andhra Pradesh and Telugus in the years to come. Venkat Narayan's account of the incident makes interesting reading:

> When his plane arrived at Hyderabad, [Rajiv Gandhi] was shocked to see the portly chief minister amidst a noisy crowd of about 200 gathered on the landing apron. This was against airport security rules and the

[16] There were also a number of Anjaiah jokes in circulation in the early 1980s, founded on his lower-class origins, "non-standard" Telangana accent, and lack of sophistication. Venkat Narayan makes a reference to stories about Anjaiah (1983: 47).

> former Indian Airlines pilot [Gandhi] lost his temper and began to yell at Anjaiah . . . The sheepish Anjaiah was on the verge of tears as a red-faced Rajiv walked into the terminal building. The MP ignored garlands and bouquets and booked himself on the next flight to Delhi . . . Five ministers had worked hard to gather the crowd and Rajiv was not even willing to go out to wave at them. After much persuasion, he obliged the crowd with a brief appearance and flew off to Tirupathi, the temple town, to fulfil an engagement. Anjaiah was deliberately left behind. Unable to bear such public humiliation by a supposedly cultured man, he now burst into tears. (1983: 77–8)

George Mathew's observation on this ill treatment and NTR's response exemplify the broader social interpretation of replacing the chief minister as an insult to the people of the state: "To crown it all, T. Anjaiah was publicly humiliated by an important national Congress (I) personality. He had to quit the chief ministership in tears. N.T. Rama Rao characterized the ouster of Anjaiah as an 'auctioning of Andhra's honour in Delhi.' A chief minister, to whichever party he might belong, symbolizes the honour of the people of the state. When he is treated in a contemptuous manner by those in power outside the state, even if they are national leaders, regional feelings rise against the offender" (1984: 169). Innaiah too mentions the incident and says Anjaiah wanted to resign from the chiefministership but was persuaded against it by his cabinet colleagues (1986: 173). In spite of everything that was wrong with Anjaiah and his government (the "jumbo" cabinet, his embarrassing displays of loyalty to the central leadership, lack of sophistication, supposed ignorance, etc.), his humiliation became an issue and was, as Guha points out (2007: 553), interpreted by the press "as an insult to the pride of the Andhras." The incident was, naturally therefore, referred to by NTR during his campaign (Venkat Narayan 1983: 48).

It is not my claim that most Telugu speakers were not hurt. It is possible that many, including NTR himself, were deeply moved by the incident. My question is how a race (as in Telugu *jati*) that could be hurt by misrule—for want of a better word to describe acts of commission and omission by those in power—came to the foreground in the early 1980s. Narratives of hurt were interpellating otherwise disparate Telugus—a "race" which had demonstrated only a decade earlier that it was invested in regional issues and which had rejected language as the basis for organizing states within the union—as a single undifferentiated political community which was, by the very fact of its origins within discussions of contemporary politics, an object of mobilization. Simultaneously, the construction of Telugu speakers as a humiliated race was so overarching in its criticism of the existing political establishment that it needed an agent from outside politics to set things right. In other words, it facilitated the retrospective naming of NTR as a saviour figure who was already anticipated by the unfolding narrative.

Eenadu's newsreports, photographs, op-eds, cartoons, and editorials underscore a similar set of issues and support the same cause. This mode of reiteration has been noted by Uma Maheswari (1999: 78–9) in her examination of the techniques used by the paper in its "war against arrack" (1992–3).[17] When we examine *Eenadu*'s coverage of the TDP during the 1982–3 campaign, it becomes clear that most of these techniques were quite developed then. News about the Congress was not blacked out. On the contrary, a great deal of space was given to the party and its leaders. At times the coverage of the Congress camp was overtly critical—like the much-publicized visit to Andhra Pradesh of Rajiv Gandhi in October 1982, which became the subject matter of a sarcastic poem and numerous cartoons. However, even when the reports themselves seemed to be matter of fact, editorials and cartoons challenged the views expressed by the Congress leaders who were quoted. Congress accusations against NTR and the TDP, including those made by Indira Gandhi, were rebutted in editorials.

The layout of *Eenadu*'s pages, especially the front page, ensured that images of NTR and/or reports of his campaign *compensated* every image and newsreport about Congress activity, in particular its political rallies. The interventionist role played by the paper is evident from

[17] Led by poor women, the anti-arrack agitation of the early 1990s swept across the state and was supported by the radical left as well as the TDP and other opposition parties. In addition to dedicating an entire page to report of the war on arrack, *Eenadu* carried cartoons, editorials, and special interviews with health experts, op-ed pieces on various issues related to liquor, etc. (Maheswari 1999: 78–9).

the way in which it mediated even advertisements by the Congress to ensure that their "message" or propaganda value was effectively undermined. For example, on 1 January 1983, an advertisement on page 10 of the Vijayawada edition, announcing Indira Gandhi's campaign schedule, was juxtaposed with an advertisement of the film magazine *Sitara*, a Ramoji Rao group publication, with a thoughtful NTR on the cover (Image 183). One of the more common techniques was to place a negative newsreport of the Congress in close proximity with the party's advertisement. The other was to place photographs of NTR's rallies on the same page as Congress advertisements.

The quality and efficacy of editorial intervention, evident from the degree of care and sophistication seen in *Eenadu*'s page layout and presentation of text and images, stands in complete contrast with *Andhra Jyothi*'s rather unsuccessful attempt at undermining NTR's campaign. Apart from editorial commentary and cartoons critical of the TDP, there was little in *Andhra Jyothi*'s reportage comparable with *Eenadu*'s handling of either Congress or the TDP. *Eenadu*'s mediation

DISTRIBUTORS
PIONEER WOOD PRODUCTS
1-1-1983
2-1-1983
3-1-1983

Image 183: Placement of images: Congress (I) and *Sitara* advertisements (*Eenadu*, 1 January 1983: 10).

was predicated on a thorough understanding of the materiality of the newspaper form and its very unique textuality: of the constituent elements—reports, cartoons, editorials, photographs, advertisements, etc.—that made meaning in conjunction with each other.

The front page of *Eenadu* on 2 January 1983 is a good example of the paper's skilful news production (Image 184). On top of the page is a photograph of NTR addressing a large rally with Maneka Gandhi (her Sanjay Vichar Manch was the only electoral ally of the TDP in the 1983 election). The photograph is as large as the quarter-page Congress advertisement at the bottom, which shows Indira Gandhi in her campaign schedule. Much of the text on the front page is devoted to coverage of the TDP–Manch rally and a summary of NTR's speech. A Congress rally addressed by Indira Gandhi, reported under a headline that translates as "Politics is not Drama" (*Rajakeeyalante Natakalu Kadu*), appears next to the party's advertisement. Halfway through this report the reader is told, as though in passing, that at a particular point during Mrs Gandhi's speech the crowd lost interest and began to leave, saying "*ika levandira*" (Get up now, folks)! This detail, and the rather dubious suggestion that the reporter had heard the impatient crowd say it had had enough, communicates with great economy Indira Gandhi's ineffectiveness as a speaker, even as it attempts verisimilitude, the experience of being there at the meeting. The report continues in right earnest to list other highlights of the speech.[18]

One of the techniques adopted by *Eenadu* consisted of coining

[18] Another page of the same day's paper has a report of a well-attended meeting addressed by Indira Gandhi in Kadapa. Here too we notice how cleverly the paper suggests that the meeting was a failure. The report, whose title declares that the audience at Indira Gandhi's meeting was disappointed, begins by pointing out that she flew in on a helicopter and was at the meeting venue for less than ten minutes (*Newstoday* 1983c: 2). The large crowd that had waited for hours was disappointed that she spoke so little. Further, the translation by Vijayabhaskar Reddy, then chief minister, was poor. Local leaders who had arrived to complain about factions within the party in the locality were disappointed that they could not get an audience with Mrs Gandhi. Worse still, one set of local Congress leaders shouted slogans against another that occupied the stage, calling them TDP collaborators.

The Largest Circulated Daily in Andhra Pradesh
ఈనాడు
2-1-1983
నూతనశకానికి నాంది: ఎన్టీఆర్ విశ్వాసం
రాజకీయాలంటే నాటకాలు కాదు
నూతన సంవత్సర శుభాకాంక్షలు.
కొత్త సంవత్సరం అందరికీ
ఆనందదాయకం, సౌభాగ్యవంతం
అవ్వుగాక!

Image 184: Making meaning from the "look and feel" of the newspaper (*Eenadu*, 2 January 1983: 1).

aphorisms, a value addition introduced by the paper around September 1982 to comment on the election campaign. These are comments on the state of the world, oracular proclamations, words of wisdom, and general statements on morality or duty. The deployment of aphorisms by the paper has an interesting parallel with the ways in which NTR used mythological speech—elevated Telugu in political discourse—over the campaign. While the aphorism tended towards the folk idiom rather than the classical, like mythological speech it too was easily recognized as being traditionally Telugu. We can see the efficacy of the aphorism in the cluster of reports and images on the front page of 2 January 1983. At the bottom of the page, below the report on Indira Gandhi's speech, is news on "atrocities" by Congress *goondas* (Newstoday 1983a: 1), and another single column report—placed immediately adjacent to the Congress advertisement—stating that the authorities had denied permission for an NTR rally in order to sabotage his campaign (Newstoday 1983b: 1). The centrepiece of the text and image cluster on the bottom half of the front page, literally holding them all together, is an aphorism. Inserted between the reports on Mrs Gandhi's speech and Congress thugs the aphorism reads: "*Sushkavagdanalu, Sunyahastalu Inkana . . . Ikapai Sagavu*"—i.e. "False promises and empty hands still? They will not be tolerated henceforth." This general statement on the rising political consciousness of the masses is made by linking two satirical puns: sunya*hasthalu* (empty hands), a reference to the Congress party's symbol; and *Inka*na which sounds like In.Con., an abbreviation for Indira Congress in the Telugu press. Such was the innovativeness of *Eenadu*'s election coverage.[19]

Ironically, the powerful Congress machinery was losing this battle of images in spite of incurring considerable advertising expenditure in *Eenadu* as well as in other newspapers, including *Andhra Jyothi*. Images of NTR from a variety of sources—such as advertisements of his most recent films and film magazines, which had his pictures on the cover—found their way into these newspapers. In *Eenadu*, virtually all images of Congress leaders—including those in party advertisements—were visually compensated either by NTR's images or by placing negative headlines. For example, on the front page of *Eenadu* on 15 October 1982, an image of Rajiv Gandhi being welcomed by a group of women and the accompanying report on his speech is literally sandwiched between an image of NTR with

[19] In the next page of the newspaper, there is a less inspired composition that roughly translates as: "Don't see the [currency] note and be fooled, brother; understand the value of your vote, sister" (*Notu choosi mosapoku tammudu; votu viluva telusukove ammadu. Eenadu*, 2 January 1983: 2).

his finger raised, as if at Rajiv Gandhi's image, and the report of an NTR rally in which the title translates as "Indira's Party Mortgaging the Country" (Image 185).

ఎంతచేయాలో అంత చేస్తుంది

దేశాన్ని తాకట్టు పెడుతున్న ఇందిరపార్టీ

E 15/10/82

Image 185: Compensation: NTR points a stern finger at Rajiv Gandhi while the headline reads "Indira's Party Mortgaging the Country" (*Eenadu,* 15 October 1982: 1).

Election Narratives: Insults to the Race

Eenadu's mediation of the campaign played no small part in authenticating NTR's self-proclaimed status as a representative of the Telugu nation and saviour of a humiliated race. The paper reported in some detail the entire gamut of symbolic gestures NTR made in his attempt to present himself as the representative of the Telugus. News and photographs of his visit to places and monuments of historical importance, as also statements on insults to the race and betrayal of the Telugus by the Congress, appeared regularly in the paper. On 6 October 1982 it carried a photograph of NTR addressing a crowd from atop his *ratham* in Warangal with the famous gateway of the Kakatiya period (*Kala Toranam*) as a backdrop (Image 186). Later the same month NTR's visit to the town of Veeravasaram (in the West Godavari district) to unveil a statue of Alluri Sitarama Raju, described by the paper as Telugu *jyothi* (lamp), was reported on the front page along with a picture of the star felicitating the rebel's brother (Newstoday 1982a: 1).

As mentioned already, NTR had a rather fuzzy conception of Telugu self-respect and pride. His speeches typically began with a sweeping critique of Delhi's rule and consequent oppression of

Image 186: Monuments of Telugu pride: NTR addresses a gathering before the Kakatiya dynasty's *Kala Toranam*.

the Telugus. He would then list the failures of the Congress party (including, for example, the growth in unemployment). Finally, he would mention local problems (the lack of proper roads, for example) and make a series of promises, including some which were specific to the locality. In the hands of NTR, any failure of the Congress became translatable as an insult to the race. As a result of this freewheeling notion of what constituted an injury, opposition to the Congress became the most immediate and important way of saving the Telugu nation. The framing rhetoric apart, there wasn't much else by way of a linguistic nationalist agenda in the NTR campaign. This is easily demonstrated by any of the multiple statements NTR made on the subject of Telugu self-respect and/or injury to the race. For instance, on 31 August 1982, at a public meeting in Tenali town NTR stated that injustice had been done to the Telugus who had been in the forefront of the struggle for Independence. By way of explanation, he drew attention to irrigation (the Right Canal of the Nagarjuna Sagar dam) and industrial projects (a tyre factory near Vijayawada and a steel plant at Visakhapatnam—the latter was an important focus of the agitation for a separate Andhra state) that had not been completed (Newstoday 1982b: 2). Some days later, at a meeting in Chittoor town, he claimed that the TDP grew out of the heartburn of the Telugu race (*Telugu jati gundello regina manta*). He lamented that the Telugus had sacrificed their lives during the Independence struggle but were not given due importance in post-Independence India. He objected to the "stepmotherly" treatment (*savati talli prema*) of the state by the central government and concluded by demanding a twenty-five crore rupee relief package for the drought-affected Chittoor district (Newstoday 1982c: 2).

He continued in this vein throughout the campaign. To cite an example from the final days, in a speech to industrial workers in Adilabad district he criticized an intra-party affair of the Congress, namely, the appointment of special officers from outside the state to oversee election expenditure. He saw the deployment of "persons imported from the North" (*uttaradi nundi digumatichesukunna vyaktulu*) as a sign that Indira Gandhi and her son Rajiv did not trust Congressmen in the state. "Is there a dearth [*karuvu*, famine] of honest people in the state Congress?" he is reported to have asked. This was a double-edged statement because, even as it lamented the Congress leadership's lack of trust in Telugu Congressmen, it suggested that the state unit of the party was so corrupt that its own leadership had no faith in it. He went on to attack the Congress for siding with the exploitative management of the company during a recent industrial dispute and promised that his party would stand by workers (Newstoday 1983d: 10).

Among *Eenadu*'s contributions to this mode of producing Telugu hurt was the anchoring of NTR's campaign to various themes related to Telugu nationalism. We have noted that it did so by highlighting NTR's statements on injured Telugu pride and his symbolic gestures—visits to historical monuments, the garlanding of statues of prominent historical figures, etc. But, most important, the paper performed a naming act: *the mobilized masses were identified as members of the Telugu nation*. For example, *Eenadu* carried an iconic photograph of NTR addressing a crowd. The low-angle shot captured NTR in profile with his hand outstretched. The large numbers of people visible in the foreground, as also on rooftops in the background, makes for an arresting image. Rather than perform a denotative function by providing details of where the speech was made, etc., the caption states (without quotation marks): "*Telugujati atmagaurava parirakshanakosam udyaminchandi*" (Agitate for the protection of the self-respect of the Telugu race, *Eenadu*, 11 October 1982: 2). It is possible NTR himself said this during a speech, but that is clear neither from the caption nor the reports in the vicinity of the photograph. The photograph and its caption constitute a standalone piece, making a direct appeal to the reader.

In the same day's paper there was a report of how two former chief ministers turned dissenters—Bhavanam Venkatram and Anjaiah—had calmed down after being summoned to Delhi and reprimanded (*Eenadu* Special Correspondent, 1982a: 5, 8). A separate article reported NTR's criticism of the Congress at the state and centre. Among other things, NTR said, state ministers had to wait endlessly on the lawns in Delhi for "*amma's darshan*" (Newstoday 1982d: 8). Reports of NTR's speech, the editorial-like direct address to the readers about the state Congress leaders' spinelessness, and a caption imploring the masses to protect the race's self-respect are all constituent elements of the big story, one centred on the narrative of injury to Telugu pride and its redressal via NTR.

As the election date approached, increasing numbers of aphorisms appeared, all appealing to the reader's Telugu identity. For example, *Tella doralanedirinchina Telugu nela, Nalla doralapalanalo nalaganela?* (Why should the Telugu land that defied white lords be crushed by black masters? 1 January 1983: 9). Historical figures were recalled, for example, on the front page of the newspaper on 3 January 1983, two days before the polling in an aphorism which translates as: "You who have Rudramamba's courage, stir yourself to drive away the vultures" ("*Rudramamba paurusham meedandi, Rabandula panibattaga kadalandi,*" 3 January 1983: 1).[20] On the day of the election a front-page editorial was titled "*Telugunata Charitra Srushtinchandi*" (Create history in Telugu land, Editorial 1983a:1). This only just stopped short

[20] Rudramamba or Rani Rudrama Devi being the thirteenth-century queen of the Kakatiya dynasty.

of asking readers to vote for the TDP (Image 187). To the editorial's right was an article titled "*Andhrula Vichanashaktiki Pariksha*" (A test of the Andhras' power of discretion, Newstoday 1983e: 1). The accompanying picture was of NTR with folded hands pasted on a map of Andhra Pradesh which, in turn, had been cut from a photograph of a large crowd at a TDP rally. Bordering the bottom right corner of the map, and adjacent to a cartoon of a voter being welcomed by politicians, including Indira Gandhi and NTR, was a warning to the voter: "*Vesavo tappatadugu, tappadu siksha,*" i.e. if you take the wrong step, punishment is inevitable. On the editorial page was an aphorism that translates thus: "Rivers of arrack will overflow, [currency] notes

Image 187: The man, masses, and map (*Eenadu,* 5 January 1983: 1).

will change hands, it will rain promises but don't sell your vote" (5 January 1983: 3).

After the election results were announced the paper carried a cartoon (7 January 1983: 4) in which "*Atma Gauravam*," self-respect, represented by NTR's *kanduva* (top cloth) outweighed numerous bags of money as well as Indira Gandhi, who was shown clinging to the scale with one hand and a sack of money on the other. NTR is seen looking on with his hands folded across his chest (Image 188).

Image 188: Top cloth of self-respect outweighs Indira Gandhi and her money bags in Sridhar's cartoon on the election results (*Eenadu*, 7 January 1983: 4).

Amma, Anna, and the Spectacle of the Mass-Nation

The NTR campaign, *Eenadu* frequently reminded its readers, was an uprising of the Telugu people. In the course of the election campaign the masses themselves became an object of textual and photographic representation. This was in part because the crowds were, in fact, mobilized in larger numbers than in any previous election. In writings and photographs of the period, as also accounts on the event produced much later, the presence of the masses is striking: everyone seems magically attracted to NTR. Press reports of the time and NTR's biographers both point out that he reached meeting venues a good 10–20 hours behind schedule. By the end of his campaign, according to Nandamuri Harikrishna—his son and the driver of the Chaitanya Ratham—he was 48 hours late (Interview, *Andhra Jyothi*, 28 May 2007: 2). Telugu culture does not seem to have been successfully interpellated within the European notion of punctuality being the politeness of kings; on the contrary, the star's unpunctuality may have enhanced his regal appeal. The crowds of people, their enthusiasm undampened, either waited for him or simply dropped whatever they were doing when they heard he had arrived and rushed to the campaign venue. Venkat Rao notes that NTR's arrival at a village was announced on the public address system attached to his *ratham*, which played the songs "*Maa Telugu Talliki Mallepu Danda*" and "*Cheyyethi Jai Kottu Telugoda*" (from the NTR starrer *Palletooru*).[21] Upon hearing the songs, villagers scampered to the venue (Venkat Rao 2003: 56). This undimmed enthusiasm featured prominently in press reports. For the most part NTR's photographs had him addressing large gatherings, the masses perched on trees and rooftops, these including old women, children, and, as chance would have it, the odd farmer with his plough. Virtually every day, reports and photographs described and showed crowds. NTR was at times either entirely absent from the reports and images, or in the distant background (Images 189 and 190).

Much effort went into the demonstration of NTR's popularity in the build-up of the confrontation with Indira Gandhi. In *Eenadu*'s scheme, the masses fitted well in the narrative of the Telugu nation's uprising against injustice and humiliation. NTR the popular leader

[21] Lisa Mitchell provides a fine translation of the lyrics of "*Maa Telugu Talliki Mallepu Danda*," the state anthem of Andhra Pradesh written by Shankarambadi Sundarachari, circa 1942 (2009: 68). Venkat Rao says that NTR revived (*tirigi jeevam posaru*, brought back to life) this and the other song used in the campaign. The latter song was written by Vemulapalli Srikrishna (2003: 56). Venkat Rao's claim is somewhat exaggerated because Sundarachari's song, as Mitchell notes, appeared in primers and school textbooks, so NTR was not really bringing it back to life. It is interesting that the Telugu dubbed version of the DMK propaganda film *Parasakthi* used this song.

189

190

Images 189–90: Masses at the rallies (Top: *Eenadu*, 9 October 1982: 1; bottom: *Eenadu*, 15 October 1982: 6).

confronted the all-powerful ruler Indira Gandhi and her "Delhi Durbar." However, such was the enthusiasm of the crowds that *Andhra Jyothi*'s photographers, who appear to have been committed to capturing the spectacle, told a story which struck a discordant chord with the newspaper's reports, editorials, and cartoons (Image 191).

Eenadu reported on the campaign as if it were a series of confrontations among competing mobilizers. Having emphasized NTR's appeal to the masses, it presented the arrival of Rajiv Gandhi (in October 1982) as a semi-final, and Indira Gandhi's tour of the state (late December–early January) as the final. During the last days of the campaign the paper drew repeated attention to the thin crowds in meetings addressed by Indira Gandhi, and the impatience and disappointment of the crowds attending them. At one point it declared that Indira's charisma was on the wane, and that NTR's meeting attracted twice as many people as her's (Newstoday 1982e: 2). In the battle between the two familial authority figures, *amma* (mother) and *anna* (elder brother)—as the two were referred to by journalists and party colleagues alike—the latter was shown as emerging the clear winner.

The climax of this strand of the election narrative was the simultaneous meetings in Tirupathi organized by the TDP and the Congress. Whether by chance or design, NTR decided to conclude his campaign in Tirupathi, in direct competition with Indira Gandhi,

Image 191: Ever-present masses (*Andhra Jyothi*, 12 October 1982: 1).

who was scheduled to address a rally there on the same day. The TDP had considerable trouble getting the local authorities' permissions to hold the meeting (Newstoday 1983b, cited above). The meeting itself is widely reported to have been an embarrassment for the Congress, with crowds gathered at Indira Gandhi's meeting rushing out of the venue, even as she was speaking, upon hearing the news of NTR's arrival in Tirupathi (Venkat Rao 2003: 72). Innaiah says that "The meetings went off peacefully but judging by the response, one could see on which side the masses were" (1986: 188). Even before the Tirupathi disaster for the Congress, *Eenadu* began to suggest that the battle was in fact already lost by Indira Gandhi: close to the election date, a tongue-in-cheek report on the thin attendance at Indira Gandhi's election meetings bore a heading that translates as "Oh mother! Why aren't there people at your meeting?" This was placed under the photograph of a lunar eclipse, bringer of bad luck, thereby mischievously predicting her party's defeat (Newstoday 1983f: 7, Image 192).

There were interesting and amusing subplots in the narrative, including one that involved Indira Gandhi's family. Rajiv Gandhi, referred to sarcastically by *Eenadu* as *yuvaraju* (prince), was an object of cartoons and a satirical poem in the newspaper. He was more or less summarily dismissed as an opponent unworthy of NTR. The Gandhi family discord, between Indira and Sanjay Gandhi's widow Maneka Gandhi, came into sharp focus because of the electoral alliance

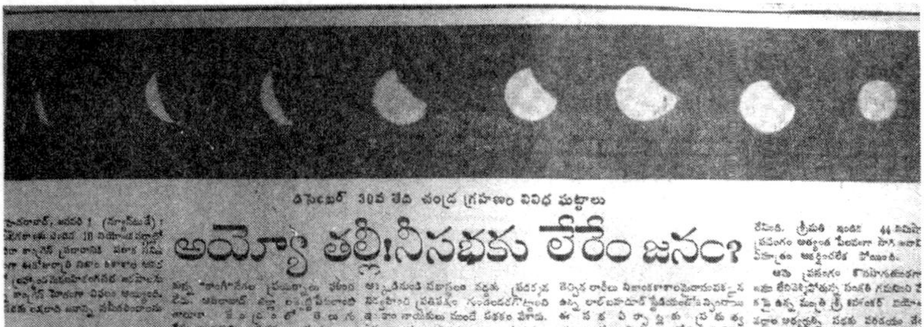

Image 192: Eclipse of the Congress (I): news of the thin attendance at Amma's meetings juxtaposed with photographs of a lunar eclipse that occurred on the night of 30 December (*Eenadu*, 2 January 1983: 7).

between the latter's Sanjay Vichar Manch and the TDP.[22] During meetings jointly addressed by NTR and Maneka Gandhi, direct and indirect references were made to Indira Gandhi's alleged cruelty to her daughter-in-law who had lost her husband and was now a young widow.[23] The production of the prime minister as an oppressive mother-*in-law* was a clever attempt at diluting her construction as the mother figure by the Congress. *Eenadu*'s coverage during the final stages of the campaign, when both Maneka and Indira Gandhi toured the state, presented them as the *atta-kodallu* (mother- and daughter-in-law) twosome who had taken their family troubles to the streets (Newstoday 1982f: 1). Simultaneously, NTR emerged as the patriarch who had offered protection to a helpless young widow oppressed by her in-laws.

The various strands of the narrative it had woven were summarized in an editorial that *Eenadu* carried on 6 January 1983, after the election but before the results were announced. The editorial's title, *Dharmakshetre, Kurukshetre*, states in so many words that the election is like the Kurukshetra war—a battle of epic proportions between right and wrong. The Congress party, likened to the Kauravas, had on its side money, the administration, past experience, *goondas* (*goondalu*), and bodybuilders (*vastadulu*). But the TDP had the support of the people. NTR's magnetism (*janakarshana shakti*) had bettered Indira's *sammohana shakti* (powers/skills of mobilization). While Indira flew by helicopter into virtually every constituency, NTR's *prachara jaitrayatra* (victory procession of a campaign) reminded the people of the need to protect the self-respect of the Telugu race (*Telugu jati atmagaurava samrakshanavasyakata*). The Congress party, the editorial alleged, was also preparing to buy off elected representatives in the event of a defeat. Regardless of the election result, the Telugu Desam had already won a

[22] Other non-Congress parties too had held talks with the TDP but with disagreements over the number of seats each was to contest there was no united anti-Congress alliance of the kind that NTR cobbled together in the years to come.

[23] Venkat Rao has an amusing story about this phase of the campaign. He reports that crowds listened in rapt attention to Maneka Gandhi's speeches in Hindi without understanding a word of what she said, and cheering loudly every time she spoke NTR's name (2003: 67).

moral victory. The party had preached (*prabodhinchindi*, a reference to the Christian notion of spreading the message of God) to the people of Andhra to fight against injustice and inspired them to do so. When the election results are declared, it said, we will know whether the winner is injustice or justice, money power (*dhana balam*) or people's power (*jana balam*). Not just the Telugus, the entire country was waiting to find out (Editorial 1983b: 3).

Drama Rao and *Cinema Janam*

That NTR's election meetings were staged as theatrical performances was noted by contemporary scholars. The sociologist Ratna Naidu (1984) drew attention to the "festive atmosphere" of the campaign and the prominence of songs, as also folk forms like *burra katha*. The campaign was drawing on the communist agitprop forms but, in combination with NTR's campaign style, the election was transformed into an extended cultural entertainment programme.

Political opponents reacted strongly, at times viciously, to NTR's campaign style. Kotla Vijayabhaskar Reddy, then chief minister of the state, reportedly dismissed the TDP as a "drama troupe" and NTR as a politically immature and ignorant film star. Some in the Congress, however, felt the star posed a serious challenge (*Eenadu* Special Correspondent 1982b: 1). Close to the polling date, as noted above, Indira Gandhi herself wondered at a rally how someone who had acted in plays (*natakalu*) till the other day could become a chief minister. She added that politics was not theatre (*natakalu kaadu*, Newstoday 1983g: 1). The nickname "Drama Rao" given to the star (Venkat Rao 2003: 58) and the condescending reference to those who thronged his meetings as *cinema janam* (film crowd/enthusiasts) alerts us to the relationship that NTR was setting up between himself and the electorate. At one point during the campaign, chief minister Vijayabhaskar Reddy cautioned NTR against trusting *cinema janam*. He also said crowds were being attracted to TDP meetings in large numbers on account of their craze for the movies (*cinema vyamoham*) and not because they supported the party (Newstoday 1982g: 1).

Andhra Jyothi and *Eenadu*, in tune with their editorial policies, made opposing claims on whether or not *cinema janam* was an index of political support. *Eenadu* reported sarcastic references to crowds (and other statements in this vein) by the TDP's opponents but countered them by showing evidence of the people's love for NTR in its reports and photographs. It repeatedly pointed out people waiting in the hot sun for hours and listening rapt to NTR even in pouring rain. In a report on NTR's tour of East Godavari district, *Andhra Jyothi* asked a question which was foremost on observers' minds: whether it was "political support or craze for the cinema" that was being witnessed during NTR's campaign (*Andhra Jyothi* 1982a: 3). The newspaper left the question unanswered but drew attention to the unusual enthusiasm of the crowds, as also NTR's habit of stopping his vehicle and making emotional speeches "wherever he found a group of fifty people." The paper listed his election promises and khaki clothes as factors contributing to his popularity. The article also mentioned the incident of a disappointed crowd attacking his vehicle and raising anti-NTR slogans when a meeting was cancelled. Both newspapers contributed to making the most routine of NTR's actions objects of spectacle, elevating the performative dimension of the campaign to a new level altogether. As the campaign progressed, there came into being a genre of photographs, as also reports, featuring the star quite literally performing to an omniscient camera/spectator, but not before an audience/crowd (Image 193).

In early October *Andhra Jyothi* carried a front-page photograph of

Image 193: The omniscient camera: the *Andhra Jyothi* version (9 October 1982: 1).

him eating "on the roadside, under the trees" (9 October 1982: 1). The picture was accompanied by a report on his daily routine during the campaign, mentioning his capacity for sustaining himself on light refreshments and lime juice and his awe-inspiring habit of sleeping in the open at night (*Andhra Jyothi* 1982b: 1).

On the same day, *Eenadu* carried similar but embellished reports. These included a boxed item saying that NTR, who till the other day lived a life of luxury, was now sleeping like a commoner on a mat by the road. His campaign tour was surprising everybody, the report added, because he never stayed in hotels and preferred to spend the night beside his parked van. Every morning he washed up in canals, kept to his simple khaki dress, had some bread for breakfast, and was back on the road. The report concluded that this sixty-year-old man who spent his entire day among the people was as active as a twenty-year-old (Newstoday 1982h: 1). On 13 October *Eenadu* published a photo of NTR snacking at a roadside eatery. Captioned "*Prajala atmeeyate annitini minchina vindu*" (People's affection is the best of feasts), it appears at the bottom left of the paper's front page, its top right showing a cartoon of Rajiv Gandhi and a satirical poem about him: Rajiv is in a helicopter carried by Vijayabhaskar Reddy in the get-up of Lord Hanuman (Images 194 and 195). The accompanying poem by Gajjela Malla Reddy, known for his satirical columns in *Eenadu*, is titled "*Rakshakudu Vachchadu*" (The protector has arrived, Malla Reddy 1982: 1).

The highpoint of this mode of presenting NTR was reached on 12 October 1982, when *Eenadu* featured a series of four images of NTR on its front page (Image 196). The first three show a perforated frame, an obvious reference to the celluloid film strip. In these images NTR can be seen shaving, washing his clothes, and bathing. He is dressed only in towel and dhoti. The last picture in the series is a larger image of him bathing.[24] *Eenadu*'s reference to the cinema is

[24] This last image reappeared, among other places, in Venkat Rao (2003: 57). This genre of photographs, notes Venkat Rao, evoked the interest of the national and international press and some of the images were picked up by agencies to be widely distributed beyond Andhra Pradesh. Congress leaders were furious with this development; one minister went on record accusing

194

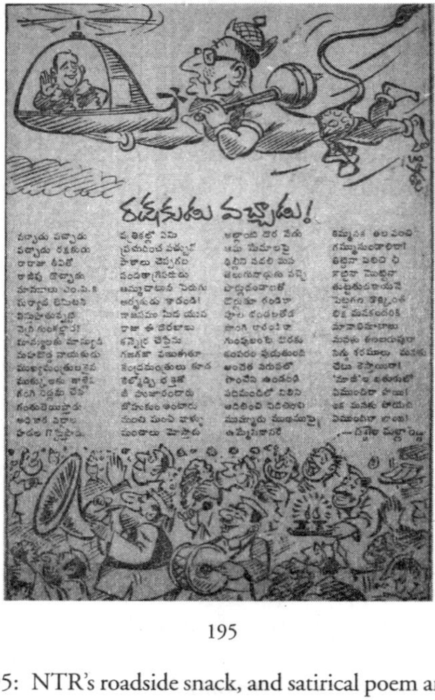

195

Images 194 and 195: NTR's roadside snack, and satirical poem and cartoon on Rajiv Gandhi (*Eenadu*, 13 October 1982: 1).

interesting because whereas the perforated frame suggests fictionality or theatricality, the images of the bath are evidently of the "real" and off-screen NTR, a man of simplicity whose commitment to the people is such that he is literally living his life in the open. Perhaps inadvertently, but with great accuracy, *Eenadu* flags the performative dimension of the "real" NTR and the manner in which his actions, even otherwise routine ones, became objects of a spectacular "show" (to use Adorno's term) during the course of the campaign. NTR's latest role is not one that has him fully made up as a youth; it shows him living the life of a commoner.

NTR's *ratham* was accompanied by press vehicles during his road shows. The constant presence of the press around him opened up the possibility of extending his performance—spatially and temporally—beyond the election rally. The positioning of the newspaper reader is similar to that of the spectator of films containing a major star. Laura

ఫిబ్రవరినాటికే రాష్ట్రంలో ఎన్నికలు

Image 196: Performing the everyday: the spectacular show on *Eenadu*'s front page (12 October 1982).

---

the press of presenting the TDP as a major force and warned that NTR, who roamed around in luxury cars, would get no votes by posing on the roadside. The TDP itself, he declared, was a *creation of the press* (*Newstoday* 1982i: 2).

Mulvey draws attention to a relevant feature of stardom: "in the star system, the stars' [centre] both screen presence and screen story as they act out a complex process of likeness and difference (the glamorous impersonates the ordinary)" (1990: 32). The genre of reporting in question quite literally makes a spectacle of NTR's *impersonation of the ordinary*. In popular cinema, such role-playing is among the chief pleasures of most films featuring major stars. For another reason, too, the spectator of the routine/mundane/real actions reported in *Eenadu* is unlike the member of the crowd at the election meeting and like the film spectator: s/he does not exist at the time-place of the event and has to be assembled in another time and place by newspapers. The reader-spectator-potential voter gets a glimpse of this performance only because the newspaper was in a place to which s/he does not have access. Newspaper readers were thus doubly constituted—by medium as also actor-politician—as variants, indeed extensions of the *cinema janam* who thronged to films and election rallies alike to watch the star perform.

Eenadu's election coverage culminated with a combination of images and reports celebrating the TDP victory and Congress defeat. "*Telugu Desam Super Hit*" reads the main headline of the day on 7 January (*Eenadu* Special Correspondent 1983: 1, Image 197). The text of the report is accompanied by a film-strip-like image series of NTR celebrating his party victory, addressing election rallies and people queuing up to vote. "Telugu race has roared like a lion" (*Telugu jati simhamla garjinchindi*), the paper declared. Juxtaposed with this report is news from neighbouring Karnataka, where too the Congress had emerged as a "super flop" (*Eenadu* 1983: 1, Image 198). The text of the Karnataka report is sandwiched between two photographs. On the left stands NTR, pointing his finger, as if warning an adversary, with the caption: "This is a victory of the poor people" (*Ee vijayam peda prajaladi*). On the right is Indira Gandhi, her head held in her hand—the picture of loss and defeat. The caption addresses her: "Mother, it is inevitable that we suffer the consequences/*karma* of our actions" (*Evaru chesina karma varunabhavimchaka evarikainanu tappadamma*!).

To the end, in 1983, the cinematic was a constant referent in the campaign. The multiple and complex invocations of the cinema were

The Largest Circulated Daily in Andhra Pradesh

ఈనాడు

Published from Vijayawada, Hyderabad, Visakhapatnam, Tirupati

7-1-1983

తెలుగుదేశం సూపర్ హిట్!!

Image 197: Announcing the election results: "Telugu Desam Super Hit" (*Eenadu*, 7 January 1983: 1).

రాష్ట్రం									మొత్తం
ఆంధ్రప్రదేశ్	180	54	1	7	5			21	268
కర్ణాటక		79	18			98		23	218
త్రిపుర		9			29			8	46

కర్ణాటక కాంగి 'సూపర్ ఫ్లాప్'

Image 198: Anna and Amma with news of Congress (I)'s "super flop" in Karnataka (*Eenadu*, 7 January 1983: 1).

not limited to the recall of the star-politician's screen role as do-gooder or god but to a performance style, as also to a spectatorial relationship. This was instituted by NTR and reinforced by the press.

But there were also developments in the Telugu cinema that NTR was not directly associated with: these show how the Telugu cinema in general, not merely the NTR film, was invested in politics.

The Other *Eenadu* in the 1983 Election: Red Films and Cinema's Political Mandate

NTR's arrival as a self-proclaimed representative of the Telugus was coeval with a churning in the film industry, which was experiencing an unprecedented phase of growth that cut across its production, distribution, and exhibition sectors. Coinciding with the election of MGR as chief minister in Tamil Nadu, the boom was not limited to the Telugu cinema but was seen across South Indian industries. MGR's election appears to have acted as a catalyst for the boom. The extent to which it was a contributing factor is not of immediate relevance, but it is interesting to note that Tamil film production reached a new high in 1978. Telugu films, which had on a number of occasions since 1968 numerically surpassed their Tamil counterparts, grew at an equally impressive rate, resulting in both southern industries matching and overtaking the production level of Hindi films. During the late 1970s and early 1980s the number of Malayalam and Kannada productions grew as well (Rajadhyaksha and Willemen 1999: 31–2).

In the Telugu cinema, we notice from the late 1970s that the spurt in production was accompanied by new experiments in genre. The social was emerging as the predominant film form and internal variations, which began to be seen in the mid 1960s, were more clearly in evidence now. In numerical terms, most films of the late 1970s were made with low budgets and introduced new actors (including Chiranjeevi and Vijayashanti, who went on to become major stars and then politicians), or cast relatively minor ones in the lead. Genre experimentation was intimately linked to the economics of film production and distribution. Low-budget films did not have access to major stars and as a result struggled to find distributors and exhibition outlets. Topicality was among the key survival strategies for the low-budget film.

Around the time of NTR's crossover to politics, popular cinema's critique of the political establishment resonated with the TDP's campaign in rather direct ways. In the early 1980s the Telugu cinema became increasingly identified with strident, albeit conservative, political criticism. The repeated targeting of the political establishment becomes noticeable; it is represented as the source of all that is wrong by a cross-section of films—including of course NTR ones such as *Bobbili Puli* and *Naa Desam*—but also genres assembled by investors and technicians working with shoestring budgets. In the early 1980s the Congress (I) was most closely identified with the establishment for obvious reasons. In the years to come, even as governments changed and individual players within the industry either grew silent or vocal according to their political affiliation, the broad pattern of attacks on politicians did not change.

In the early 1980s the Telugu film industry assembled a new genre locally referred to as communist- or *erra cinemalu*, i.e. red films. This genre's concerns can be traced to the landmark "Naxalite film" *Bhoomikosam*, which was centred on the mobilization of the rural masses against feudal landlords and their class allies. Over the next few years, films on feudalism, made by directors associated with the New Indian Cinema, were a huge influence on the Telugu cinema including, as we saw, NTR films. By 1980 there was already a body of low-budget political films that adopted the representational techniques of the New Indian Cinema, as also the latter's focus on the "backward" countryside as the home of the feudal oppressor. Communist films in Telugu were coeval with I.V. Sasi's Malayalam red films of the early 1980s. Ratheesh Radhakrishnan notes that Sasi and scriptwriter T. Damodaran, the latter a known sympathizer of the Left, worked together on the "mass film" or "red film" (2010: 37–40). The distinguishing feature of this genre in Malayalam, Radhakrishnan argues, is that, unlike films made by communist sympathizers in the 1970s, there is no investment in socialist realist aesthetics. Like the films of the Sasi–Damodaran team, Telugu red films featured Communist Party activists as mobilizers of the masses, fighting corrupt and morally degenerate political elites. Interestingly, however, these two parallel developments do not seem to have been influenced by each other. With the exception of the Telugu film *Eenadu* (P. Sambasiva Rao, 1982, discussed below), which is a remake of Sasi's Malayalam film with the same name made earlier in the same year, I have not found evidence of the Malayalam counterpart being a point of reference for the Telugu red film, or vice versa.

The Telugu red film was largely a creation of relative newcomers to the industry. Like other contemporary low-budget films, the genre introduced new actors, directors, lyricists, script and dialogue writers, and was made by debutante production companies. The success of early 1980s red films ensured wide distribution and exhibition of the genre.

The move away from Madras played an interesting role in shaping the red film. To keep budgets low, most films of the genre were shot on location in Andhra Pradesh in towns or villages close to a railway station with a direct train to Madras (where film was processed).[25] Cast and crew stayed in inexpensive hotels or in the homes of locals working on films whose stories dealt with the social, economic, and political problems of ordinary people. The scenario recalled KoKu's prediction that the relocation of the film industry would not only affect its economics but also its aesthetics. In the red film we notice a great deal of local geographical detail but no explicit invocation of Teluguness. However, low-budget "Made in Andhra" films' increasing preference for political themes is too striking a coincidence to ignore. This preference suggests that if owning real estate was one form of asserting the industry's commitment to the Telugu nation, acquiring a stake in politics was another. Both were responses to the gradual shift away from Madras as the centre of Telugu film production.

Some of the industry figures associated with the red film, such as the veteran actor (and NTR's contemporary) Nagabhushanam, the chief villain in *Kathanayakudu*, were Communist sympathizers or party cardholders. Many others, including the genre's leading star and producer Madala Ranga Rao, were drawn directly from the Communist Party of India (CPI) and Communist Party of India Marxist (CPM) affiliates, such as Praja Natya Mandali. Murari (n.d.: 283) says Madala Ranga Rao had acted in "hundreds" of Praja Natya Mandali plays before he entered the film industry, first as an actor and

[25] I am grateful to M.V. Rayudu for drawing my attention to the importance of railway lines to outdoor shooting locations.

then as a producer. He is also credited with introducing to the industry two other CPM sympathizers who went on to become leading lights of the 1980s red film: T. Krishna (director and actor), and Pokuri Babu Rao (producer) who established Eetaram Pictures, a major low-budget film production company.[26]

The red film was attacked by Naxalite literary and cultural organizers and party sympathizers (see, for example, the essay on Madala Ranga Rao by Jinka 1982 published in the official journal of VIRASAM). In the 1980s, even as the red film continued to be made, it gave rise to two distinct genre tendencies, each focusing on the degeneration of the political system and questioning a number of its key components including electoral politics. The first was the Naxalite film (called Naxalite *cinemalu* in Telugu) which revolves around underground armed squads of Communist Party of India (Marxist-Leninist) groups and represents them as heroes. The Naxalite film came into being in the latter part of the 1980s largely due to the efforts of R. Narayana Murthy who starred in, directed and produced films of the genre till they became profitable enough for the entry of major stars and production companies in the late 1990s (Murari n.d.: 270–3). Narayana Murthy began his career as an actor and assistant director in low-budget films in the early 1980s. He began directing films with *Ardharatri Swatantram* (1986) and dedicated the film to T. Krishna who also played the role of a revolutionary singer modelled on the popular Naxalite poet/singer Gaddar.[27]

[26] The red film has a link, albeit a tenuous one, with the Rayalaseema faction film of the late 1990s as well. This genre played an important role in reviving the careers of both Balakrishna and Chiranjeevi. B. Gopal, the director most closely identified with the faction film at the turn of the century, began his career as an assistant in Madala Ranga Rao's red films. Interesting in this regard is a "snippet" in the magazine *Suprabhatam*, which lists over a dozen key industry figures, including actors, directors, and producers who were introduced by the red film (5 May 1995: 67). This list does not mention the director Mutyala Subbaiah, who went on direct Chiranjeevi in *Hitler* (1997).

[27] Gaddar (Gummadi Vithal Rao) of the Jana Natya Mandali, the cultural front of the CPI (ML-People's War) was a major figure in the Naxalite movement from the 1970s—indeed its public face—throughout the 1990s.

The second genre offshoot was centred on the middle-class vigilante who cleansed the polity of corruption. Eetaram Pictures was largely responsible for the evolution of the red film into the vigilante film. Among the most important films of the latter tendency are *Neti Bharatam* (T. Krishna, 1983, Image 199), *Pratighatana* (T. Krishna, 1985, produced by Ch. Ramoji Rao of *Eenadu* fame), and *Kartavyam* (A. Mohan Gandhi, 1990)—which laid the foundations for Vijayashanti's emergence as the "Lady Superstar" who did away with the need for a male lead in her films.[28] In spite of their ideological divergences, the red film proper, the Naxalite film, and the vigilante film are characterized by sympathetic but populist interpretations of revolutionary politics in the post-Emergency period.

Image 199: "Lady Superstar" Vijayashanti in her early career as female vigilante on the VCD jacket of *Neti Bharatam*.

He continues to be politically active as a key organizer of the Telangana Praja Front. For an account of Gaddar's career in the 1980s, see Somasekhar (1990). For an analysis of his work, see Venkat Rao (1999).

[28] Vijayashanti's 1990s work has been discussed by Lalitha Gopalan (2003) and Tejaswini Niranjana (2004).

The feudal lord inspired by the New Indian Cinema appears in the red film as the member of a grand exploitative alliance which includes corrupt government officials, politicians, and industrialists. *Yuvataram Kadilindi* (Dhavala Satyam, 1980, Image 200), the trend-setting red film, is set in the Coastal Andhra town of Ongole—home to some prominent red film producers and technicians—and shot on location there. The film begins with a detailed and seemingly pointless account of the mischief of students in a college. We soon realize that this universe of the students is about to change: Satyam (Ramakrishna), a new teacher, arrives to transform these youth into agents of socio-political change. As the film progresses, all sections of the student community—even the most rowdy ones—are won over

Image 200: Screening the revolution: Madala Ranga Rao wielding an axe in *Yuvataram Kadilindi* (VCD jacket).

by Satyam. Later, as Satyam accompanies the students on a study tour to his own village, the revolution spreads to the countryside. Here we discover a feudal lord in exactly the position of unquestioned authority that the New Indian Cinema found him some years earlier. A flashback reveals that the protagonist Satyam was the servant of the local zamindar (Chalapathi Rao) and that the latter had killed Satyam's brother (played by Madala Ranga Rao).[29] The students join Satyam in carrying out a campaign against the landlord by staging a *burra katha* performance. Their campaign later leads to a rebellion in the village—when the lower castes and the poor boycott the feudal lord. We soon discover that the zamindar is a member of the governing body of the college where the story began. Other members of the governing body include a corrupt politician and a woman who runs a prostitution racket. This mode of creating an ensemble of villainous class enemies is directly traceable to *Bhoomikosam*, where the zamindar, the rich model farmer, the moneylender, and the gambling-liquor-den owners form a syndicate to punish the villagers. The students and Satyam return to the city and soon confront the chief villain, Salahala Rao (meaning Advisor Rao, played by Nagabhushanam), the politician who is in league with the zamindar and his friends. Satyam is killed by the villains. The youth however (quite literally) mobilize the masses and attack Salahala Rao's house. In an obvious reference to Shyam Benegal's *Nishant*, the film's climax has the villains being chased by the crowd. The crowd gathers at a crossroads and there is a freeze frame on a top-angle shot of the crowd. A card showing "*Yuvataram Kadilindi*" (The young have moved/risen) appears. A voiceover narrator warns that Satyam/truth cannot die and any attempt to bury it will be given a fitting response by the *nyaya peetham* (seat of justice: referring to the masses).

Yuvataram Kadilindi established that political commentary was a reliable thematic foundation for the red film and low-budget films in

[29] Although the film does not credit Ranga Rao as producer, Murari points out that he had started the film's production company Navataram (New Generation) Pictures, which in the years to come was closely identified with the red film (n.d.: 233). Subsequently, a number of red films highlighted the special place of the actor by carrying the credit line "Madala Ranga Rao *Sardhyamlo*"—i.e. "under the guidance of Madala Ranga Rao."

general. In the early 1980s the genre did not make direct references to the Naxalite movement that was spreading through the Telangana region of the state in the post-Emergency period. Communist propaganda nevertheless figured prominently in the genre, in particular in song sequences. For its part, *Yuvataram Kadilindi* has inspirational and propaganda songs, one of which is in the form of a *burra katha* performance. The film also has a sarcastic song ridiculing the chief villain in a folk tune, thus gesturing twice over towards the communist parties' cultural agenda to adopt "people's forms." Songs found wide acceptance as the red film's highlights, and circulated widely beyond the cinema hall. The transformation of Leftist propaganda into mass culture is a development that would also figure in the business model of the Naxalite film some years later. One of the red film set-pieces is the May Day song, inevitably showing processions of workers. The genre's songs had a striking and ironic presence on All India Radio, even as the genre itself repeatedly faced censor trouble. The May Day song in *Erra Mallelu* (Dhavala Satyam, 1981, Image 201) continues to be featured on television to this day on 1 May; in fact most private satellite channels show at least one red film or Naxalite film to celebrate Labour Day.

Murari's entry (n.d.: 233) on Madala Ranga Rao is a chronicle of the genre's censor troubles. While *Yuvataram Kadilindi* was judged "best film" by the state government and awarded the Golden Nandi, *Viplava Sankham* (Beeram Mastan Rao, 1982) was denied a censor certificate. Madala, the star-producer of the red film, went on a hunger strike to protest against the Regional Office of the Central Board of Film Certification (CBFC) in Madras. Murari reports that through an emissary Indira Gandhi herself tried to get him to withdraw his hunger strike but failed. Eventually, his sheer determination prevailed and the film had to be given a censor certificate. Another film, *Prajasakthi*,[30] was completed during the 1982–3 election campaign but denied a certificate. The producer advertised his protest in newspapers (Images 202

[30] Rajadhyaksha and Willemen (1999) credit Navataram (as in Navataram Pictures) as the director of the film. The film's advertisements do not mention the director's name and it is likely that the production company was credited with directing the film. I have not been able to locate the film.

Image 201: VCD jacket of *Erra Mallelu* with a shot from its hit May Day song.

and 203). Incidentally, earlier in 1982 NTR's *Bobbili Puli* had faced censor problems (*Andhra Jyothi* 2007b: iv). Ranga Rao appealed successfully in the supreme court and *Prajasakthi* was eventually released in March 1983. When *Janam Manam* (D. Mohan Doss, 1984) faced trouble, prominent communist leaders in the state went on a hunger strike. *Erra Matti* (Dhavala Satyam, 1984) was held up for five years.

Although the political films of the early 1980s did not directly endorse NTR, they reinforced his critique of the Congress and the claim that political degeneration had set in during its rule of the state. Moreover, by explicitly concerning themselves with violent rebellions and/or mass mobilization, and by relentlessly attacking politicians, they gave the impression that the political establishment was in dire need of cleansing. When NTR arrived on the scene, it

Image 202: "Long live world peace! May destruction befall Imperialism! May revolutionary forces unite!" reads the heading of Madala Ranga Rao's signed statement condemning the delay caused in the release of *Prajasakthi* due to censor troubles (*Andhra Jyothi*, 1 October 1982: 1).

was as if the industry as a whole had thrown up the agent of change after demonstrating the need for it. Illustrating the general sense that the cinema had turned against the political establishment—the party in power in particular—are two half-page advertisements in *Andhra Patrika* (25 June 1982: 8). The first is an invitation by the Kurnool unit of the TDP to participate in the "great procession" (*brahmandamaina ooregimpu*) of supporters through the town's main thoroughfares and via a public meeting later in the evening. This was accompanied by an advertisement for the latest red film on offer, *Mahaprasthanam* (1982), featuring Madala Ranga Rao in the lead and directed by

Image 203: Madala Ranga Rao thanks the public for their support in the successful battle against obscurantist forces and announces the theatrical release of *Prajasakthi* (*Andhra Jyothi*, 6 March 1983: 8).

K. Hemambaradhara Rao of *Devata* fame. Named after a collection of poems by Sri Sri, this film was scripted by the poet, who is also credited as its presenter. Madala is seen shirtless and tied to a horizontal pole in the foreground of the advertisement, while line drawings of thin men and women with communist flags confront obese gun- and knife-wielding men in Gandhi caps—the masses have risen against their exploiters—easily recognized as politicians (Image 204).

In a number of political films of this period, including this particular red film whose release coincided with the early stages of NTR's campaign, violent rebellion is not only justified but presented as necessary. More important for our purposes, the masses were directly addressed as objects of mobilization. There is a textual manifestation of the direct address which cannot be missed in the red film, no more than it can in NTR's films like *Naa Desam*. Enormous crowds

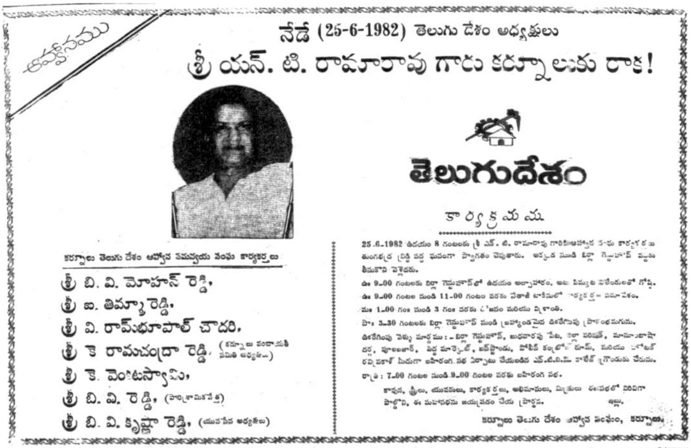

Image 204: Advertisements for a TDP election rally in Kurnool and the latest red film, *Mahaprasthanam* in *Andhra Patrika* (25th June 1982: 8). Source: Manasu Collection, M.V. Rayudu.

of people begin to make an appearance on the screen, either as addressees of a political discourse or as vigilantes. In fact, the red film thrived in an environment in which the cinema began to represent the government and political establishment as a whole as an illegitimate source of authority and power. *MLA Yedukondalu* (Dasari Narayana Rao, 1983), released after NTR's election, exemplifies the nature of the critique. In this political satire the barber Yedukondalu (Dasari Narayana Rao) is elected as a member of the legislative assembly (MLA) and is instantly transformed into a corrupt and greedy politician. The illegitimacy of the MLA's actions is reinforced by his lower-caste origins. The film ends with a speech by Yedukondalu, who reveals that he has all the time been motivated by the desire to expose the system.

Among the films that had a direct resonance with the TDP campaign was *Telugunadu* (Lakshmi Deepak, 1982). While I have not been able to locate the film, a review and advertisements of the film in *Andhra Jyothi*, prominently featuring the map of Andhra Pradesh, provide sufficient grounds for this assertion (Image 205).

Image 205: Advertisement for *Telugunadu* (*Andhra Jyothi*, 22 October 1982: 4).

According to one reviewer, the film makes a strong case for a unified Andhra (Krishna Babu 1982: 7). *Telugunadu* was reportedly made during the Emergency but censor troubles held up the release for seven years. It had sequences depicting political speeches and rallies in support of the Telangana and Andhra agitations. Curiously, even in 1975 when the film was made, the two agitations for statehood were already old news. It is therefore likely that *Telugunadu* was merely using these agitations as cases in point to make a more general statement on the threat to the Telugu land (*Telugunadu*) from manipulative politicians. It is possible that the film posits a negative equivalence between the two, anticipating NTR's logic of interpreting bad politics or poor governance as attacks on the linguistic nation. As we know, *Telugunadu*'s political concerns and overt references to the unity of Andhra Pradesh do not have parallels in NTR's own film career.

The other film that was related to NTR's campaign is *Eenadu*, arguably the most important political film released in 1982. Even though it did not feature NTR, it was virtually a campaign film.

Eenadu—the Film: Revolution under the Sign of the Cinema

After the election results were declared, a full-page advertisement appeared in the *Eenadu* newspaper highlighting the convergence of different strands and tendencies within the industry. This makes explicit the connection between the rise of the TDP and popular cinema's perspective on politics. Issued by the film star Krishna and his Padmalaya Studio, the congratulatory advertisement had an image of Krishna from the film, and that of NTR. The text, referring to the election results that had only just been announced, claimed that *Eenadu* (the movie) was the unanimously elected film (*ekagreevamga ennikaina chitram*) and the TDP the party of unanimous choice (Image 206).

Eenadu the film is Krishna's home production and features him in the lead. Its release in October 1982 coincided with the second phase of NTR's campaign, when the yellow-flag-waving mass was ubiquitous in Andhra Pradesh. The film does not openly endorse the TDP and, given the history of rivalry and competition between NTR and

Image 206: Film and party elected unanimously (*Eenadu*, 8 January 1983: 8).

Krishna, there is no reason to believe that the latter was acting in the interests of the older star.

Like the Malayalam original, the action of the Telugu *Eenadu* is framed by rallies and crowds marking the film's beginning and end. The remake opens with a reference to Alluri Sitarama Raju, the rebel whose role, as we know all too well, Krishna had played some years earlier in the eponymous film. The Krishna character leads a procession of workers and sings, imploring them to rise. He identifies himself as Rama Raju and assures them that he will be with them to the very end. Soon enough a statue of Alluri Sitarama Raju is seen prominently in the background while the procession moves along. Gathered around

Rama Raju are groups of people holding banners such as the RSU (Radical Students' Union), affiliated to a Naxalite group (CPI-ML People's War) as well as mainstream trade unions affiliated to the CPI and CPM (All India Trade Union Congress, AITUC; and Centre of Indian Trade Unions, CITU, respectively). Scenes of this procession, which attracts impressive crowds of curious roadside onlookers, are intercut with documentary footage of actual communist rallies (red flags and banners are clearly visible) in Delhi, as also unidentifiable cities. The song initially gives the impression that it is a red film set-piece and has little connection with the story. Halfway into the song, however, there is an unexpected transition to agitated factory owners who have presumably heard about Rama Raju's procession. For the rest of the song's duration, scenes of the rally are intercut with those of factory owners. The song ends with the procession reaching a factory's gates and workers raising slogans against an illegal lockout. Upon reaching the factory Pulla Rao (Jaggaiah), a fellow worker and friend of Rama Raju who has been in league with the owners, invites Rama Raju inside for a discussion. The owners attempt to bribe Rama Raju but the latter leaves their office, issuing them an ultimatum. On the way out the peon Koteswara Rao (Rao Gopala Rao), his brother-in-law, asks Rama Raju to reconsider his decision. Upon refusing to do so, Rama Raju is attacked by a gang led by Pulla Rao. When the police arrive Pulla Rao kills a member of the gang and implicates Rama Raju, who is arrested and sentenced to three years in jail. The jail barber Govindaiah (Kanta Rao), a convict who is about to be released, tells Rama Raju that he will give up his profession and join politics because he is hopeful of it yielding good returns.

The credit sequence now begins, with documentary footage of crowds waving red flags and shaking fists at the camera. We also see Congress and TDP supporters waving their respective party flags. We even get a fleeting glance of NTR's Chaitanya Ratham engulfed by a massive crowd. These shots of crowds are superimposed with scenes depicting the rapid rise of Govindaiah and Koteswara Rao as politicians. They are garlanded, make speeches, and greet people with folded hands. When the credit sequence ends, Koteswara Rao, now an MLA, is approached by a group of *basti* dwellers who request him to take action against a polluting factory. He assures them help but his speech to his constituents is intercut with scenes of a street conjurer's tricks, leaving little doubt that he is fooling them. Koteswara Rao is shown being bribed by the factory's owners (those who put Rama Raju in jail) and pays a part of it to Govindaiah, now a minister. Between them the minister and Koteswara Rao decide that they will not touch the factory. Rama Raju is released from prison. The rest of the film depicts the corruption and decay of various state and non-state institutions and the rise to further prominence of a troika consisting of Koteswara Rao, Govindaiah, and Pulla Rao (now a liquor baron). As the story progresses we realize that the superintendent of police (Satyanarayana) is on the side of the villains, government offices are plagued by corruption, students have become criminals, and their teachers strike irresponsibly for higher salaries.

Rama Raju sets about undoing the damage. He works with the *basti* dwellers to clean up the pollution caused by the industry and improve civic amenities. The activities of the villains, however, constantly impinge on the lives of the common people. Pulla Rao's brother Pratap (Sudhakar) tries to rape a college-going *basti* girl. She commits suicide. Pulla Rao hides his brother, and when Rama Raju and an honest police officer (Sridhar) capture him, the villain contacts the superintendent of police and has his brother released. Pulla Rao then sends his brother out of the country. Koteswara Rao encourages his henchman and ex-convict Anjaiah (Tyagaraju) to start a liquor shop in the *basti*. Rama Raju destroys it. Koteswara Rao gets Anjaiah a licence from Pulla Rao to run a government-sanctioned arrack shop. Rama Raju prevents the *basti* dwellers from drinking. Koteswara Rao then plots with Pulla Rao to set up a liquor shop at the venue of an all-party meeting which, ironically, is being organized to demand prohibition. Anjaiah says he cannot brew the large quantity of liquor that is required for the occasion. Pulla Rao sends him spirit (methyl alcohol) from a government hospital and has his men teach him to brew a lethal concoction without informing him of its ruinous potential. Back at the *basti* Anjaiah grudgingly agrees to the marriage of his son Suri (Chandra Mohan) and Malli (Radhika), the daughter of another *basti* dweller Ranganna (Gummadi). He decides to distribute some of the deadly brew to the *basti* dwellers during the wedding celebration. Rama Raju blesses the newly-wed couple and leaves to attend the all-party meeting. In his absence, with no one to counsel them, the villagers drink the spurious liquor. At the all-party meeting and in the *basti* a total of 2500 people perish, including Suri and most of the *basti* men.[31] Anjaiah makes a dying declaration that Pulla Rao supplied the spirit and is responsible for the tragedy. The hitherto honest police officer takes a bribe from Pulla Rao and destroys Anjaiah's statement. Even the superintendent of police is shocked by his subordinate's action but is forced to remain silent when reminded by the inspector that senior officials like him had destroyed the system by siding with powerful people. Koteswara Rao now decides to stake a claim for chief ministership because minister Govindaiah is discredited after the liquor tragedy. He approaches Pulla Rao for financial backing to set up his own party and buy the support of legislators of other parties. Between them they also decide that Rama Raju is to be killed. Pulla Rao's wife Lakshmi (Jamuna) overhears the conversation and informs Rama Raju, who refuses to take any precautions and is attacked and injured by Pulla Rao's men.

During the film's climax a large crowd of people, led by Rama Raju, prevents Koteswara Rao from reaching the venue where he is to be sworn in as chief minister. Pulla Rao is arrested when Lakshmi arrives on the scene to reveal that he was the mastermind of the plot to murder Rama Raju. The protesters, identified by the hero as voters from the MLA's constituency, join Rama Raju in forcing Koteswara Rao to resign from the assembly because he was elected under a different

[31] This tragedy has many parallels in real life. James Manor (1993) draws attention to the regularity with which death and disability have resulted from the consumption of "hooch" in cities across India. Citing newspaper reports, he points out that between 1972 and 1992 there were at least fifteen major incidents of liquor poisoning that claimed the lives of around 2000 people in various parts of India. In 1981, the worst of these incidents took place in Bangalore, killing more than 336 people. In 1982 there was another incident in Vypeen, Kerala (ibid.: 18). That the film was not off the mark in directly implicating powerful politicians and the police in the tragedy becomes clear from Manor's study. Manor notes that the man alleged to have brewed the poisonous liquor in the Bangalore tragedy was released on bail due to the efforts of "a senior figure in the Congress (I) Party" who visited the accused in jail (ibid.: 139).

party's banner. The villain is told that people had not voted for him but for his party's leaders. Left with no option, he resigns. Interpreting the developments, Rama Raju says that the people's action is a lesson which history has not yet taught chameleon-like politicians. He adds that that day's incident will become a *silasasanam*, a law written in stone, the foundation stone for democracy, as also a *vedam* for future generations. He raises slogans: *Bolo Swatantra Bharat ki jai* and *Vande Mataram*, then falls down. There is a freeze-frame on the collapsing hero, and a card with *Eenadu* (this day) written in red brings the film to a close.

The Star and *Cinema Janam*

The general drift of the film is in support of NTR's campaign. There are throwaway references to how the actions of politicians are shaming the entire Telugu race (*jati*), recalling the NTR–*Eenadu* newspaper discursive construction of the injured race. Extending the film's political critique, the principal villain is made to bear some resemblance with Chenna Reddy, wielding a baton like the former chief minister. Defections engineered by Koteswara Rao recall Chenna Reddy's success in winning over opposition MLAs after the 1978 election. There are also sarcastic references to the chief minister, whom we don't actually see in the film, spending most of his time in Delhi. As if to lend authenticity to this reference, the dates of his Delhi trips are mentioned. However, story-level references to the contemporary are not the only pointers of the convergence between this film and NTR's campaign. What is of interest is the manner in which the film envisages the location of the star *vis-à-vis* the fiction but also politics, inserting him into contexts in which the masses are in dire need of new leadership.

The Telugu remake creates multiple equivalences between the cinema and politics which are absent in the original. In the Malayalam film the character Krishna Pillai (Balan Nair), on whom Rama Raju is modelled, is a middle-aged communist who has been in jail while a new generation rose to power. During his absence the Communist Party itself has been corrupted by the entry of a manipulator who is in league with the class enemy (the Pulla Rao character in Telugu). In the Telugu film, in spite of references to communism and the ubiquity of red flags, Rama Raju's relationship with the Communist Party or politics remains fuzzy. Moreover, unlike Krishna Pillai who loses his lover to his corrupt party colleague, Rama Raju is a pure political agent—he has no life outside politics, nothing that can be called personal. There is no history of intimacy between Rama Raju and Lakshmi (Pulla Rao's wife). His doting sister's attempts to integrate him into her family or share its wealth fail repeatedly.

Radhakrishnan (2010: 40) proposes that the Malayalam version "presents us with the possibility that a film star could be replaced by a political 'star'." Krishna was already a major star, so there was no question of replacing the film star with another kind of star. The Telugu *Eenadu*, too, makes an interesting link between the political churning of the period and the film star, albeit one very different from the original's attempt at assembling a political star. The line-up of the entire spectrum of communist organizations (from the RSU on the extreme left to the mainstream left trade unions) behind Rama Raju is accompanied by repeated references to Krishna's films. The opening sequence seems to suggest that our star-protagonist is inserted in the contemporary political context—marked by political turmoil and agitating crowds waving all kinds of flags. We are thus not introduced to a new kind of star but one whose political mandate is inextricably linked to his superstardom. The juxtaposition of documentary footage of generic crowds and "real" crowds of diegetic onlookers and fans—who wave, run, or simply gather in strength around Krishna in outdoor locations—offers a demonstration of the power of the star as a rival, and indeed superior, rallying point to the political party. In *this* star-protagonist, around whom the masses gather spontaneously, we have found the agent of the revolution. Whereas the red and yellow party flags demonstrate the political intent of the masses, the star-protagonist alone can ensure that their energies are channelled towards transformative ends. Notice that the villains rise to power during Rama Raju's absence, as if unsupervised political unrest has somehow thrown up false leaders.

Whereas in the Malayalam version communist graffiti provides the backdrop to some of the action, especially in the *basti*, in this film such pedestrian realism is shunned. Instead we see posters of Krishna's earlier films marking the diegesis as a space under the constant gaze of the star.[32] At one point in the film we see a poster of *Alluri Sitarama Raju* pasted on the foundation of a Gandhi statue and the hero points in the general direction of the statue/poster while reminding the MLA about sacrifices made by freedom fighters for the nation. The cinema itself figures in the film as the site for resolving the crisis of political representation, one where the agitating masses are condemned to be ruled by manipulative and self-seeking leaders. During the climax Rama Raju refers to the crowd as an ocean (*praja samudram*) and also as a gathering of *Telugu biddalu* (Telugu children). The gathering is also compared to the collective that brought the mighty British empire to its knees. The power and purposefulness of the mass is thus stressed, but in effect it is the magnetism of the leader that is foregrounded. There is a memorable scene of Rama Raju blocking the path of Koteswara Rao's procession by lying on the road. Instantly, the entire crowd follows his example.

What do we make of the crowds in the film? Murari points out that Krishna had instituted the practice of incorporating crowds of curious onlookers and fans (who inevitably materialize at shooting venues) into the action of his films. The climax of his home production *Devudu Chesina Manushulu* (V. Ramachandra Rao, 1973), with NTR and himself in the lead roles, was shot against the backdrop of such crowds. Soon after, Krishna produced *Alluri Sitarama Raju*, in which the onlookers became bit-role players in the film as Rama Raju's constituency and members of the Telugu/Indian nation. The practice that Murari (n.d.: 182) credits Krishna with inventing is the incorporating of *cinema janam*, who hang around shooting venues, into the fiction. The Telugu cinema thus began to double back on itself by depicting the star and his fans in the same frame. This is particularly telling in *Eenadu*, which is among the few Telugu films ever to have been shot in Vijayawada. Here we see the city's thoroughfares choked by thousands of people and the camera packs

[32] The films include *Alluri Sitarama Raju*, but also for example *Mayadari Malligadu* (Adurthi Subba Rao, 1973), in which he plays a village ruffian sentenced to death by hanging for a crime he did not commit. He accepts his fate, spreads cheer among his fellow prisoners, and is saved at the last minute when the truth is discovered.

them into the frame like newspaper photographs of NTR's campaign. During the film's remarkable climax, Krishna and the crowds that have gathered to see the shooting are seen together in the Gandhinagar area in Vijayawada, the location of hundreds of film distribution offices and over a dozen cinema halls. The final confrontation between the villain and the masses can easily be identified as Sanyasi Raju Road, whose entrance in the 1980s was flanked by Dr Rai's Sex Clinic (now Bakshi Hospital) on the left and Alankar Theatre on the right. Today, Gudavalli Ramabrahmam's statue, installed after the film was made, stands a few yards from this street, as if overseeing the health of the film industry while its customers are taken care of by Dr Rai's successor (Images 207 and 208). Coincidentally, this is the exact point at which a visitor to the city, making her way from the railway station or bus stand, would turn into streets housing the city's film-related real estate—no doubt a location thronging with *cinema janam*. The climax has the crowd making its way *out* of the Gandhinagar area—in the same direction that filmgoers move after screenings—to confront the villain. Referred to by the hero as the ocean of humanity and labelled as Telugu *biddalu*, the on-screen mass is, in all likelihood, composed of the locality's morning show crowd.

There is a further layering of the references to the cinema in the climax when, at the very end of the film, Rama Raju bares his chest, daring the police to shoot him in precisely the manner that the rebel does in *Alluri Sitarama Raju*'s climax. When the hero exposes his body we see that it already has bleeding wounds, as if the rebel has travelled across time to make an appearance in the here and now. But of course it is Krishna we see playing two roles simultaneously and, in the process, offering an insight into the star's ability to transform the film spectator into a mobilized political subject. The invocation of history to authenticate present-day politics is thoroughly mediated by the star's own cinematic past. The star as mobilizer stands before the *cinema janam*, recalling his screen roles and re-enacting them to mobilize them.

Building on NTR films, *Eenadu* suggests much more explicitly than the older star's campaign films that politics is a field crying out for the intervention of the cinema. The political intent of the crowd and the complete mastery Rama Raju has over it, and the references, even in

207

208

Images 207 and 208: The statue of Ramabrahmam (top) looks on as *cinema janam* are seen milling around Sanyasi Raju street on a late April afternoon in 2011. A vinyl hoarding of Vangaveeti Mohana Ranga, the popular Kapu MLA who was murdered in 1988, can be seen on the left side of the entrance of the street, in a fan promotion of the film *Mr. Perfect*, starring Krishnam Raju's nephew Prabhas.

his death, to the other (Alluri Sita) Rama Raju, are all pointers to the fact that the cinema is now a key political player. Its role is to bring the masses face to face with its political responsibilities—and lead them along the path of revolution. The crowd does not have a voice. Yet the leader will not only speak on its behalf but also interpret its silence. At a time when the true leaders of the nation are but statues and memories, the screen will produce the new leader.

It is erroneous to assume that films transmit political messages. The Telugu cinema presents us with a convincing case of cinematic pleasures assuming retroactive significance in the wake of an atypical and paradigm-changing election campaign. And yet NTR was absolutely right in asking us to watch his *Bobbili Puli* to find out what his political agenda was. He was cobbling together the Telugu nation through his films at a time when political movements in the Telangana and Andhra regions had demonstrated that the foundations of the Telugu nation were pretty shaky. A new logic, and of course a new centre, was needed to hold the pieces in place. The Telugu cinema had come further from the grand unification proposed by Ramabrahmam than ever before. The link between a location-specific realism and language had been upturned. The Telugu nation now became that entity which is addressed by the cinema, its constituent parts held together by the star.

The story of the Telugu cinema is not the biography of NTR, unless we conceive of NTR as the name of an organizing principle and not just an individual. By the late 1970s, with the rise to prominence of Krishna and Sobhan Babu, a second generation reinforced the male star's centrality to the film industry as well as his continuing ability to initiate fan mobilization around himself. Around this time the competition between NTR and Krishna spread to the sphere of fan activity where, in spite of their relatively small numbers, Krishna fans ensured a high visibility for the star in the public domain.[33] With NTR attempting a crossover into electoral politics, this ability of younger

[33] Fans of Krishna and NTR got into violent confrontations in the late 1970s. Krishna's fans are rumoured to have rigged box office collections by buying up the tickets of their star's film to prolong the length of a film's run. For details of fan activity, including their rivalries, see Srinivas (2009: 3–69).

stars to gather the masses around them too assumed a direct political significance. Yet another generation of stars, the third after 1956, was already waiting in the wings. During *Eenadu*'s climax, coincidentally, we see a huge hoarding for a Chiranjeevi film. Like Krishna in his generation, Chiranjeevi too would demonstrate the complex links between stars and mobilization, both on and off screen.

Within months of NTR's ascent to the chief-ministership, there appeared ominous signs of the future. Krishna's Padmalaya Studio, then under construction on ten acres of land given by the state government at subsidized rates, ran into trouble with the Municipal Corporation of Hyderabad for violating municipal regulations (*Andhra Jyothi* 1983a: 1). The star's fans were quick to accuse the TDP government of sabotaging his interests. At one point fans threatened to hold a black flag demonstration at the venue of the first post-victory TDP Mahanadu (*Andhra Jyothi* 1983b: 1). The confrontation did not occur and the studio was not, after all, demolished. But in the 1984 parliamentary election Krishna campaigned for the Congress. In the late 1980s he made a number of hard-hitting political films, including *Naa Pilupe Prabhanjanam* (which he starred in and directed in 1986), attacking NTR and his government. In the run-up to the 1989 assembly election, which the TDP lost, both Krishna and Dasari Narayana Rao attacked NTR in their films, even as a spate of low-budget political satires lampooned the star-politician.[34] In 1989 Krishna was elected as a member of parliament on a Congress ticket (he lost the seat in 1991). His interest in political cinema persisted well into the 1990s, when he starred in a home production of a Naxalite film, *Encounter* (N. Shankar, 1996), playing the revolutionary and dying all over again.

[34] Anti-NTR political satires of this period include *Mandaladheesudu* (1988?) and *Gandipeta Rahasyam* (1989), directed by the noted screen villain of the 1970s, Prabhakar Reddy; and *Kaliyuga Vishwamitra* (Pradeep Sakthi, 1989).

Conclusion

Politics as Pathetic Performance

In retrospect it seems possible to assert that NTR's campaign, of which his election speeches were constituents, was part of a naming act: it labelled the mobilized masses as members of the Telugu nation. It also rendered this mobilized collective, which in fact had no antecedent, timeless. His projection of a Telugu political community back in time had parallels with the Dravidian movement's invocation of antiquity. As Bernard Bate says, "Dravidianist oratory, a speech genre modeled on a written form that sounds old, is an iconic index—an emblem—of antiquity deployed at the very moment when a modern institution emerges" (2009: 185–6).

The long decade of the star-politician in Andhra Pradesh, from 1982 to 1996, spanning the period between the establishment of the Telugu Desam Party and NTR's death, corresponds with the highpoint of theatrical exhibition in the state. This was also a time when it appeared that a Telugu nationalism complete with paraphernalia for state sponsorship—including institutions promoting the language and statues recalling the glorious dead—was firmly in place. The cinema was deeply implicated in this project. However, there was never a time in the state's post-1956 history when language fanned political passions of the kind Sumathi Ramaswamy (1997) and Lisa Mitchell (2009) draw attention to in their studies of Tamil India, and the Andhra region's agitations that followed Potti Sriramulu's death, respectively.

From the vantage point of the present, the decade of Telugu nationalism comes across as an interlude. The edifice has disintegrated since, and predictably, along the axis of colonial political geography.

During NTR's reign too there were intermittent calls for a separate Rayalaseema state. But at present there is no doubting the truth that the very idea of the Telugu nation has been fundamentally challenged. Underscoring this shift is the spectacular symbolic gesture by a group of pro-Telangana activists who demolished the statues of eminent Telugus on the banks of Hussain Sagar Lake in Hyderabad in March 2011.[1] The statues had been commissioned in 1986 during NTR's chief-ministership as part of the Telugu Velugu project, which is believed to have been wholly conceived by him. Undamaged as of now, but seriously imperilled by the political climate in Hyderabad, is the statue of Telugu Talli, Mother Telugu, which stands outside the state secretariat, barely a kilometre away from the demolished statues. Mitchell notes that this particular statue was installed in 2002 by the chief minister, N. Chandrababu Naidu, as a replacement for another statue of the Mother that NTR had commissioned nearby and which had been damaged during the construction of a flyover (2009: 91). A decade after its much-publicized inauguration, the Telugu Talli statue finds itself surrounded by several coils of razor wire and guarded by armed policemen (Image 209).

I began writing this book at a time when it became more evident with every passing month that economic and political considerations, and not emotional bonds or cultural affinities, held Andhra Pradesh together. Further, over the past decade, it was the movement in support of Telangana that showed all the signs of a classic nationalism. An affective community was formed around Telangana, and so strongly that "Telangana sentiment" is now a key phrase in discussions, widely used by politicians, activists, and journalists to underscore the emotional foundations of the demand for statehood. As in instances of classic nationalism (Weber 1946: 176), the formation of the political community here is a matter of sentiment. The movement's fascinating iconography, including the images of a new mother goddess, Telangana Talli, the deity personifying the region, is evidence of a nationalist imagination at work (Image 210).

[1] The incident occurred on 11 March 2011. The *Hindu* reported that 7 (of the 33) statues were destroyed and 1 thrown into the lake (City Bureau 2011: 1). Other reports claimed that as many as 19 statues were destroyed and 11 thrown into the water (Sudhir 2011).

Image 209: Imperilled Telugu Talli statue against the backdrop of the secretariat (October 2011).

Image 210: The ascendant goddess: innovative T-shirt design put out by a supporter of Telangana which shows Telangana Talli against the backdrop of a map of the proposed state and "official stamp" of the future government in the foreground. Source: https://picasaweb.google.com/102613673111603566632/SatishkumarTG#5570161819640257746, visited on 16 November 2012.

The prospect of the formation of a Telangana state—coinciding with the exhaustion of the opportunities and promise of 1956 for all regions—and the rapid rise of television as the form which assembles the nation in the early twenty-first century, are pointers to the fact that the Telugu cinema's relationship with political geography is no longer what it was in the second half of the twentieth century.

Even as the Telugu film industry began to earn half its gate collections from the Telangana region, the cinema was named by pro-Telangana commentators as causing hurt to the people of the region by ridiculing their dialect and also representing them in poor light. One article argues: "During the last 20 years, the Telugu film and entertainment industry dominated by coastal Andhra capital has consistently portrayed Telangana people as either villains or comedians. Belittling of Telangana culture, language and life has become the norm in Telugu films and television" (Melkote *et al.* 2010: 11). Telugu films, like most other popular films, are laced with stereotypical representations of women, oppressed classes—including Dalits and indigenous peoples—and religious minorities. Brahmins and Reddys too have on occasion protested against their own screen images. The images of Telangana people, in addition to being politically incorrect, are pointers to a critical development in the history of the Telugu cinema: the establishment of studios in Hyderabad and the practice of shooting films in Hyderabad city and its surroundings. The city's geography and the Telangana region's dialect became a noticeable presence in the Telugu cinema as recently as the late 1980s, with *Siva* (Ram Gopal Varma, 1989). In this film, for the first time in popular Telugu cinema, the local specificity of the city was foregrounded, the action being set in the narrow bylanes of the city's *bastis* and Irani tea shops, against the backdrop of the odd historical monument. Characters also spoke accented Telugu, allowing for a clear distinction to be made between those arriving from Coastal Andhra and local people. *Siva* was made by Annapurna Studio, owned by ANR's family, and launched Varma as the specialist in *urban nativity*. It was not just paddy fields and palm trees but also street signs and accents that marked the specificity of a story's location in Telugu films from this point of time.

What more can the history of Telugu cinema and NTR's career

tell us about the present than the problem of misrepresentation? The question is best located against the backdrop of the growing interface between political mobilization, especially electoral campaigns, and news media and entertainment within Andhra Pradesh and beyond. This allows us to see that neither the South Indian star-politician nor the celebrity-turned-politician is a necessary condition for the dovetailing of politics with entertainment in the mass media.

In their examination of "elections as popular culture in Asia" contributors to Chua (2007) on the theme draw attention to how politics becomes entertainment. The role of the media, in particular television coverage, is brought into sharp focus by M. Madhava Prasad, who points out that in India "Reporters followed leaders on their campaign trail, from morning to evening, showing them eating, sleeping, talking, walking, and sharing intimate details, during car rides, about their private lives and personal difficulties" (2007: 146). Arguably, television is to today's election campaigns what newspapers were to NTR's, although newspaper coverage of his campaign never attempted to create intimacy between him and the reader-voter. Yufen Ko, writing about elections in Taiwan, gets even closer: we are told that candidates indulge in a variant of Japanese "Cosplay" to impress their constituencies (2007). Cosplay (derived from costume play), is a pop cultural form of Japanese origin in which fans dress up like their favourite animation characters and participate in competitions or public performances. Ko points out that in the run-up to the 2004 parliament election "Many candidates adopted cosplay as their first impression maker: one candidate dressed like the Hollywood film character 'The Terminator'; and other impersonated Hong Kong comic movie star Stephen Chow . . . Several female candidates dressed like the most popular female figure of the year, a woman therapist . . . who featured in a Korean epic [television] drama" (2007: 27). Cultural performance associated with transnational fandom proper, and with no discernible connection to local politics, thus made its way into the election campaign.

With increasing degrees of the electronic mediation of elections, the question is no longer whether the performative element plays any part in politics. NTR's campaign demonstrates the continuity between popular cinema and the election campaign. The star's campaign style, combining speech in classical-sounding Telugu with theatrical body movements and gestures, was of crucial importance for the leakage of the cinematic into the electoral. The press, expectedly, picked on NTR's performative excesses and went on to make a spectacle of his most routine acts. In the process it constructed readers and an electorate as members of a spectatorial collective. There was a perfect fit between the star who insisted on showcasing his histrionic skills during his election rallies and a print medium only just learning to have "fun with democracy" (Prasad 2007). This began the era of mass electoral politics in Andhra Pradesh.

I propose that the distinguishing feature of NTR's campaign was his *pathetic performance.* NTR staked his political future on a performance that was pathetic in both senses of the term: it was at once saturated with affect and laughable in the sense of being worthy of contempt. First, it was centred on a display of the star's sadness at the plight of the suffering multitudes: his Telugu brothers and sisters, who were not just poor like the majority of the population in India but were suffering *because* they were discriminated against, subjected to stepmotherly treatment by rulers in distant Delhi. Simultaneously, the performance was pathetic in that it was unabashedly theatrical and excessive, evoked contempt, and invited ridicule. NTR was at once visibly moved, delivering moving speeches, and laughable.

Insights into the issues thrown up by his campaign style are offered by a video that has now found a new life on YouTube.[2] Titled "TDP History: NTR's Emotional Highly Applauded Speech," this video was originally distributed by the TDP during its silver jubilee celebrations in 2007. A minute-and-a-half excerpt has been posted separately on YouTube under the title "NTR Emotional Speech."[3] The excerpt is a studio recording of a speech made during the 1985 election

[2] Rajeshbits, "TDP History: NTR's Emotional Highly Appaluded Speech." Uploaded on 24 June 2009. Stable url: http://www.youtube.com/watch?v=LjFTE7iZjFA&NR=1. Last accessed on 15 December 2011. I am grateful to T. Vishnu Vardhan for alerting me to this video.

[3] Kaiannantr9, "NTR Emotional Speech." Uploaded on 18 October 2008. Stable url: http://www.youtube.com/watch?v=nHNkBDUtvmw&feature=related. Last accessed on 15 December 2011.

campaign. NTR is seen in saffron clothes, speaking to the camera. Shots of crowds from rallies are intercut at regular intervals while canned applause punctuates his lines. In its YouTube avatar, the clip is so completely dislocated from the original context that NTR—his voice made hoarse by the campaign, his numerous gesticulations at the camera, his frequent facial changes—comes across as hilarious. It would be natural to mistake him for a clown, he seems so unlike a serious politician. At a particularly memorable moment in his speech he says his party was born out of the sweat of labourers. As he says "sweat" (*chemata*), looking directly into the camera, he flicks a non-existent drop of perspiration from his brow. This is vintage NTR: so focused on the generation of affect that he risks coming across as ridiculous (indeed the nickname Drama Rao stuck).

In my discussion of Adorno's essay on fascist propaganda (Chapter 4), I argued that the masses at NTR's rallies, as also those who read newspaper reports of them, were invited to be a part of an exchange in which they were offered an entertaining performance in return for political support. There is no reason for us to assume that the crowds at his rallies were unaware of the excessive nature of his body language, speech, and rhetoric. My point is not the translation of this exchange into voting behaviour, but the positioning of the political subject and voter as spectator. The researchable problem about the mediatization of politics is not whether the masses believe false promises and vote for the wrong people—that mistake we are capable of making all by ourselves, without inputs from newspapers and television. The question is what happens to politics in the presence of an omniscient media. The NTR instance tells us that the one thing we can expect to find is an increase in instances of the pathetic performance, which is no longer limited to right wing mobilizations—what Adorno calls the "psychotechnics" of applied irrationality (1994: 223). The 1982–3 campaign benefited from the entropy of the masses (manifest in changing caste alignments in the electoral domain and armed insurrections alike) and a host of contingencies. The analysis of political shifts of the period remains incomplete without a discussion of the performative dimension of politics and its mediation by modern industrial-cultural forms addressing the restive masses as objects of mobilization. Almost three decades after the event, we notice a slew of political leaders across the country—regardless of language, caste, and gender—acquiring mastery over a performative idiom eminently suited for television. Andhra Pradesh continues to provide stunning examples of the complex links between media consumption and political mobilization.

NTR's lasting influence is evident from the movement for the formation of a separate Telangana state. On the face of it, this appears to be a counterintuitive and even disingenuous claim because the differences between NTR's agenda and demands for the creation of a Telangana state are glaring. The ongoing Telangana movement is committed to undoing NTR's ideological suture, which had temporarily resolved the identity question in the early 1980s. The beheaded statues of Hyderabad's Tank Bund are doubtless a part of that move. It is useful to see the two mobilizations as mirror opposites. Like all mirror opposites, they have much in common.

Striking in this regard are abusive speeches by the Telangana Rashtra Samiti (TRS) leadership, K. Chandrasekhar Rao (KCR) in particular. He has an excellent command of Telugu and his public statements are usually laced with clever and witty insults against his opponents. He has on occasion threatened opponents of Telangana state formation with violence, threats that he has been careful enough not to translate into action. Sometimes this rhetoric—such as the one warning Coastal Andhra politicians that their dhotis would drop when they were chased and thrashed by the people of Telangana—evokes the comic. On camera he speaks only in the Telangana dialect. Typically, his insults make headlines on television and in the newspapers. As with NTR before him, KCR's speech with its Telangana dialect facilitates a strong identification with the political cause that he espouses. There is also no denying the performativity of his utterances—they are meant to draw attention and circulate as headlines and soundbytes. As in 1982–3, the symbolic gesture is central to the TRS campaign. Among other things, the party frequently invokes Telangana Talli.

And then there is Y.S. Jaganmohan Reddy (known as Jagan), son of the former chief minister, Y.S. Rajasekhar Reddy, who died in a helicopter crash in September 2009. Jagan chose to mobilize the masses by engaging in what he calls the *odarpu yatra*, the tour of consolation. This *yatra* was purportedly to console the families of those who reportedly committed suicide on learning of Rajasekhar Reddy's death. The real intent, to mobilize support for Jagan's bid to capture power, was hardly in doubt. During the *yatra* he was often seen with inconsolable family members of his father's deceased supporters. It is another matter altogether that there were media reports suggesting that most of these deaths had natural causes unconnected with the death of Jagan's father.

Ironically, even as the performative idiom became ubiquitous across the political spectrum in Andhra Pradesh, Chiranjeevi, the most popular post-NTR film star, has enjoyed a rather limited success in politics. From the late 1980s, the expansion of the industry, the exhibition sector in particular, and the exponential rise in fan activity made Chiranjeevi a more visible presence in the public domain than NTR was at any point in his career. Like NTR, he was approached by political parties before starting the Praja Rajyam Party (PRP) in 2008. The PRP initially appeared to have broad-based support cutting across regional and caste divisions. However, the party won only 18 seats in the 2009 assembly election—i.e. only about half the number predicted even by the least favourable pre-election surveys. The party did not win even one parliamentary seat, and Chiranjeevi himself lost one of the two assembly seats he contested. A number of reasons were offered by observers for the PRP's poor showing: caste equations did not work out, the party was too closely controlled by the star's extended family, there was no clarity in his agenda, and so on.

Against the backdrop of NTR's 1982–3 campaign, a crucial difference between the two stars becomes clear. Chiranjeevi's campaign, which too began in Tirupathi and with references to his film career, was notable for the star's rather surprising inability to deliver a satisfying speech on the political platform. This is not to say the obvious: his public speeches lacked the rhetorical finesse of NTR, and were at times faltering. For all his popularity, acting abilities, and symbolic gestures, Chiranjeevi appears to have had difficulties in making the transition to the idiom of performance in which NTR excelled. Still, although the figure of the star-politician seems now on the decline, the idiom itself has become the hallmark of mass mobilization in Andhra Pradesh and beyond. NTR's career, and its resonances in the crop of charismatic leaders who came after him, suggest that even if these are not "passions of the tongue," passions are, all the same, the stuff of democratic politics in this part of the world.

Bibliography

Adorno, Theodor W. 1994. "Anti-Semitism and Fascist Propaganda." In *The Stars Down to Earth and Other Essays on the Irrational in Culture*. London and New York: Routledge, pp. 218–31.

Amin, Shahid. 1984. "Gandhi as Mahatma: Gorakhpur District, Eastern UP, 1921–22." In Ranajit Guha, ed., *Subaltern Studies III*. New Delhi: Oxford University Press, pp. 1–61.

Ananth, S. 2007. "The Culture of Business: A Study of the Finance Business in the Vijayawada Region of Andhra Pradesh." Unpublished Ph.D. dissertation. University of Hyderabad.

Andhra Bhoomi. 1962. "Vinadapapanunu Parisramabhivruddhikey Viniyoginchali." 7 April, p. 5.

Andhra Film Chamber Journal. 1964a. "Chitranirmanamlo Andhrula Pettubadi Vivaralu." Vol. 9, nos 5–6. March–April, p. 41.

———. 1964b. "Andhra Jillalalo Gala Theatrelu." Vol. 9, nos 5–6. March–April, p. 56.

———. 1964c. "Andhralo Telugu Chalanachitra Pradarsanasalala Abhivriddhi." Vol. 9, nos 5–6. March–April, p. 83.

———. 1964d. "Sri Sarathy Studios." Vol. 9, nos 5–6. March–April, p. 38.

Andhra Jyothi. 1982a. "Idi Rajakeeya Abhimanama? Cinema Moja?" Vijayawada edition (21 October), p. 3.

———. 1982b. "Pongi Poralina Abhimanam." Vijayawada edition (9 October), p. 1.

———. 1983a. "Padmalaya Koolchivetaku Notisu." Vijayawada edition (22 May), p.1.

———. 1983b. "'Indulo Mee Prameyam Ledantara?'" Vijayawada edition (24 May), p. 1.

———. 2007a. "Telugu Desam Vijayavani Mundugane Vinipinchina *Justice Chaudhury*." In "Chitra Jyothi" (28 May), p. iv.

———. 2007b. "Sanchalananiki Maru Peru *Bobbili Puli*." In "Chitra Jyothi" (9 July), p. iv.

———. 2008. "Telugu Chitra Parisrama Swarashtramlo Sthirapadadaniki Karakulu Akkineney." In "Chitra Jyothi" (15 January), p. iv.

———. 2009. "Chetulu Kadigesukovadame." *ABN-Andhra Jyothi* Interview. Bangalore edition (22 November), p. 8.

Andhra Patrika. 1980. "NTR Cinecreations Patakamlo Mahaniiyula Chitralu" (13 September), p. 13.

Andhra Pradesh Film Chamber of Commerce. 1981a. "Cinemas in India." In C.V.V.R. Prasad, ed. *Indian Talkie Golden Jubilee Celebrations Andhra Pradesh 1931–1981: Souvenir*. Hyderabad: Andhra Pradesh Film Chamber of Commerce, p. 131.

———. 1981b. "Navayuga Films." Advertisement in C.V.V.R. Prasad, ed. *Indian Talkie Golden Jubilee Celebrations Andhra Pradesh 1931–1981: Souvenir*. Hyderabad: Andhra Pradesh Film Chamber of Commerce, p. 163.

———. 1981c. "Veterans Honoured." In C.V.V.R. Prasad, ed. *Indian Talkie Golden Jubilee Celebrations Andhra Pradesh 1931–1981: Souvenir*. Hyderabad: Andhra Pradesh Film Chamber of Commerce, pp. 43–55.

———. 1981d. "NTR's Estate." Advertisement in C.V.V.R. Prasad, ed. *Indian Talkie Golden Jubilee Celebrations Andhra Pradesh 1931–1981: Souvenir*. Hyderabad: Andhra Pradesh Film Chamber of Commerce, p. 160.

———. 1981e. "Sowing of the Seed: The Hyderabad State Film Chamber of Commerce." In C.V.V.R. Prasad, ed. *Indian Talkie Golden Jubilee Celebrations Andhra Pradesh 1931–1981: Souvenir*. Hyderabad: Andhra Pradesh Film Chamber of Commerce, p. 59.

———. 1981f. "Andhra Pradesh State Film Development Corporation Limited." Advertisement in C.V.V.R. Prasad, ed. *Indian Talkie Golden Jubilee Celebrations Andhra Pradesh 1931–1981: Souvenir*. Hyderabad: Andhra Pradesh Film Chamber of Commerce, p.158.

———. 1995. *Andhra Pradesh Film Diary 1995*. Hyderabad: Andhra Pradesh Film Chamber of Commerce.

Arnold, David. 1985. "Sitarama Raju's Rebellion: A Response." *Social Scientist*. Vol. 13, no. 4 (April), pp. 44–9.

Balagopal, K. 1984. "A False Resurrection: Rise and Fall of Rama Rao." *Economic and Political Weekly*. Vol. 19, no. 45 (10 November), pp. 1901–4. Stable URL: http://www.jstor.org/stable/4373737.

———. 1985. "The Karamchedu Killings: The Essence of the NTR Phenomenon." *Economic and Political Weekly*. Vol. 20, no. 31 (3 August), pp. 1298–1300.

———. 1986a. "Review: Agrarian Struggles." *Economic and Political Weekly*. Vol. 21, no. 32 (9 August), pp. 1401–5.

———. 1986b. "Anti-Reservation, Yet Once More." *Economic and Political Weekly*. Vol. 21, no. 36 (6 September), pp. 1572–4. Stable URL: http://www.jstor.org/stable/4376086.

———. 1987a. "An Ideology for the Provincial Propertied Class." *Economic and Political Weekly*. Vol. 22, no. 50 (12 December), pp. 2177–8.

———. 1987b. "Censorship by Force: A 'Telugu' Prescription for the 'Yellow' Virus." *Economic and Political Weekly*. Vol. 22, no. 26 (27 June), pp. 1022–3. Stable URL: http://www.jstor.org/stable/4377142.

———. 1987c. "Karamchedu: Second Anniversary." *Economic and Political Weekly*. Vol. 22, no. 33 (15 August), pp. 1378–81.

———. 1989. "A Year of 'Encounters'." *Economic and Political Weekly*. Vol. 24, no. 2 (14 January), pp. 66–8. Stable URL: http://www.jstor.org/stable/4394239.

———. 2000. "A Tangled Web: Subdivisions of SC Reservations in AP." *Economic and Political Weekly*. Vol. 35, no. 13 (25–31 March), pp. 1075–81.

Barnouw, Eric and S. Krishnaswamy. 1980. *Indian Film*. Second edition. New York, Oxford, New Delhi: Oxford University Press.

Baru, Sanjaya. 2007. "The Local and the Global in Hyderabad's Development." *Economic and Political Weekly*. Vol. 42, no. 43 (2 November), pp. 31–6.

Baskaran, S. Theodore. 1981. *The Message Bearers: The National Politics and the Entertainment Media in South India 1880–1945*. Madras: Cre-A.

———. 1996. *The Eye of the Serpent: An Introduction to Tamil Cinema*. Madras: East-West Books.

Bate, Bernard. 2009. *Tamil Oratory and the Dravidian Aesthetic: Democratic Practice in South India*. New York: Columbia University Press.

Bhageeratha. 1980. "Hyderabadlo Chalanachitra Parisrama." *Jyothi Chitra* (Sankranti Pratyeka Sanchika), n.d. CSCS Media Archive Record Number Te180020.

———. 1986. "Hyderabadlo Chalanachitra Parisrama Bhavitavyam?" *Jyothi Chitra* (Ugadi Pratyeka Sanchika), pp. 70–4.

Bhrugubanda, Uma. 2011. "Genealogies of the Citizen-Devotee: Popular Cinema, Religion and Politics in South India." Unpublished Ph.D. Dissertation. Columbia University.

Bommakanti, Subba Rao. 1964a. "*Doctor Chakravarthy:* Bengali Taipu Sunnita Chitram." *Krishna Patrika* (18 July), n.d. CSCS Media Archive Record Number Te110003.

———. 1964b. "Rama Rao Studio." *Krishna Patrika* (18 July), n.d. CSCS Media Archive Record Number Te110003.

———. 1965. "Kalla Tuppu Vadilinchina *Thene Manasulu*." *Krishna Patrika* (24 April), pp. 16, 17, 30. CSCS Media Archive Record Number Te110018.

———. 1991. "Film Journalismlo Parinamam." *Vijayachitra* (July), pp. 43–5.

Bowser, Eileen. 1990. *History of the American Cinema Vol. II: The Transformation of Cinema 1907–1915*. Berkeley, Los Angeles, London: University of California Press.

Brown, C.P. 1903, rpt 2006. *Telugu–English Dictionary*. Achanta Satyanarayana, ed. Vijayawada: Victory Publishers.

Bruhaspathi. 1949. "Janapada Chitrala Peeda." *Telugu Swatantra* (16 September). Translated and reprinted in *Workshop on Telugu Cinema: History, Culture, Theory*, 1999, "Dossier." Organized by Anveshi Research Centre for Women's Studies and Centre for the Study of Culture and Society, Hyderabad (13–16 August), pp. 57–8.

Chakravarthy, Pritham K. and Venkatesh Chakravarthy. 2008. "A.V.M. Studios: A Historical Reading." Paper presented at the Regional Film Industries: The Formative Years. Organized by the Department of Cultural Studies, English and Foreign Languages University, Hyderabad (14–15 November 2008).

Chinanarayana, Pulagam. N.d. Online edition titled "About the Film [*Dana Veera Sura Karna*]." Stable URL: http://www.telugucinema.com/c/publish/movieretrospect/retro_dvskarna_printer.php.

Chua Beng Huat, ed. 2007. *Elections as Popular Culture in Asia*. London and New York: Routledge.

City Bureau. 2011. "'Million March' Turns Violent in Hyderabad." *The Hindu*. Hyderabad edition (11 March), p. 1.

Dakshina Murthy, Patibandla. 2006. *Kalatmaka Darsakudu B.N. Reddi*. Hyderabad: Creative Link Publications.

Damodaran, Harish. 2008. *India's New Capitalists: Caste Business, and Industry in a Modern Nation*. Ranikhet: Permanent Black, in association with The New India Foundation.

Damodaraswamy, P. 1986. "Hyderabad Nagaramlo Pata Theatrelu." *Jyothi Chitra* (Ugadi Pratyeka Sanchika), p. 58.

Das, Veena. 1980. "The Mythological Film and Its Framework of Meaning: An Analysis of *Jai Santoshi Maa*." *India International Centre Quarterly*. Vol. 8, no. 1 (March), pp. 43–56.

Das Gupta, Chidananda. 1991. *The Painted Face: Studies in Indian Popular Cinema*. Delhi: Roli Books.

Dechamma, Sowmya C.C. and Elavarthi Sathya Prakash, eds. 2010. *Cinemas of South India: Culture, Resistance, Ideology*. New Delhi: Oxford University Press.

Deshpande, B.L. 1948. "Bezawadalo *Balaraju* Satadinotsavamulo Prekshakulapai Lathiprayogam." *Roopavani* (July), p. 68.

Devulapalli, Krishna Shastri. 2011. *Ice Boys in Bell Bottoms*. New Delhi: HarperCollins India.

Dickey, Sara.1993. *Cinema and the Urban Poor in South India*. Cambridge: Cambridge University Press.

Dwyer, Rachel. 2006. *Filming the Gods: Religion and Indian Cinema*. London and New York: Routledge.

Dyer, Richard. 1991. "*A Star is Born* and the Construction of Authenticity." In Christine Gledhill, ed. *Stardom: Industry of Desire*. New York and London: Routledge, pp. 132–40.

Editorial. 1951. *Roopavani* (March), pp. 7–8

———. 1983a. "Telugunata Charitra Srushtinchandi." *Eenadu*. Vijayawada edition (5 January), p. 1.

———. 1983b. "Dharmakshetre Kurukshetre." *Eenadu*. Vijayawada edition (6 January), p. 3.

Eenadu. 1983. "Karnataka Congi Super Flop." *Eenadu*. Vijayawada edition (7 January), p. 1.

Eenadu Special Correspondent. 1982a. "Delhiki Taloggatam Alavate." *Eenadu*. Vijayawada edition (11 October), pp. 5, 8.

———. 1982b. "Telugu Desam O 'Drama Troupe'." *Eenadu*. Vijayawada edition (11 October), p. 1.

———. 1983. "Telugu Desam Super Hit!" *Eenadu*. Vijayawada edition (7 January), p. 1.

Elder, Joseph W. and Peter L. Schmitthenner. 1985. "Film Fantasy and Populist Politics in South India: N.T. Rama Rao and the Telugu Desam Party." In Robert E. Frykenberg and Pauline Kolendaeds. *Studies of South India: An Anthology of Recent Research and Scholarship*. Madras: New Era Publications and New Delhi: American Institute of Indian Studies, pp. 373–87.

Forrester, Duncan. 1970. "Subregionalism in India: The Case of Telangana." *Pacific Affairs*. Vol. 43, no. 1 (Spring), pp. 5–21.

———. 1976. "Factions and Filmstars: Tamil Nadu Politics since 1971." *Asian Survey*. Vol. 16, no. 3 (March), pp. 283–96.

Freud, Sigmund. 1921, rpt 1985. *Group Psychology and the Analysis of the Ego*. In idem. *Civilization, Society and Religion: Group Psychology, Civilization and Its Discontents and Other Works*. The Penguin Freud Library, Volume 12. Harmondsworth: Penguin, pp. 91–178.

Golconda Patrika. 1962. "Manodaurbalyaniki Manchi Mandu Uttama Chitralu" (7 April), p. 4.

Gopalakrishna, Parachuri. 2003, rpt 2008. *Telugu Cinema Sahityam: Katha-Kathanam-Silpam*. Hyderabad: V-Tech Publications.

Gopalan, Lalitha. 2003. *Cinema of Interruptions: Action Genres in Contemporary Indian Cinema*. New Delhi: Oxford University Press.

Gray, Hugh. 1971. "The Demand for a Separate Telangana State in India." *Asian Survey*. Vol. 11, no. 5 (May), pp. 463–74.

———. 1974. "The Failure of the Demand for a Separate Andhra State." *Asian Survey*. Vol. 14, no. 4 (April), pp. 338–49.

Guha, Ramachandra. 2007. *India After Gandhi: The History of the World's Largest Democracy*. London: Macmillan.

Guy, Randor. 1985. *B.N. Reddi: A Monograph*. Pune: National Film Archive of India.

Hansen, Miriam. 1991. *Babel and Babylon: Spectatorship in American Silent Film*. Cambridge, MA.: Harvard University Press.

Hansen, Thomas Blom. 2004. "Politics as Permanent Performance: The Production of Political Authority in the Locality." In John Zavos, Andrew Wyatt and Vernon Hewitt, eds. *The Politics of Cultural Mobilization in India*. New Delhi: Oxford University Press.

Hanuman Chaudhury, Tripuraneni. 2011. "Manava Dharmoddharakulu." *Andhra Jyothi* (15 January), p. 4.

Haragopal, G. 1985. "A Socio-Economic Study of Modern Andhra." *Social Science Probings* (March), pp. 37–77.

Hardgrave, Jr., Robert L. 1973. "Politics and Film in Tamil Nadu: The Stars and the DMK." *Asian Survey*. Vol. 13, no. 3. (March), pp. 288–305. Stable URL: http://links.jstor.org/sici?sici=0004-687%28197303%29 13%3A3%3C288%3APATFIT%3E2.0.CO%3B2-8

———. 1979. "When Stars Displace the Gods: The Folk Culture of Cinema in Tamil Nadu." In *Essays in the Political Sociology of South India*. New Delhi: Manohar, pp. 92–122.

Hughes, Stephen Putnam. 1996. "Is There Anyone Out There? Exhibition and the Formation of Silent Film Audience in South India." Unpublished Ph.D. Dissertation, University of Chicago.

———. 2007. "Music in the Age of Mechanical Reproduction: Drama, Gramophone, and the Beginnings of Tamil Cinema." *The Journal of Asian Studies*. Vol. 66, no. 1 (February), pp. 3–34.

———. 2010. 'What is Tamil about Tamil Cinema?' *South Asian Popular Culture*. Vol. 8, no. 3 (October), pp. 213–29.

Hyderabad State Film Chamber of Commerce. 2007. *Hyderabad Film Diary 2007*. Hyderabad: Hyderabad State Film Chamber of Commerce.

Innaiah, N. 1986. *State Government and Politics: A Study of Andhra Pradesh Politics, 1885–1985*. Hyderabad: Scientific Services.

Jaganmohan, T.S. 2011. *Abhyudaya Chalanachitra Sarathy Gudavalli Ramabrahmam*. Hyderabad: Creative Links Publications.

Jeevan, P. 1948. Letter in the column "Mana Theatrela Dustiti." *Roopavani* (June), p. 61.

Jeffrey, Robin. 1997. "Telugu: Ingredients of Growth and Failure." *Economic and Political Weekly*. Vol. 32, no. 5 (1–7 February), pp. 192–5.

———. 2010. *India's Newspaper Revolution: Capitalism, Politics and the Indian-language Press*. 3rd edition. New Delhi: Oxford University Press.

Jinka, Nagaraju. 1982. "Madala Vastunnadu Tappukondi". *Arunatara* (June), pp. 54–9 and 61.

Juluri, Vamsee. 2010. *The Mythologist: A Novel*. New Delhi: Penguin Books.

Kaali, Sundar. 2000. "Narrating Seduction: Vicissitudes of the Sexed Subject in Tamil Nativity Film." In Ravi S. Vasudevan, ed. *Making Meaning in Indian Cinema*. New Delhi: Oxford University Press, pp. 168–90.

Kameswara Rao, Kamalakara. 1980. "Mookila Nunchi Talkiela Yugam Prarambham." *Jyothi Chitra*. [Sankranti special issue. January.] No page numbers. CSCS Media Archive Record Number: Te180001.

Kannala. 1996. "The Ebb and Flow of the Tide." In K.N.T. Sastry, ed. *Telugu Cinema*. Hyderabad: Cinema Group, pp. 21–37.

Kantha Rao, M.L. 1999. "Study of the Socio-Political Mobility of the Kapu Caste in Modern Andhra." Ph.D. Dissertation. Hyderabad: University of Hyderabad.

Kapur, Geeta. 1987. "Mythic Material in Indian Cinema." *Journal of Arts and Ideas*. Nos 14–15 (July–December), pp. 79–107.

Keathley, Christian. 2000. "The Cinephiliac Moment." *Framework*. No. 42 (Online Edition), http://www.frameworkonline.com/42ck.htm.

Ko, Yufen. 2007. "The Festive Machine: Taiwan's 2004 Elections as Popular Culture." In Chua Beng Huat, ed. *Elections as Popular Culture in Asia*. London and New York: Routledge, pp. 22–37.

Krishna Babu. 1982. "Samaikhyata Vadanni Balapariche *Telugunadu*." In *Andhra Jyothi*. Vijayawada edition (26 October), p. 7.

Krishna Patrika. 1962a. "*Palleseema* Darsakudu." In "Chalanachitra Vartha Tarangini." *Krishna Patrika* (20 June), p. 22. CSCS Media Archive Record Number Te110020.

———. 1962b. In "Cineprekshakulapai C. Pullaiah Abhiprayalu." *Krishna*

Patrika (20 October), pp. 16–17 and 30. CSCS Media Archive Record Number Te120019.

———. 1962c. "Hyderabadlo Annapurnavari Chitram Shooting." In "Chalanachitra Vartha Tarangini." *Krishna Patrika* (1 September), p. 26. CSCS Media Archive Record Number Te120015.

———. 1962d. "Nag Sankalpam." In "Madras Cineranga Viharam." *Krishna Patrika* (1 December), n.d. CSCS Media Archive Record Number Te120021.

———. 1963. "1963 Samvatsaram Antamlo Film Parisrama Dustiti." *Krishna Patrika* (21 December), n.d. CSCS Media Archive Record Number Te110007.

———. 1964a. "Madras Cinerangamlo Vinutna Sobha". *Krishna Patrika* (8 August), pp. 14–15, and 17. CSCS Media Archive Record Number Te110004.

———. 1964b. "Naa America Yatraanubhavaalu." *Krishna Patrika* (15 August), pp. 20–1. CSCS Media Archive Record Number Te110038.

———. 1964c. "Rama Rao Bruhat Vidyasahaya Padhakam". In "Avi, Evi." *Krishna Patrika* (12 September), p. 18. CSCS Media Archive Record Number Te110005.

Krishnabai and Prasad. 2000a & 2000b. "Cinema Teerutennulu" [Preface]. In *Kodavatiganti Kutumba Rao Vyasa Prapancham IV, Cinema Vyasalu.* 2 vols. Andhra Pradesh: Virasam, pp. v–vii.

Kusuma, Krishna Kumar. 2010. "Dalit Image in Telugu Cinema Since 1947." Unpublished Ph.D. Dissertation. Jamia Millia Islamia.

Kutumbarao, Kodavatiganti ["KoKu"]. 1964. "Telugu Films: An Industry in Exile." *Andhra Film Chamber Journal.* Vol. 9, nos 5–6 (March–April), pp. 3–7.

———. 2000a & 2000b. *Kodavatiganti Kutumba Rao Vyasa Prapancham IV: Cinema Vyasalu.* 2 vols. Krishnabai and Prasad, eds. Andhra Pradesh: VIRASAM.

Laclau, Ernesto. 2005. *On Populist Reason.* London and New York: Verso.

Lai, Linda Chiu-han. 2001. "Film and Enigmatization: Nostalgia, Nonsense and Remembering." In Esther C.M. Yau, ed. *At Full Speed: Hong Kong Cinema in a Borderless World.* Minneapolis, London: University of Minnesota Press, pp. 231–50.

Lakshminarayana, Edara. 1997. "Naaku Telisina Chakrapanigaru." In Velaga Venkatappaiah, ed. *Chakrapaniyam.* Tenali: Chakrapani-Kolasani Foundation, pp. 22–31.

Lakshmi Parvathi, Nandamuri. 2004a. *Edurileni Manishi: NTR Jeevita Charitra.* Hyderabad: Sri Gayatri Publications.

———. 2004b. *Telugu Tejam: NTR Rajakeeya Jeevitam*. Hyderabad: NTR Educational Society.

Liang, Lawrence. 2011. "Media's Law: From Representation to Affect." *BioScope: South Asian Screen Studies*. Vol. 2, no.1 (January), pp. 23–40.

Lutgendorf, Philip. 1990. "*Ramayan*: The Video." *The Drama Review*. Vol. 34, no. 2 (Summer), pp. 127–76.

———. 2002a. "A Superhit Goddess: *Jai Santoshi Maa* and Caste Hierarchy in Indian Films." *Manushi*. No. 131 (October–November), pp. 10–16.

———. 2002b. "A 'Made to Satisfaction Goddess': *Jai Santoshi Maa* Revisited." *Manushi*. No. 131 (October–November), pp. 24–37.

Maclean, C.D., ed. 1885, rpt 1987. *Manual of the Administration of the Madras Presidency: In Illustration of the Records of Government and the Yearly Administration Reports, Volume 1*. New Delhi: Asian Educational Services.

Madhusudhana Rao, D. 1981. "Samasyalu Parishkaralu." In C.V.V.R. Prasad, ed. *Indian Talkie Golden Jubilee Celebration Souvenir*, pp. 148–51.

Madras Representative. 1964. "Swatantra Varshikotsvanantaram Telugu Cinemarangam Dusthiti." *Krishna Patrika* (29 August), p. 29.

Maheswari, Uma. 1999. "Anti-Arrack Movement, Prohibition and After: *Eenadu*'s Strategic Support and Silence." *Journal of Arts and Ideas* 32–3 (April), pp. 73–85.

Malla Reddy, Gajjela. 1982. "Rakshakudu Vachchadu." *Eenadu*. Vijayawada edition (13 October), p. 1.

Mana Samskriti. 2004. "Venkataramamurthy Gidigu (1862–1940)." *Mana Samskriti*. No. 80 (September). Stable URL: http://www.vepachedu.org/manasanskriti/ gidugu.html.

Manigopal. 2007. "*Justice Chaudhury* ki Patikella Vaibhavam." *Sitara* (10 June), p. 4.

Mankekar, Purnima. 1999. *Screening Culture: Viewing Politics: An Ethnography of Television, Womanhood, and Nation*. Durham and London: Duke University Presss.

Manor, James. 1993. *Power, Poverty and Poison: Disaster and Response in an Indian City*. New Delhi/Newbury Park/London: Sage Publications.

Manuel, Peter. 1993. *Cassette Culture: Popular Music and Technology in North India*. Chicago: Chicago University Press.

Mathew, George. 1984. "Primordiality in Indian Politics: The Case of 1983 Elections in AP and Karnataka." In George Mathew, ed. *Shift in Indian Politics: 1983 Elections in Andhra Pradesh and Karnataka*. New Delhi:

Christian Institute for the Study of Religion and Society & Concept Publishing Company, pp. 165–77.

Melkote, Rama S., E. Revathi, K. Lalitha, K. Sajaya and A. Suneetha. 2010. "The Movement for Telangana: Myth and Reality." *Economic and Political Weekly*. Vol. 45, no. 2 (9 January), pp. 8–11.

Melly Maitreyi, M.L. 2011. "Will 'Resurrection' Retain Same Magic?" *The Hindu* (13 March). Online Edition. URL: http://www.hindu.com/2011/03/13/stories/2011031363840600.htm.

Metz, Christian. 1982. *The Imaginary Signifier: Psychoanalysis and the Cinema*. Bloomington: Indiana University Press.

Mikkilineni, Radhakrishna Murthy. 1975. *Teluguvari Chalanachitrakala*. Hyderabad: Andhra Pradesh Sangeet Natak Academy.

Mitchell, Lisa. 2009. *Language, Emotion and Politics in South India: The Making of a Mother Tongue*. Bloomington and Indianapolis: Indiana University Press.

Mulvey, Laura. 1975, rpt. 1990. "Visual Pleasure and Narrative Cinema." In Patricia Erens ed. *Issues in Feminist Film Criticism*. Bloomington and Indianapolis: Indiana University Press, pp. 28–40.

Murali, Atlury. 1984. "Alluri Sitarama Raju and the Manyam Rebellion of 1922–1924." *Social Scientist*. Vol. 12, no. 4 (April), pp. 3–33.

Murali, K. 1995. "Upper Caste Violence on Dalits: Case Studies of Karamchedu and Chundur Massacres." Unpublished M.Phil. Dissertation. University of Hyderabad.

Murari, Katragadda, ed. n.d. *Telugu Chalanachitra Nirmatala Charitra 1931–2005*. Hyderabad: The Telugu Film Producers' Council.

Murthi Sri. 1993. "Abhyudaya Darsakudu Gudavalli." *Suprabhatam* (5 August), p. 57.

"Murthy." 1948. "Prekshakulapai Lathi Prayogalu Inka Kaavali." In the column "Tarapadhamlo." *Roopavani* (July), p. 7.

———. 1962. "Chalanachitra Varta Tarangini." *Krishna Patrika* (31 March), pp. 16–17. CSCS Media Archive Record Number Te12007.

"Naa Peru Kankara Chandrayya." 2011. In "Navya." *Andhra Jyothi* (8 October), p. 1.

Naidu, M.D. Narayana. 1995. *NTR: The Man of the Masses*. Tirupathi: Shobha Lata Publications.

Naidu, Ratna. 1984. "Symbolic Imagery Used by the Telugu Desam in Andhra Elections (1983)." In George Mathew, ed. *Shift in Indian Politics: 1983 Elections in Andhra Pradesh and Karnataka*. New Delhi: Christian Institute for the Study of Religion and Society & Concept Publishing Company, pp. 129–38.

Nair, Janaki. 2005. *The Promise of the Metropolis: Bangalore's Twentieth Century*. New Delhi: Oxford University Press.

Narasaiah, K. "1981 Telugu Film Parisrama." In C.V.V.R. Prasad, ed. *Indian Talkie Golden Jubilee Celebration Souvenir*, pp. 145–7.

Narasaraju, D.V. 1986. "Naaku Aidu Lakshalu Nashtam." *Jyothi Chitra* (Ugadi Pratyeka Sanchika), pp. 186–8.

———. 2006. *Tera Venuka Kathalu*. Hyderabad: Creative Links Publications.

Newstoday. 1982a. "Veeravasaramlo Veera Puja." *Eenadu*. Vijayawada edition (14 October), p. 1.

———. 1982b. "Anyayala Palaina Telugu Jati." *Eenadu*. Vijayawada edition (1 September), p. 2.

———. 1982c. "Telugu Jati Gundello Regina Manta." *Eenadu*. Vijayawada edition (11 September), p. 2.

———. 1982d. "Delhi Velte Mana Mantrula Mokham Choosevarevaru?" *Eenadu*. Vijayawada edition (11 October), p. 8.

———. 1982e. "Indira Jaalam Matu Maayam." *Eenadu*. Vijayawada edition (4 October), p. 2.

———. 1982f. "Andhraku Atta Kodallu." *Eenadu*. Vijayawada edition (12 October), p. 1.

———. 1982g. "Ee 'Cinema Jananni' Nammaku. Bolta Padtav." *Eenadu*. Vijayawada edition (3 October), p. 1.

———. 1982h. "Vaagula Pakkane Visranti." *Eenadu*. Vijayawada edition (9 October), p. 1.

———. 1982i. "Telugudesam Sakthi Patrikala Srushtey." *Eenadu*. Vijayawada edition (15 October), p. 2.

———. 1983a. "Goondala Kiratakam." *Eenadu*. Vijayawada edition (2 January), p. 1.

———. 1983b. "Ramarao Sabhaku Anumati Nirakarana." *Eenadu*. Vijayawada edition (2 January), p. 1.

———. 1983c. "Indira Sabhalo Prekshakulaku Nirasa." *Eenadu*. Vijayawada edition (2 January), p. 2.

———. 1983d. "Andhrulaku Adugaduguna Avamaname." *Eenadu*. Vijayawada edition (1 January), p. 10.

———. 1983e. "Andhrula Vichanashaktiki Pareeksha." *Eenadu*. Vijayawada edition (5 January), p. 1.

———. 1983f. "Ayyo Talli! Nee Sabahaku Lerem Janam?" *Eenadu*. Vijayawada edition (2 January), p. 7.

———. 1983g. "Rajakeeyalante Natakalu Kadu." *Eenadu*. Vijayawada edition (2 January 1983), p. 1.

Niranjana, Tejaswini. 2000. "Reworking Masculinities: Rajkumar and the Kannada Public Sphere." *Economic and Political Weekly*. Vol. 35, no. 47 (18–24 November), pp. 4147–50.

———. 2004. "Vigilantism and the Pleasures of Masquerade: The Female Spectator of Vijayasanthi Films." In Preben Kaarsholm, ed. *City Flicks: Indian Cinema and the Urban Experience*. Calcutta: Seagull Books, pp. 237–54.

Omvedt, Gail. 1981. "Capitalist Agriculture and Rural Classes in India." *Economic and Political Weekly*. Vol. 16, no. 52 (December), pp. A–140–59.

Online. 2010. "Kamma Brahmaloo Unnaru." *Adivaram Andhra Jyothi* (9 May), p. 23.

Paidipaala. 1992. *Telugu Cinema Paata* [Telugu Film Song]. Madras: Sneha Prachuranalu.

Pandian, Anand. 2008. "Cinema in the Countryside: Popular Tamil Film and the Remaking of Rural Life." In Selvaraj Velyutham, ed. *Tamil Cinema: The Cultural Politics of India's Other Film Industry*. London and New York: Routledge, pp. 124–38.

Pandian, M.S.S. 1991. "*Parasakthi*: Life and Times of a DMK Film." *Economic and Political Weekly*. Vol. 26, no. 11/12, Annual Number (March), pp. 759–70.

———. 1992. *The Image Trap: M.G. Ramachandran in the Film and Politics*. Delhi: Newbury Park, London: Sage.

Pandurangarao, Yinaganti. 1951. "*Patala Bhairavi* Mota." In "Prajabhiprayam." *Roopavani* (August), p. 40.

Parthasarathy, D. 1997. *Collective Violence in a Provincial City* New Delhi: Oxford University Press.

Parthasarathy, G. 1984. "Growth Rates and Fluctuations of Agricultural Production: A District-Wise Analysis in Andhra Pradesh." *Economic and Political Weekly*. Vol. 19, no. 26 (30 June), pp. A74–A77 and A80–A84.

Pillai, Swarnavel Eswaran. 2010. "Tamil Cinema and the Major Madras Studios (1940–1957)." Unpublished Ph.D. Dissertation. Iowa: University of Iowa.

Pingle, Gautam. 2010. "The Historical Context of Andhra and Telangana, 1949–56." *Economic and Political Weekly*. Vol. 45, no. 8 (26 February), pp. 57–65.

Pinney, Christopher. 2004. *Photos of the Gods: The Printed Image and Political Struggle in India*. New Delhi: Oxford University Press.

Prabhu. 1993. *Swarnayugamlo Annapurna*. Hyderabad: Annapurna Pictures Private Limited.

Prakasam, Vasiraju. 2006. *Chalana Chitra Chakravarthy Dr. D. Ramanaidu*. Hyderabad: Rajeswari Publications.

Prasad, A.A.V. 1996. "Bahudoorapu Batasari Bahumukha Vyaktitvam." *India Today Varshika Cinema Sanchika* [Annual Special Issue on Film], pp. 60–8.

Prasad, M. Madhava. 1998. *Ideology of the Hindi Film: A Historical Construction*. New Delhi: Oxford University Press.

———. 1999. "Cine-Politics: On the Political Significance of Cinema in South India." *Journal of the Moving Image*. No.1 (Autumn), pp. 37–52.

———. 2006. "From Virtual to Real Political Power: Film Stars Enter Electoral Politics." *Asia Research Institute Working Paper Series*. No. 59. Asia Research Institute, National University of Singapore, Singapore (March).

———. 2007. "Fun with Democracy: Election Coverage and the Elusive Subject of Indian Politics." In Chua Beng Huat, ed. *Elections as Popular Culture in Asia*. London and New York: Routledge, pp. 139–54.

———. 2009. "Fan *Bhakti* and Subaltern Sovereignty: Enthusiasm as a Political Factor." *Economic and Political Weekly*. Vol. 44, no. 29 (18–24 July), pp. 68–76.

———. 2011. "Genre Mixing as Creative Fabrication." *BioScope: South Asian Screen Studies*. Vol, 2, no. 1, pp. 69–81.

———. N.d. "Human and Divine: The Mythological Film." Unpublished essay.

Radhakrishnan, Ratheesh. 2010. "What is Left of Malayalam Cinema?" In Sowmya Dechamma C.C. and Elavarthi Sathya Prakash, eds. *Cinemas of South India: Culture, Resistance, Ideology*. New Delhi: Oxford University Press, pp. 25–48.

Raghavendra, M.K. 2011. *Bipolar Identity: Region, Nation and the Kannada Language Film*. New Delhi: Oxford University Press.

Rajadhyaksha, Ashish. 1993a. "The Phalke Era: Conflict of Traditional Form and Modern Technology." In Tejaswini Niranjana, *et al.*, eds. *Interrogating Modernity*. Calcutta: Seagull Books, pp. 47–82.

———. 1993b. "The Epic Melodrama." *Journal of Arts and Ideas* 25–26 (December), pp. 55–70.

——— and Paul Willemen. 1994, rpt 1999, eds. *Encyclopaedia of Indian Cinema*. New Delhi: Oxford University Press.

Rajamani, Radhika. 2009. "Nativity and Narrative Themes in Telangana

Art." In M. Bharath Bhushan and N. Venugopal, eds. *Telangana: The State of Affairs*. Hyderabad: AdEd Value Ventures, pp. 147–51.

Raju, D.V.S. 1986. "Oka Dasabdamlo Telugu Chalana Chitra Parisrama Pragati." *Jyothi Chitra* (Ugadi Pratyeka Sanchika), pp. 141–2.

Rama Rao, N.T. 1982. "Naa Manoratham." Pamphlet. Hyderabad: Telugu Desam.

Rama Rao, Veeranki. 1942. *Madras Film Diary 1942*. Madras: Veeranki Rama Rao.

Ramabrahmam, Gudavalli. 1940. "Telugu Film Parisrama Labhadayikamga Undgalante." *Andhra Patrika*. Vikrama Samvatsaradi Sanchika [Special Annual Issue 1940], pp. 95–9.

Ramachandra Murthy, Jeedigunta. 1996. "Marapurani Madhurachitralu." *India Today Varshika Cinema Sanchika* [Annual Special Issue on Film], pp. 46–52.

Raman Rao, A.V. 1993. *Andhra Pradesh Economy Since Independence (1947–1992)*. New Delhi: Kalyani Publishers.

Ramaswamy, Sumathi. 1997. *Passions of the Tongue: Language and Devotion in Tamil India, 1891–1970*. Berkeley, Los Angeles, London: University of California Press.

Ramaswamy, Uma. 1978. "The Belief System of the Non-Brahmin Movement in India: The Andhra Case." *Asian Survey*. Vol. 18, no. 3 (March), pp. 290–300.

Ranga, N.G. 1926. *Economic Organisation of Indian Villages, Vol. 1, Deltaic Villages*. Vijayawada: Vani Press.

Rao, R.V.S. 1964. "Andhra Rajadhanilo Venditeraku Bangaru Bhavishyattu." *Andhra Film Chamber Journal*. Vol 9, nos 5–6 (March–April), pp. 97–101.

Raraju. 1941. "Cinema Simhavalokam: Telugu Parisramadarulaku Konni Soochanalu." *Andhra Patrika*. Vrisha Samvatsaradi Sanchika [Special Annual Issue 1940], pp 22–4.

Report of the Film Enquiry Committee. 1951. Chairman S.K. Patil. Delhi: Ministry of Information and Broadcasting, Government of India.

Report of the Indian Cinematograph Committee 1927–28: Vol. III. 1928. Madras: Government Press.

Report of the States Reorganisation Commission. 1955. New Delhi: Government of India.

Rosen, Philip. 2006. "History, Textuality, Nation: Kracauer, Burch and Some Problems in the Study of National Cinema." In Valentina Vitali and Paul Willemen, eds. *Theorising National Cinema*. London: BFI Publishing, pp. 17–28.

Roopavani. 1951. "Film Vartalu." *Roopavani* (March), pp. 17–18.

Sastry, K.N.T. ed. 1986. *Telugu Cinema*. Hyderabad: Cinema Group.

———. 1993. *L.V. Prasad: A Monograph*. Pune: National Film Archive of India.

Satyanarayana, A. 1995. "Dalit Protest Literature in Telugu: A Historical Perspective." *Economic and Political Weekly*. Vol. 30, no. 3 (21 January), pp. 171–5.

Sayana, V.V. 1949. *The Agrarian Problems of Madras Province*. Madras: The Business Week Press.

Shanti Kumar. 2006. "Mapping Tollywood: The Cultural Geography of 'Ramoji Film City' in Hyderabad." *Quarterly Review of Film and Video*. Vol. 23, pp. 129–38.

Shatrugna, M. 1984. "Emergence of Regional Parties in India: Case of Telugu Desam." In George Mathew, ed. *Shift in Indian Politics: 1983 Elections in Andhra Pradesh and Karnataka*. New Delhi: Christian Institute for the Study of Religion and Society & Concept Publishing Company, pp. 95–112.

Simhadri, S. 1997. "River Water Politics in Drought-Prone Telangana." *Economic and Political Weekly*. Vol. 32, no. 37 (13–19 September), pp. 2315–17.

Sivaram, Peketi. 1964. "Andhra Rajadhani . . . Telugu Parisrama!" *Andhra Film Chamber Journal*. Vol 9, nos 5–6 (March–April), pp. 60–3.

Sivathamby, Karthigesu. 1981. *Tamil Film as a Medium of Political Communication*. Madras: New Century Book House.

Special Correspondent. 1983. "Casteism through Elections." *Economic and Political Weekly*. Vol. 18, no. 7 (February 12), pp. 213–15.

Somasekhar, N. 1990. "The Movement and the Song: Portrait of a Cultural Army." *Economic and Political Weekly*. Vol. 25, no. 29 (21 June), p. 1570.

Srihari, Gudipoodi. N.d. *Telugu Cinema 91*. Hyderabad: Gudipoodi Srihari.

Srimantu Raja Yarlagadda Sivaramaprasad Bahadur Challapalli Rajavari Shastyabdapoorti Sammana Sanchika. 1966. N.d.

Srinivas, G., M. Shatrugna and G. Narayana. 1984. 'Social Background of Telugu Desam Legislators." In George Mathew, ed. *Shift in Indian Politics: 1983 Elections in Andhra Pradesh and Karnataka*. New Delhi: Christian Institute for the Study of Religion and Society & Concept Publishing Company, pp. 113–28.

Srinivas, S.V. 1999. "Gandhian Nationalism and Melodrama in the 30's Telugu Cinema." *Journal of the Moving Image*. No. 1 (Autumn), pp. 14–36.

———. 2003. "Hong Kong Action Film in the Indian B Circuit." *Inter-Asia Cultural Studies*. Vol. 4, no. 1 (April), pp. 40–62.

———. 2005. '*Kung Fu Hustle*: A Note on the Local.' *Inter-Asia Cultural Studies*. Vol. 6, no. 2, pp. 289–95.

———. 2009. *Megastar: Chiranjeevi and Telugu Cinema after N.T. Rama Rao*. New Delhi: Oxford University Press.

Srinivasulu, K. 1994. 'BSP and Caste Politics.' *Economic and Political Weekly*. Vol. 29, no. 40 (1 October), pp. 2583–6.

Srivatsava. 1964. "Filmparisrama: Sahitya Samskrutulu." *Andhra Film Chamber Journal*. Vol 9, nos 5–6 (March–April), pp. 69–75.

Sri Sri [Srirangam Srinivasa Rao]. 2010. *Cinema Patalu*. In Challasani Prasad and M.V. Rayudu, eds. *Sri Sri Kavita Prasthanam Vol. III: Kavita Prasthanam*. Hyderabad: Manasu Foundation.

Subba Rao, A.H.V. 1964. "Bhyagyanagaram Bhagyasali." *Andhra Film Chamber Journal*. Vol. 9, nos 5–6 (March–April), pp. 90–3.

Subbarao, C.R. 1951. "Tenali Prekshaka Sangham". In "Prajabhiprayam." *Roopavani* (September), pp. 41–2.

Sudarsanam. 1964. "Avi Evi." In *Krishna Patrika* (3 October), pp. 18–19, 22.

Sudhir, Uma. 2011. "Million March: Hyderabad's Prized Statues Wrecked". Stable Url: http://www.ndtv.com/article/india/million-march-hyderabads-prized-statues-wrecked-90934&cp. Last visited 12 December 2011.

Sundarayya, P. 1973a. "Telangana People's Armed Struggle, 1946–51. Part One: Historical Setting." *Social Scientist*. Vol. 1, no. 7 (February), pp. 3–19.

———. 1973b. "Telangana People's Armed Struggle, 1946–1951. Part Two: First Phase and Its Lessons." *Social Scientist*. Vol. 1, no. 8 (March), pp. 18–42.

———. 1973c. "Telangana People's Armed Struggle, 1946–51. Part Three: Pitted against the Indian Army." *Social Scientist*. Vol. 1, no. 9 (April), pp. 23–46.

———. 1973d. "Telangana People's Armed Struggle, 1946–51: Part Four: Background to a Momentous Decision.' *Social Scientist*. Vol. 1, no. 10 (May), pp. 22–52.

Suri, K.C. 2004. "Telugu Desam Party: Rise and Prospects for Future." *Economic and Political Weekly*. Vol. 39, no. 14/15 (3–16 April), pp. 1481–90.

Sushil Rao, Ch. 2011. "Freedom Curtailed? Cinemas Closure Plan Hits Roadblock." *The Times of India*. Hyderabad Edition, 12 January, p. 2.

The Hindu Business Line. 2008. "Rajasekhara Reddy Unveils Ramanaidu Film

Studio." 18 August. Online edition. Url: http://www.thehindubusinessline.com/2008/08/18/stories/2008081851201500.htm.

Thirumali, I. 1992. "*Dora* and *Gadi*: Manifestation of Landlord Domination in Telengana." *Economic and Political Weekly*. Vol. 27, no. 9 (29 February), pp. 477–82.

———. 1997. "Language, Communists and Vishalandhra." S. Simhadri and P.L. Vishweshwer Rao, eds. *Telangana: Dimensions of Underdevelopment*. Hyderabad: Centre for Telangana Studies, pp. 15–23.

Times News Network. 2008. "Unfair Deal: Cinema Owners to Blackout Big Players." *The Times of India*. Hyderabad edition, 6 July, p. 3.

Upadhya, Carol Boyack. 1988a. "The Farmer-Capitalists of Coastal Andhra Pradesh." *Economic and Political Weekly*. Vol. 23, no. 27, 2 July, pp. 1376–82.

———. 1988b. "The Farmer-Capitalists of Coastal Andhra Pradesh." *Economic and Political Weekly*. Vol. 23, no. 28, 9 July, pp. 1433–42.

"Ushasree." 1949. "Cinema Theatrelalo Anuvadalu." *Roopavani* (July), pp. 43–5.

Vakulabharanam, Vamsi. 2004. "Agricultural Growth and Irrigation in Telangana: A Review of Evidence." *Economic and Political Weekly*. Vol. 39, no. 13 (27 March–2 April), pp. 1421–6.

Vardhan, T. Vishnu. 2006. "The Emergence of New Star Body and the Death of Mythologicals during the 1970s: Exploring the Film (and) History of Telugu Cinema." The Eleventh International Cultural Studies Workshop on Cultures of the Body. Organized by Centre for Studies in Social Sciences, Calcutta, in Goa, 23–28 January.

———. 2007. "After Godhood: The Political Career of N.T. Rama Rao." Paper presented at the International Conference on "Asian Cinema: Towards a Research and Teaching Agenda." Organized by Centre for the Study of Culture and Society, Bangalore, 2–4 February.

Vasudevan, Ravi. 2010. *The Melodramatic Public*. Ranikhet: Permanent Black.

Velayutham, Selvaraj. 2008. "Introduction: The Cultural History and Politics of South Indian Tamil Cinema.' In Selvaraj Velyutham, ed. *Tamil Cinema: The Cultural Politics of India's Other Film Industry*. London and New York: Routledge, pp. 1–15.

Venkat Narayan, S. 1983. *NTR: A Biography*. Sahibabad: Vikas Publishing House.

———. 1985. "The Phenomenon Called NTR: Actor-Turned Politician." In T.M. Ramachandran, ed. *70 Years of Indian Cinema (1931–1983)*. Bombay: Cinema India International, pp. 203–14.

Venkat Rao. 1999. "Writing Orally: Decolonization from Below." *Positions*. Vol. 7, no. 1 (Spring), pp, 253–67.

Venkat Rao, I. 2003. *Oke Okkadu*. Hyderabad: Monica Books.

Venkatasubba Rao, K.N. 2007. "The Glory and Fall of Kannada Cinema." *The Hindu*. Bangalore edition, 14 August, p. 6.

Venkateswara Rao, Kommineni. 2011. "*Patala Bhairavi*: 60 Yella Jaitrayatra." In "Chitra Jyothi." *Andhra Jyothi* (15 March), p. iv.

Vijayachitra. 1980. "Chitrayatralo *Vijayachitra*" (October), pp. 46–7, 49.

Weber, Max. 1946. "Structures of Power.". In *From Max Weber: Essays in Sociology*. Ed. H.H. Girth and C. Wright Mills. New York: Oxford University Press, pp. 159–79.

Willemen, Paul. 1994. *Looks and Frictions: Essays in Cultural Studies and Film Theory*. London: British Film Institute and Bloomington: Indiana University Press.

Yamada. Keiko, 2010. "Origin and Historical Evolution of the Identity of Modern Telugus." *Economic and Political Weekly*. Vol. 45, no. 34 (21 August), pp. 57–63.

Index

(*Numbers in bold indicate pages with images*)